# Drift Net

# Drift Net

## THE AESTHETICS OF LITERATURE AND MEDIA IN MIGRATION

Chris Campanioni

LEVER
PRESS

Lever Press (leverpress.org) is a publisher of pathbreaking scholarship. Supported by a consortium of higher education institutions focused on, and renowned for, excellence in both research and teaching, our press is grounded on three essential commitments: to be a digitally native press, to be a peer-reviewed, open access press that charges no fees to either authors or their institutions, and to be a press aligned with the liberal arts ethos.

The complete manuscript of this work was subjected to a fully closed ("double blind") review process. For more information, please see our Peer Review Commitments and Guidelines at https://www.leverpress.org/peerreview

DOI: https://doi.org/10.3998/mpub.14606494
Print ISBN: 978-1-64315-080-2
Open access ISBN: 978-1-64315-081-9

Library of Congress Control Number: 2024948048

Published in the United States of America by Lever Press, in partnership with Michigan Publishing.

*Table of Contents*

## *Member Institution Acknowledgments*

Lever Press is a collective effort. This work was made possible by the generous support of Lever Press member libraries from the following institutions:

Amherst College
Atlanta University Center Consortium
Berea College
Bowdoin College
Carleton College
Central Washington University
Claremont Colleges
Claremont Graduate University
Claremont McKenna College
Clark Atlanta University
College of Saint Benedict & Saint John's University
The College of Wooster
Davidson College
Denison University
DePauw University
Grinnell College
Hamilton College
Hampshire College
Harvey Mudd College
Hollins University
Iowa State University
Keck Graduate Institute
Knox College
Lafayette College
Macalester College
Middlebury College
Morehouse College
Morehouse School of Medicine
Norwich University
Occidental College
Penn State University
Pitzer College
Pomona College
Randolph-Macon College

Rollins College
Santa Clara University
Scripps College
Skidmore College
Smith College
Spelman College
Susquehanna University
Swarthmore College
Trinity University
UCLA Library
Union College
University of Delaware
University of Idaho
University of Northern Colorado
University of Puget Sound
University of Rhode Island
University of San Francisco
University of Sheffield
University of Vermont
Vassar College
Washington and Lee University
Whitman College
Whittier College
Willamette University
Williams College

# INTRODUCTION. /

# "I AM LOOKING FOR THE MOMENT A PAST BECOMES A POST"

## *On Introductions, Limitations, and Inquiries Outside the Frame*

What's the difference between raw matter and ruin, ruin and debris? The drift floats, it doesn't submerge; it isn't assimilated as waste and expelled or renovated. Broken down without being sorted, abandoned drift abandons any original form or allegiance to singular constitution in pursuit of momentary and undetermined detail. But cropping the whole in order to tailor another image or recognize the parts for their dissolvable plenitude requires care; demands that we, at the very least, come closer.

The making of this book and its research that began, officially, in the summer of 2017 but which I've reckoned with since my birth, has been marked by experiences of thrilling discovery, the continuous exchange between anxiety and urgency, and a pulsating sense of home that I've carried with me my whole life, a sense of home that I've been carried by, which is to say that I've both internalized and imagined. These are obligatory preconditions for most children of migrants, especially those of us born to two exiles: those persons, perhaps now adults, perhaps now with children of our own, who can only remember the places we've come from in stories. And I guess that is the point, of all of this, the research and the study itself, what the research found, if it found anything besides the fact of moving, of being moved by a necessary lack. I learned, from such an early age, a common narrative, which was in fact the absence of it. The self-silencing I became accustomed to as a child, through which my own past so often felt irretrievable, turned me into a reader, a reader into a writer, a writer into a teacher, who could only theorize a migratory text by looking, first, at his own life: my own life, where so much of the personal has been deferred or diminished through the institutionalized agenda of objectivity and distance, of specialization and separation and the cultured language of the intellectual. Everything I wish to theorize first goes through the body, what it can and cannot say, or more specifically, the trauma which is both unspeakable and transmittable, inchoate, and yet undeniably passed down. What else have I inherited but each of my parent's desires to change, and so to change the present means to alter the outcome, but also the trajectory. How we got here. And where were we, or: how do we begin?

The discourse of migration is fraught with academic, literary, and political spokespeople, conditions which leave little room for self-representation and pathways for self-determination. What I want is to pay careful attention to the moments that contradict these regular and regulative state and cultural practices, moments in which the partial, piecemeal, and processual texts by persons on the move have been able to enact the possibilities of something else, beyond being spoken about and spoken for, or otherwise made legible through assimilation in a dominant language and logic. And I began, in the summer of 2017, or rather, I continued, in June of that same year, by walking in the footsteps of Walter Benjamin, traversing the numerous sites of his seven-year exile while reading the letters he wrote at each waypoint, while writing him letters when I arrived.[1]

The occasion for meeting, for convergence, takes time, and specifically, a time that is not ordered and uniform, that is not linear, that does not separate the *before* and the *after*, that does not repeat this violence (which is all separation) through monumentalization (which is history), a time that is not about closure but about the opening up of another narrative, neither public nor hidden, but nascent: the diffuse ways in which our lives are unfolding in relation to each other. I am looking for the moment a past becomes a post. Or rather, when *past* and *post* become part of the same transmission, belonging to the same space, the same breath, a moment to read and be read in all its dimensions—awaited and remembered and hallucinated and hypostatized—this thin paper surface as Möbius strip.

Through a discursive model I call a migratory text, *Drift Net* seeks to recognize the diversity of experiences of migration, displacement, and exile, and the manifold ways of addressing them in art; and seeks to recognize a set of formal properties that are shared by the texts that make up such a corpus. This analytical approach both deepens and broadens our conceptualization of migrant literature, allowing us to open up other areas of literary study—Modernism and the twentieth-century avant-garde, the prose poem, digital poetics, documentary, autofiction, personal criticism, the broader field of life writing—through a focused treatment of migration and displacement. The migratory text—media that includes notebooks, correspondences, self-portraiture, diaristic video, auto-archival installation, and immersive performance—does not reproduce itineraries of passage so much as reveal alternative mobilities, to the extent that its textual framework allows us to read developments in creative expression alongside migrant coalition. To theorize this work is thus to encounter how migrants have mobilized autobiography—a literary-artistic mode with a long history of appropriation and exploitation by the state—to open it up from a representative territory of the individual to a porous space of collective passage. My use of *migrant* here is significant, indicative of *Drift Net*'s reassessment of the limited scope by which cultural mediators, and their audience-readers, understand migration and, by extension, the material realities of persons—a group that includes refugees, asylum applicants, exiles, displaced, stateless, and otherwise unprotected persons—who have been rendered il/legible by frameworks of legality that presuppose hierarchies of human value. Instead of consenting to a subject-position that is always and already circumscribed by ethnic, racial, national, or regional markers, the migratory texts attended to in this study can be read as performing both a renunciation and a renewal, wherein the refusal of identity—to be identified—in the *first person* is a refusal to move from one form of dispossession (containment) to another (fetishization).

As scholars before me have shown, the scope of refugee studies and the growth of the field across diverse disciplines have both been tied to policy-oriented research, always at risk of being co-opted by the organizations that fund it. Adding to these ethical dilemmas are the academic virtues or veils of critical distance and objectivity, each with the potential to obscure the particular political or bureaucratic interests of the agencies that have empowered such research. Richard Black, in his 2001 retrospective analysis of "Fifty Years of Refugee Studies," points out that even prior to the establishment of the United Nations High Commissioner for Refugees (UNHCR) in 1950—and the coinciding production of the first international organization devoted to the study of refugees, the Association for the Study of the World Refugee Problem—scholars of migration took their cue from intergovernmental organizations, beginning in the interwar era with the League of Nations.[2] At once sweeping and insular, the operation of reifying the shifting and overlapping categories of migrants—and naturalizing their differential qualities—as empirical study on the basis of policy, to influence policy that directly affects the lives of millions of people, reminds scholars of the dangers of confusing academic investment with independence. Indeed, if the birth of the study of "the refugee problem" in the interwar era and its resurgent proliferation at the end of the Cold War provides a ledger of displacement across mutable names and landscapes, it must also include the potential reinscribing of a circular knowledge production, a positivist retrieval in which we look for what we already know, that is to say, what has already been named as knowledge.

Rather than conforming to the individualization or universality of the "refugee" label prevalent in the field of refugee and forced migration scholarship,[3] these creative expressions—far from denying the actuality of inscribing one's individual experience—all yet move beyond a subject-centered ontology and toward an identity position that is collective and often anonymous. What I am interested in is how these specific texts, in reformulating modes of authorship and identity, reflect and have also reshaped contemporary digital norms—networked affect, copresence, produsage, transmedia—as well as earlier formal and aesthetic categories of artistic production ranging from autofiction to intertextual narratives and découpage. Close observation of the migratory text's material conditions and aesthetic makeup both extends and informs the legacy of Cold

War era samizdat—roughly translated as "we publish ourselves"—that flourished throughout the Soviet Union following Joseph Stalin's death in 1953, and which owed its existence to remediation, the multiple and displacing adaptations of what's already been produced in other formats.

Sharing similar timelines across various time zones, the concept of "intermedia" would also begin to circulate among the transnational coterie of Cold War artists, architects, and composers assembled under Fluxus, many of whom were incarcerated or disappeared throughout the Eastern Bloc during the three decades that followed. Intermedia, named by Fluxus cofounder Dick Higgins in 1965 and rematerialized a year later with his *Intermedial Object #1*, served to describe an art form that lies between several different media—a way of making art that had already existed and which, in being named, could be recognized anew.[4] Fluxus's output of alphabetical texts, performance and video art, and installations, and its combinatorial approaches to configurations of media as a form of art crossed not just borders of media but also lines of artistic production and critical theory, so-called artistic and scholarly practices. I want to consider how our reading of a migratory text that is produced through the movements *across* languages and media types also deepens relations of hybrid art forms and methodologies, recovering, in the process, an understanding and application of transmedia that predates digital cultures while contributing to a recently renewed intermedial studies. And yet, far from serving solely as a comparative analysis of personal texts produced in transit from the turn of the twentieth century through today, or performing as an abstract theoretical model for critical and pedagogical endeavors, this study aims to take scholarly questions and apply them to public, civic discourses.

How does a corpus of texts that are born in translation respond to a multiculturalism that is calibrated to the metrics of the nation? What can closer consideration to this corpus teach us about ways in which to reimagine the relationship between state, law, and citizenship? This study wants to pay attention to the moments where public policy, the publication and circulation of world literature and literary translation, and academic scholarship align to produce representations of migration and migrancy that are then reproduced and codified, as law or literature, in fact or in fiction. In this book, I argue that the migratory text raises important revisions for the field of world literature and models of translation both old and new—including prevalent one-to-one translations generated through machine learning—while questioning the efficacy of national literature's traditions of monolingualism and academic conventions of periodization. The migratory text subverts the hierarchical relationships between "author" and "translator" and "original" and "translation," changing our approaches to the practice of translation and the ways in which we read works in translation.

It is no secret that the vast majority of English and comparative literature departments are organized through an engagement with various national literatures, or through the study of world literature and literature in translation, informing curricula that are predicated upon colonial discourse and national thinking (along with an increasing awareness and attention toward postcolonial theory), within institutions that are similarly compartmentalized and confined to selective appropriations. The migratory text proposes a third approach, neither nationalism nor globalization, asking readers, scholars, and instructors not to place ourselves in a linear national or linguistic tradition (the originary fiction of national nativity or the polarization of universalizing totality) but to persistently displace ourselves through a relational, interactive model: textual encounters with works that are neither inside nor outside (absent, against, et cetera) the border but that dwell in the verbal transition of *border*, where to pass and be passed on is as much a language as it is a methodology.

To engage in a methodological project is not just a tactic of resistance by scholars of color but a way for us to seek revision in the language and discourse associated with the minoritized subject. This methodology, in other words, is part and parcel of the theory it sets out to develop and apply. In my investigations of a minoritarian aesthetic and a formulation for migrant subjectivity, and as someone who has traversed many roles, languages, spaces, and their borders as first-gen citizen, as Cuban and Polish, as media scholar and artist but also media commodity, as the first in my family to be here—in so many senses—it became necessary to heed the many different registers of "migratory" to labor within paradoxes surrounding citizenship and make visible the interrelations of race, sexuality, gender, and migration; to make visible, too, the interrelations of publishing, scholarship, humanitarian practices, and public policy. Perhaps, then, it is no surprise that in *Drift Net*, I locate the site of transformation, the site of agency, for these producers and in these texts, in the moments of their mediation, a movement within and without, where collaboration, polyphony, archive, and abstraction work to produce a text that could have only been produced in passage.

My desire to activate theory to apply it in public discourses outside of academia—a convergence of literary criticism and migrant activism—is mirrored by *Drift Net*'s critical-creative and autoethnographic approach, which has allowed me to develop ideas about the migratory text by reenacting its formal components within the study's analysis, contributing to the field of autoethnography and a developing body of critical-creative scholarship in different disciplines. How can we, as scholars and researchers, privilege the processual elements of our work and our writing, while shedding light on the many different voices, elements, progressions—and detours—that constitute academic discourse and, ultimately, research and publication? In pursuit of an interpretive mode of reading—to read event and encounter as one would read the text—to reassess literature and art with lived experiences, in the hopes that greater transparency in our research may also yield greater accountability to the subjects we draw upon in our scholarship.

In my investigation into a social and political commons concretized through migratory media, I join scholars such as Sarah C. Bishop, Rebecca M. Schreiber, Long Bui, Graziella Parati, Eva C. Karpinski, Mieke Bal, and others, whose significant work has formed connections between narrative, performance, autobiography, audience reception, and affect. By bringing together and building on recent scholarship from seemingly disparate fields, this book also signals a series of important departures.

Taking Alessandra di Maio at her word when she asserts that migrant writings have long been considered as "mere testimonies, sociological texts, and have been denied any literature value,"[5] I not only treat migrant literature through literary analysis, but theorize an aesthetics of transmedia in and of migration, which can be employed to read similar work, as well as to reconsider and retrieve such "testimonies" that have been obscured through their relegation to certain disciplines or spheres of culture. Lest we conflate a word and its terminological deployment, my treatment of *transmedia* differs greatly from the eminently cited "transmedia storytelling" coined by Henry Jenkins early in the new millennium and enriched, in the ensuing years, by related scholarship exploring how the franchises of corporations, and their fans, construct more expansive and immersive stories than would have been possible across a single medium.[6] My focus isn't entertainment, it's itinerary and errata, it's errantry and detritus. Though in my reading of texts whose conditions of production require movement across sign systems, I want us to think, again, about how the artifacts of "new media" phenomena—Jenkins's elaboration of transmedia storytelling included—can actually be traced to migration; that new media practices didn't begin through networked computing and interactive entertainment, the emergence of social media or the convergence of media and the concentration of media companies, but the displacement and dispersal of bodies. What I'm interested in is the material excesses inherent to the operation of transport and transformation; what I'm interested in is loss and, more specifically, lost histories, a loosening present, about how learning to read a text that moves across sign systems can nurture a more general intermedial literacy that might allow us the means to glimpse underneath the surface of our machines and the bodies that handle them, whether to recognize the complex interactions occurring whenever we switch between and combine media or, moreover, to understand how the processes that continue to shape our digital leisure also generate—in the form of container tracking software for logistics information systems—the organization of unprotected labor and exploitation of already displaced workers, people who are neither legally a "refugee" nor recognized, in popular parlance, as a "migrant" because they do not exist on land and have not, unlike the goods transported on floating shipping containers, arrived anywhere.

My theorization of an aesthetics *in and of migration* deviates from the video-centric analysis contributed by Mieke Bal, whose principal thesis is that "migratory culture [...] is best grasped in the moving image."[7] Whereas Bal relocates the act of migration itself to read it as a metaphor for a cultural condition exuding sensorial traces that have "a particularly overdetermined connection"[8] with scopic formats, my study focuses on media which, through various strategies, work to decenter visual modalities. As such, my treatment of these texts asks us to complicate hierarchies of Western perception and, specifically, the relationship of representation to visibility. Moreover, I contend that migrant authors have not only remade the traditional scope of autobiography and documentary but, in doing so, have evaded what Sandra Ponzanesi has called the "postcolonial cultural industry"[9] rife with exoticism, tokenism, fetishization, and, ultimately, the cultivation of cultural difference-as-commodity. To understand how this study of the migratory text allows us to read a blueprint for a broader intervention on the local and organizational levels of asylum, integration, public housing, and, ultimately, membership, is to also mark the ways in which migrant producers have reformulated subjectivity through the same genres and modes that have otherwise contributed to their devaluation as minoritized subjects.

Indeed, rather than understand the "limitations of [...] first-person narratives"[10] as impediments for migrants' creative responses to oppression, as Bishop does, or characterize such instances of "talking back" as sites "of compromise,"[11] in Parati's interpretation, *Drift Net* takes these limitations and interferences as the necessary conditions for collaborative, transmedia production, contributing to an examination that calls into question the *first person* of personal narratives by exploring how migratory texts have produced a collective expression while remaining unbound to the collective—the fixations of politics or descriptive institutional categories that fix one in place. To think life writing through process and affect, as Karpinski does, is to consider not only how the genre is always en route to change but moreover, how these formal shifts—what Karpinski calls "their migrations and metamorphoses"—can change the *habitus* that defines the rules and practices of legitimacy and possibility in the arena of thinking, feeling, and imagining. Whereas Karpinski contends that life writing has stretched the terms of "life" and "writing," my study asks us to think about how the migratory text, as a problematization of these terms—a *life* that is not just "a property of the subject of consciousness and perception"[12] and a *writing* that is collaborative, open-sourced, mediated in multiple ways—has altered the possibilities for autobiography and the larger field of life writing by turning such metaphors of "plasticity" and "migrations and metamorphoses" into material acts of passage and mobility.

Schreiber, who looks at how Mexican and Central American migrants have produced, curated, exhibited, and circulated photography, film, video, and audio, locates 9/11—and the ensuing polarization of world politics—as the cultural-artistic boiling point for the creative self-representations of undocumented persons that followed.[13] In contradistinction, my study traces specific strategies of migrant self-representation much farther back than the early aughts, the Bush Administration's war on terror, global neoliberalism, and digital technology. As I chart the reevaluation of archive and autobiography by migrants and internally displaced persons, this book calls for a closer look at the different hemispheric valences of postwar geopolitical alliances. By elucidating links between Eastern Europe and Latin America, the Cold War and the twenty-first century, I also want to reclaim the epistemological and intertextual advantages of "autofiction"[14]—not as an aesthetic move by literary theorists and metropolitan authors, but as a subversive detour with specific political and social aspirations by migrants and minoritized subjects.

Building on my previous scholarship traversing autobiography, translation, migration, and surveillance studies—including an investigation of the state processes and systems of capital that generate refugees, linking labor, resource extraction, militarization, and humanitarian aid to theorize a refugee-celebrity dialectic; a reassessment of audience reception theories with close attention to the social and political potential of play, reading social media as the open source from which minoritized subjects embody a self and a belonging premised on the staging of transparency; and a theorization of the glitch that connects contemporary creative strategies with a history of maneuvers by migrants of becoming imperceptible—I suggest, furthermore, that these creative practices of/at/against the border serve as a paradigm for structural shifts in user interaction and co-production within contemporary digital discourse, which may inform how users and readers approach increasingly liminal and liquid genres and modes of textual production. By reading the migratory text alongside developments in media distribution, convergence culture, and the frameworks of transmedia storytelling and produsage,[15] this book shows how migrant authors have forecast *and* reshaped new media practices and norms. In recasting a narrative of metropolitan media practices through the pipelines of migration, *Drift Net* engages with issues raised within the fields of media ecology and media archaeology. That the refugee is the vanguard of their peoples, as Hannah Arendt once wrote,[16] is evident; *Drift Net* contends that migrants must also be considered as vanguards of the cultural phenomena that have today become increasingly commonplace and which will, in years hence, be virtually normalized.

The ideas that cohere in the following chapters have emerged from intimate archival fieldwork with refugees and asylum applicants and shelter and community center staff from 2018 through 2020. This series of interactions and interviews that occurred across Europe continues to reorient my conceptual framework, which devotes close attention to queer migrants and the politics of sexuality at the border. The need for greater attention to gender and sexuality studies within the field of migration is well-documented;[17] it is worth noting here that during the three days of proceedings at the largest global scholarly conference on migration in 2019, the number of presentations totaled over five hundred; only one—a multimedia version of chapter 4's fieldwork—addressed queer migration and the specific experiences of LGBT+ migrants.

*Drift Net*'s mobilization of textual analysis to reassess the study and politics of migration is in conversation with recent scholarship contributing to a discourse Espiritu has called "critical refugee studies." Aided by a theoretical repertoire that includes queer theory and media theory, alongside gender and sexuality studies, performance studies, and translation studies, *Drift Net* critiques prevailing assimilationist models of migration that reproduce policy-based conceptions of people on the move. My investigation into the industry of literary translations and the discourse of forced migration and refugee studies testifies to the project's scope: a movement from text to authorship, and the possibilities for marginalized persons to redeem themselves and the terms by which they've been hailed through self-representations that evade the frame of recognition and a representational economy rooted in visibility. This is not a study about the "connected migrant,"[18]—Dana Diminescu's fraught conceptualization in 2008—and the ways in which this mythical figure has mobilized ICTs, so much as it explores specific ways in which migrants have reconfigured digital norms by reworking how these technologies have, at times, been used against them. Besides forging a translocal space of belonging—a transitional, fragmented, and heterogeneous membership not based in an origin, or destination—such migrant self-representations have also liquefied lines between media production and distribution. In this sense, migrants have responded to the material realities of unequal access, exploring and exposing their own desubjectification through what I identify as an aesthetics of transmedia that employs elements of autobiography, literary criticism, notebook, photo album, and correspondence.

Among my aspirations: to break down these texts into common components that may allow us to trace large-scale shifts in how textual production, consumption, and distribution occur today. To trace, as we well know, in spite of whatever painstaking care we put to the task, is to copy out *imperfectly*. It is this degree of imperfection that I want to hold onto as we examine such texts in light of the discrepancies—glitches, gaps, accretions, and "mistranslations"—intrinsic to their movement across sign systems. And although I advance the migratory text here as an object of study, a method of study, and a theory about object and method, my hope, in opening up the migratory as a practice, is that we can think about the migratory text's relevance *outside* of literature and art—that this study's inquiries necessarily exceed the scope of the disciplines and fields that have nourished it.

This book, then, wants to perform a double move: a theorization of the migratory text that is an invocation to a corpus characterized by collaboration, polyphony, archive, and abstraction; and an analysis of such texts. How do these properties play out for discourses of immigration? Or, put another way: can we employ this literary theory for a political practice? To find out, I began to investigate alternative migrant-integration models at community centers and shelters throughout Europe in the summer of 2018. I was driven by these questions—a desire to test my own study and moreover, to trouble the wider field of migration research and scholarship. When we complicate the ways in which migration has been formulated in much refugee and forced migration studies, might we recover other histories and other temporalities of passage that are not legible to a UNHCR framework, experiences of migration that do not serve and that are not guided by Western political policy or discourses of migration?

As I probed deeper into my theorization and began conducting qualitative interviews to consider my literary analyses in relation to housing initiatives and asylum reform efforts by local organizations, I began to employ the migratory text as a framework for civic activism, aiming to address a primary intervention in the field of migration studies, which has historically been framed by the UN's own policies, categories, and bureaucratic labels,[19] and that of media studies, which has largely been grounded in a universalized Western narrative of media archaeology and practices.[20] With consideration to these gaps in scholarship, it became clear to me that it would be necessary to integrate my theorization of the migratory text with studies of media ecology, and moreover, to reevaluate my suppositions outside of the academy: a reading that intervenes in refugee and forced migration studies, areas of knowledge production which have in turn shaped migrant-assimilation protocols by state actors and nongovernmental organizations (NGOs).

In continuing to explore the ways in which the academy, and the cultural productions that surround the academy, shape—and are shaped by—the legal systems that govern migration and that configure the material conditions of migrants, this study identifies the figure of the queer migrant and the space of the queer refugee camp as enacting a response and also a question, through which the Western rubric and criteria of assimilation and asylum are problematized, alongside the limits of such alternative approaches that, as of yet, proceed from a Western framework. Not unlike the migratory text that constitutes my study, the queer refugee camp thus attends to its source code as a site of collaborative interrogation and relation: a site of critique, which includes its own organization.

This book acknowledges that the lack of a nuanced, comprehensive understanding of migrant and migration in both popular culture and policy-oriented academic research are further complicated by the social-political terms and criteria for parsing the queer migrant. While a generalized and cosmopolitan literature of migration has a tendency to import further indistinctions of im/mobilities, I want to insist that our reading of the migratory text—a treatment of migrant-produced literature and art that foregrounds archive, abstraction, polyphony, and collaboration—can also deepen our consideration of persons obscured by both borders and passages, the manifold experiences of people in movement. As a work that undoes binaries of author-translator and boundaries of language and national literature, the migratory text is a queer production; throughout

*Drift Net*, my engagement of a variety of research methods and archives to observe literary-artistic developments alongside contemporary social and political organizing also highlights the queerness that is already installed in the migratory's textual makeup.

And here I begin, or return, to the beginning, a repetition[21] that is countered by its (eventual) redaction. In 2017, my starting point was to redraft Benjamin's seven-year exile from Paris to Lourdes, Lourdes to Marseilles, Marseilles to Port-Vendres, Port-Vendres to Portbou. In my endeavor to converge past and present, I collaged letters written by Benjamin during his exile; scenes of departure culled from interviews, photographic evidence, and testimonies; reportage of political and social upheaval in Europe in the same summer; and finally, my own letters, written to Walter as I read him back. During the composition of "In Parallel with My Actual Diary," during the process of our parallel encounters, it became clear that it would also be necessary to reevaluate the xenophobic culture of the European cities that we each had traversed. It became clear that it would be necessary for this study, too, to bridge but also complicate the gaps between the interwar era and today to shed light on the undocumented microhistories of migration. In *Drift Net*, I similarly invite you to attend to what is missing, what begins and what has been redacted as beginning, reminders and residue which inevitably exceed the text, so that the trace of the action becomes another node of connectivity to the (net)work proper, and in this abbreviated, constellatory, and self-referential manner, a work in itself.

For a project that asks critical questions about mobility and the ways in which the personal text has been employed and ultimately altered in service of migrant self-representation and, elsewhere, safe conduct, the readers that approach the following pages might take *Drift Net* as more than an overdetermined title or representative description but as instructions for use. Put differently: if this book can be thought of as a network, then I'd like us to read the chapters herein as sites of connectivity and detour, each of which are organized by their attention to a specific characteristic of the migratory text. Both network and crosscurrent, *Drift Net* wants us to think, too, of trapping and extraction, but also the perforations in a net that allow bodies to sift through without being sorted, without retrieval, an eliding of hard force through the fluidity of tides.

Like Kale Bantigue Fajardo, who reorients traditional geographic cultural frameworks as *oceanographies of culture* to identify the "maritime border zones" where race, class, gender, and sexuality are intermittently and inherently translated and reconfigured,[22] I want us to read beyond centers and margins to heed such spaces and subjects in between.

Although I consult the interwar period in chapter 1 to distill certain textual markers through a close analysis of notebooks and correspondences produced in transit, it is the Cold War that *Drift Net* takes as central and that this study continues to broach in its analysis of the different political maneuvers, geographies, and genealogies which inform a migratory text spanning the plastic arts, performance, and literature. The mutability of literary and artistic categories, as I detail in the first chapter's coming pages, is here only overshadowed by the mutable nature of a form that might encompass them in a single text. Without any desire for unity or synthesis, it is likewise capaciousness, the generosity of form—the multiplication of differences, which yields similarity—that has been both inspiration and aspiration, and which serves this book as its author's own memento, a memory and a sigil: what I want, I remember thinking, as I am thinking now, is to understand my parents' distinct passages as parallel currents; to rethink the frame—which is always a border—of the "East" and the "West" before, during, and after the Cold War; to return to recent history to continue to imagine alternative forms of government to colonial rule, to consider the routes out of empire today as in the past as manifold and necessarily intersecting.

## STRUCTURE OF THE BOOK

What is brought to light when we converge studies of migration with media theory? Chapter 1, "Tracing Imperfections for an Amateur Aesthetic: A Genealogy," charts the movements of errant, personal accounting by migrants and displaced persons from the turn of the twentieth century through today. In attending to an orbit that includes letters, notebooks, CVs, and fabricated broadcasts during the interwar era, I argue that the aesthetics of migrant self-representation and the cultural norms of digital culture are intimately connected. Multiplicity of address, self-reflexive performativity, interactivity, anonymity, immersion, appropriation, copresence, and glitch—today's aesthetic strategies to compose content and identity across digital media aren't unique to the internet; the strategies of new media users, in other words, are neither new nor exclusively digital, they're migratory. These formal markers, chapter 1 shows, are a response to the material experience of displacement and drift during the interwar period, and the proliferation of de/nationalization, statelessness, detainment, and exile that would follow, across diverse landscapes, throughout the Cold War. And to examine pre-internet writing to make a point about digital culture is also to make a point about how the migratory text proposes not merely a mode of textual production, but a mode of reading, in which we can engage with these notebooks, letters, and assemblages of criticism anew, to illuminate their migratory context.

As I link the manipulation or disappearing of genre—a response to a porous and performative sense of self that is today more about (mutable) presentation than (fixed) content—with the publication and distribution of the migratory text, I argue that it is not just autobiography—the first person of personal texts—that migration calls into question, but the system of trackable "category" as a normalizing logic for the literary-art structure and its community. Through a combination of close readings and cultural theory, and guided by recent scholarship on the ways in which migrants, refugees, and asylum applicants have used digital mediation and correspondence, virtual memorialization, and networked activism, chapter 1 establishes a genealogy of the migratory text by looking closely at the amateur aesthetic and processual aspect of the scrapbook as a form and method, a fuzzy realism which, unlike the precepts of today's new media, does not erase the traces of mediation but rather embeds them as textual archive, a point of contact I will return to throughout each chapter to follow.

How does the migratory text question, contest, revise, and respond to realist documentarian narratives—the language of the UNHCR and humanitarian-focused NGOs—as well as to their generic literary and cultural representations, of being spoken for and spoken about? In the 1995 edited collection *Writing Across Worlds*, editors Russell King, John Connell, and Paul White set out to investigate the ways in which creative work may inform the work of sociology, and in particular, how "'non-academic' literature, written often (but by no means exclusively) by migrants, can offer insights into the nature of the migration process and the experience of being a migrant," a narrative, they contend, that is commonly accounted for—and delimited by—social-scientific research that "fails to capture the essence of what it is like to *be* a migrant."[23] To understand international migration, which they identify as "a dominant feature of world literature from both post-industrial and developing countries," the editors contend that it is necessary to bring together "the social scientist's concerns with explanation and the student of literature's expertise in the handling of text."[24] Lest we take this disciplinary intervention as anything more than an entry point into parsing the artificial distinctions—"'non-academic' literature," "fully-fledged creative literatures," or any other (see the editors' "evolutionary series of forms of migrant literature," a model laid out in the book's preface)—brought by the academy, while continuing to place migrant literature and art more centrally in analyses of migration, we should read any attempt by white metropolitan scholars to "capture the essence of what it is like to *be* a migrant" as another conquest—an embodying and an erasure.

In contradistinction, by bringing into focus a critique of world literature—"all literary works," in David Damrosch's oft-cited definition, "that circulate beyond their culture of origin, either in translation or in their original language"[25]—and advancing scholarship in performance studies, translation studies, and autobiography studies, my second chapter, "Migration as the Primal Scene of Narrative and a Model for its Reconfiguration," demonstrates the significance of storytelling in transmitting not only a migrant's singular experience of passage, but also a collective condition of mobility and a collaborative model for detouring traditional narrative structures.

World literature, as Lawrence Venuti has argued, cannot be conceptualized apart from translation;[26] likewise, as a work produced in movement, the migratory texts examined throughout *Drift Net* cannot be read without attention to the ways they reformulate each of these systems. Rather than consent to a universalizing and generic world literature, the migratory text circulates beyond its culture of origin by calling the origin—the source, the site of textual nativity, the native tongue—into question, evading the national and revising the framework of world literature through collaborative, multi-sourced, and mistaken translations.

My attention to the "remainder," here and throughout *Drift Net*, as the signifier of non-equivalence *and* convergence inherent in all acts of documentation and retrieval, reevaluates Venuti's concept of the remainder, after Jean-Jacques Lecercle, as the "textual effects that exceed transparent uses of language geared to communication and reference and may in fact impede them, with varying degrees of violence."[27] This study contends that the remainder—not merely as an effect but as a mode of exposure—specifically through revealing such traces of mediation, allows for a more nuanced understanding of translation's limitations, but also its possibilities: the complications and interferences in every *intended meaning*.

In relating translation's mutually transformative process, the works discussed throughout chapter 2—Edward Said and Jean Mohr's *After the Last Sky: Palestinian Lives*, Edgar Garcia's *Skins of Columbus*, Craig Santos Perez's *from Unincorporated Territory*, Brent Armendinger's *Street Gloss*, Fernanda Farias de Albuquerque's *Princesa*, and the embroidered paintings of Klára Hosnedlová—propose a radical reinvention of the source *as* the trace. In selecting texts that straddle distant geographies, generations, genres, and media, I wish to emphasize the breadth of this corpus while recognizing its proximity to Caren Kaplan's early nineties formulation of an "out-law genre"[28] and its properties of autobiography (practice) and autobiographical critique (theory), each of which are mobilized, alongside the transitional material relations embedded within the work (process) as key ingredients of the migratory text.

Striving to raise further questions about audience and address, and aided by scholarship that examines the "refugee repertoire" of performance (Bui 2016) and the function of audience members as somatic collaborators activated by a "spectator consciousness" (Freedman 1991), this chapter juxtaposes the migratory text with generic representations of migration commonly circulated as world literature, including the serialized anthology *Refugee Tales* (2016–current). As scholars such as Liisa H. Malkki have shown, humanitarian practices tend to silence refugees, specifically by stripping them of the authority to produce narrative evidence of their own conditions;[29] my analysis shows, furthermore, how capitalist globalization and liberal humanism have spurred a literary-art cultural industry rooted in literary translation and the literature of exile and migration, and how universalizing trends in publishing and translation have reproduced such practices of silencing. In continuing to observe the manufacturing of intimacy and transparency alongside the processual architecture of the migratory text and its invitation for immersion—as demonstrated by Syrian filmmaker Reem Karssli's 2013 video diary, *Every Day, Every Day,* and her more recent co-production with Caroline Williams, *Now Is the Time To Say Nothing* (2017–current)—I again look to contemporary digital culture, juxtaposing the migratory's potential for empathic labor with current technology to reevaluate the techno-utopian promise of virtual reality as an empathy machine.

How have migrants and other displaced and internally excluded persons used both self-forgery and erasure in service of mobility? How can we read an aesthetics of disappearance as more than just an artistic choice but as a source of activism? Following Jacques Rancière, I understand that such aesthetic acts are capable of creating "new modes of sense perception"[30] and, in doing so, they produce alternative forms of political subjectivity. In my third chapter, "Documenting Disappearance: Self-Forgery and Erasure as a Means of Mobility," I continue to draw from a range of media—including Eastern European and Latin American avant-garde poetics, Caribbean abstract expressionism, Palestinian scrapbooks, and Soviet Bloc self-portraiture—while comparing migrant self-representations and creative tactics of camouflage, mimicry, and dissembling with public practices. The extraterritorial space of the makeshift camp—in Calais, in Rome, along the Balkan Peninsula, and elsewhere—is read in my analysis as a site of question and crossroads, a self-organized refuge and a paradigm for preserving invisibility and anonymity that brushes up against Karma R. Chávez's investigation into a queer migration politics, in which "queerness" is linked with "coalition": the moment in which "distinction between entities blends and blurs"—that moment that resists "permanent incorporation into one body."[31] If *passing* can be read as a restoration, as C. Riley Snorton, in his *Black on Both Sides: A Racial History of Trans Identity*, has argued,[32] then we might read *fugitivity* in this context and for my study as a resistance: not only a reimagining of the normative system and logic of race and gender, but also as a reimagining of the terms of belonging and community—to flee citizenship so as to reinvent it.

The migratory text signals just this movement; this study, likewise, calls for a shift from discussing who makes art (producer) to whom art makes (subject): the production of self, in view of an/other, where, as we know, politics is played out, in the gathering between stage, audience, and the performer's body. And yet, it is not just that aesthetic acts have the potential to produce novel forms of political subjectivity, as Rancière understood, but that, in order for the latter to be true, the equation needs to be reversed: political subjects *must first be recognized as aesthetic subjects*. To elaborate this distinction, I juxtapose Eastern Bloc self-portraiture prior to the fall of the Soviet Union with the self-representations of undocumented migrants in the wake of 9/11, demonstrating common markers across different generational fabrics.

As I place the mixed-media work of East German artist Cornelia Schleime in conversation with the contemporary glitch art—drawings, paintings, video—of Kon Trubkovich, who was born in Moscow and left, at age eleven, following the Chernobyl disaster, my aim is also to continue to broach the multiple, intersecting, and extant repercussions of the Cold War, geographically and generationally. By calling attention to the documentation of performance and the performance of documentary, I show how migrants have implemented a scrapbook aesthetic in the creation of their own self-representations—returning themselves to the public as aesthetic subjects—a strategy that not only destabilizes the borders between autobiography and fiction, but also undermines the power structures of identitarian subjectification. Forced to negotiate overexposure and omission in the public sphere, migrants have returned to the aesthetic forms that have too often represented them by producing *themselves* on their terms—a break from the oscillation between subject and object, whereby political subjectivity is enacted through the evacuation of subjectification; to reorient the terms of visibility it becomes necessary, this study asserts, for subject-producers to *stage the gaze* that would otherwise objectify them.

How has the parallel rise of refugee studies and world literature in the late eighties obscured certain structural and policy issues of migration that remain present today? How can a comparative analysis bring together different disciplines to critique current practices in scholarship, publishing, and public policy? How can the queer migrant—and the space of the queer migrant camp—present a foundation for integration techniques that upends traditional hierarchies and power structures between empowered citizen-actors and politically and socially disempowered migrants? And how might this social-cultural intervention, as the seeds of an alternative political ecology, contribute to the discourse of decoloniality, from which a growing body of scholarship on migration has drawn?

Bringing together an array of scholarship on world literature (Denning 2004; Kadir 2004; Mufti 2016, et al.) and informed by critical examinations of postcolonialism (Appiah 1991; Loomba 2005), postmodernism (Mignolo 2018), transnationalism (Balibar 2004), and decolonialism (Tuck and Yang 2012; Garba and Sorentino 2020), my closing chapter, "Remapping the State and the Academy from Within and Without," reads literary, cultural, and academic representations of migration against models for migrant coalition produced by community organizations, art centers, and shelters across Central, Southern, and Northern Europe. Alongside interviews and interactions at the Schwulenberatung and the Kreuzberg Initiative against Antisemitism (Berlin), the Trampoline House and the Center for Art on Migration Politics (Copenhagen), and the Sigismondo Castromediano and the Ribezzo cultural centers (Puglia), I revisit scholarship on queer migration, including work by Martin F. Manalansan (2006), Lionel Cantú Jr. (2005), Chandan Reddy (2005), and Héctor Carrillo (2004), to historicize and address extant racialized and gendered labor migration and the twinning of migration and sexuality through their dual control by the state, as I continue to underscore the fraught nature of "visibility" in all its valences.

Returning to the Cold War concept of Négritude that emanated from the Caribbean (Césaire 2000; Glissant 2020) while revisiting chapter 2's critical discussion of the publishing and translation industries—linking art and scholarship with public policy and social practices—my hope is that we might begin to envision the migratory text as an alternative to the fetishization of exile and displacement as a subject, and the global circulation of national literatures in translation as a method. In the final analysis, I argue that we can apply critiques of migration studies (Espiritu 2006; Hayden 2006; Bakewell 2007; Treitler 2015; Chatty and Marfleet 2013, et al.) to a larger critique of migrant-assimilation techniques by state organizations and NGOs, and that these connections should be read alongside the publishing industry and the academy that sanctions a world literature. Representations of migrants and migration in journalism, academia, and art should be read alongside one another, yielding a critique that implicates state and humanitarian aid actors, but also scholars, publishers, and writers.

Among the recurring maneuvers in this study is the contention that such connections beg others, and that to analyze a migratory text within the wider scope of comparative media studies is to interrogate the same technical processes that have further obscured—or else depoliticized and rationalized—migrant exploitation. As indispensable labor to the organization of the global supply chain for retail conglomerates, and silenced phantom in the social-economic-political organization of everyday life, the migrant worker relates our moment's unsustainable (and paradoxical) tenets of "transnational flow" and "national borders," to the extent that the migrant body unsettles the body politic by revealing the logistical assembly of raw materials that in turn assemble the vast swath of free citizens' lives. To return the migrant worker to visibility thus converges not only the inside/outside (and more specifically: the inclusion/exclusion of national or supranational memberships) but also the East and West, colonialism and imperialism, global capitalist processes (accumulation, extraction) and governmentality (sovereignty, law).

For all protected, free, or enfranchised persons, the task becomes not a matter of choosing sides—party lines, political programs, ideologies—nor even of recommitting one's self to the practice of democracy and a celebrated humanism—moral or ethical codes of freedom, justice, liberty, the rights of the individual—but, on the contrary, to admit the limitations of these credos while imagining ways in which to modify a membership that is not tied to the inclusion-exclusion dialectic of a "universal" citizenship, the paradoxical arrangement of the "rights of man" *and* a "common" birthright—mythos, heritage—under a singular nation-state. Indeed, this study finds that as coalitions endeavor to educate and empower migrants in civic practices, even the most alternative integration models produced by local community organizations, arts centers, and shelters reveal the restraints of institutional membership and organizational language and logic—echoes of an interpretive paradigm that reproduces exclusionary and normative practices on the ground—while raising further questions about what democracy means, within and without the transnational political space.

Why is art useful in this context? Why would an annual art festival—the Refugee Festival in Malaysia, Bristol's Refugee Festival, Manchester's Journeys Festival International, the One Journey Festival in Washington, D.C., the Global Festival of Dignified Rage, among many others—matter during this moment of institutionalized debt, rising global inequality, the normalization of risk, disproportionate vulnerability, resurgent racism and xenophobia, and the proliferation of borders both digital and material?

Another way of asking this is asking ourselves: what is it we turn to when we turn to the arts? And what is it we find? In theorizing a corpus of texts produced by migrants and their kin—an analysis that foregrounds the production of agency *and* a recognition of the complex fabrics of power negotiated by persons whom society too often considers weak and powerless—this book wants also to reconsider the work of affect as a generator of events, where the event and its materials are at once too personal, too collective, too clumsy, too fugitive, too slippery to fit neatly into any *right space*. The reconceptualization of space, and the movement from the space of art to the art space as a creative, social, and political locus all at once seems to me to signal the trajectory tendered or perhaps more accurately tended to by the migratory text.

To feel affective force—the movement of language after language—is the occasion for what we think of when we think of a work as "poetic," however far, Brian Massumi reminds us, its actual relation to poetry.[33] To be poetic is thus to be a generator of affective intensities that might be carried by language and which most certainly are carried long after the author-artist-producer has stopped, which is to say long after the text in question has been resolved as "finite" and "fixed." In this sense, immediation, as the immediacy of affect's occurring in the event, exceeds subjects just as it exceeds form, *even as it comes into being and because it is not limited to being*. This surplus of sense, of preexisting meanings and meanings still to come, what Massumi has called the "autonomy of affect,"[34] is exactly what might precipitate, in all its uncertainty and indeterminacy, a reinvention of representative democracy as a politics of emergent subjectivities: a subjectivity without subjects.

Yet rather than see *mediation* and *immediation* as disparate and even mutually exclusive, as process philosophers such as Massumi and Erin Manning have asserted, this study understands each phenomenon as partner, as agent in the collaboration of an alternative politics and an ethics of care that takes as its premise differential subjectivities rather than the zero-sum situation of mutual exclusion and competition for security, competition of identity. I want to read immediation in this project as the event of mediation ... the moment when an aesthetics of transmedia unfolds into the realm of the public and the everyday. Immediation may very well be the middle, the "middling"—against which, in Manning's supposition, mediation comes between "to parse [...] existing terms" and ultimately, in her understanding, to preserve them.[35] But it is also and moreover, as I've witnessed during the daily "Parliament" of the Trampoline House in Copenhagen, as I've encountered in my interactions with staff and shelter residents at the Schwulenberatung Berlin, as I've recognized in the pedagogical interventions within the institutional spaces of art and education in Puglia's "Welcoming Museums" and KIGA's "Discover Diversity" programs, the potentiality of mediation as it has been staged—as it has been enacted *in stages*—by the migratory text. What I am trying to straddle—without any attempt at grasping—is a development without denouement, an eventuality that arises if and when we mobilize theory for the seeds of a political ecology. How does the occurrence of event—its taking place; both the particulars of space and the unindexed potentialities of mobility—inform and shape the event itself? The migratory text is what happens—what might occur, as potential *and* as trace—when we move from the subject to their staging; a focus on mediation and its preservation allows us, in this study, to read the shift from who makes art to whom—and what—art makes, as a metatextual interval: from the multiple and discontinuous stages of fabrication to exhibition, through which arises an occasion which is never merely "creative" or "artistic" (let alone "poetic"), but social and political.

There is always a displacement within the processes of trapping that gathers garbage and sentient life one and the same, the incommensurable trauma that nevertheless provokes overturning, inversions, undecidability, indeterminacy: the momentary melting point of objects becoming subjects, or vice versa. When Timothy Morton, in 2012, reorients the coordinates of what we call the Anthropocene, is it any wonder that he can only theorize his *hyperobject*—and its belated deliverance; the potential bearer of the justice to come—through the mushroom cloud of the atomic bomb, in the thin layer of radiation bubbling within the Earth's crust, upon the shallow iceberg tip of a perennially intensifying global warming? I prefer his essay's closing example, when Morton, taking Percy Shelley at his word, thinks the poem as a hyperobject whose meaning *is* its future, its spectral futurality, "the gigantic shadows," as Shelley once wrote, "that futurity casts upon the present"[36]—shadows, which, in their protean contingency, exceed form, which is to say, exceed presence, exceed *a present*, in order to accommodate the heterogeneity of pasts and futures, the gathering of relations that would productively entangle otherwise perpendicular timelines and spacetimes. If the poem-as-hyperobject can only be seen, that is heard, in its capacity for withdrawal, then what is needed, in our reading of the migratory text within and outside this book, is a refocusing of aesthetic awareness.

## TO END IS TO BEGIN: CURRENT LIMITATIONS AS FURTHER INQUIRIES

What are the limitations of this project? In lieu of a conclusion, I offer a(nother) set of questions. If our work as researchers, instructors, and organizers is to track and respond to the simultaneous processes by which citizens and non-citizens become "strange," or estranged from the countries in which they live and work ... as *l'étranger*, both stranger *and* foreigner in the French, or, alternatively, as both "more than foreign" and "less than foreign," assimilated and excluded, as residents and employees in the spaces in which they have become or remain unprotected, what might we encounter through a closer look at logistics, casting our eyes, moreover, to the ways in which the software systems used in coordinating supply chain infrastructures function within our own universities?[37] Such an interrogation implicates the industrial and the institutional to probe further into the inquiries this *Drift Net* casts as a starting point.

Elsewhere, I've written that nothing is wasted, not even waste.[38] But waste is not exactly or ever only *nothing*; waste is neither accident, excess, or junk but a sprawling business, a generator of spatial relations, and one that literally connects—as zonal residue of exception—data management and collection with the collection and management of moving bodies, through which the seamless flow of labor mobility is not understood as migration at all. What fails to disappear completely, what closer attention to logistics—the interface of technical systems, management software, and supply chain infrastructures—wants to retrieve, account for, is more than trash but the *refusal* of bodies: evidence of exploitation, extraction, collection, and aggregation in special, exempt, and interstitial locations; reference points in which to imagine social-political alliances among transnational workers.

As we know from the proliferation of biometric practices at border control checkpoints, asylum application interviews, admittance to refugee shelters, residence and naturalization processes, and evaluations of eligibility for basic human rights, technology has for years legitimized claims to security, mobility, and community; such exclusionary measures conducted under the auspices of transnational ideals have only intensified in years and in light of a global pandemic experienced unequally throughout the globe. The impact of COVID—racialized and gendered—has been particularly detrimental for migrants because of border closures and the suspension of asylum procedures, against which existing marginalization—poor infrastructure, overcrowded housing, the inability to move, let alone *socially distance*—inevitably escalates.

What are the wider social and political consequences of the prevailing logic—and desire—for immediacy? The aesthetic and political dimensions of omnipresent optimization, streamlining, and rationalization in our social and institutional spaces, our geographies and ecologies, the precincts of law and governance, amidst the time of pandemic and the amorphous spaces of the extraterritorial camp? In French, it is revealing in and of itself that a *parasite* may also refer to the static in a communication act, what we think of as interference, the often inaudible "noise" intrinsic to every transmission. So a virus invades a body; so noise leaks out from the surface skin of a machine otherwise humming with the fiction of immediacy—in either case, what becomes exigent is adjustment, modulation, hospitality: the readjustment of our internal organisms as a means of survival, and a survival contingent upon copresence. In the company of virus, we are compelled to change, to surrender ourselves and our ideas about ownership and autonomy, to give up, and in giving up, to give ourselves, as nascent host, completely and unconsciously, over to our desiring guest. Neither subject nor object, parasite serves the artery of mediation, which provokes the passage of emergence: another I, whom I feel, in such moments, below my skin, as I learn about myself through the other.

The migrant, the human made illegal and alien, the asylum applicant existing between borders and nationalities, the undocumented body eliding the biometrics and data of surveillance and collection, the unreturnable exile, all of these persons appear to the state as noise and parasites; all of these persons are articulated by the state and its politicians in the language of plague and infection, as vector of disease and contamination, as leech of social resources and economic opportunities; all of these persons, neither subjects nor citizens under the law, indistinct and unanticipated like the noise embedded in every message, teach us about the limitations of the state and the conditions in which it operates, the state of exception that produces political legitimacy and legitimize a politics of exclusion; the virus that is no longer a guest but a hostage: ransomed and renounced, castigated and expelled.

In this study, as I continue to develop my earlier conceptualizations of noise as revelatory metatext and informational accomplice, I take as paramount the political dimensions of mediality itself, where the affective capacity of the *in between*—the midway point of transmission, of transit—relates itself as a space of transformation. The migratory text, through its capacity to represent both the event and its recording, can be read as a form of noise, which, just as in communication theory, forces a crisis, the etymological turning point that implies a change to the existing system or its pattern of relations.

Prior to our current pandemic, the camp and the city were already indistinguishable. Sites of violence and industrial capital—Berlin's Tempelhof camp, Paris's Centre Humanitaire—have ghosted the present as municipal spaces of mobility and detainment. At the same time, 60 percent of all refugees and 80 percent of all internally displaced persons live, today, in urban areas rather than organized camps.[39] Closer scrutiny of the state's detailed organization and implementation of complex operations and movements yields still other inquiries. How has the pandemic challenged urban development agendas, while provoking the recurrence of colonial governance as a recurrent state of emergency in cities across the world? How has the multiplication of material and immaterial borders in the city been reified, in parts, by the city's function, in the time of pandemic, as a landscape of timed and coordinated movements of distant bodies and things?

In many ways, these questions are beyond the scope of this project, and I suppose that, too, is the point. The migratory text as a site of tension and paradox, of productive discord echoed by its polyphonic composition, reminds me that this book sets forth a framework, not a formula, for returning our scholarship to the communities in which and for which we work. I believe the formal properties theorized throughout *Drift Net* are useful in signaling the plot—the conceptual groundwork—for sowing concrete political actions in the day-to-day of our lives. This, too, is not and can never be a conclusion but only the interlude, equally *no longer* and *not yet*, a moment that redirects our gaze, that dislocates our place of enunciation, that provides nothing if not continuance and discontinuity, the duration necessary to envision *something else* in its place: a transformation of the relationships between state, law, and citizenship. The migratory text can be our source code.

## CHAPTER ONE: ARCHIVE. /

# TRACING IMPERFECTIONS FOR AN AMATEUR AESTHETIC

## *A Genealogy*

Exiled in Berlin during the disintegration of the USSR, Dubravka Ugrešić, who was born in Yugoslavia after the country split from the Soviet Union and before it was wiped off the map, speaks about a childhood game she often played. "That most elementary child's game," she writes, describing how, in view of others, she would cover her eyes with her hands and say, "I've gone," and then, opening her hands, announce: "Here I am," to which the children around her would respond, in agreement: "There you are!" A game, nevertheless, which Ugrešić insists, "fixed certain concepts in the consciousness: here I am, I exist (therefore, I see), and I've gone, I don't exist (therefore, I don't see)."[1]

Yet this game of make-believe, for Ugrešić as for other persons on the move and those displaced and detained in a radically territorialized world, is not just about *fixing* a concept of consciousness, but *breaking* the borders of representation, whereby appearance and disappearance may coincide, and moreover, may be deployed, amidst the reality of indefinite detention, amidst the reality of interminable passage, through enacting a different mode to articulate the "I" of identity. Coming into the world, Ugrešić writes, at a time when people destroyed everything—not just towns and other people but memory—even the act of remembering would have to be revised; at a time in which, as she points out, "the word 'identity' resounded everywhere like the holy word of God, and people were killing one another with divine ease in its name,"[2] one would have to refuse the first person, or learn to fuse it with a collective body. Ugrešić's anecdote reveals a post internet approach to artistic production and identity formation that was already happening in migrant communities well before the convergence of information and communication technologies (ICTs) and the emergence of the World Wide Web. How can we learn from other persons on the move who have resisted both the subjectification and commodification brought by global capitalism?

Collaboration, polyphony, archive, and abstraction—such are the formal characteristics of what I call in this study a *migratory text*. This chapter wants to chart the movements of errant, personal accounting while at the same time demonstrating its political function across digital discourses, particularly for the construction of identity by migrants and displaced persons. In doing so, I wish to cast a wider net, as this book's title suggests, for a hybrid poetics that has been for far too long theorized through a monochromatic Western genealogy; by employing this study to retrace this lineage, I want to call attention to the patterns of migration and displacement that have continuously advanced this discourse of hybridity and been obscured by it.

When does the migratory text appear? Why does it emerge? Where—and in what ways—does it circulate? Why should we care? I believe that we can distill certain markers of this corpus through a close analysis of notebooks and correspondences produced in transit—those degraded diaristic forms, which formalists like Viktor Shklovsky and Yury Tynyanov endeavored, in the interwar era, to push into "literary facts"—and that we can employ these findings to study the self-representations of migrants today. Closer attention to the formal markers of these personal accountings, I argue, can yield instructions on how to read contemporary migrant refusals to be thought of as commodity or victim, their maneuvers for producing themselves not only as subjects, but as agents of social and cultural change. The potential of these traversals depends, of course, on eliding the frame—dodging cultural and literary representations, along with their systems' prescriptive blueprints, so as to reconfigure them. At stake, too, is not just a negotiation of the cultural industry's commodification of identity but the academy's privileging of specific literature and its periodization.

If it is true, as Fredric Jameson asserts in his 1981 methodological guide, *The Political Unconscious*, that every hermeneutic is dependent upon a particular historical and social condition, what is ours in relation to the migratory text?[3] Any discussion of "a third digital revolution"[4] characterized by an Internet of Things that send and receive data demands that we think about the networks of data that send and receive people, and moreover, the transmission of texts situated in the breaks of route and movement. And yet, I want to make clear that today's aesthetic strategies to compose content and identity across digital media are not unique to the internet; the strategies of new media users—multiplicity of address, self-reflexive performativity, interactivity, anonymity, immersion, appropriation, copresence, and glitch—are neither new nor exclusively digital, they're migratory. It is not, this book contends, exposure to the internet that helps produce them, but *exposure to migration.*

To study the migratory text is to read migration not merely as subject but as paradigm: the recuperation of media that have been born in translation and produced in passage, or alternatively, in detention or exile, a state of indeterminacy that manifests in each work's anonymous/collective accounting and in its nonlinear form and intermedial structure. Likewise, we can understand these texts as migratory because of their ability to embody a heterochronic "migratory aesthetic," which I wish to push outside of Mieke Bal's limited sphere of video[5] and toward a wide range of old and new media: notebooks, correspondences, self-portraiture, diaristic video, auto-archival installation, immersive performance, and other uncategorizable texts, which similarly place the self in question, and question the terms of representation. As in the everyday act of passage, migratory texts invite emergent and unplanned interactions as a form of authorship, what I describe, in later chapters, as *the staging of co-incidence*. This convergence, or slippage, between distant temporal, spatial, and linguistic zones, carries a particular resonance for reader/user collaborations, including translation, as well as the indiscriminate resignification of a work in alternate formats. A migratory text—through its imperfections of reproduction and unplanned exchanges—makes visible the event of mediation that is too often erased or otherwise streamlined by emerging media.[6]

Of course, to examine pre-internet writing to make a point about digital culture is also to make a point about how the migratory text proposes not merely a mode of textual production, but a mode of reading, in which we can engage with these notebooks, letters, and assemblages of criticism anew, to illuminate their migratory context. These formal markers—collaboration, polyphony, archive, and abstraction—are a response to the material experience of displacement and drift during the interwar period, and the proliferation of de/nationalization, statelessness, detainment, and exile that would follow, across diverse landscapes, throughout the Cold War.

To understand these creative strategies by migrants, we need to understand how the notebook and correspondence—as a mode and a methodology—inform a broader archival impulse shaped by an amateur aesthetic. If one function of writing is not merely to explore one's subject but to also explode it, transforming it into something else, the privileging of the processual elements inherent in the act of personal accounting—the documenting of the immediacy of thought, and its progression—make it a particularly instructive form in the sphere of social resistance, a how-to for reevaluating the current moment, through which the act of keeping a notebook serves as a tracing of the history of thought and art, as well as its transcribed preparations. Susan Sontag, in her own notebook, believed that the notebook was simultaneously an art form, a thought form, and a philosophical form.[7] The notebook can be all of these things, I argue, because it is none of these things in name, escaping the literary markers that accompany designations of genre and mode, not in spite of but because of its cultural dismissal as an inchoate, incidental, patchwork text.

Nevertheless, to locate the charge of the migratory text—an aesthetics of transmedia that employs elements of autobiography, literary criticism, photo album, correspondence, and notebook—means not only continuing to position its orbit of influence alongside the archival urges of social media feed, but also a parallel surge of critical-creative scholarship within academia. Nancy K. Miller, in her 1991 book, *Getting Personal*, gives this "new" discourse a name: *personal criticism*, the "confessional, locational, academic, political, narrative, anecdotal, biographematic" performances within the act of criticism, by which self-narrative, theory, and the use of interstitial material coalesce into the attempt "to mark the body's presence." Miller likens personal criticism to a "passport," whose author is always specified and singular, identified "by gender, color, and national origin."[8] Through digital mediation, migrants and asylum seekers are today able to both mark—inscribe, efface—and remark upon their presence, to stay in touch with other migrants they've encountered along the way and family members they've left behind. In doing so, migrants have become alternately perceptible and imperceptible, able to speak for themselves while refuting the connotations of lack and deficiency associated with the socially undesirable categories to which they've been placed, as well as the identity constructions—"gender, color, and national origin"—which have been used to sort them.[9]

Virtual practices of self-presentation, copresence, and mobilization are common tactics used by today's asylum seekers, including those I met in Berlin in 2018; I want to think about how, in converging political demands with social urges, these habits challenge borders through the partial disclosures offered by open access technologies, tending to a networked affect that relies on both attachment and dispersal, the serendipitous or systematized encounters that emerge between bodies, not all of which are human.[10] A decade earlier, Jodi Dean described the flows of communicative capitalism as affective networks, which "capture subjects, intensities, and aspirations," while interrupting singular content in favor of seriality.[11] Content, thus, is overridden by contribution. Verbs replace nouns. Action doesn't replace feelings but is driven by them: desire strives toward jouissance, which can only arrive, Dean argues, from communication for its own sake.[12] What is perhaps obscured by this excess, this accelerated movement from information to affect, is the internal transport between users, in which thoughts and memories that are not our own move us beyond ourselves. We are captured because we enjoy, Dean says. I say, we enjoy because we are captured, and this *capture* allows us to transcend bodily, spatial, and temporal constraints, an important consideration that informs the ways in which migrants continue to shape digital discourse from the periphery. By relating qualities that we often associate with new media users to make mediation *visible*, the migratory text does not just trouble new media customs and characteristics—the futurological tropes of transparency and perfection—but asks us to reconsider the trajectory and location of new media: a departure from white and Western centric narratives of technological progress and hubs of interactivity.[13]

At the turn of the new millennium, scholars of gender and sexuality were beginning to understand that theorizations of globalization and transnationalism could learn from critical studies of sex. Their novel proposals were rooted in the earlier assessment that the opposite was in fact also true: Sex has learned from globalization and transnationalism. Elizabeth A. Povinelli and George Chauncey, in their introduction to *GLQ*'s final issue of 1999, "Thinking Sexuality Transnationally," accounted for the "explosive" diversity of sexual identities and practices in New York throughout the twentieth century by tracking migration to the United States' largest city: first the arrival of southern and eastern European Catholics and Jews in the interwar era, then the migration of Puerto Ricans to Manhattan in the 1950s. "It is impossible to understand the sexual history of New York, Rio de Janeiro, San Juan, and other cities in the Americas," they insisted, "without coming to terms with the implications of such transnational movements and the tremendous translocal mobility of every city's residents."[14]

Though I want to go further. Not only has sex and transnationalism learned from each other, but both have learned from the digital technologies that have re/produced the global and glocal of embodied experience tethered to media, the markers of "hybridity" and "liquid modernity" that characterize platform capitalism and, more broadly, twenty-first century social life. Bodies, languages, desires—a whole grammar of sexuality with which to learn about one's self through another—are channeled, not just through the migration of persons but through the movement of media across different sign systems, which conveys nothing if not a critical discrepancy between sender and receiver, "source" and "destination." Who speaks—when and from where? It's not just that the time and space of desire has changed through our mediated practices, but that what has been converted, in the friction between bedroom and chatroom, is an address and a subjectivity that is at odds with any binary assumptions between the public and the intimate, global institutions and local practices, the "West" and the rest of the world as it has been drawn up and imagined by Western thinkers.

Whereas greater attention to gender and sexuality in migration studies has today demonstrated that the internet has become the primary medium for facilitating non-normative migration—a movement neither generated for productive labor, nor conforming to the state model of assimilation or reproductive family, but one rooted in pleasure and desire—we should also acknowledge that digital transnational connectivity today is not without its own frictions, instances in which migrants have reevaluated digital norms through reclaiming alternative copresences, the exchange of physical letters as a practice of self-care that disavows instantaneity for the contemplation and reflection afforded by spatial and temporal distances.[15] As in any journal or correspondence, authorial agency is located in the uncovering of self—both a fundamental loss and revelatory gain, the possibility for sharing and recovering collective memories—and the liminal form of its delivery, a transmission that neither depends on genre and generic constraints nor on the gloss of a team of editors and producers, a fuzzy realism that I link with imperfections and amateurism, and which I locate in this study as fundamental to the fostering of alternative media landscapes and, ultimately, to the formation of new models of political citizenship. I want to continue to read these mediated practices by migrants alongside the slippery notebook form and the virtual physicality of correspondence to consider how the migratory text harnesses both transparency *and* abstraction in its production as archive.

Fuzzy realism can appear to be, at first glance, a paradox. The cult of realism, after all, relies on a documentarian aesthetics that itself relies on the illusion of objectivity and the fiction of recording. Realism is receptive, delivered to reader-viewers as a fixed, rigid "reality" that is pre-established and naturalized via its own reproduction. Reality is taken to be the real, and the latter's mediation is obscured by the flash of visual evidence or the bounded testimony. What becomes normalized is not a certain truth but the certainty of truth, an idea about truth that does not reflect reality so much as reference it. The photograph is considered as an object of evidence only because we've believed, in the past as today, that a photograph is not an interpretation of reality but its neutral proof—artifactual aura as the availability to see what happened, and to see it clearly. The intimacy born through latent exchanges, though—the play of veiling and unveiling, the tension between the possibility and impossibility of knowing the authentic individual—relies on exactly this paradox, a resistance to and reliance upon transparency, or its manufacture.

The amateur gaze, I argue, is exactly the means to achieve such a fuzzy realism—an intimacy that implies or relies on the promise, but only the promise, of physical contact; not the effect of the camera so much as the hand that holds it up. In this hand-held production, each slight or shaky movement awakes our own bodily gestures, a haptic encounter with the subjects but, moreover, the subject-producer, a cruising that is haphazard and accidental but also inevitable. The amateur gaze intervenes in the manufacturing of transparency by showing us the processes of its mediation, the slippage between narrative event and narrated event, the experience and the story: fault lines we can read or which we can map on the surface; fault lines, geologically, which tell us about *prior structural movements*. It is not, in fact, that the amateur act—analog or digital—remains original, intact, objective, unrehearsed, or unmediated, but that through its shaky transmission, it holds up these fictions—the aspiration or ideal of representation—to viewers.

Put another way: organizing a family album, exiled author Dubravka Ugrešić writes, is a deeply amateur activity. This is because, she clarifies, its curation is devoid of artistic pretensions. The organization of a family album, then, is an inward-facing activity, it is an act that remains concerned only with itself: collection and assembly, a shaping that begs repetition (to be looked at) and yet resists finality. Photo albums don't end, their pictorial narratives only exist to be rearranged—and shared—according to the patterns desired by their curators-viewers. Ugrešić, though, reflects on this amateur activity in her own personal accounting, a scrapbook of photographic captions, memories of a native country that has been removed from cultural cartography (Yugoslavia), and observations of her own present exile (Berlin, before and after the fall of the Walls): *The Museum of Unconditional Surrender*, originally published in Dutch translation in 1997 and then in several other languages, including English (by Celia Hawkesworth), before being printed, five years later, in the language in which Ugrešić wrote it—part list, part series of letters: an autobiographical novel which includes a family recipe for caraway soup. This compendium suggests that the only way to tell one's history of exile and displacement is to do so through melting the borders between fiction and autobiography, novel and journal.

Indeed, such creative expressions by migrants as a mode of survival and memorial—a strategy to re-member the past, to prevent its material abolishment—necessarily intervene in documentary through the insertion of interstitial elements: elements of composing on the move that relate the imperfections of documentation, the fraught processes of mediation. When Ugrešić writes about the distinctions between amateurism and what she calls "professionalism," a difference "contained in the point of indistinct pain, pain which an amateur work (like extrasensory perception) can *touch and thus provoke the same reaction in the observer/reader*,"[16] I am reminded of novelist Sarah Manguso's acknowledgment in her own diary cum theorization of the diary form: "I often prefer writers' diaries to their work written intentionally for publication. [...] The goal being a form no one notices, the creation of what seems like pure feeling, not of what seems like a vehicle for a feeling. Language as pure experience, pure memory."[17] What could be a better strategy for excavating—and restoring—a home that is no longer returnable, a country that is no longer represented on the world map, than a linguistic vehicle for pure memory, which is never, in fact, pure, absolute, or unclouded but rather *transparently opaque*: to revel, then, in the text's own discrepancies, by exposing its performative lack of staging. Amateur acts, *because* of their inward-facing practice, have greater potential to interact with a community of others, engendering an impossible empathy, the pinnacle of expression that "so-called works of art,"[18] in Ugrešić's estimation, can rarely achieve.

The incitement of feeling through the invitation of caress, tactile and mutual, illuminates this fuzzy realism—a realism that depends, not on seeing, but on the solicited glimpse of what's behind the image: the imperfect—perhaps, at times, anonymous—human hands behind it; and in capturing the processes of documentation, fuzzy realism also documents a memory that testifies to the human past, an *act*uality that we will return to throughout this study. Against the rigid paranoia of the present and the prescriptive determinations of much contemporary theory,

Eve Sedgwick has discussed recuperating the "skill of imaginative close reading," which might lead to reading from "a reparative position"—an engagement that requires surrendering to surprise, hope, trauma, all of these, from which to "organize the fragments and part-objects she encounters or creates."[19] We might read Sedgwick's theoretical position in 2003 alongside the scrapbook format and amateur aesthetic of the family photo album, the curatorial production of which is not utopic but *rehabilitative*—not only a vision of alternative futures but an act that announces that the past, too, could also be different, which is to say multiple. *Things change once they land in a book.*

Alongside Sedgwick's reparative readerly position, I want to insist on the specific magnitude of the amateur while locating it among José Esteban Muñoz's blueprints for a queer futurity, in which Muñoz reads the gesture as both a resistance to "the goal-oriented tautological present" and an auguring of "another time and place"[20] made possible only because of every gesture's suggestiveness and imperfections. The gesture becomes, in this sense, by not becoming, serving as both excess (supplement) and abbreviation (incomplete or uncompleted) of movement. In *Drift Net*, I want to suggest that the gesture, as the intermediary moment of movement—where nothing is communicated except the act of communication—can be read alongside the glitch of transmission, the noise embedded in every message, the residue of media, of mediation, a representational excess that informs how migrants have refashioned autobiography and documentary from a space of insecurity, of illegibility and failure: not a hole but an opening. Amidst the proliferation of flawless selfies and fabricated deepfakes, the amateur aesthetic has today become an instructive guideline for migrants in the production of their own self-representations. Migrants' specific interests in material that can be appropriated and repurposed—at times, reanimated—informs the endeavor to remake the terms of representation, not only of one's life but of one's death, the commemoration of which, as extant process, produces forms of public evidence *and* social engagement: both memorial and activism.

It is not the sheen of the product but the inherent instability of the process—which is always ongoing—that provides such accountings with a liminal migratory charge. The permission to narrate a history is also a reconstruction of the present public sphere, allowing not only a virtual refuge, a networked fringe from which to develop a counter-public based on the aspiration of self-narrative, but moreover, a political tool for mobilizing local and transnational activism from within or below, the emergence of what anthropologist Miriyam Aouragh has termed, in relation to glocal political mobilization in Palestine, "cyber intifada."[21] These personal accountings not only help migrants cross territorial borders and organize migratory routes through the dissemination of crucial information, but also track, record, publish, and archive movements by the state, and its surveillance and security apparatus meant to detain people on the move. Such productions of self thus serve as an alternative form of documentation and mapping, a strategy of self-surveillance that other scholars have only recently taken up.[22] Indeed, these autobiographic, second-hand, and remediated interventions by migrants have remade documentarian markers while at the same time dodging a predatory representational economy established through facial recognition.[23]

Any discussion of digital technology and its uses, of course, requires critical attention to issues of access, infrastructure, literacy, and the gender and age gaps that reveal their limitations as a tool of empowerment for migrants, whether they've already reached a host community or remain in transit. Great attention to the digital border, and of the convergence and interactions between the symbolic and the territorial in defining and diffusing its lines, also troubles the celebrated narrative of the "connected migrant"[24] and the well-researched role of ICTs in giving a voice to migrants and diasporic communities by asking to what extent such voices are heard, by whom, and to what effect. These considerations raise important questions of audience and address as well as narrative framing, strategies and negotiations centered in *Drift Net*'s second chapter.

To understand how migrants have used emerging media to produce agency and subjectivity as a mode of transit, it's important to identify border studies' longstanding separation between the material and symbolic, which obscures their interpenetration, their joint production and legitimization of the border. Indeed, today's borders are hardly static or conspicuous[25] but distributed, networked, malleable, myriad, ephemeral, impalpable, electronic, non-visible, and—at the same time—visual, contingent upon the (b)order of visuality within a politics of representation. In the same fashion, the biopolitical/biometric regime of control exercised at the border is no longer confined to a single dividing line, checkpoint, or territorial crossing. These surveillance-security measures, in other words, are not only situated at specific points, but themselves cross—into and beyond the networked communications and digital surveillance of social media and data collection, where they continue to perform the work of detaining and sorting persons after they've moved past state borders.

Within this security apparatus, how do we move while staying put?—and how can this mode of mobility, as a remaking of space through one's position within it, serve a poetics that has less to do with distance than depth?[26] The migratory text does not only make possible the recording of external events and narrative interiorities of history's commentary, but more essential, narrates the inchoate *consciousness* of its author at the permeable moment of the text's inscription. As we continue to explore contemporary strategies by migrants, and their reshaping of contemporary digital norms, it is fruitful to look, once again, to the past. To think about the social and political agency of personal accounting, specifically the personal text that moves between the philosophical, lyrical, and processual, as the migratory text does, is to place this corpus of media in connection with the *denkbild*, or "thought-image" so celebrated by the Frankfurt School, whose project of turning to art to find a way—or more precisely, turning art into a way—for critical theory to bring about "a transformation of consciousness that could become," as Theodor Adorno remarked, "a transformation of reality,"[27] should similarly be read through the drift of movement and displacement in the years following the First World War but also with attention to the emergence of visual cultures, and their possible repurposing in the landscape of the alphabetical text. In this sense, Walter Benjamin's endeavor to employ the cultural residue of modernity to address its traumas and rework its source code—not to elevate the everyday and banal into the realm of abstraction, but to attend to and *celebrate* their banality on the level of form—does not simply serve as an aesthetic precursor to the fragmentary, discontinuous, polyphonic, and provisional migratory text, but also locates its potential political charge and social dynamism: the ingredients of critical theory, art, activism, and, as this study attests, the necessary interaction between all three. Benjamin, with whom I continue to form or forge a correspondence, offers for this study a prototype in the interactive and unfinished *Arcades Project*, a theoretical and literary entry point to encounter other works by persons who are likewise composing in transit and detention, yet writing with, near, and through so many others—not quite Nancy K. Miller's vision of a celebrated "personal criticism" that reinscribes its author's identity as a form of authorization so much as a decentering of the narrative "I" for the amorphous positionalities born through passage.

In demonstrating shared qualities between the notebooks and correspondences of writers on the move, the verbal-visual *denkbild*, a critical-creative personal criticism, and the migratory text, I also wish to make abundantly clear that these poetics are neither new, nor are they the product of the "powerful white male scholars" to which composition and rhetoric theorists such as Patricia Bizzell have attributed the "compelling nature of this new intellectual work."[28] Just as Muñoz endeavored to reorient the field of queer theory from "a place where a scholar of color can easily be lost in an immersion of vanilla while her or his critical faculties can be frozen by an avalanche of snow,"[29] it is my hope that this study can provide a more nuanced, comprehensive understanding of the link between such discourse-blending personal criticism—the genealogy of which Miller traces to Western, white feminism—and the migratory texts produced by those on the periphery.

As I've shown in my re-writing of "the American" in the life and work of Gertrude Stein and Henry James, the link between Gertrude Stein's privileged exodus to Paris, and the composition of her national literary epic, *The Making of the Americans* (1901–1911), is not coincidental.[30] What gets elided is not the movement of a modern American literature, or its introduction to literary modernism, but the forced movement of bodies, or conversely, their interminable detention; the genocide of Armenians, Assyrians, and Greeks, which preceded its publication in 1925; the mass displacement and denaturalization of persons with which its celebrated appearance coincided.

The institutional impulse to theorize certain strains of decades-old artistic production and call it *new* is indeed not new, but only as serial as the social media timelines through which recent scholarship has linked a "new autofiction," a mode of art that has been attributed, not surprisingly, to a Rolodex of white writers.[31] Just as new media's glitch aesthetic can be read in postwar texts prior to digital cultures, as this study shows, what scholars have recently called "new autofiction" to describe the strategic substitution of narrativity with interactivity has roots that stretch far beyond the recombinant zones of encoded networks, conditions that we can trace to migration in the interwar era. Locating a lineage for new media in often disregarded contexts means also restoring overlooked practices, unconsidered futures.

## STATUS UPDATE

It should come as no surprise that Walter Benjamin's strongest vision of a form outside the novel appears in his unpublished notebooks from 1931. "The complete takeover of literature by the newspaper," he writes, in "Diary from August 7, 1931, to the Day of My Death," "[...] is in fact a dialectical process. On the one hand, it spells the demise of literature in contemporary social conditions, but, on the other, it prepares the way for its reinstatement when conditions change."[32] The conditions were already changing, even before Benjamin fled Paris, writing letters on the move, even before Benjamin said goodbye in a room on the second floor of the Hotel Francia, in Portbou. The popular nature of production—and its integration into the production and circulation of commodities—ushered by the declining barrier between author and public, Benjamin writes, would be the site of the printed word's "regeneration in a new society."[33] The new society is our own, the "collective intelligence" that forgets or obscures the body in its march toward dematerialized distribution 140 characters at a time, permitting the conditions for mass political protest and the proliferation of fake news and echo chambers in parallel keystrokes; the new society is our own, one that has gone *live* to jolt the discontinuous temporality of the past into the double ground of the present, crowdsourced and curated a version of Benjamin's own meticulously arranged *Arcades*: the hyperlinked segments and sequences that accumulate, crisscross and cross-reference, in an attempt to avoid being crossed out. Hovering between commentary and quotation in its devotion to the leftovers of daily life, *The Arcades Project*'s spectral assemblage is as much a response to the cultural passage of authors into producers configured, as Benjamin understood, by the "literarization" of all the conditions of life and living during the interwar period as it is a presaging of contemporary consciousness, and its possible resistances, under a data economy that absorbs and flattens in its unrelenting spread. The conditions for the emergence of *the public as writers* is of course contingent upon the realization that writing could be public as soon as it is written. The frequency by which today's users publish their daily stories is not only an embrace of discursive relation but, moreover, a resistance to relation's assimilation into linear narrative chronology. Each message—image, video, voice memo, alphabetical text—that is posted is also responded to, screenshot, annotated, appropriated, and republished, a gathering of relations and narratives whose addresses and timelines branch out and multiply within a space that is likewise distributed unevenly.

The call for the self is a call for a new social subject and thus a call for the reconfiguration of the public—the structures of genre and mode, the structuring of narrative and address—that circumscribes an audience. For nearly a decade, on every Friday beginning in April of 2011, the anonymous Syrian video collective Abounaddara would publish a new "bullet film" on its Vimeo, communicating its weekly dispatch on Facebook and Twitter moments later. Abounaddara, whose name, loosely reconstructed in Arabic, can be read as "the man with glasses," references a nineteenth-century Egyptian journal outlawed for its revolutionary content, a periodical which, after its founding editor's exile to France, was reproduced by lithograph, translated into French, and smuggled inside larger Egyptian newspapers, circulating across classes and countries. *The man with glasses.* At stake, indeed, in Abounaddara's project is the reorientation of the gaze: how the Syrian body is seen; the terms of dignity in death as in life; the right to a dignified image. Its self-trained videographers—mostly women or women-identifying; all but two anonymous—are explicit in their aims: the transformation of media representation, which necessarily entails the transformation of both a mainstream media that desires images of atrocity and a social media that turns users into data, experiences into ornamented content, both "old" and "new" media culpable as a conduit of the banalization, and aestheticization, of death and the suffering of life, each of which today can be recorded and broadcast in real time, neither consent nor acknowledgment needed. It is not just the human image that is for sale in a post internet economy but the human being ostensibly behind any image.

Unlike both the spectacle of violence and mourning merchandised by mainstream news outlets and the "goodbye messages"[34] of Twitter users turned citizen journalists, the user-generated content picked up and republished by mass media (a list of curators that included, during the early years of the Syrian Civil War, the *New York Times*, *Time*, *CNN*, and the *BBC*), violence in Abounaddara's revision of documentary is represented through sounds off screen and a sense of motion that interrupts the eye of the otherwise fixed camera, while appropriated media footage of the ongoing crisis—news reporters thrusting microphones in the face of wounded survivors to demand further exposure and exploitation: "Tell us who did this to you"—serves to undermine the media's own presumed ethics and authority. Any possible answer to the reporter's question, of course, must necessarily include the political and economic systems that insist that some lives are more representable than others; that some lives are more representable when they are dead.

What does it mean to create an alternative archive of Syrian life whose materials are broadcast on the same media platforms that perpetuate the exploitation of image and the imagined intimacy mobilized by pixelated portraiture? What are the limits of any call for "a dignified image," which depends, nevertheless, on the close-up of facial recognition? Besides "The Witness," a series of testimonies in which each subject's face is blacked out, many of Abounaddara's documentarian shorts insist upon the aesthetic of realism solicited and solidified by the face. "We invite you to look at [the subjects'] face …," Abounaddara cofounder Charif Kiwan acknowledged in October of 2015 during "The Right to the Image" conference, a symposium that coincided with a three-week exhibition of the group's works at The New School's Arnold and Shelia Aronson Galleries in New York City.[35] "If we want to resist, we need to show the faces of people." More telling than any reliance on an already objectified subject's face, however, is the possible resistances glimpsed by knitting Abounaddara's calls for human recognition on the basis of a revision to citizenship and its concomitant rights—the group's transformative interpretation of international human rights law—with the anonymous collective's mission to create, collect, and archive an alternative representation of the human being that has been dispossessed of humanity by political and cultural actors. The revolution, in Abounaddara's vision or version—the return, as Benjamin had once sought, of the storyteller and their displacing relations—will happen "side-by-side with the world's image makers,"[36] side by side with the information economy through which communication is replaced with content and content replaced or simply mistaken for ads, side by side with the world's most profitable exploiters of images and intimacy, or not at all, perhaps understanding the importance of the self-reflexivity garnered by any attendance to one's own archival process; that any glimmer of emancipatory potential borne by a new social subject bears traces, too, of the modern communication technologies that articulate their novel modes of production; that such traces serve as more than just memory of mediation but also its own critique.

Thus in Benjamin's unpublished hypotheses of 1931 as in Abounaddara's contemporary emergency responses, what remains to be seen is not just how we use social media to represent our social conditions and communities in the aim of transforming them, but, in view of the extant practices in which social media uses us as both product and labor—users who are subject to invasive surveillance; objects who are susceptible to monetization—how migrants today as in the past have repurposed the infrastructure designed to individuate and commodify in order to resist subjectification and commodification *on the basis of the collective and collaborative*. Here we might also observe Benjamin's notational observations from Svendborg, during the summer of 1934, in which he takes note of several long conversations with Brecht, with whom he shares his "Author as Producer" manuscript. Brecht disagrees with the idea of the revolutionary function of literature and the technological advances necessary for the transformation of artistic forms and intellectual means of production—not that technology wouldn't convert the artist-intellectual into an agent of political expediency, but that the proletariat would have a part in this subversive expression. "Brecht," Benjamin clarifies, "was willing to concede the validity of this thesis only for a single type—namely, the upper-middle-class writer."[37] On the contrary, Benjamin, who, like Brecht, included himself among the upper middle class, nevertheless understood that art could only alter reality if it extended itself outward, not upward. "The collective is a body, too," Benjamin writes earlier, in his 1929 essay on "Surrealism": "[...] Only when in technology body and image so interpenetrate that all revolutionary tension becomes bodily collective innervation, and all the bodily innervations of the collective become revolutionary discharge, has reality transcended itself to the extent demanded by the *Communist Manifesto*."[38]

Benjamin disliked ideology because he didn't trust it. To the extent that he trusted Marxism or Surrealism, it was only so that he could critique each, revise them to match his ideas about historical materialism, an always-volatile past, and a present bodily collective for which everything one encounters can be integrated toward a passionate revolt borne on anthropological inspiration: the self as our ultimate case study. If we take feminist historian Antoinette Burton's idea that any autobiographical act is in itself political, that every act of autobiography is also, always, an archive, then what happens—what is made possible—when the documentation of a work of art occurs alongside its assembly? A double gesture of self and self-appraisal, a movement—amateur and imperfect—within and outside the art object, those traces of event—fuzzy, though transparent—that inform, and occasion, the writing of them, which are so often erased; in absence of nothing then, this superscription becomes a productively unstable force, an arena for networked testimony.

The autobiographical work, Burton asserts in her 2013 essay, "'An Assemblage/Before Me,'" *must* be productively unstable. Without its polysemy and fractures, without its "multiple singularities" and "centripetal forces,"[39] its inherent incompleteness, the autobiography would not be representative of history itself, it would not be able to re-present history, and to imagine the histories of a people that remain unthinkable, let alone unwritten. In my notes, I've written: how can the sharing of our stories promote activism, healing, and survival?

Today we can track a collective, unconscious mood through the marking of the mundane, whose flow relies on the redundancy of every day and everyday redundancies. And what's more, this ambient awareness has the tendency to alight upon the moments when the ordinary shifts into emergency, an indexical activism that becomes itself and also its own record or trace. I want to return to an earlier point about the counterpublics cultivated by the migratory text, and how greater attention to such personal accountings can engage questions necessary to a reevaluation of our norms and forms within today's post internet culture—the post that comes before and comes after, etymologically *behind* and also *toward*, *to*, *near*, *late*, *close by*, but also *away from*, which is to say both, or all. To signal *post* is to entertain the multiple singularities of correspondence, the addressee and the event of address—*I am writing to you*—and when I write to you *I keep you close at hand*, a coinciding of proximity and distance which demands closer attention in the chapters to follow.[40] And yet I want to linger here, within or in the midst of the post, in large part because of its function as keyword in the academy, with particular relevance to experiences of migration codified as world literature and deliberated upon in fields such as area studies, cultural studies, and postcolonial studies.

In pursuing the distinctions between the "post" of postcolonialism and the "post" of postmodernism, Kwame Anthony Appiah, writing at the moment in which refugee studies was beginning to expand as a multidisciplinary field in the academy, raised similar questions about the need to reevaluate extant terms and the practices scholars and artists employ on their behalf.[41] In the process of becoming institutionalized in the Western academy, the "postcolonial" itself has become shorthand, Ania Loomba suggests, "for something simultaneously fashionable and marginal."[42] And as the *postcolonial* flattens differences of colonial rule and historical moments, "postcoloniality" is reduced to "a vague condition of people anywhere and everywhere." Such generalizations premised on cultural opposition—without any discussion of cultural differences (race, class, gender, location)—prevent meaningful investigations of the colonial power matrix at work today, while blanketing past colonial opposition in a universal narrative. "[T]he term," Loomba has cautioned, "begins to obscure the very relations of domination that it seeks to uncover."[43]

The work that postcolonialism does or cannot do in the institution is not the subject of this project, although it is worth considering how a critique of postcolonialism informs structural critiques embedded in the institution, namely how the history of specialization within Western systems of knowledge is tied to the growth of racial theory.[44] The histories of such disciplines have not only been shaped by colonial discourses, they have produced colonial discourses. Among this book's tasks, thus, is to reconsider the relationship between a "world literature" that circulates a representation of the experience of migration, exile, and diaspora, and the academic scholarship—whether housed in English literature, comparative literature, sociology, anthropology, political science, or any other discipline—that endeavors to do the same.

In this study, post internet culture thus reflects the implications for any possible futures and also a contemporary mode of self-publication and circulation, the ways in which media are exchanged and capital is produced. At once noun, verb, and prefix, *post*—set aside, divested of hyphen—calls attention to the binary between historical time and personal time that is problematized by the migratory text. Historical and personal: it is a mistake to think that one is shared and one is solitary. It is a mistake to ignore the exigency of the anecdotal; incidental situations have a spiritual weight that intervenes in the stack or stockpile of history.

Francis Ponge's postwar notebook, *Nioque de l'Avant-Printemps*, recorded in the French countryside of Les Fleurys over the first two weeks of April 1950, and then in Paris at the end of May and June of the same spring, propose an alternative to the earlier twentieth-century political programs—Bolshevism, Marxist-Leninism—that stifle instinct, sacrificing desire and impulse for what its author called the creation of "a dried-out pretension, a ridiculous and trying rigorism."[45] Not a decade removed from the Second World War and its annihilation, Ponge posits an altogether different manifesto, one not interested in an ideology or a polis, but a poetics: a practice that privileges the minutiae, the discarded, the neglected, the abandoned, the remains—and each of their repetitions; seasonally, vocally, bodily, elementally.

> We will not look for anything (to say) about what is "significant" about our epoch (this will work itself out on its own; we are all too immersed in it). We will search (on the contrary) for what does not appear as significant, what does not return to its symbols (into its symbolism): whereof serial time (or eternity) is.[46] (April 8, 1950)

However, Ponge's poetics are not concerned with looking so much as *looking forward*—an anticipation of regeneration, with a difference, an iteration that resembles the (silent) joy of discovering one's self coupled with the vocal enunciation—and repetition—of words, of speaking so as to be heard. Indeed, Ponge affirms, "we have to *resay* April (or October)."[47] The physicality of words—and the foraging *for* words, not unlike the haptic act of correspondence—is an act that always goes through the body, a mirroring or mimicking of seasonal passages. One clears the throat to speak the way rain rinses debris so as to build upon itself, vegetate, disperse.

Ponge's work, which is traditionally studied through the lenses of modernism, the prose poem, and the aesthetic concerns of metropolitan avant-garde poetics, cannot be treated without due attention to the German occupation of France and its author's role as political courier in the French Resistance, an undercover errantry in exile which shapes his self-reflexive, archival poetics. What else is brought by the invitation to open up these areas of literary study through the interventions of migration and displacement? How, in other words, does re-reading Ponge's work as migratory trouble our specific formulations of the avant-garde, while provoking broader reassessments for scholars working in fields *outside* of modernism and the postwar prose poem, accounting for the portability of the migratory text, and its application as theory and practice beyond studies of migration and media?

Indeed, the knowledge that lives inside the notebook title's *Nioque*—the Greek *gnosis*, which relates both observation and experience—implies a reassessment marked by the expansiveness of what it means "to know." In the continuous accumulation of knowledge, one can only advance deeper by retracing earlier steps, questioning one's self as one questions others. And so Ponge advances a task for the artist that is less interested in completing ideas than returning to them. The idea abbreviated, interrupted, elongated, extended, attenuated, and tenuous, the attentive idea. This is an originality insistent upon objects, not subjects—and their difference, their "differential qualit[ies]"[48] that demand struggle, opposition, friction, vexation ... an irritation, which is a *sensitivity*, necessary for the distillation of a "brief gleaming"[49]—the illumination of consciousness. By giving primacy to the idea of illumination rather than the illuminated idea, Ponge's work evades the finitude and linearity of much other knowledge production, producing instead a conjectural form that self-reproduces based on association and proximity, a poetics of partiality—having both total fondness and a fondness for unfinished things. Even within the virtual presence of the text, Ponge straddles a hypothetical future, one in which his notes become directions for the reader:

> In several days it will be too late, we will be at ease, the comforts of true spring [...] We will have forgotten this sensation (emotion). We are no longer able to say anything about it.
>
> So, will it be necessary to wait for the next year to retake these notes and finish the picture?
>
> No, it is necessary to complete it (in stride) immediately. (April 6, 1950)[50]

Witness this desire—this necessity—to get it all down in one sitting, if only because what would be written now could not be written otherwise. These are a poetics of imperfection and improvisation, a conditional poetics in which cycles of (ex)change can only arrive by way of a passage's own abrupt eruption—unsought and unforeseeable. In the rhetoric of the pear tree of Ponge's daily scenery, even effacement becomes a confirmation of existence; "[t]hus, often, when one trims (practices amputation on) the language (a sentence), certain words [...] swell up interiorly, regain strength [...] become thicker [...] in trimming something, one automatically confirms what remains."[51] It isn't just the physical act of removal that interests Ponge, but the interior redactions that constitute a forgetting: "A certain senility: naiveté refound," he writes, "to restart from stammering, from zero."[52] And as I read these lines I, too, find myself in my notebook; I am refound; I am reminded of Duchamp's fascination with Francis Picabia's gift of total forgetting, which allowed Picabia, as Duchamp explains, in his own notebook, "to launch into new paintings without being influenced by the memory of preceding ones."[53]

The gift of forgetting encounters a choreography that is interested in marking its deviated flow. Ponge notates, not with the intention of drawing out a definitive work but a work that remains indefinable and unfinished. The culmination of these instructions to readers involves the dissolution of all boundaries, chief among them, the one between reader-writer in the text: "Westerly come huge worries [...] at the top (the two upper thirds) of the page, and at times soaking it completely, dampening, at times sprinkling all the way to the reader (in their window frame)," Ponge writes, adding parenthetically, "All the space between the reader and the page swept elsewhere across by the wind [...]."[54] As Ponge reimagines his reader's body, so too does he reimagine the body of the book, or how it might be reinhabited, so as to be read differently as a corpus of copresence.

Likewise, perhaps it should come as no surprise that the occasion for Franz Kafka to articulate his theory of small literatures—decades later taken up and renamed by Félix Guattari and Gilles Deleuze as "minor literatures"—arrives through the ritual notations permitted by his journal.[55] The social and political agency of the personal text is here underscored by the date of the note's inscription: December 25, 1911, the eve of the First World War. As Pascale Casanova has pointed out, every emerging literature exists within a structurally unequal relationship, not only to its nation of origin but especially to world literature at large: the large literatures of the dominant republics of letters. And yet, the notebook form provided Kafka a way out of conforming to—and thus confirming—both the obligatory relationship writers have to their national origins and the center's wholesale absorption of peripheral literatures. By looking more closely at the effect and function of migratory flows through and against denationalized literary capitals, I want to reevaluate Casanova's normative and prescriptive "obligatory itinerary" of every underprivileged writer: the choice between assimilation and difference.[56] It is not just that migrants help bolster the "boundaries [...] capitals [...] highways [...] and forms of communication"[57] characteristic of Casanova's world literary space, but in providing essential literary infrastructure, migrants also produce necessary intersections and detours.

The coinciding of history and literature is doubly significant for a people without a recorded history; there is perhaps no other way of entering the world's stage on one's own terms than by writing the history of one's self. And to do so, one would have to portray not the relation of event, but its relationship to one's inner world, the work of *working things out*. As Kafka himself considers in his *Blue Octavo Notebooks*, a series of eight slender notebooks maintained from February 19, 1917 to June 1919, which mark a departure from the diary entries he stopped producing during this same period: "The history of the world, as it is written and handed down by word of mouth, often fails us completely; but man's intuitive capacity, though it often misleads, does lead, does not ever abandon one."[58]

These collected notebooks, representative of the artistic traditions that migratory texts have mobilized, comprise excerpts of unpublished short stories, philosophical dialogues, annotations of other texts, lists of books recently read and books to read, definitions of common Jewish words, aphorisms—repeated and resignified pages later as one hundred and nine "Reflections on sin, suffering, hope, and the true way"—drafts of letters, and desultory observations. The lack of signpost or separation between any of these—besides the itemized "Reflections"—allows readers to enter Kafka's collected—and conflated—works without filter or finality. *The Blue Octavo Notebooks*, as a compilation of fuzzy traces, provokes us to question how we—readers, scholars, instructors—come to texts, and to reassess the ways in which our reading is mediated through generic expectations, which the notebook dissolves. These moments—when the usefulness of the memory of a staircase is considered alongside a description of the funeral rites of a mouse, a businessman's decision to close up shop for the day on account of "one's own free will," a young prince's visit to a prison where he encounters a man who had just completed the twenty-third year of his sentence, and a first-person account of an encounter with "a large, an overlarge, egg" from which hatches a "stork-like, still featherless bird, beating the air with wings that were too short"[59]—nourish the charge of discontinuous and amorphous encounters, the rapid shifts between imagination, observation, and fictionalization presented piecemeal. The migratory text not only troubles the division between original and copy but melts their borders through *forging*—a craftwork that relies on continual pressure and the effort of manipulation.

What distinguishes these octavo notebooks from Kafka's diaries is not an indexical attachment to one's outer world, but, on the contrary, their disjointed investigation into one's *inner* world—not the account of events but the event of accounting. To begin with, which is to say our preparation; what is stirring in the pot and how; what stirs us. These are the stakes of the notebook; this is when the personal becomes positional, relational, where the refusal to be inscribed by formal structures of the state and the institution becomes an occasion for inscription. What does notebook consciousness accommodate? How does the decision to write in one's notebook inform what one will write, which is to say what one will find? A thinking, moreover, that can only be produced by writing, and a writing produced by movement, by mediation. That the act of notation shapes not only the past but the events to come—unintended futures—is worth re-marking upon; one's thinking changes even prior to inscription in light of the choice to notate thought. What we are talking about is a newfound sensitivity and receptivity to thinking and feeling in our bodies and to the spaces we traverse; the subjects and objects that move with(in) us.

To acknowledge that narrative displaces the events it contains, resolving them as either "facts" or "fiction," is also to recognize that the notebook, as a second-hand relation, at once preparatory and unpremeditated, deters the allure of documentarian proof, the fetishization of unmediated experience that obscures the role of the materials we use to render thinking and feeling into words, words into meaning, meaning into materiality: not facts so much as diverse acts of composition. Miguel Á. Hernández-Navarro, who, with Mieke Bal, curated the now well-traveled *2MOVE: Double Movement/Migratory Aesthetics* multiple-city exhibition in 2007, contends that visual art can make us better understand migration—which he brackets within our "contemporary problems"—while minimizing the "humanist practice of writing."[60] In contradistinction, I want to relocate the charge of the migratory to a realm distinctly outside the scopic. And although this study analyzes a range of media, including visual art, I want us to observe the ways in which each of these texts, through various strategies, work to circumvent the optical illusion that equates seeing with paramount perception or knowledge.

Without deleted scenes, we wouldn't have scenes. Without imagination, we would be forced to see everything around us; to take everything at face value; to never get beyond the finite art objects that hang on a wall or in our screens, sacred and silent. Today's personal texts beg such participation and retrieval, inviting us to become accomplice and archivist. Index, portfolio, errata—isn't it true that the virtual gesture always anticipates the physicality of form, and the form of physicality? "In the age of the vanishing book and the virtual text in which we live," Antoinette Burton writes, "we should linger on the embodied form: its conditions of production, how it was handled and circulated, the practices of borrowing and annotating in which it participated, the dangers and the pleasures its embrace entailed."[61] Reader-response theorist Wolfgang Iser understood the urgency of the "living event" made possible through reading, and yet acknowledged that it must always remain unlocatable. Because our reading cannot be pinpointed or fixed, the potential for its mediation is both inevitable and non-indexical, due to the interplay between the memory of a text and the reader's perception of it at present. "Thus the reading process," Iser writes in his phenomenological examination, "always involves viewing the text through a perspective that is continually on the move."[62]

I would like to add that it is not just the reader who is tasked with the complications—and capacity—of this time-sequence, but the writer. How there is a general desire to be endlessly remembered and endlessly repeatable, a political philosophy rooted in (r)elation, pleasure, and the continual penetration of sensitive contact with language, as well as a now-ness that can be likened, today, to a screen grab or GIF, both premature and portable, half-frozen between the pose of permanence and the shudder of in-formation: a detail from which to recognize a stochastic hybrid form and, moreover, a mode of reading engendered as a result. As observations expand in real time, the notebook transforms *how* we perceive narrative; accountings are not rendered retrospectively or diagrammed in advance but tune to the register of the thinking-feeling body, a narrative transparency I want to compare to the hyper self-awareness that literary theorist Matt DelConte has characterized as the "four-wall present tense structure"[63] capable of provoking the reader to ethical action. In gathering information as it happens, readers become witnesses but also recorders; there's no border between the narrative-I and the experiencing-I; the story of the event and the story *as* event.

The "event of art," and its staging, is fundamental to a political aesthetics, because these interactions shift identitarian representations to relational ones, displacing the individual, whether author-artist-producer or reader-viewer-audience, and our binary relationship to one another.

Immersive media producer and curator Jill Bennett has described this movement as "an exploration of *communality as a process*":

> In other words, rather than merely giving an account of an event that has already happened (and which may have informed the work's production and form), it [the exhibition] serves to generate a set of possibilities, which may in turn inform political thinking with regard to particular circumstances.[64]

Bennett's exhibition space where *art happens* concurrent to a virtual politics and Iser's unlocatable virtual convergences within the *living event* of reading might be read together to inform the migratory text's application of theatricality, precariousness, contingency, improvisation, and constant revision, a space where relationships are incessantly formed, and diffused. Transmedia mobilization[65] in our current moment fosters greater accessibility—for users, for producers—while connecting specific content to broader organizational movements. These strategies of dispersing media across multiple platforms and in alternative formats turn personal narratives into public projects. Even more relevant to this study is how migrants, by repeating and restaging stories—their own and others—have produced a political resistance across borders by remarking—remaking—the architecture of the alphabetical text across different formats; the book, the page, the screen, as such, becomes an unravelable fabric. These personal texts are distinguished by the ways in which they render such borders indistinguishable, merging the private and public, autobiography and fiction, the individual subject and the desubjectified collective: a fuzzy realism rendered by imperfect reproductions, and the exchanges of an amateur gaze.

Recall Dubravka Ugrešić's monumental task of staving off an annihilation that was, after the dissolving and disappearing of Yugoslavia, more than bodily, but cultural. What mattered most to *The Museum of Unconditional Surrender*'s narrator was collecting sounds, protecting the memory of domestic tenors. Is it any wonder that Palestinian American poet Fady Joudah, during a conversation with ABC News in the midst of Israel's unremitting siege of Gaza in October 2023, pointed to the primacy of everyday objects for preserving the history of a people? "How many times can a people be displaced?" Joudah asked a reporter across the screen, a response to ABC's routine questions about how Joudah was doing after losing several family members in the ongoing bombardment, what news he had, and what had happened. "How many times can a people be on the verge of having their lives and their memories displaced?"

> Homes hold memories [...] even if they are vacant of their residence, there is a mass murder to memory. These people will lose all their papers, their photo albums, their children's toys. Yes, they are simple material things to regain but these are the stories we need to understand about Palestinians who have endured this relentlessly for decades.[66]

Weeks later, Joudah's essay "A Palestinian Meditation in a Time of Annihilation" would appear in Grove Atlantic's *LitHub*; his discursive text, organized into thirteen maqams or Arabic melodic patterns, begins with a tribute to Hiba Abu Nada, a thirty-two-year-old Palestinian poet identified among the countless civilian casualties in Gaza during the month of October in 2023, before displacing the reader to August 2017 and central Texas, to a flooded home, and amidst the flood: to the marginalia, etchings, and underlinings of his own reading, rescued and reanimated, upon encountering his books again while sifting through the damage wrought by Hurricane Harvey. These rediscovered annotations articulated personal memories—and primary acts of expression—of their own, "modes of signs and signals I had left behind," Judah writes, "like a map for myself in an afterworld I was certain would come but didn't know how or when," unboxed runes that conjure the presence of the past, however distant and however certain its annihilation appears to be.[67] These thirteen maqams and their notation of things and thoughts, versions of self both lost and found, are also, in its author's own words, burial rites, for those persons who have been divested of their dignity, deprived of the right to be recognized as worthy of life and recognizable in death.

The relationship between the familial and the collective, innocuous objects and political subjectivity, is not coincidental. It is because our objects, like our homes, hold memories of their own that spaces of refuge are not confined to their materiality; that shelter might depend on the collecting of lapses, intervals, absences, unsettlements. "Enshrouded in political domination and conquest, cultural memory atrophies and disintegrates," warns Khatharya Um, describing the layering of war, genocide, occupation, and forced dispersal among the Cambodian and Champa communities. Such a sense of loss, Um makes clear, "stirs not only a personal feeling of dislocation but also a *collective* sense of anxiety about national survival."[68] For writers who can only begin with/in the non-space of redaction, the act of memory—imperfect, unreliable, fragmentary—the act of memory, which is to say the act of forgetting, subverts a total and totalitarian history. "In articulation," Um writes, "we give form and meaning to that which is still unnamable, still incomprehensible, still unacknowledged."[69] The tenuous fabric of the migratory text—a surface flimsy enough to allow the traffic between autobiography, fiction, theory, diary, myth, correspondence—are the very conditions for its mobility.

Recall that Jacques Derrida first introduces his notion of "having-been present in a past *now*" or a present, "which will remain a future *now*" in 1972's "Signature Event Context," the *maintenance*—his imperfect French rendering of Benjamin's *Jetztzeit*—(l)inked with the formation, and formalization, of a holding place (for another); for an-other's taking (the) place (of): the signature that stages one's susceptibility to duplication, substitution, transmission, copresence, risk, vulnerability, surrender, all ingredients necessary to intimacy. "In order to function, that is, to be readable," Derrida explains moments later, "a signature must have a repeatable, iterable, imitable form; it must be able to be detached from the present and singular intention of its production."[70] To say "iteration" and hear the Sanskrit itara, meaning *moveable bodies*, or *another*, or *the other*, or *the remaining one (of the two)*; another way of saying this is *I am lending you my voice.* What Derrida finds in the place without place is not nothingness, but immediacy, proximity, and imminence, which is justice—the "*just* happens, *just* happened, is *just* about to happen [...]," Derrida declares almost two decades later, "no longer lets itself be inscribed in the ordered sequence of a history."[71]

I want us to read deconstruction's spectral hauntology of the virtual alongside the broader turn toward systems thinking brought by cybernetics at the advent of the Cold War to deepen the entanglement of environmental and technological networks—ecologies and information—that characterizes the signs and signals through which we live today. Tuning our frequencies from texts to systems, from the literary to the network, allows us to reassert the importance of breakdown: the political-ontological pulses of what fails to break down, that is, become total and totalized. But how to gather what resists cohesion? Research engineer and complex systems philosopher Paul Cilliers imagines mesh-like spaces, which would allow fruitful interaction—the "'play,'" he writes, "in the space between signs"—that could account for relationships and experiences that transcend neat spatial and temporal boundaries.[72] Likewise, Timothy Morton centers the space between object and observer, and moreover, between event and appearance, to declare the exigency of the delay; "that's the whole point;" Morton insists, describing the radioactive layer in Earth's crust, "its detection must be belated."[73] What's the whole point? Or rather, what's the whole, when there is always a surplus, which is hidden, given to any object's desire to conceal itself? Presence, or what we might revise as its return, occurs during failure, a glitch, as I've elsewhere written, that can only ever reveal, that can only ever relate that excess, which both roots a text as an aesthetic object and moves it beyond itself, toward reembodied experience, the forces and flows, often nonvisible, of information and aesthetic energies.[74] Networks can be understood, after all, not by what they enclose, but what gets lost in the drift, what leaks out. Turning to systems thinking in relation to the migratory text as both material text and mode of reading can help us graph the relationship between the forces underlying human displacement and the freedoms proposed by digital media.

## A DIFFERENT HISTORY MAY EMERGE

Start with a rendering: to give again, to give back, to yield, as in letting go, giving up or giving in, surrendering; to pay up, give out, give off, or bring up, as in vomit, throw back; the act of returning or restoring something, or to bring forth, bring about: to cause to be or become. Some of this has to do with memory, with remembering. The haphazard sign system of internal storage, when what leaks out is not the fidelitous translation of an original but its stuttering utterance. The way that the tradition of storytelling counters capitalist logic; how nothing here really gets accumulated, only retrieved and redeemed, only repeated differently with each successive rendering; how the sometimes inaudible and extant cry or call of the flesh staves off the singularity of narrative for its multiple and displacing versions.

The work of poet Anthony Cody, a descendant of the Bracero Program that brought so many low-paid and temporary guest workers from Latin America to fulfill labor shortages during the interwar period and the Cold War, is rooted in the complex and transactional maneuvers of identity and belonging; the polyphonic speakers of his poems a testament to the striations of a memory fragmented but also flattened by historical trauma, by the variegated residues of colonialism and its attendant massacres: ecological and economic precarity, the extraction of human labor and natural resources, the rehearsal of ethnic cleansing, xenophobia, mass deportation, and nationalism; all of the above, and then some. Cody's poetics—his use of lineation and arrangement as a form of division and dispersal—indexes both the excess and scarcity brought by democratic capitalism, registering the absences and omissions intrinsic to any operation of representation, as well as to the pathways and divergences of migration and dispossession that have been produced in its wake. Cody's 2023 collection, *The Rendering*, serves as more than a direct follow-up to his award-winning debut, *Borderland Apocrypha*, published four years earlier, but rather deepens these formal maneuvers to exhilarating depths: a hypnotic investigation employing sound sculpture, image, and text, including assembly rituals with QR code accompaniments, that endeavors to render a network server as a book of poetry, or the reverse.

Early into the collection, "Elegy with Barbed Wire Swaddling a Fortunate Child, as Barbed Triptych Assemblage" signals Cody's aspirations toward abstraction, his imbrication of three distinct speakers whose voices begin to resemble the murmur of a multitude; who speaks, and when? Individual subjectivity—coded as hashtag, square bracket, and brace—is displaced for the primacy of interaction; linear progression temporality is problematized by a piecemeal and collaborative recitation that can only be related through repetition, exchange, and interference. Unforeseen and embedded disorder, what we think of as *noise* in communication theory, informs much of Cody's application of glitch to trigger a relationship between disparate spaces (source-destination) and bodies (sender-receiver), in a transmission that is similarly nonsequential. A page earlier, opening poem "Cada día más cerca del fin del Mundo" stages the parsing of content in platform capitalism, the scaling and refraction of rolling windows, each containing only more windows from which to detour, in which the *closer* of the titular "más cerca" gestures toward *enclosure*: the rub of an always-on synopticon that returns one's gaze in real time. "In the scrolling, witness," Cody writes, "a logging machine annihilate/a tree into parts. This is social [...]."[75]

Enjambment in Cody's work isn't constrained by the unit of a line; instead, his poems offer multiple pathways for reading; proposals for partition and redirection in "Cada día" are accompanied by annotative arrows pointing to several more text box stanzas and graphics—including the aforementioned logging machine: a photograph digitized and destroyed—below and across the page, at times degrading, like a panorama of command prompts, to near illegibility through the performance of iteration. The velocity and fragility of communication passing, the excess of content's cascade in post internet culture, are each negotiated in *The Rendering* by the ostensible agency of the user-reader, we who implicate ourselves in the products we consume or eventually become. Cody's use of the archive, extending from his debut collection, has often been rooted in a critique that desires, like the glitch itself, to reengineer the medium of representation from the inside. Photojournalist Dorothea Lange's photographs of the Dust Bowl—several dozen of which have been laid over Cody's irradiative textual track—are likewise appropriated, fragmented, used as palimpsest but also as formal mediator, as intermediary between past and present, politics and advertisement, the border of the frame which, in *The Rendering* as in today's superstructure of algorithmic governance, is impalpable, porous, omnipresent.

Inside a rendering is the word *rending*, and Cody's attention to the rupture enacted by contemporary paradigms of political economy orients his formal application of syntactic and verbal deconstruction, a narratorial cleaving that demonstrates language's role and function in reproducing a global coloniality, the grammar and rhetoric that both shapes and is obscured by public policy. In "Calculating the Load of Wind at the Weather Bureau Station," the mutations and permutations of language unwind in hypnotic repetition: *presses* becomes *erases* becomes *pares* while, in an adjacent column, *hearth* becomes *heart* becomes *earth* becomes *hear* becomes *ear* becomes *per* becomes *seer* becomes *sparse* becomes *reaps* becomes *eras* becomes *as*, as if to say, with no sense of finality: there is no commensurate relation for tabulating a metrics of tragedy. A page later, the impossible task of inventorying calamity becomes a diptych; "It was conditions of this sort which forced many farmers to abandon the area, Spring '35, New Mexico" schematizes the vestiges of abdication, while nevertheless acknowledging their unforeseeable aftermaths. Bracketed statistics append each category of "umbra," disintegrating, by the end of Cody's ritual accounting, to an indistinct stamping of the mantra "the umbra of" that approximates a barcode and, below that, the final line: "the umbra of sign that reads, *if you can read this, we are gone* [4]."[76]

These strategies of il/legibility in service of documentarian performance recall Sabato Visconti's DACALOGUE (2018), a series of digital paintings which uses the Brazilian-born multimedia artist's own DACA[77] application as its source material, responding to the cost—and privilege of protection—for a program that requires an application fee of nearly four hundred dollars, plus a required biometric scan that costs another hundred. For DACALOGUE, Sabato physically manipulated his application materials as he scanned them, pushing and pulling his identity documents as they were recorded, rendering them discursively unreadable. The bureaucratic language of inhospitality ingrained in the fabric of US Citizenship and Immigration Services applications—"Not valid for reentry to U.S.," "This card is not evidence of U.S. citizenship or permanent residence," and "This notice does not grant any immigration status or benefit"—must be literally held up to the mirror in order to be made out. Cody contributes to this tradition of migrant self-erasure and reappropriation, employing absence (sonic, visual) as much as material collage, as when he reenacts the recording of a Dust Bowl field recording in Arvin, California, in 1940 or, a page before, prefigures the interior of a photograph through a series of distant coordinates, in which the narrative is (re)cast as legend, shepherded by footnotes constellating the exploded white space of a vacant or vacated stretch of land, the perimeter of which might be read as a fence. In *fence*, a leitmotif of this collection, lives the word *defence* (defense); nourished by Cody's fertile adaptations of public domain content, *The Rendering* rarely strays from an investigation of manifest destiny, as well as the necropolitics that make the conditional freedom of the United States of America (as any other "free nation") possible.

To read Anthony Cody's poetry is to engage in a retinal aerobics that reconsiders Mary Ann Caws's conceptualization of an "architexture" that attends to the conditional building of a text *at the moment* it is seen and reconstructed by the reader, "a poetics of perception," as Caws wrote in her 1981 study, *The Eye in the Text*, that "insists upon the immediacy of the eye and upon an *intertexturality* of the visible and the audible and the understandable in their mobile interrelations."[78] To be sure, Cody's poetry requires more than just "a passionate reading," but, moreover, a reading that advances through *misrecognition*. The erotics of overhearing, the inventiveness of mishearing—and thus passing along the hearsay as material relation—the gloss of misreading, misrecognition, is here leveraged to exploit discrepancies between the documentarian truth of official record and the inner world of the individual, whose material history is passed down as notation, as testimonial and scraps, as corrigenda related as counternarrative.

In Cody's voluminous card catalog, there is no complete picture, no full story; neither is there one story being told. Readers are thus asked to reenact the labor of sifting through an archive; the swerves, the detours, the dead ends, and revelations pile up, mimicking the flux and entanglement of task-switching amidst the clutter of digital flotsam that serves *The Rendering* as both material and methodology. What is a fragment but the clue (and only one among m/any others) to the whole it might have been? What we are thus considering is nothing less than the abundance of every partial reading, every partial rendering. Where is the center? What is the primary narrative? We read *The Rendering* as an experience of skittish transit, of unconsummated transfer; Cody's poetry, scaffolded by both generosity and obstruction, edges readers between lines, across pages, and, especially, to the omissions and aporias of relation and expression: everything words cannot say but for the breakdown of language. The trouble with words is they are everything they are not, which is too much. Words, divested of their intentions, which are our own, can offer something, which is themselves.

So Cody observes the silence, allows the language of silence to be read, to be interpreted, ultimately, to be heard, which is to say: to allow the language of silence to speak. And yet—and yet—to admit or begin to understand the story that even silence cannot tell; this, too, is the task of *The Rendering*: to recognize that "the story"—all stories—are fallible, tend to fallacy. As an inquiry into documentation's assumed transparency, Cody's text modulates as fugue, as counterpointed constellation detonating clusters of words, as verbal clouds diffused across an interpenetrating interface, forcing us to retrain our own habit of reading—and seeing—as if to remind ourselves that language itself is inherently chaotic, contradictory, manifold, and, yes, fragmentary—the language of submersion and subversion. Of sound, not words. Of phatic communion. Preverbal. Of long and uninterrupted sequence. Of code.

In "Everywhere I sleep, I see Dust Bowl, 14.0," Cody manipulates a graphic of a giant, centuries-old tree falling in a series of seven, each one more faded than the one before it, transposing text across each whited-out replica at various lengths of the page: a reverse palimpsest in which readers are forced to reckon with the destruction of time (the destruction of the past) upon all things living, while reckoning with a tenuous documentarian infrastructure that is susceptible, itself, to entropy. To uncover the whole, it is necessary to scan each image and accompanying text against its ritual serialization to glean a narrative that must be continuously retrieved in order to be reassembled; the labor of redemption, of renewal, Cody's poetry reminds us, takes time, and through each conscious act of returning to a source, the present, too, will have been irrevocably altered.

Somewhere alongside or around a rendering is the word *rendition*, and Cody's work, through all of its formal maneuvers and intratextual accompaniments, sustains an interrogation of the processes of seizure and detainment that link the Cold War with contemporary neoliberal globalization; the economic and agricultural collapse of Depression Era North America with the food insecurity, water scarcity, and rising sea levels exacerbated by climate change, which continues, every day, to uproot persons in the most vulnerable regions of our world; the postwar guest workers imported by the thousands who were deemed illegal in their new homes after their contracts expired and the thousands of persons stranded between the Americas in the twenty-first century, detained indefinitely or deported without trial. Cody's paternal grandparents were Dust Bowl refugees and the severe dust storms and drought that wrecked the North American prairies throughout the third decade of the twentieth century is unmistakably the specter that haunts *The Rendering*, the heart of which is "Everywhere I sleep, I see Dust Bowl," a procession of fifteen poems that successfully mediates Cody's innovative formal aesthetics and the political charge vibrating underneath the structural reassessment of syntax and speaker. "He never says home," Cody writes against the gray sky above a railroad crossing and the scattered tent homes of Dust Bowl refugees in "Everywhere I sleep, I see Dust Bowl, 5.0":

> I say home, knowing there was once a place and, now, there is not. Nothing exists on the other side of the tracks. I confuse today near the Fresno Rescue Mission with 1939. This is not the dream. Someone says it is getting warmer. [...] Someone says the other side of the tracks is the past. Another, the future. I am learning. I / am learning. I / am learning. I / am learning to understand the nature of this displacement.[79]

What would it mean to write a book by listening? Walter Benjamin's insistence, that prior to literature there was only the "anonymous storyteller,"[80] reminds us that the rise of an information economy and the novel coincided with "the rise of the solitary individual," she who is without counsel, she who, in addition, no longer has the means to counsel others. Narrative thus has been removed "from the realm of living speech,"[81] speech, which as we well know, heralds the political subject, speech, which, furthermore, serves as the means through which the political subject might resignify themselves. And yet, just as other histories, like the persons they dispose, live inside the one that has been passed down, Cody's text—found, appropriated, iterative—suggests that words, too, live within one another, and that they might form an associative narrative out of their own dismemberment. The language of the law and the language of poetry, after all, each yield texts which rely on density, specificity, obfuscation; in *The Rendering*, wherein words routinely break and are broken, Cody reappraises how we conceive of the past, as well as how we might account for the imperfect mediations of our present. In his frequent memo to readers to treat the book as waystation, Cody makes explicit that stories are not only survivable but susceptible to re-writing, to re-reading, should we key to their gaps, to their breaks and pauses. So Cody lets the text speak. It is these voices, these versions of a history untold, that haunt *The Rendering* and thus become the text—a text which, like all texts, is nothing if not a copy. That Cody's work troubles the site of the origin as well as the model of traditional authorship is no coincidence; each of these moves remains inextricable from a larger intervention that questions national polities and our rubric for reading their histories.

Cody's terminal iteration of "Dust Bowl" suggests the indexical universe characterized in Jorge Luis Borges' 1941 short story "The Library of Babel." Instead of the capture and accumulation of information as an infinite library of indefinitely ordered books, "Dust Bowl, 15.0" pantomimes contemporary surveillance culture and compulsory biometrics through a prosaic dataset in which everything that is known and unknowable and not yet known is mappable and thus capable of being cataloged and conquered. The parable charted in this rendition does not just condemn the pursuit of absolute codification and systemization normalized by containerized transport and supply chains infrastructure, but serves, moreover, as a critique of visibility as it is commonly construed as "representation" within a literary-art market that fetishizes identitarian authorship and pledges allegiance to an individual "I" tethered to national citizenship, boxed in the Western categorical constructions in which we house ourselves (in which we are contained).

"[Y]ou are not one," Édouard Glissant reminded Manthia Diawara in 2009, as the two skimmed the Atlantic aboard the *Queen Mary II*, "you are multiple, and you are yourself. You are not lost because you are multiple. You are not broken apart because you are multiple," Glissant said, all the while being filmed, in a series of cuts over six days and five nights, for Diawara's documentary that would screen the same year. "[...] It's difficult to admit this because we're afraid of losing ourselves."[82]

Cody's work elicits the space carved from variable evacuation, the challenge that diaspora poses to a system of unity, to a structure of the universal. The conclusion of "Everywhere I sleep ..." initiates the engine for another sequence of poems that resemble program commands, server errors, unencrypted file names, unintended user actions. As Cody collages climate catastrophes from distinct moments and the wholesale digitization of sensation, he also tracks our consumer complicity, ventriloquizing Jem Bendell's ongoing 2018 study, "Deep Adaptation" as a trendline scrolls the page's footer like an ominous forecast. What is said? What is left out? What is implied? What is foreseen? Cody's reader labors as archival accomplice, gleaning incomplete details from multiple sources, attuned to the text's call for errant movement and unmeasured receptivity: the blur of cropped exposure, hasty tempos.

What is any poem but a place of passage? What is any poem but a site of refuge? The violence of language cannot be undone but it can be replayed, it can be subverted, it can be cut open and reassembled as ruins, ruins that are a surface ledger of historical trauma, ruins that are also the materials with which a different history may emerge, a different grammar.

## GENERATIVE FICTIONS AND TEMPORAL DISCREPANCIES: COPRESENCE AS A WAITING GAME

> *Ladies and Gentleman, Perhaps you are going to listen ... You have, in any case, begun to hear ...* BOOM! *(Are you listening?) You are now hearing the first lines of a text, ... the reading of the German translation of a text, written originally in French ...*[83]

So read the opening words of Francis Ponge's *Le Savon*, in English, which begins by imagining, not only its own translation, but its adaptation into radio *soap opera*. Ponge, in exodus since the German occupation of France in 1940, writes, first on the move with his family in the unoccupied zone of Roanne in April 1942, then, indefinitely interned, in Coligny (June 1943), from which he (outside the text) narrowly escapes deportation, and, finally, from Paris, twenty-one years later, at the dawn of three-world atomization and Cold War, tracking the body's movement through memory and fantasy, a cultural history repressed and re-written, the desire for self-sovereignty in the midst of global war and pervasive exile. The plea, then, to direct one's own movements, which requires restaging and rehearsal, recombination and annotation, the repetition of thought as the mind goes forward. "No," Ponge writes, on the same first page of the same book, "I have not written *this*, I write it, *I am in the act of writing it, German listeners, for you to hear. I am in the act of writing these first lines. I am no more along in it than you. I am not more* advanced *than you. We are going to* advance, *are* advancing *already, together; you hearing, me speaking; aboard the same train, or the same boat*."[84] The four-wall simultaneous present tense frame, for which time and space flatten into the immediacy of the moment, here becomes a flattening of the mountain between writer and reader, not merely an invitation but an insistence on cohabitating the book which will be written together—and in transit—or not at all. Power structures dissolve in the hypnotic rhythm of movement. Movement, in fact, becomes the *occasion* to tell one's story, a story which is about commonality *and* self-negation, the disappearance of the subject in which we realize ourselves: "[o]ur *paradise*, in short," reads *Le Savon*'s penultimate passage, translated for English readers by Lane Dunlop: "will it not have been *the others*?"[85]

What is soap (*Soap*) but an object that relates its form through dispersion?—the shape of which mutates with each convergence between us and it; the labor of *rubbing it in*, which accentuates a certain effect while providing the means to vanish—recall, with me, the negotiation between transparency and blur, the amateur gaze that invites user-readers to witness the text's production as a form of media, the haptic action of mediation. What is *Soap* but a seminal publication of transmedia storytelling?—an attempt to bring the modality of music into literature, to turn literature into music, music as fugue—a book that translates and is translated; a book that is translating itself through redaction and reprise, the intentional describing of what's been purposefully destroyed so that it might be taken in pieces, a framework for productive effacement in which Ponge staves off authorial agency to signal the dislocated space from which to enter his book's first page. Outside the text, Ponge, perhaps unbeknownst to his readers, was preparing to deliver an actual audio recording of *Le Savon*'s manuscript for Stuttgart radio listeners in Cold War fragmented Germany in 1964. In rediscovering his long-untouched MS and preparing it for broadcast decades later in a different medium, *Le Savon* mutates yet again, foaming, ultimately, into the 1967 alphabetical publication in French, the most significant of the "book-poems" that would later characterize Ponge's poetics. In this sense, *Le Savon*, like the object it is named for, needed to interact with other bodies to serve its purpose: to disappear (disperse) as an act of immersion.

Indeed, Ponge's inclusion of his own *notes to self*, as when he interrupts his observations about serving as a recorder to events so terrible, such "that no other age could have witnessed," to remember, too, to "(Develop this a little)"[86] mark the impossible task of saving everything, even everything that eludes one's writerly purview. The migratory text—as errata and erratic—serves as a reclamation, not only of the marginal but the miscues and omissions. Yury Tynyanov's well-known assertion of linguistic slips in the 1924 essay "The Literary Fact," his claim that every mistake in "normative poetics is, potentially, a new constructive principle"[87] can and should be evaluated outside of the limiting perimeter of normative poetics. Moreover, as I will show in later chapters, an aesthetics of failure, of glitch, of being mistaken, can produce intentional and unintended advantages for marginalized people on the move and those detained.

Under these considerations, Ponge's note dated December 29, 1964, from Paris, as he ruminates on the "abstraction in [...] memory, of the exodus of 1940," prompts revelations for this present study, even if his own question—an invitation for readers, for scholars, to attend to the migrations and dislocations that instigated this book—remains too often unexplored. Yet Ponge's comparisons of soap (the object, the text) to defeat, a defeat that is excessive, enveloping, developmental, purificatory—a defeat that *celebrates* its own withdrawal—exemplifies an alternative approach to practicing mobility, a "way of giving up yet occupying space, a very particular way"[88] that shares much in common with practices of mobility exercised by other migrants to advance both artistic production and cultural activism. Perhaps, then, *Le Savon* should be read as a toolkit or, in its author's own words, "a sort of universal *key* or *cipher*," the pages of which only appear "as if they were good for nothing."[89] It is exactly the appearance of serving nothing and no one but a communion with one's self—the solitary joy of self-collection—that allows such texts to move beyond the structure of representation whose most characteristic condition is, as we well know, absence.

Unlike the generic rules of the novel, the migratory text is not predetermined but permeable; the relation of event—and, moreover, its staging—unfolds and sprawls like language and its social uses, the promises projected out into the world through words. When Marina Tsvetayeva wrote letters to Rainer Maria Rilke, she tried her best to annul the time and space that separated them, she in Western France, he in Western Switzerland, letters impeded by more than borders but by an unreliable postal service and the inevitability of their interception by state actors during moments of emergency and emergence: between world wars and cultural revolutions. Tsvetayeva postdated her letters to Rilke, so they'd arrive faster. Sometimes Tsvetayeva's letters arrived before she wrote them; here we are reminded that migration involves not just temporalities of conflict but, moreover, *temporalities in conflict*—events that coincide, contradict, or come out of order if they come at all. The migratory text thus can be thought of as a vector, which carries more than one's ambulatory passages, more than affect or emotion, but also unresolvable conflicts and tensions, not all of them geographically defined or temporally confined, nor experienced as an exterior flux but psychic, deeply interior, symbolic, heterochronic, imagined and imaginary. "Marina Tsvetayeva," Rilke writes back, on May 10, 1926, "Were you not here just now after all? Or *where was I?* It is still the tenth of May—and, strange thing, Marina, Marina, that was the date you wrote above the concluding lines of your letter (cast forward into time, forward into the timeless moment when I was to read you)!"[90]

In its instability, its porous non-locations, its discontinuous encounters, the migratory text, not unlike transnational correspondence of the past, reflects the complex routes of its own navigation, becoming both self-reproducing and combustible, a form charged with a way of crossing: a mode which is both conditional and a condition. Take, for instance, the instructions yielded from the collected letters of the Zapatista Army of National Liberation (EZLN)'s longtime and erstwhile unofficial spokesperson. On the eleventh of May in 1995, a year after the Zapatista uprising, Subcomandante Marcos writes to Eduardo Galeano with no purpose in mind except the act of writing itself. I am writing to you, Marcos writes, "because I have no reason for doing so, which means that *I can tell you things as they occur to me*, without worrying that I stray from the purpose of this letter."[91] Perhaps more accurately, in the act of correspondence, the purpose *is* to stray. Marcos, writing from the jungles of Chiapas, from the mountains of the Mexican Southeast, from the Lacandon Jungle, strays often; this correspondence, he makes the Uruguayan novelist aware, will take time, takes time; Marcos begins writing on Children's Day, the thirtieth of April. The message will be sent out eleven days later. What happens in the interval, besides the scene of composition?—the text as landscape: both verb and noun.

A day later, in reply to John Berger, who'd pointed out that writing is the approximation of experience, Marcos asks the English art critic, painter, and philosopher if it isn't the reverse, in fact, that is true, that "the writing, and above all the reading of the written text could be an act of distancing."[92] That written word and image could serve, instead, as vehicles to "create distance in order to stay on the other side."[93] The negotiation between proximity and distance in the act of correspondence is not only inevitable, but necessary for the production of intimacy: the reading *from a distance* that any receiver allows themselves while being close enough to touch the printed words, a hand held to the slip of paper or one's screen: haptic reminders of being exactly *on the other side*. The point is not to enact a bridge. And yet the fact of traversal—the movement itself, the inability to converge or consummate fully; to be, at points, refusing of assimilation—should be read as correspondence's kinetic charge. The imagination to fill that gap—between Berger's approximation and Marcos's distancing—constitutes the agency of the person on the other end, but also the person whose message they await, the one writing, and imagining, as they write, the distances that cannot be carried by transmission.

Transnational digital correspondence today as in the past doesn't just facilitate an aforementioned copresence, but also (re)produces the experience of waiting, a waiting that is both heightened and flattened through the always-on assemblage of mobile devices, and which, because of this interplay—and slippage—between the bodily and the virtual, intensifies longing, an aspiration for contact. These encounters of drift—between orbiting and absence—among diasporic communities can tell us more about the cultural norms from which the vast swath of citizen-subjects operate within post internet culture. Just as the digital world is shaped by the material world and a material infrastructure that pipes in the illusion of placelessness under our feet, the material world is increasingly shaped by digital forms. No longer do we think of the "virtual" and "real" as separate or distinct but mutually constitutive, interpenetrating, and continuously entangled elements of everyday life. These convergences should be read as *generative fictions*, as I've argued elsewhere; moments where the real and the irreal don't clash or collide but in fact collapse allow the leakage of a new language, and language which means the imagination of a new form of life.[94] Is it any wonder that in Italian—migrante, immigrato—there is today a new word to describe a person in transit, through a redefinition of what it means to move? "Immigrante" as present participle here denotes the subject of the migrant by emphasizing their interminable passage; someone who has *not yet arrived.*

## DEATH OF THE ~~AUTHOR~~ POET

HERE LIES A GERMAN POET, reads the inscription, in Catalan, at the gate of the community cemetery of Portbou. Walter Benjamin's greatest aspiration was to be nothing less (and nothing more) than Germany's foremost literary critic. But his processual, roundabout, and fragmentary essays are equal parts poetry and prose, straddling the liminal spaces made possible by each, and moreover, by the gaps created when they intersect, overlap, cut into each other. *The Origin of the German Tragedy (Ursprung des deutschen Trauerspiels)*, his early try, and the study which ultimately served as his dissertation in 1925, was a failure, at least on the job market. No one at any university would hire Benjamin as a professor. "How were they to understand a writer," Hannah Arendt writes in her introduction to Benjamin's posthumous essay collection *Illuminations*, "whose greatest pride it was that 'the writing consists largely of quotations—the craziest mosaic technique imaginable'."[95] As he emphatically insisted to childhood friend Gershom Scholem in the same letter Arendt quotes from, "no one could have collected any more valuable or rare."[96] We might consider how all quotation is a form of documentation, but Benjamin's work seems also to assert: *All documentation is quotation.* In a new light, surrounded by a different combination of words, sentences that have been retrieved so as to be reconceived, the words of others harness a charge that is both artifactual and relational: Benjamin's *Arcades Project* invites the historical into the nascent awareness of its redeployment. Here the future in fact ghosts the past, sourced, in its thirteen years of development, from over 850 bodies in multiple languages. When Benjamin decides to render, at times, the French excerpts into his own German, the text becomes more than a kaleidoscopic mixtape, but a meta-translation that remarks upon its own passages—between languages, cultures, countries, centuries—the moment of spatial-temporal trespass performing as a reprise, in which every sampling of the before changes all the other records, or recordings, around it. The *be-for*, the after: in devotion to the latent interactivity of every text.

Greater than the vast collection as a whole is the inability to separate or determine its parts: the annotations from the analysis, the secondary from the primary, the critical from the personal—what has been copied out, what has been written. What is a citation but a calling forth and a divestment? To cite is to engage in extraction and extradition; citation, thus, is both a referral and a retrieval, a joining-together but through deposit and deposition, the substitution of a second hand through a convergence, which is also a removal. In Spanish *citar* can refer to an appointment or arrangement; to be anointed or assigned to, to plan for an eventual encounter.

Among the primal charges of the migratory text is its fluidity, its resistance to periodicity, of where and when constructions of narrative and annotation end and begin, its dissolution of borders—between writer and reader, between journal and fiction, between self and source: between, as this chapter has hoped to make clear, the mediation of experience and its imperfect reproductions. Benjamin, too, understood the power of escaping the finality of so much form, toward the agency of anonymous encounters. Take, for instance, his explicit mandate within his seminal *Arcades*: "This work has to develop to the highest degree the art of citing without quotation marks."[97]

The question we should ask ourselves is, why? What is the effect and function of reading, in which thoughts and voices are continuously embedded without demarcation or pause, absent a signpost where the past stops to let the present in? As in any anonymous encounter, the intimacy lies in not knowing who is speaking to whom, of who gives and who takes in. The intimacy of anonymous encounters, even in public, comes from the certain uncertainty of not knowing if I'm still me, or who else I've become. Of who else is becoming me, and how. "It's as if you had conjured me or assigned me to my own private Pythia," Boris Pasternak writes to Marina Tsvetayeva, on May 5, 1926, from Moscow, the two of them crossing letters and desire with Rilke. "I have, insanely, begun to confuse two words: you and I."[98] How does this undressing—unmaking—of author and address, the reversibility of subject and object, instigate the pattern for a new form, or a new landscape through which it might alight?

In his 1928 "Curriculum Vitae," the third version, as represented by the parenthetical Roman numerals appending its title, Benjamin explains his critical endeavors:

> The idea of casting light on a work by confining my attention purely to the work itself [...] Just as Benedetto Croce opened the way to the individual concrete work of art by destroying the theory of artistic form, I have thus far directed my efforts at opening a path to the work of art by destroying the doctrine of the territorial character of art [...] unconstrained in any way by territorial concepts.[99]

But even Benjamin acknowledged the limits of his goals, if only because literary criticism, not unlike the mass ornament of pop culture, or the notebook and correspondence as lower forms than "literary facts," was widely considered to be an amateur activity. "If you want to carve out a reputation in the area of criticism," he writes to Scholem in a later letter, "this ultimately means that you must re-create criticism as a genre."[100] Brecht, during the same summer encounter in Svendborg described earlier, criticizes Benjamin for descending into the depths, looking at useless things, things which "escape," as a Chinese parable goes, in Brecht's words, through the second-hand reporting of Benjamin, "the sufferings of usefulness."[101] But depth—the foraging *for* mystery—is crucial to Benjamin's dialectical materialism, a prerequisite to his "journeying to the antipodes."[102] Brecht chided his friend for failing to "escape the charge of writing in diary form," and yet Benjamin understood, deeply, and without regret, that he felt "at home in [its] marginal space [...]."[103]

Something becomes available to us through an embracement of scarcity, and the imbrication between disclosure and its resistance, wherein the resistance of *usefulness*—recall Francis Ponge's own desire for *Le Savon*'s pages to appear "good for nothing"—so often bears fruit.

## WORD PROCESS(OR): A WAY OUT OF THE WHOLE

We tend to think of the production of knowledge as a process of finality. In fact, our over-determination of knowledge production has turned it into a finite product, and accompanying it, the widely held worldview that a finished work of art must be always already defined and demarcated, draped around an aura of mysticism, that "atmosphere of entirely bogus religiosity"[104] that John Berger critiqued in *Ways of Seeing*. We should be at odds with this tendency of the academic expert and cultural gatekeeper to safeguard knowledge and to value its mere production instead of the various processes—and persons—that contribute to its formation.

In "The Author as Producer," a 1934 address that was never presented, to an institute that did not exist—"The Institute for the Study of Fascism"—Benjamin writes: "What matters [...] is the exemplary character of production, which is able, first, to induce other producers to produce, and, second, to put an improved apparatus at their disposal. And this apparatus is better, the more consumers it is able to turn into producers—that is, readers or spectators into collaborators."[105] We are reminded of Roland Barthes's essay "The Death of the Author" and later, *S/Z*; Barthes who, like Benjamin, used Brecht to illustrate how a text comprises multiple writings, several bodies entering into dialogue with one another at any moment and at every moment, all of this "because the true locus of writing is reading."[106] Barthes's ideal text unfolds an unrestricted "galaxy of signifiers" that has neither beginning nor end—no enclosures, only holes.

Benjamin, too, anticipated a culture of crowdsourced annotation and appropriation, and the conditions that have nourished an aesthetics marked by distance but also immediacy, remediation, homelessness, and popular culture; work heightened, moreover, through its resignification of seminal texts; these canonical framing devices are meant to insinuate proximity and multiplicity: the expansion of address, as well as the repositioning of artificial categories from which we define or demarcate a text. The text, like its user-producer, is expected to be liquid and thus correspondent and compatible, reformattable: *mobile friendly*. Linger in the span of our last quick decade: erstwhile "out-law" modes—such as speculative autobiography, or the cross-genre, critical-creative, and hybrid text—are now commonplace. I'm interested in how this manipulation or disappearing of genre amidst the increasing dematerialization of media is also a response to a porous and performative sense of self that is today more about (mutable) presentation than (fixed) content; genre as a determining marker becomes increasingly irrelevant, at least outside of the mainstream publishing industry, whereas formats—filetypes, markup tags, mediums—provide an opportunity for seeing how a single text can be presented, repackaged, and disseminated in several different ways, so many of which alter the outcome, which is to say the experience of consumption *as* production. As I wish to make clear here: it is not just autobiography—the first person of personal texts—that migration calls into question, but the system of trackable "category" as a normalizing logic for the literary-art structure and its community.

Channeling the complexity and plurality of the art object proposed by Barthes, as well as the polyvalent "open work" of clustered constellations theorized by Umberto Eco in his early writings,[107] today's "produser" doesn't create content so much as continue it, engaging in a palimpsestic curation of unfinished artifacts that does not merely call a stable authorship into question but, moreover, advances the notion that composition is only ever a continuous process and, likewise, that the text is not a specific, locatable constant but in fact a variable. Six years after coining the term "transmedia storytelling" in a 2001 article of *MIT Technology Review*, media theorist Henry Jenkins revisited his ideas about convergence culture on his blog, *Pop Junctions*, describing a process "where integral elements of a fiction get dispersed systematically across multiple delivery channels for the purpose of creating a unified and coordinated entertainment experience."[108] In my brief treatment of transmedia storytelling for the purpose of this study, what I want to direct attention to is not the economic imperative that enables media conglomerates to exploit the influence and popularity of their franchises as well as their consumers' fluency to read seamlessly and simultaneously across diverse modes of media, but the "gaps and excesses in the unfolding of story" that Jenkins understood as providing readers with a role and goals or incentive to elaborate and expand upon a story that we can read as being neither unified nor original but atomized and iterative. Traces of Jenkins's vision of "knowledge communities" in which consumers become "hunters and gatherers moving back across the various narratives trying to stitch together a coherent picture from the dispersed information" in an era of "collective intelligence," recall both Benjamin's mobilization of the ragpicker (der Lumpensammler) as both forager of the past and harbinger of now-time and his insistence of Surrealism's potential for bodily collective innervation to re/turn as revolutionary discharge.[109] I want to insist: within a culture of convergence characterized by the dispersal of media and the disappearance of its mediation, today's encyclopedic impulse of readers as archivists and archivists as curators, curators as co-composers, draws from the desire to author an unauthorized text, scraped from various sites and reinserted into a space-time in which chronology is displaced by simultaneity, in which cultural memory and personal forgetting work in tandem, each agents of an archive that is also a junkyard.

We can read such hypertextual, recombinant, and anonymous maneuvers as constitutive of a broader departure from modernity's alienated individual and toward a refracted and aggregated identity, serving a growing digital modernism[110] with work that mimics the distribution of media by network technologies and renders a subject-position liquid and libidinal, which is to say deeply attracted and also curious about its own pleasures: a fascination for trace, residue, and scent, the exaltation of the trail as sacred, where pattern displaces plot. But is this methodology any different from the one employed throughout the correspondences and notebooks of migrants during the interwar period, including Benjamin's own *Passagen-Werk*? In forging a method built on excess and ellipsis, Benjamin was not only endeavoring toward a poetics of unsettlement, but the preservation of the original work's "intention," as he writes in a letter to Hugo von Hofmannsthal, poet, librettist, and publisher of Benjamin's 1924 essay, "Goethe's Elective Affinities": "to plumb the depths of language and thought ... by drilling rather than excavating."[111] Even Rolf Tiedemann, editor of Benjamin's posthumous *Passagen-Werk*, was skeptical, admitting, "it is tempting to question the sense of publishing these oppressive chunks of quotations," while understanding that all of the citations—75 percent of *The Arcades Project*'s 250,000 words—were necessary and served, in its author's own words, "to discover in the analysis of the small individual moment the crystal of the total event."[112]

It is this total event that Benjamin, at a moment of unprecedented mass displacement that presaged our own, drilled, that is burrowed, but also tested out, repatterned through repetition, the fugitive exercise of reading. The embrace of the fragment, the friction of the passage, the fissure of the cut, the reawakening produced by the return of a single sentence or strain of thought—that repetition that mimics a choral, crowd-backed recitation—is not a way out of the whole, but a way to reveal it: the emergence of textual layers that were always already there. The migratory text reflects this personal accounting, while ultimately rendering a form of public resistance. "Significant literary effectiveness [...] must nurture the inconspicuous forms that fit its influence in active communities better than does the pretentious, universal gesture of the book—in leaflets, brochures, articles, and placards," Benjamin writes in a section titled "Filling Station" of *One-Way Street*, a dress rehearsal, in 1928, for the unfinished *Arcades Project*. "Only this prompt language shows itself actively equal to the moment."[113] Of course, what is "equal to the moment" need always be up for critical reevaluation.

Fredric Jameson, like Adorno before him, understood that what drives modernism is not some vision of the future or the new, but the belief that certain forms and techniques can no longer be used and should be "creatively avoided."[114] By contrast, Benjamin recognized that the dead end of creativity and cogent action lies in the belief that there are matters already at our disposal that are off-limits, insisting on a critical engagement of things that have *gone out of use*. What is the difference between refuse and refusal? Benjamin turns from the habits of historicism to reorient his gaze upon the garbage and ill-begotten, what society deems inadequate, unworthy, trash. This philosophy of history has its roots in Benjamin's philosophy of language and of naming, a citability that presupposes a call to appear, a call to authority, a call to attention, a method of investigation that implicates its author in their own bibliography—their own biography—like the collector of Benjamin's unpublished essay "Unpacking My Library," who melts into his collection as the last sentence halts. "And now he is going to disappear inside," Benjamin writes, "as is only fitting."[115]

To be named is to be called. To be called is to become, or come into action.

## ADDRESSES

Life enters literature the same way literature might enter a life. When this happens, we can mark the evolution of the "literary," particularly by what many literary critics consider to be distinct from literature, the facts of everyday life that Yury Tynyanov understood, by contrast, as being only the undercurrent of the *objet d'art*, something that "play[s] out its literary role, sinks once more into everyday life," and returns—"when circumstances are right"[116]—into a literary fact. Thus a receipt can become, not evidence of something provided or consumed, but a token of a forthcoming feast *to-go*. The mutability of these categories—"slovesnost" (letters), "literatura" (literature), and "poeziya" (poetry)[117]—is here only overshadowed by the mutable nature of a form that might encompass them all in a single text.

Tynyanov, writing in the fraught years following the First World War, has in mind nonsense languages and the vast field of nineteenth-century letter-writing, both of which, he writes, "operate with unusual material; they have enormous significance for the evolution of literature, but escape any static definition of the literary fact."[118] I would amend his assessment only by saying that it is precisely *because* these dynamic, overlooked phenomena "do not leave enough striking, static 'traces' behind them"[119] that they can both escape static definitions of the literary fact *and* remake it, not from the inside or from the outside, but through straddling the in-between zone of the periphery.

It is because the specific form of notebooks and letters—their lineation and lineaments—bears fruit as to how we might read the migratory text today that Tynyanov's tracing of the nineteenth-century's literary correspondence to the "small talk" of drawing rooms, then games, and finally, the letter, is equally important to understanding our contemporary intensification of the convergence between the private and public realms, particularly through the synthesis of ludic practices and venues across social media: life as game, countable through metrics.

Closer attention to the common stylistic devices of fragmentation, partial reveals, and the erotic negotiation between suggestion and "leaving things unsaid"—a marked turn, as Tynyanov points out, from the "'grandiose' devices of the eighteenth century"[120]—informs how the migratory text has prefigured and advanced new media practices and digital norms. Remember Francis Ponge, who had to imagine the reception of "German ears" in order to actualize the wish fulfillment of the book as a landscape of past occurrences, nascent encounters; what Ponge was also doing was negotiating the limitations of one-to-one correspondence, expanding his address to not only include user-readers across different languages, but also across different media; expanding his address as a way of considering how such a correspondence would and *could* be received; what it means to read and be read as an account of emerging media.

◆

What is exile but a way of life that demands the arrangement of certain interludes? Enter: Arnaldo Calveyra's debut, *Cartas para que la alegría*, published in 1959, translated into English in 2018. Between them: a terminal exile, an intermittent movement, its author's death but also a second life, an "already all back at the beginning-ginning again."[121] Calveyra, who was exiled in France alongside fellow Argentine writer Julio Cortázar during the US-assisted death squads of the Cold War and the Videla dictatorship, turned to correspondence—with Cortázar, with the geography of the countryside and the language of the past, with its future translation into French, in his adopted country, where he would ultimately receive its highest literary honor. If *Letters So That Happiness* is a series of correspondences, these are letters written to their own author, a shift in address that anticipates Susan Sontag's own predictions of the "[d]ecline of the letter, the rise of the notebook." As she elaborates in a note dated April 26, 1980: "One doesn't write to others any more; one writes to oneself."[122] In the same way, Calveyra's missives are mementos, discontinuous jottings, jagged and whimsical descriptions of Entre Ríos, of tiptoes and startled chickens and big balloons, suspended, veering, propulsive, all of these and all at once, a poetics of departure so as to elongate the thrilled charge of waiting, lengthening time so as to look at it now, and look at it for later, as when Calveyra beholds his own "childhood of us above us."[123] And yet, despite its wish to be haunted, these are notes toward the future; a project of returning to one's history not merely to relive it but in order to restage it, to see it again and to see it differently. This old-new landscape thus becomes subjected to the temporal and spatial restructuring amended by Calveyra's cartographic grammar: the recovery of a culture and a people, a syntax borrowed from the language of the campo, unrecoverable but for its retrieval in the landscape of the text. If these *Letters* are incomplete, it is because all archives are necessarily extant *and* effacing; as readers, we, too, are tasked with the responsibility of impossible renderings: to both stay and rise, to leave the text so as to remake it, but also to plumb deeper while reveling, nevertheless, in the work's desire to evade, elude—"This is my chance [...]" Calveyra writes in the book's penultimate poem, "This is my little chance."[124] It comes, after all, only when the letter itself slips away, toward some distant pleasure.

"In some ways, perhaps, translation is another leg in this journey of distances," Elizabeth Zuba, Calveyra's posthumous English translator, suggests in her "Translator's Note," "to near by way of distance, to identify by obscurity, to be in many places at once, and at once, remember the many kinds of forgetting—dispersion and through dispersion, preservation."[125] Translation here should be thought of as a re-writing of the original through the circuitous routes of materially unreturnable passages, an accumulation of inexact movements and moments. Calveyra's lean book marked the beginning of his exile—first from the campo of childhood to the city of Buenos Aires, then from an Argentina of authoritarian dictatorship, where he would never return amidst the turbulence of the Cold War's Guerra Sucia. More important to this study, however, is that the letters themselves reinscribe a new language for articulating exile, and furthermore, for inhabiting its disruption: a reorientation situated on restless paradox, on memory and forgetting, on leaving, but also and always, on leaving a space for later—not necessarily the discovery of the new but something newly visible, a revelation that is contingent upon the emergence of what could heretofore not be perceived. How can this insight—the pull of a text that is both testament and sigil—be read against the assimilation impulses of state and system?

Between 1931 and 1932, just as Benjamin was preparing to flee Germany and begin an exile that would terminate only in death, he collected and edited a collection of German letters for the *Frankfurter Zeitung*. "The intention of this series," Benjamin writes in an unpublished, undelivered talk meant to herald its publication:

> [...] to reveal the lineaments of a "secret Germany" that people nowadays would much prefer to shroud in heavy mist. For a secret Germany really exists. It is merely that its secretness is not simply the expression of its inwardness and depth, but—albeit in a different sense—the product of raucous and brutal forces that have prevented it from playing an effective role in public life. [...] It is because these letters make this so clear that they have remained so unknown.[126]

In another undelivered talk called "On the Trail of Old Letters," Benjamin illuminates the political potential of these correspondences, on the condition that they are made available to the public instead of being relegated to "the preserve of scholars—indeed of specialists."[127] As though echoing Benjamin several decades later, Félix Guattari reminds Maurice Nadeau: "Theoretical work shouldn't be reserved for specialists."[128] Rather than centering the primacy of the individual author-producer envisioned by Guattari's fantasy of "another breed of intellectuals, another breed of analysts, another breed of militants, with the different types blending and melting into each other," I want to call attention to the ways in which public access to personal correspondence can engender *another text*—an alternate text, not unlike the two versions of every letter allegedly written by Mark Twain and Alexander Pushkin: a double letter, always multiple and multiplying, multiplied by the vision and version of so many others, so many others.[129] In this sense, Ponge's 1950 notebook, *Nioque of the Early-Spring*, becomes exactly this alternate text, serving to complete the recto verso of the codex initiated by *Soap*, which comes before (April 1942) and leaves off after (January 1965), and which, in doing so, reveals the ways in which one never ceases to be a migrant, suggesting that migration and displacement, too, are not extraordinary and finite events so much as everyday occurrences that convey enduring conditions. Reading these two texts together forms a composite portrait of an exile that is not a solitary experience so much as a collective condition of abbreviation and addenda, the yearning to articulate one's own "nervous modification[s]"[130] through the reciprocal act of inscription: a correspondence with one's self.

Benjamin's early task in collecting and editing a series of German letters can be understood as our own task, here in these pages, of recollection and retrieval, the gathering of migratory texts to be read against occupation, exile, forced acculturation, and nationalization, the gathering of such texts if only so that they might look at one another, understanding, as Viktor Shklovsky once wrote, in his own compilation of anecdotes and quotations, that "things change once they land in a book."[131] Through the personal correspondence, especially those which trace a route of migration and situate the microhistory of persons on the move, we are asked to question as readers—as recorders—that which has been shrouded in heavy mist, whether by brute force or more insidious, implicit means. Each voice in a streaming feed can interrupt the one preceding it, or allow the pause of a breath in the one that follows; what we think of as disruption can be a diversion: to redirect one's attention, to recall a prior moment, to insert other voices onto the track, to loop and overlay. To straddle, to ride, to hover. Given up to the soft drift of the text and the drift of your own thoughts that form another.

Sample, first use: 1985. An excerpt of recorded sound or music reused or modified as part of a new recording or performance. But to what ends? A sample renders a finite part of a statistical population to gain information about the whole. As we have already seen, Benjamin grapples with concepts that foreshadow twenty-first century textual cultures; the form of his intertextual, translingual *Arcades* presages our everyday browsing habits in which users don't necessarily read—or rather, don't only read—but scroll, parse, detour, annotate, copy, paste, disseminate, writing back in a polyglot, pictorial language often transliterated through speech recognition. Anticipating the sample as a standard of writing and listening, Benjamin also provides his readers with the permission to move through his text at our discretion, if only to let the eye, and mind, wander, as we become not only writer of the text but also its subject: the flâneur. We breathe as we read and the text breathes too, widening its margins: a sigh, not of relief but with the deep exhalation that comes during contemplation, and the discovery of something I had not previously thought of. "And today," Benjamin writes in another section of *One-Way Street* titled "Attested Auditor of Books": "the book is already, as the present mode of scholarly production demonstrates, an outdated mediation between two different filing systems. For everything that matters is to be found in the card box of the researcher who wrote it, and the scholar studying it assimilates it into his own card index."[132]

Benjamin here suggests that as writers and thinkers, we would be better served reading everything an author ever read than everything they ever wrote. Translation, thus, is nothing if not a mode of experience, where to copy something out is also to relive it, a mode of passage that includes the reader's footsteps, and crucially, constitutes a refusal to separate the annotating of experience and the experience of annotation. Through a closer attention to such functions of second-hand inscription in the chapters to follow, we can begin to see how the migratory text prefigures our current phenomena of "produsage"[133] and the vast assemblage of user-generated content that characterizes today's P2P sharing economy. At stake in this discussion is not just the democratization of art but troubling the very idea of intellectual property, which is to say the very concept of ownership and authorship.

Long before the internet was rerouted from military servers and then mainstreamed, Michel Foucault understood the efficacy of anonymous interactions on the level of literature, imagining a culture where discourse would circulate without any need for an author. But what he was asking in 1969 is something we can better answer today—and only with attention to movements that predate Foucault's own analysis—because it seems less germane to call into question the need for an author in a culture in which everyone is reading, producing, and reproducing text, and more effective to think about the migratory text's invitation to reevaluate the notion of a single author, or what it means to *write by yourself*. One would have to testify to the media we have at our disposal; the opportunities the internet has provoked for dis/placement and distribution, and, moreover, our ability as producers of content to *cut out*—the abandonment of our own authorial expertise and ownership. One would have to surrender the idea that authors own anything besides our will to keep producing, and our desire for change; and to modulate means to resist without negating, to alter without omitting, to enable something new to come forward: the unfolding of the text into the anonymity of a murmur.

We should remind ourselves that "to author" all the way down to its Latin roots signifies advising, witnessing, and transferring. We should be reminded that to author something means to forget the act of saying "I," to forget it or to make the I recede in service of the other or others, on behalf of a community, for the sake of an audience. Author, from *auctor*, which designates a source, such as a vendor or assignor, of a particular right or title, who thus enlarges it, confirms it, produces it. Not coincidentally, auctor, today, can be used to describe the person who donates the genetic material used to create a clone. In this sense, original and copy are in fact inextricable. The decentralization of web development and programming from the early nineties through today informs these poetics of relation, an always-open structure in which, as Édouard Glissant has said, "the creator of a text is effaced, or rather, is done away with, to be revealed in the texture of his creation."[134] When a solid melts, it reveals something always underneath, something at the bottom, something inside—something new and something that was *always already there.*

The mix is a remix but also a mixtape: a carefully curated arrangement of tracks overlaid onto hard disk or digital space, capable of being heard or re-written. What good is our work for our communities, I often think—from the privileged space of the classroom—if we write only for ourselves? What good is our work for our communities if we speak for them instead of allowing them to speak to us? What happens when we hold, together, literary criticism and "creative writing" and the academy and the community and the theoretical and the personal? What happens when we hold them up to critical inquiry and pedagogical, political, and artistic possibilities? At stake is choice; the ability to choose, as much a proposal as it is a defense of heterogeneity, access, and inclusion. I say this with the conviction that if I get to the bottom of theory—not yet or ever to the bottom, but even, only, to brush up against it, to lay beside it, to reach out for it and to be received in return—something of that theory will be given to me and in turn given back. From theory to theory, and toward theory. Always on the way, en route, and effluent. I say this with the conviction that all theory is not only personal—the raw material from which a detached abstraction emerges—but also reciprocal and reciprocating.

Speaking about antiquated—yet still championed—definitions of an author, Foucault, in "What Is an Author?" answers: "the ideological figure by which one marks the manner in which we *fear the proliferation of meaning*."[135] The italics are mine, but everything else is shared. And within these margins is the sight of another great feast: "For to some degree," Benjamin writes, "all [...] texts contain their potential translation between the lines."[136] Reading this assertion, from "The Task of the Translator," alongside Foucault's identification of a *transdiscursive author*, whose work, Foucault writes, "contains characteristic signs, figures, relationships, and structures that could be reused by others,"[137] allows us to see how new discourses are created through opening up existing texts, for an analysis that yields more than just criticism, but a rubric for imitation that masquerades as obscurity. It is the very act of writing that creates, as Foucault understood, "a space into which the *writing subject constantly disappears*."[138] Desubjectification and polyphony and the murmur of collaboration as a framework for narrative and authorial dispersal, the terms for a migratory poetics. A way out of consensus is in the celebration of difference, not as a way to assimilate the other through the conversion of language but as a form of translation through the empathy made possible by walking in another's footsteps.

Boris Pasternak, writing during the Second World War about his youth and friendships during Russia's Bolshevik Revolution, proceeds, in his own words, at random. Of course, nothing is more random than *Safe Conduct*'s opening pages, in which Pasternak begins his autobiography by stating: "I am not writing my autobiography," a deferral that is actually an invitation, since one's autobiography can't be found under one's own name but "must be sought under those of others"—and this is because the "more self-contained the individuality from which the life derives, the more collective [...] is its story," a paradox resolved only by considering Pasternak's call for the accumulation of "unessentials": everything that has happened and continues to occur, not to the author, but to their readers—in short, everything that necessarily escapes an authorial purview.[139]

Hugo Ball, likewise, begins his diary in 1914, in the midst of an unprecedented bodily violence and the stifling of civilian movement, by telling us who is passing through him. "At the moment I am reading Kropotkin, Bakunin, and Merezhkovsky," Ball writes, in November, from Berlin. "I have been at the border for two weeks. In Dieuze I saw the first soldiers' graves. Fort Manonvillers had just been shelled, and in the rubble I found a tattered Rabelais."[140] Here, literature and death converge, as if to say that the art obscured by violence and the violence obscured by art, or its production, can also be reversed; that we can uncover life and literature—and life as literature—through divesting ourselves of our own insistence on individuality. That, on the contrary, to tell one's story one has to tell about all the people—real or imagined—who accompany us. Isn't every notebook or journal also a correspondence? The negotiation between absolute solitude and intense communion, to be in another's orbit, to be in their purview and in their story, an approximation of another's presence, and also the desire for proximity; is this not the promise of a book that merges observation and aside, itemization and reflection, narrative and citation?—the fulfillment of Friedrich Schlegel's aphoristic inquiry: "aren't there individuals who contain within themselves whole systems of individuals?"[141] Even so, the migratory text affirms the unmaking of systems through exactly this radical displacement, which is actually a meeting, a confluence. Tsvetayeva's letters to Rilke and Pasternak were lost during the course of transit; we are able to read them today only because of the drafts made in her notebooks. These preliminary letters replaced the originals; or rather, the originals became copies, from which readers now draw.

What does careful revisitation and revision offer as a framework toward further structural interventions? In her call for reorienting the scholarly tradition of neutrality and distance, and the common academic practices of relativizing and universalizing, Susan Buck-Morss demonstrates the historical moment in which "theory and reality converged [...] by which philosophy burst out of the confines of academic theory and became a commentary on the history of the world."[142] In excavating both Hegel and the birth of Haiti at the turn of the new millennium to argue the need for radically rethinking institutional methodology—"[d]isciplinary boundaries allow counterevidence to belong to someone else's story"[143]—Buck-Morss also provides ample evidence for the agency of auto-archival practices. In raising possibilities for the telling of "*un*disciplined stories,"[144] Buck-Morss is only able to tell Hegel's by privileging what the German philosopher was reading—gleaned, not coincidentally, from Hegel's own letters. Perhaps most interesting for any analysis aiming to contextualize the personal text in our present moment is the well-traveled nature of the journal in question. *Minerva*'s articles were taken up by countless other newspapers within Germany but also largely outside of Hegel's native land; its writers, too, borrowed from a mix of German, English, and French sources, a system of transnational, translingual, and open communication that can be likened to an early internet.

Yet at stake in Buck-Morss's project of revealing the glaring discrepancy between thought and practice to reclaim historical narratives and undo institutional and institutionalized silences is much more than academic interdisciplinarity but actual representation, whether the extant practice of slavery or all other dehumanizing practices that remain largely undocumented in our own time—the reality that inside the First World's global postmodernism is not just "a veritable Third World" but as Aijaz Ahmad reminds us, "perhaps two or three of them."[145] Inside such an insular global postmodernism are also the everyday limitations for transit, mobility, and connectivity; the reality that within Africa, as we know, the most effective way to travel through air, even between contiguous countries, is by going through Europe. Here, as elsewhere, "internationalization" remains a localized, centralized concept, where communication and consciousness are configured through metropolitan elites and the streamlined chronology of transnational capital flow.

To think through and past the production of knowledge we have reproduced as scholars, as instructors, our task becomes to entangle representation and recuperation. Stripped of legal protection and removed from public awareness, undocumented migrants and those who endure outside cultural and legal frameworks are also removed from public memory, the right to be remembered. Of course, every narrative is not only composed by but comprises an authority—premised on history, legality, legitimacy. Such conditions, Edward Said suggests, govern the "permission to narrate," whereby persons, such as the Palestinian people, can only ever arrive in a degraded present, without a history, without a future.[146]

What could be a greater exercise of power than the appropriation of a nation's social memory? *Pero mientras sea desaparecido, no puede tener ningún tratamiento especial, es una incognita, es un desaparecido, no tiene entidad, no está, ni muerto ni vivo, está desaparecido.*

In a press conference in 1979, Jorge Rafael Videla, dictator of Argentina between 1976 and 1981, said exactly that.[147] What does it mean to be *un desaparecido*? To not have any entity; to be neither dead nor alive. What does it mean to be permanently *missing*?

Mansour Omari, a Syrian human rights activist who in the years following the Arab Spring and the Syrian Revolution of Dignity was imprisoned and tortured by the Assad regime, is a human recorder, whose archive of bodies signals the importance of naming—not of the past but of the present reality that would otherwise be snuffed out, not unremembered but unseen. In the 2018 documentary *82 Names*, Omari talks about how the idea came to the group of prisoners in Syria's Fourth Division, a detention center run by President Bashar al-Assad's brother, outside the institutions and courts of the state. Unsatisfied with the daily ritual of remembering and reciting the names and contact information of five inmates, a jailed journalist (later killed in prison) suggested using a chicken bone to pierce the flesh, to form the ink of blood, to mix the blood with rust from steel bars, to write each prisoner's name out from the body, to place it back on the body. Omari eventually delivered this counter-archive on strips of cloth, hidden in the neck collar of his shirt, when he was released from prison.

In Assad's totalitarian Syria, where self-documentation is an act of espionage, there are very few photographs[148] rescued from a regime that has alternately overseen and denied the systematic disappearance of Syrian citizens, many of them perishing in the same prisons where Omari smuggled out his own testimony of detainment. His next act, to lend this cell-sourced documentation to the United States Holocaust Memorial Museum, which has restored much of its legibility, is a museal glance that is less toward the past—this happened last year, two years ago, a decade earlier—than the present, pointing to the importance not merely of documentation but also to the archiving of the process. "Keeping this alive and telling people what is going on [...] this is not just reminding people but telling them what is happening now—at this moment,"[149] Omari tells his interviewer, an insistence he repeats several times throughout the film's 53 minutes. This is still happening.

How do our notebooks give us away, which is to say, how do they deliver us? How can our notebooks give us insight into how we read our past, how we remark upon our present? How can our notebooks allow us to access—and understand—the manifold experiences of a single event since reduced to the annals of fact and the formulations of narrative? To see is to know, a student once told me during our seminar on interpreting literary testimony. I asked the class to probe further. They'd been keeping their own logs—what we called our *records of experience*—for the past several weeks, and they were beginning to consider the ways in which their daily annotations were shaping how they interacted with the world, which had begun, in its own way, to imperceptibly alter, a newfound susceptibility nourished by the embodiment beneath inscription. "To know is to experience," the student continued, without so much as a pause. "To experience is to feel. To feel is to understand." What I want to hold on to is where we left off; what we are left with. What I want to hold on to is feeling; what it feels like, a precursor to understanding but also imagination and displacement, the ingredients necessary for empathy. How the notebook, unlike documentarian reportage, is not so much concerned with what one did on any given day but rather what one was thinking; what, and who, one kept in their thoughts despite the material unsettlement of the present and the ceaseless destruction of the past, which is memory; what it feels like to be in the midst of thought, and how it feels to be inside another's. To know, in some interpretations, might be to experience, but so is, unquestionably, *to not know*. The desire—remember—is not an exact recording but an imperfect one: approximate, incomplete, annotated, transparent, fuzzy, fragmentary, discontinuous, remediated. Maybe the imperfections in such irregular accountings are the necessary cracks by which we might enter another's life and experience. What it might mean to place our hand here, too, and inscribe the words that would constitute this text.

And there's something I want to say about copying things out, about the slippage of writer and reader, and the writing of a composite text passed along from every person who has been here and who remains here in the here-after. I situate *Drift Net* as a diasporic, phenomenological, processual, and ever-personal study that locates the migratory as a key site through which political and social action may be practiced, recounted, and ultimately, enacted.

And in the margins—memoranda, or an invitation: *(Develop this a little.)*

# CHAPTER TWO: POLYPHONY. /

# MIGRATION AS THE PRIMAL SCENE OF NARRATIVE AND A MODEL FOR ITS RECONFIGURATION

The story of migration is migration as story. Not one story but multiple, intersecting, divergent, continuous; migration both provokes and requires its own narrative repetition, its own non-narrative influx, its own dissemination, which is to say its own movement, precisely because of the fact of any passage's incompleteness, its desire not to be *told in full*, its inclination and capacity to reconstitute itself in fragments.

Open hangars, fenced-off stretches of earth, aircraft aisles, train terminals, prison cells, cargo decks, checkpoints and chokepoints, shipping lanes, ports and consulates, the archive of the street, the periphery of the city. These are the contact zones of the migratory text. Someone is telling a story. Someone is listening. A story is told so it can be heard. And in being heard, it is told again. The point of the story is to keep moving; to pass and so to pass on. The listener, the reader, becomes more than a receiver of such stories but a narrator; storytelling becomes dynamic and participatory, capable of transmitting not only a migrant's singular experience of passage, but, moreover, a collective condition of mobility and a collaborative model for detouring traditional narrative structures, the political impact of which so often depends on how the story is framed.

I want to start here, with the challenges and perceived constraints of personal narrative, if only so I can complicate authorial notions of the self that require or demand solitary experience. Linking the literature of testimony to the primal story of migration to draw out the *act*uality of inscription—a marked departure from the criterion of "factuality"—allows us a better understanding of how a text's migratory context informs its processual, partial, and piecemeal structure, an unsettling that has allowed persons on the move, as well as those who have been internally displaced, to map their tracks of experience.

Such narratives, often co-authored or anonymous, translingual and remediated, have the potential to re-read the notion of a national literature—by putting it into question—but also posit a re-writing of the nation. The focus thus shifts from the ability to tell one's story to the ability to *construct* one's story, a privileging of the material, archival, and formal dimensions of the work I've identified in this book as migratory. Such texts do not end but in fact begin in translation, and to read this intervention is to make a further critique about world literature and the industry of literary translation which the international book trade relies upon. I want to propose that we pay closer attention to how the literal and literary are mutually constructed; as I will show in later chapters, we can read this literary critique alongside critiques of migration studies, a comparative analysis that informs a framework for alternative refugee integration models and migrant coalition.

"Each Palestinian structure presents itself as a potential ruin,"[1] Edward Said says, writing in the last decade of the Cold War about the fractured consciousness of a people without a home. I would add that the reverse is also true, and in fact fundamental to our understanding of the charge—political, social, affective—of such migratory texts. Indeed, each ruin—produced by migration, dislocation, displacement, colonization, exile—presents itself as a potential structure. The possibilities for productive displacement are rooted in the question of form, but also the manipulation of frame. It is the migrant who, in providing the primal scene of narrative, also subverts the consecrated scene of nativity, the very idea of an origin. Put another way, the migratory text provides a new source code: texts that are in fact instructions for reassembly and collaboration, and the displacement of the original through its copies.

## PERSONAL NARRATIVES, PUBLIC ENGAGEMENT

What are the prospects and limitations of storytelling for developing a public and political voice? Sarah C. Bishop, who conducted interviews with undocumented immigrants in New York City from 2015 to 2016, set out to explore this question while researching autobiographical story-sharing in advocacy and social action, the "reclaimant narratives" that proliferate throughout the immigrant rights movement: "experiential, *partial*, public, oppositional, and *incondensable* stories" that have been used by marginalized persons "to assert their right to speak and *reframe audience understanding*."[2] According to Bishop, while these stories open up the possibilities for understanding, sympathy, and a point of commonality within the larger public sphere, by privileging an experiential and individual narrative as a model to reclaim a cultural representation, they also elide the reality that individuals experience cultural conditions, such as globalization and migration, with immeasurable difference. Bishop links reclaimant narratives with performance and strategic omission, aspects that are read in her analysis as deficiencies—"they will necessarily leave out the 'hidden transcript'"[3]—private stories, she cautions, when delivered to the public, can never tell *the story in full*.

Possibilities for autonomy thus diminish; in Bishop's scenario, storytellers must decide between simplification and universal humanism or the specificity and diversity of human experience; issues or individuals; structures or selfhood. But perhaps more troubling than these alleged defects of personal narrative are the repercussions of its delivery to a public that is so often sated with merely being well-informed, a narrative fatigue produced in an age of information abundance in which knowledge replaces action, where knowing replaces doing, forcing marginalized producers to think about how to equip their audiences with information *and* cultivate the means for engagement. This aspiration, to inform and engage, pushes back on the public's compulsion for sympathy and familiarity, a retrieval, I want to read, of the kind of "counsel" that Walter Benjamin, writing in 1936, already saw as diminishing in an age of information, in which the communication of experience had been similarly outmoded.

Counsel is a purpose, a policy or plan of action or behavior, a deliberation and consultation. More importantly, as Benjamin also understood, counsel establishes "a proposal concerning the continuation of a story *which is just unfolding*"[4]—not so much the right to tell one's story as the right to be listened to and thus repeated, in memory or otherwise, an imminent relation that is subject not to closure but rather indefinite returns. To consult is always an invocation, whether to a person or group of people in body (to ask the advice or opinion of) or in spirit (to refer to, to be in dialogue with), what we might think of as the spectral or ghostly audience members of past and future tellings—an interpenetrating space of reception facilitated, today, through mobile technology's contestation and reshaping of borders, gaps in the ground plan through which to enter virtual experience as real time. Counsel posits a togetherness that does not flatten differences but invites them, as iterations of narrative *and* narrator. However, as Benjamin warns in "The Storyteller," "the gift for listening is [already] lost and the community of listeners disappear[ed]."[5]

And yet—what communication does not require a sole representative or spokesperson? What mode of meaning-making does not require the language of bureaucracy to push it through or to prevent it from advancing? And how might we relocate a text from the privileged location of Bishop's *full story* and toward incompletion and imperfection, toward the sketchy, the tentative, the rough and unfulfilled—meaning that is found, and found wanting. Or, in other words: what does it mean to work in translation, to work on translation; indeed, to work translation through a collaborative social-literary practice activated by noise—by gaps, by slips, by non-lexical awareness, by an awareness of the word as autonomic: language, which no longer posits a relation of property—this language does not *belong-to*; it is neither mine nor yours—but, on the contrary, proposes a tenuous communion, a recognition and embodiment moved by encounters?

Gestures of the body and related performance strategies have long been thought capable of breaking the hierarchical relationship between visitor and exhibit, stimulating forms of constructive participation and learning: a space within space, in which the private and public converge as a co-produced locus of lived experience. In this exhibit it is neither the artist nor the work of art and its curators but the guests who become a key element in the production—ongoing, and ever-changing—of narrative. Somatic enactments have the potential to awaken other forms of memory—intuitive, sensorial—while subverting the hierarchy of knowledge reception rooted in visuality, the common perception that, above all, *seeing necessarily means knowing.*[6]

As scholars such as Liisa H. Malkki have shown, humanitarian practices tend to silence refugees, specifically by stripping them of the authority to produce narrative evidence of their own conditions. Read against a dehistoricizing universalism buoyed by the moral obligation for "exemplary victims," the perception of the refugee as a storyteller can in fact have negative implications.[7] In a visual economy where wounds, not words, signify value, displaced and disenfranchised people, such as the Hutu refugees described by Malkki in 1996, are discounted by experts and organizers alike as "persons who [are] always 'telling stories',"[8] whereas photographs, such as the one that appeared in *Life*'s feature, "Eyewitness Rwanda," begin and end with self-conclusive captions. The refugee, in this scenario, is thus incapacitated on the levels of expression *and* representation. *Life*'s affirmation, made during the genocide in Rwanda, that its six-page full-color photograph spread "require[s] no elaboration"—that it is specifically and especially the image's "silence" that "tell[s] the story of Rwanda"[9]—underscores both the gross overvaluation of scopic documentarian evidence, and the media's concomitant absence of accountability in its dispersal of such visual proof. Recall the fetishization of unfiltered proximity and immediacy of participatory journalism countered by the Syrian anonymous video collective Abounaddara, and their resistance to the user-generated content shot on the front lines of the Syrian Civil War, whose spectacle of violence offers its own critique: that "independent" authors capable of producing their own images could also become the "subcontractors" of a representational regime whose golden rule remains "if it bleeds it leads."

However, it is not just the role and function of the media—and its official and unofficial correspondents—that requires reexamination, but international organizations like the UN, which privilege the photograph as an object that stands on its own, requiring little or no critical engagement, only the tacit directive to *look*. Edward Said, reflecting on the genesis of the collaborative text-image project *After the Last Sky: Palestinian Lives*, discusses exactly this command, after being told that the photographs of Palestinian life to be hung in the main entrance hall of the United Nation's International Conference on the Question of Palestine (ICQP) in Geneva could only be hung up, affixed to the corridor and fixed in place, with no writing displayed. "No legends," he writes, "no explanations. [...] It was then that Jean Mohr and I decided to work together. Let us use photographs and a text, we said to each other, to say something that hasn't been said about Palestinians. Yet the problem of writing about and representing—in all senses of the word—Palestinians in some fresh way is part of a much larger problem."[10]

Here, as elsewhere, we can see how the refugee can be silenced and yet still speak to us, through our own language, in our own voice, raising questions about authorship, framing, audience, and address, and raising, for me, another. How does the migratory text question, contest, revise, and respond to such realist documentarian narratives—the language of the UNHCR (United Nations High Commissioner for Refugees) and humanitarian-focused nongovernmental organizations—as well as to their generic literary and cultural representations, of being spoken for and spoken about? It is, indeed, this "much larger problem" suggested by Said that I would like to expose and address here, this much larger problem that demands we move beyond the reductive and circular witness-testimony binary, that we move beyond the binary of subject and object, and that, through these movements, we parse the distinctions between language and speech.

The material realities of migrants, particularly those without papers, and the crisis of visuality under platform capitalism is, as I've shown elsewhere,[11] rapidly escalating, through the network storytelling circulated by digital technologies, as well as journalistic narratives derived from descriptions offered by police and politicians, yet I'd like us to reconsider the potency of the partial and piecemeal, a narrative frame that is meant to be perforated and penetrated, by audience members and readers, archivists and accomplices. I'd like to think of these limitations, not as built-in impediments toward the transmission of experience in and of migration, but on the contrary, as a kind of prerequisite toward literary and literal passage. I want to insist that in eschewing formal markers both national and narratorial, such personal texts produced in transit also call into question traditional notions of authorship and translation, and they do this *through these very limitations*: friction and interferences that are actually fault lines, fault lines which can make the earth swell—and shift—below our feet.

## THE COUNTER-SLIPS OF PERFORMANCE: AUTOBIOGRAPHY AS RELATIONAL PRACTICE

How to mobilize autobiography—the only mode of production available to writers of color, especially writers of the diaspora, according to a range of theorists, instructors, and other authors[12]—so as to open it up from a representative territory of the individual to a porous space of collective passage? Rather than be "condemned to write only autobiographical works," filmmaker and theorist Trinh T. Minh-ha describes how migrant authors may choose to relate the details of their individual life while understanding that their account "no longer belongs to them as individuals." Instead of consenting to a subject-position that is "always politically marked (as 'colored' or as 'Third World'),"[13] in Minh-ha's words, or colored by ethnic, racial, national, or regional markers, the migratory texts attended to in this study can be read as performing both a renunciation and a renewal, wherein the refusal of identity—to be identified—in the first person is a refusal to move from one form of dispossession (containment) to another (fetishization); to evade the circuit of differential supervision and supervised difference; to restore the origin story in the shape of an itinerary. What is most clearly marked in these autobiographical narratives is not the past—the home, the source, the native land, the mother tongue—but the future of mobility: a crowdsourced choreography of passage, which is still occurring.

How do strategies of immersion—not a reconstruction of experience but its reimagining—work to engage empathy *and* activism for audience members, a response tended by relation and affect, from work that is instructional, participatory, and intermedial, work that performs as a close encounter of displacement? Syrian filmmaker Reem Karssli and Caroline Williams's production, *Now Is the Time To Say Nothing*, enacted at London's Young Vic Theatre in 2015 as part of Shubbak, a festival of contemporary Arab arts, and at other venues across the United Kingdom through today, proposes exactly this communal reenactment, an empathy-driven aesthetics that exceeds the limits of the technical, visual, and solitary experiences offered by virtual reality, for instance, or the spectatorial passivity required by mass media. No longer directed to the purely optical experience, *Now Is the Time To Say Nothing* asks audience members to sit in darkness, on VB armchairs, backs to each other, facing several screens, wearing headphones that provide a soundtrack, from which instructive voice-overs cut across various footage, including on-the-ground, lo-fi, poorly lit sequences of Karssli's migratory passages and life in exile; public demonstrations by London youth for migration reform; and news headlines sliding along the staged monitors as a constant reminder of the distancing rhetoric of so much media. In its collaging of vastly different modalities and experiences, and with the awareness of the screen as a tool for participatory poetic exploration—an awareness of the power of telling stories that require imaginative engagement and self-reflexive practice—this installation-performance aspires to the endeavor of recognition *by dodging visibility*.

Karssli's 2013 film, *Every Day, Every Day*, documented family life in exile in Damascus through short and disconnected diaristic recordings made during the onset of the Syrian Civil War.[14] *Every Day, Every Day*'s non-narrative approach has become common in other refugee theater productions across Germany, including Maxim Gorki Theater's "Exile Ensemble" (Berlin) and Münchner Kammerspiele's "Open Border Ensemble" (Munich), both groups comprised entirely of refugees. During the last five years, each company has staged various meditations on exile that serve as anti-dramas; these are stories, like the Exile Ensemble's 2017 production "Winterreise" (Winter Journey), that abandon plot for the discontinuous invitation of occasion: to rove, sensitive to transit's variables.

To read this immersive and interactive corpus of media, it is necessary to re-read the refugee experience through nonlinear, achronological narratives, a frame that is not limited by the scope of the author's own subject-position but instead adopts and adapts to the reception of an audience. By positioning the *repertoire* (as reiterative and traversing) against the museum (as locatable and contained), Long Bui has argued that the cultural forms facilitated by performance can exceed the one-way traffic and passive documentarian functions of most archival practices.[15] The refugee experience, too, manifests as multidimensional and intergenerational, marked by the memory of the past—even the memory of events that have preceded one's birth—as well as the lived experience of the present. Repertoire, of course, suggests what a performer is capable of—the list or supply of pieces or parts that a company or person is *prepared* to perform. I want to insist that because of its emphasis on anticipation and performativity, as well as the skill-set and experiences of the past, Bui's "refugee repertoire" also posits a fundamental notion about the power of a refugee identity spurred by its interminable and elastic nature, a migratory subject-position that reappropriates the very conditions imposed on migrants by the nation, among them: the temporary status that state processes frame in their image of the migrant-as-aspiring-citizen, and the indeterminate nature of detainment amid asylum processing and restless camp life.

An examination of the "storyteller" and their political-ethical functions necessarily implicates the "tale," which has been characterized by literary critics as the portable art par excellence, a mobility conditioned by its account of a highly specific, localized landscape, whose enduring narrative propels it across cultural and regional boundaries. The tale as both an emblem of nativity and transnationalism extends another paradox, to the extent that the genre performs as both mirror (of the storyteller) and "depersonalizing [...] tool"[16] for provoking further tellings (by the audience). "The tale is of all countries," declared literary critic Mohamadou Kane, in translation.[17] To read Kane's assessment, or Minh-ha's translation, is to understand the ways in which the tale belongs, in fact, to no nation, exceeding the parameters of the territorial and the individual, and also any allegiance to completion.

At stake is not just the story of migration but how that story is told, and in turn, how, and with what imbrication, it is read and returned. It is not coincidental that Said, in order to compose *After the Last Sky*, insists upon the "essentially unconventional, hybrid, and fragmentary forms of expression"[18] as fundamental markers in the endeavor to represent a Palestinian existence. Dispossession and dispersion constitute tragedies on the individual and collective levels, but together might serve as the bearer of power. "How rich our mutability, how easily we change (and are changed) from one thing to another, how unstable our place," Said writes, "and all because of the missing foundation of our existence, the lost ground of our origin, the broken link with our land and our past."[19]

Said's analysis is of the eternal exile, whose absence is not just a home, but a nation, not just a nation but an origin story, not just an origin story but the chronology which connects the past to the present. And yet what gets produced in that catastrophe is another break: spatial, temporal, national, ontological—the means to remake one's relationship to space. I want to read the mutability and instability through which Said characterizes Palestinian subjectivity in relation to the queerness of the migratory text—its inversions, in-betweenness, stealth, partiality, porousness, permeability, all of which bode or body its radical potentiality—*queer desire* as disruption to the violence of normative valuation. In my notebook, I've written: *To what extent does a queer aesthetics operate within and without the institution as a working in and against, and even more: working near other discourses (such as feminism, hybridity, diaspora, deconstruction, decoloniality, etc.)? I want to invite, to continue to invite an aesthetics of attraction, which is about nearness but also about similitude (doubles, correspondences, resemblances).* Like: *to welcome other discourses/traditions/methodologies/technologies as a queer aesthetic (so as to work with them and work on them).*[20] Picture, again, the net of this study's title, what it holds and what necessarily cannot be held, that is contained. It is this excess of life and language that undoes the order of heteropatriarchy undergirding white supremacist settler logic—unplaceable, but not, as Said contends, without a home.

Writing in 1986, Said described the Palestinian people's current moment as the juncture when autonomy and autobiography intersected in pursuit of a possible politics of dispossession: "for the first time in our history, one can see Palestinians in a sense *producing themselves* as they go about their work in a new environment of Palestinian self-consciousness [...]."[21] How are these self-productions representative, not only of a migrant self-consciousness, but, as we've seen with Sarah C. Bishop's conversations with undocumented storytellers, symptomatic of our current norms across social media, in which migrant self-actualization informs a cultural shift in networked identity and production?[22]

As I've shown elsewhere, the normalization of networked file distribution in the nineties deepened the convergence of previously demarcated media, genres, and cultures, a constellation that signaled the emergence of the cover and the glitch as both artistic techniques and art forms in and of themselves.[23] What does this mean for any study of the migratory text, twenty years later? "[H]ybrid genres and interactive platforms have retrospectively altered our understanding of the historical development of the novel," the Warwick Research Collective (WREC) concludes, "prompting reappraisal of its strategies and affinities in light of an expanding communicational economy."[24] But why limit the scope of inquiry, as WREC has, following Fredric Jameson and Franco Moretti, to the privileged and prefab form of the novel? The contemporary collapse of boundaries between genres and media have not only altered our reading of the novel, but, moreover, helped prompt a retrieval of exactly the hybrid, stochastic, and interactive forms of the past that have replaced it, in the present, as an agent of potential political expediency.

Tuning to the valences of performance helps us to rethink the script of resettlement and the scope of conventional narratives with clear beginnings and finite endings. We are reminded that one never ceases to be a migrant; that communities have the power to transmit their stories of the past; that future generations of migrants are capable of mounting their own productions of memory, a recall that is not total or complete but *necessarily fragmentary*, and even formless. We are urged, ultimately, to complicate the negative connotations of the partial narrative linked, by Bishop, with lack and absence, by exploring how the migratory text, not in spite of its fractured nature but precisely because of it, enables the transmission of embodied experience that is unmistakably individual yet also intergenerational. The temporal-spatial slips fostered by performance are inherently mingled with a possible politics because the power to affect and be affected rims a transition, the iterative passage that tends presence and trace, the evocation of the exhibition space as a relational event that plays out between experience and memory, and the mediations of each.

A related question or series of questions: In what ways does the selection of materials influence how and when and where we write? And upon what, in the end or at the very beginning, we write down; what we find when we become present with ourselves and for ourselves, when we allow the back of our minds to come forward?

This was the idea we had, because whenever I feel an awe in the back of my ribs, I try to return that moment of susceptibility to my students, so many of whom, like me, are children of migration, persons who cannot or have never returned to the places where they've come from, the people that remain there. I'd invited us to undertake the challenge of composing on the move, reflecting on and envisioning new possibilities for writing and reading through specific moments of emerging media. Haven't you ever thought, I'd ask, just as writing allows us to think, to make a thought and to mind its erratic passage, so, too, might we retain the residue of the media that conditioned the act of writing? That what is produced by the writing act isn't only rhetoric or narrative, but the occasions from which thought arises. The landscapes and lineaments we might trace, with our forefinger, as if we were reading a map, or another book below this one.

◆

The three works by Czech artist Klára Hosnedlová on view in August 2022 at Berlin's Boros Foundation, a Nazi air-raid bunker turned private collection, all depict a mobile phone, one hand clutching the rectangular portal, the other holding a magnifying glass to its touchscreen.[25] Each composition is cropped to draw attention to the flexed fingers and open palms, the tactile handling of immaterial cultures, or perhaps the attempt to move beyond or further penetrate the sleek aura of disembodied digital presentations. The ambiguity is intentional; just as ICTs provide us with the disguise of anonymity, so too does the invisible and electronic surveillance of our movements curtail any consummation of a space for refuge. The inner workings of contemporary phenomena, these dislocated and anonymous subjects seem to suggest, are questionable, unless the details, which are grainy not in spite of but because of their enlargement, provoke exactly an intimate, haphazard gaze. Cellular phones are not allowed within the Boros Foundation's gallery space, so I'm doing this from memory. Look again. The painting (each untitled, from a 2020 series called *Nest*) isn't really a painting, or at least Hosnedlová doesn't use a brush to produce her embroideries, whose materials are unrecognizable from a distance.

Before the time-consuming process of threading silk on canvas and mounting the panels on terrazzo, Hosnedlová begins by directing performances, or what she calls "a sketch of something that is about to come"; site-specific interactions are digitally photographed and then degraded through pixel reduction. Sustaining Hosnedlová's meticulous preparations, though, are chance and collaboration; the architectural settings she selects guide her to the persons whom she will direct, strangers who become possible characters in an interwoven narrative, a text that can only emerge through the mediation of its composite elements, and furthermore, through the preservation of their traces—a handbag cradled on blue jeans in one composition; the assemblage of a dismantled vehicle's metal parts in the background of another—which resist disappearance from the completed whole *because* of the artist's heightened use of extraction, which urge viewers to participate as if we ourselves were the people who once were staged as roving ensemble and arranged for the camera. "My work is literally waiting for someone who is about to enter," explains Hosnedlová, who was born a year after the Iron Curtain fell and Czechia became a democratic country. "Performers are leaving items after themselves as evidence of some activity in the space."[26]

If I were a possible character instead of a gallery visitor who's paid thirty-six euros for my reservations-only admission to the erstwhile Reichsbahnbunker, I would think about leaving something behind, too. The way that every viewer of Hosnedlová's work is asked, on behalf of its implied origins, to remember the false memory of *what may have taken place* after the performers have left the scene that has been reconstructed, again and again and again, and placed, as if a sequence of unidentified excerpts, or annotations of a floating signifier, before us. Look closer. The magnifying glass over the cell phone's screen in one embroidery reveals amorphous shapes that resemble a mouth, jagged teeth, perhaps a tongue: silk filaments capable of instigating self-estrangement in the viewer. In another, through the magnifying glass, we can make out half a miniature face in profile, the mouth agape as if captured mid-shout. Tools are assembled on the table: flashlight, Swiss Army knife, screwdriver—things meant for making, or unmaking. The metal instruments become increasingly difficult to identify as the eye travels along the array of silver toward the painting's edge. Invited into this oblique moment as if looking through our own magnifying glass, or a keyhole, we gather meaning through what's been left out, what we've been equipped to imagine, and thus re-create. Nothing is uncovered except the act of uncovering.

I want to insist that the utopic temporality of plausible space(s) orients Hosnedlová's work as a revisitation of Cold War urban planning and the austere organization of mobilities, the bureaucratic management of public space in a culture of internal borders. Hosnedlová's chosen installation sites—the Ještěd Tower in Czechia, Berlin's Tempelhof Airport, the aforementioned Reichsbahnbunker—each signal foundational moments in pre- and postwar Eastern Bloc Europe. Not coincidentally, the architects of DDR-era Berlin turned to collage—cutting, combining, and pasting photographs from Western fashion magazines—to present planned projects to their superiors in a way that was both legible and convincing, despite the existing ideologies of design, the architectural language of national(istic) traditions being pursued, each found image from the West blurring into a new scene in the East: a blueprint for a moment that is not yet here but could be. Since the past—attested to by the leitmotif of Hosnedlová's hand-held lens—is more uncertain than the future.

Perhaps, then, it is too easy to assign Hosnedlová's artwork that resists both completion and disappearance to a general insecurity and anxiety of social media's surveillant assemblage. What's at stake in her project, I want to make clear, is not the recovery of the alienated individual under late-stage capitalism but the recovery of the past within a possible present. Ambiguous temporalities like those nested in Hosnedlová's embroideries activate the migratory text as a work that skirts the normative trajectory of *original* and *translation* by confounding both source and trace, origin and afterlife, without closing off either event's undiscovered encounters. And yet, as we move from a people deprived of their land as well as their history to the former Nazi bunker of historical violence housing Hosnedlová's artwork—the economy of death and dispossession undergirding the art market's commodity exchange, which permitted Jacqueline Lichtenstein the hallucination, upon visiting Auschwitz, that she was in a museum of contemporary art[27]—what is obscured in the hypnotic desire to collapse into the anonymous and ambiguous? Indeed, attending to the multiple and overlapping gaps, variations, and in/commensurable materialities of migration subsumed by the confluence of migratory groups wrought by ongoing settler colonialism offers, at the very least, a reminder that one's migration might well be another's displacement.

Informed by the invitation for readers to become producers of a text that has been opened for the contributions of a community—the occasion for correspondence through accident and interface, sense and memory, recitation and citation, what I refer to in this study as a *staging of co-incidence*—I wish to make clear that the migratory text is both intensely here and now, imbued with the charge of nearness signified by the dated inscription common to journal entries and correspondences, which is reanimated upon each reading, and also then and there, an *aboutness* harnessed by the slippages between the event and its recording.

How can we better understand these occasions for correspondence—the migratory text's devotion to copresence and its own staging—by reading them against earlier theories of language, audience reception, and autobiography? Michael Fried, in his 1968 essay, "Art and Objecthood," argues that art ends where theatricality begins, since theatricality implies another participant[28]—a viewer, a reader, someone who is a part of the performance while at the same time observing it. In contradistinction, I understand that art *begins* at or rather in this moment of transitional affect, the perception of staging at present, which includes our own. Our own presence, our own staging. The potential for reversibility between beholder and beheld turns all spectatorship into an interaction of "fractured reciprocity"[29] that renders a gaze—a reading—capable of placing *and* displacing the reader. We are invited, and implicated, by the awareness of our look, but also by the sight of our being looked at—the awareness of our role as subjects, and as objects, for others. Not content to separate seeing from showing, such a subject-object relation can achieve or employ both, in service of a reading that engenders intimacy and empathy, but also blur, the withdrawal of self that occurs as a necessary precursor to the adoption of another's point of view and position—a resistance to the public's aforementioned compulsion for sympathy vis-à-vis familiarity; one cannot attend to another without first giving up, and giving something of themselves. I want to make clear that this self-(dis)covering, akin to what Barbara Freedman has called a "spectator consciousness,"[30] relies on misrecognition and error as much or much more than when the act, in the parlance of J.L. Austin and his performative utterances, "comes off," a "misfire" built on the discrepancy between intention and outcome. In this sense, the migratory text is not only performative; these works also reconfigure the rules of a "successful utterance": that which depends on felicitous conventions and appropriate circumstances.[31]

Of course, it is not that, in misfiring, nothing happens, but that *something always happens*. Attending to the incidental, the inadvertent, the provisional and improvisational, harvests ingredients that make translation possible as a mode of incantation and swerve, risk and vulnerability, encounters that rely on *exposing* one's point of view; in making this view visible (as failure), one can ultimately expose the limitations of every representation, every speaking for and speaking about which involves not just who is speaking (subject), who is spoken of (object), and who listens (audience), but the environments in which these interactions take place. Taking Gayatri Spivak's call for speaking to the oppressed in order to produce a *countersentence* that can inaugurate a new historical narrative,[32] Linda Alcoff insists on the transformation of social spaces, such as classrooms, workplaces, universities, and, tellingly, institutions for international development and aid, while acknowledging the potential for existing communication technologies to facilitate important interactions.[33] We might re-read Alcoff's confidence in the role of ICTs and Freedman's assessment, that "[o]ur continued work [...] depends upon our willingness to displace our look, to stage it, and so to keep it on the *move*"[34]—both of which were made in 1991—by considering the prevalence of co-creation, and its reconstruction of individual subjectivity in our age of heterospatial self-mapping and the synthesis of ludic practices and venues across social media, the simultaneous tethering and outsourcing of identity, along with social media's invitation, or provocation, of life as a game—a game that has the potential for empowering social change by transforming one's position in space, and thus, the practices and relationships therein. As Alcoff acknowledges, the entire crisis of representation is thrown into stark relief in any situation in which one participates in the construction of another's subject-position.

Of course, this investigation into what I earlier called the transmission of a migrant's singular experience of passage, which is also a collective condition of mobility, poses an obvious question: How to produce a collective expression while remaining unbound to the collective—the fixations of politics or descriptive institutional categories that fix one in place? Rather than passively accepting integration into a polis, the migratory text provokes the possibility of other arenas from which to participate and perform alternative political and aesthetic forms that aspire to reassess and reimagine representation. As I will advance in the following chapters, in decentering individual identity through an aesthetics of displacement and disappearance, the migratory text also develops alternative political strategies that elide representational politics and practices, employing strategies that involve improvisation and recycling, the organized spontaneity offered by the stage, and the performance of authorship as ensemble.

Retracing her theory of narrative criticism a decade later, Nancy K. Miller asserts that every autobiographical act—self-effacement notwithstanding—requires a partner.[35] I want to insist, however, that the relational model binding self to other that has historically shaped the narrative of autobiography can also be ascertained in the *reading* of autobiography, an "autós" that offers, in its Greek origins, less attention to the exempt self than the *self together with*—the Biblical "we ourselves, not thou only" (Luke 22:71). Writing—and reading—memoir thus constitutes sketching out a composite picture of cultural memory, yet I argue that the collective memorialization contributed by the migratory text does not in fact provide "building blocks to a more fully shared national narrative," as has been attributed, by Miller and others, to autobiography.[36] Rather, in revealing and relating the double movement of time and space, the memory of mobility and the mobility of memory, migrant expressions of autobiography upend a national narrative that begins and ends with the fetishization of the original, the fiction of origin stories, and the artificial demarcation of borders, both material and discursive.

"Since our history is forbidden," Edward Said writes, "narratives are [...] broken, often wayward and meandering in the extreme, always coded."[37] And Said's conception of Palestinian narrative can also be read, not unlike the intermedial accountings of Hosnedlová, as an altogether different conception of time; a broken time marked by unsynchronized rhythms; a coded time, private, secret, marked by the recording of *another* history, one that neither takes the shape of nation, nor moves through the procession of narrow nationalist discourse; one that disturbs and disorients—an intervention on the level of form, on the collaging of modes, on the *writing over* of image.

*After the Last Sky*, first published in 1986, a year after newly sworn in US President Ronald Reagan announced that his administration would arm and support "freedom fighters" against communist regimes across Latin America, Africa, and Asia (later known as the Reagan Doctrine), is Said's attempt, in his own words, to render the Palestinian condition—which he links with African Americans, Armenians, Jews, Cubans, and Poles—"not from the viewpoint of policy-makers but that of memoirists and unregimented historians."[38] For a people whose history is in fact forbidden, it is not that there is no better way to tell the story, but, more clearly, that there is *no way* to tell the story other than through another's hand, another's eyes; Jean Mohr's "listening" photographs record faces that are evidence, then, of another ecology, an ecology, as Said writes, that is "neither symbolic nor representative in some hokey nationalist way."[39] Rather than relating atrocity, or politicizing ritual, or underscoring religion, Mohr's photos allow viewers—readers—to enter into a scene where "some offstage catastrophe"[40] has occurred. Perhaps we need to rethink the strategies in which we present—and in which we receive—such untellable trauma. And in their ordinariness, their being represented *outside* the debilitating confinements of exile, *outside* the debilitating confinements of history, Palestinians become identifiable as people; their world becomes identifiable as contemporary, as immediate; readers no longer encounter such figures as objects and as objects of catastrophe—no longer I and you, us and them—but on the contrary, can imagine their interiorities as if they were their own.

Said and Mohr's *After the Last Sky* thus serves an alternative mode of expression, one that is contrary to the version encountered in the media, the social sciences, and in literature, a constellation that reminds us of the interconnected relationship between institutions within the continuous negotiation between being spoken for and spoken about amidst the fraught ventriloquizing of *speaking as*. How do these photographs—we might recall: no longer divested of legends, explanations—reframe not just a version of a people but our vision of them, and, moreover, our vision of ourselves? "Many Palestinian friends who saw Jean Mohr's pictures thought that he saw us as no one else has. But we also felt that he saw us as we would have seen ourselves—at once inside and outside our world."[41] Said acknowledges, likewise, that as he wrote the text that would eventually accompany Mohr's photographs, he found himself switching pronouns; no longer reduced to the first person or third person, Said shifts, indeed, from "we" to "you" to "they" to "I" in the space of a few pages. And if this shift—this series of shifts, this lack of distinguishing between you and I, us and them—is a response to a stateless, dispossessed, and de-centered people, it is also a response constituting the processual, collaborative, and piecemeal nature of this book. "I look at them without precise anecdotal knowledge, but their realistic exactness nevertheless makes a deeper impression than mere information. I cannot reach the actual people who were photographed," Said admits, early on, "except through a European photographer who saw them for me. And I imagine that he, in turn, spoke to them through an interpreter."[42] That *After the Last Sky* is in fact a book of translation is not quite the point; the point is that migration relates and reveals to us that translation abounds in *every* story of passage, in every retelling. In these mediated encounters, which are numberless, the migratory text provokes an impression that exceeds information, a movement beyond meaning and toward an experience of empathy and intimacy: an arena for immersion, its stage directions of identification and surrender, the kind of empathy-generating maneuvers outlined earlier in contemporary refugee theater productions.

Is it any wonder that the last photograph of *The Last Sky* is captioned: "The photographer photographed?"[43] In this palindromic inversion, the search outside ourselves leads us back to ourselves, but differently. Now the photographer becomes the subject of their photographs; now the photographer is captured, and in the publication of this photo, we (and I include the photographer here, occluded, as he is, by his own camera) come to better understand the terms of all representation, the power dynamics between subject and object and audience but also the critical engagement of what's behind the photo—or rather, what the photo can never show, and yet does: its limitations as representation.

If the book invites this representation, what Judith Butler has in the past called a "critical image,"[44] it is to be found several pages earlier, in the portrait of a Palestinian villager wearing glasses, the right lens smashed.

Yet, as Said explains: "The blotch is on the lens, not in him [...] and even if his vision is a little smudged, he can still see more or less everything there is to be seen."[45] Except I would want to go further, and remind us that he can even see (more or less) everything there is to be *unseen*, or not represented, not available to be represented. This persistent interference in vision informs the structural imbalances between photographer and the subjects within their viewfinder, or the border of the frame and its periphery. Instead of an unmediated or intentional reality, this critical image shows the reality of incoherence, the reality of disorganization, the reality between fact and fiction (which is to say, their convergence), memory and media, which constitutes the blurry consciousness of the migrant, and the ways in which they must navigate such a fraught landscape—a lens that might be broken, yes, but one that is their own. This photo, paired with the book's final image—the capture of two Palestinian children holding up their own camera to the gaze of Mohr, who doubles as the viewer-reader—reminds us that every objectified subject is not only seen and looked at but also looks back, returning a counter-gaze that has the potential to alter not just how we write our stories, but how we read another's.

## THE ANONYMOUS SUBJECT AS A STAGE OF HOSPITALITY

In John Berger's visual-verbal documentation of the material conditions of male migrant workers in the 1970s—another co-production with photographer Jean Mohr—it is exactly this question of narrative framing which carries the story of combined and uneven development, of departures and returns. And yet the project's record of labor exploitation, the extraction of land and resources, and Cold War colonialism is only an opening for another narrative, the one begged by the story of migration, filled in by the reader.

> His prestige as a returned and successful migrant is considerable. [...] The villagers now respect him as a man of different experience. He has seen and received and achieved things which they have not. He is the

*interpreter*, the *transmitter*, the *conveyer* of these things to them; the things range from money through commodities to information. They seize upon them to put them to *their own use*.[46]

The migrant, upon arrival, becomes both author and translator; a translator of their own text, which has elsewhere been re-written by others, state officials and company overseers. The migrant becomes empowered, reclaims their identity, but only by divesting themselves; they become reconstituted only by giving themselves away, only by feeding their audience with their own body; their bodily experience, "stripped," as Berger writes, "of what he [*sic*] came back with."[47] The migrant is always a translator, always a storyteller, tasked with shuttling between cultures and languages, and everything that cannot be said, that cannot be shown; or rather, that must be shown by revising—remediating—the parameters of the visual. Berger's and Mohr's *A Seventh Man* is a collection of such moments, arranged in three sequences which resemble, as Berger writes in his preface, rolls of film. The emphasis on framing and staging, and the language and techniques of the camera, becomes explicit in the authors' attempts to "get as near as possible to those moments—as with close-ups."[48] Close-ups, which, as we know from the words of its own inventor, D.W. Griffith, had the capacity to turn acting into "a duplicate of real life,"[49] a trick of authenticity tied to spatial manipulations and the (mis) recognitions of another.

If it is true, as Berger professes, that abstract political and economic theory each fail to explain and reflect upon the lived experience of the migrant, what is needed is more than just metaphor, but entering another's subjectivity through a constellation of facts, fantasies, images, and perhaps most importantly, a narrative devoid of characters and places, the narrative tropes of plot and setting. Proceeding from the vantage point and with the advantages of anonymity, Berger and Mohr's alternative documentarian gaze deliberately withholds information, understanding that "[t]o be homeless is to be nameless."[50] Thus, nearly everything in *A Seventh Man* is accounted for with shifting pronouns and a narrative frame that is intermittently interrupted by dialogue without quotation marks or identifiers. Names reduce to "he" and "they"; the third person inexplicably assumes the "I," a slippage of identity that is doubled in the defamiliarization of spatial and temporal markers; the setting can be anywhere and so it becomes *always here*, bestowing an urgency and a presence to a book produced over half a century ago. By withholding specificity, Berger and Mohr drape their account of Cold War mass economic migration with an erotics afforded to anonymous interactions in public. The viewer, then, is forced to enter the text as a witness and as a respondent, as someone who must imagine—who is forced to imagine—the person, or people, who are now addressing them, an interaction that collapses the border between storyteller and listener, the singular and the collective, the frame of narrative and its mediation. Reading becomes a mobile experience where information is withheld so that it can be accumulated. In this negotiation between offer and deprivation is the gift of narrative, which gets returned each time it is read.

To acknowledge that migrants are tasked, always, with being both storyteller *and* translator is to ask what is yielded in the unequal exchange brought by each textual convergence. How, in other words, does this simultaneous mediation reconfigure the narrative frame which the migrant takes up? Ralf Simon, in his 2016 essay "The Temporality of Hospitality," calls the guest "a figure of the third,"[51] a useful metaphor for this study that evokes the guest's perennial straddle between the alleged *us* of assimilation and the *dis-integration* of self-storage; in hovering over two edges or endpoints, the guest also resists becoming anything other than what they already are. And yet: what is the guest but a person who epitomizes the paradoxical inclusion-exclusion dialectic of modern citizenship, someone who can only ever be themselves; someone who can never be themselves? The narrative event is innately a moment of border crossing, a disturbance and a negotiation undertaken.[52] In this fictive scenario, the protagonist becomes the reader's guest, and in the primal scene of hospitality, the guest offers a gift to their host: the story of where they came from, how it was they left and why.

The origin story, which is always a story of arrival, but an arrival, I want to remind us, that is *not* foreclosed, becomes the gift; the story becomes an offering: translation as transaction. And yet, this fundamental exchange thought to be rooted in narrative in fact develops *inside* language, evidenced by the German word for host—*Gastgeber*—wrapping itself among the gift (*Gabe*) and also the act of giving (*geben*). This gift derives from a power and a privilege that is spatial as well as temporal. Were a guest to endure, they would become a part of the host community. Were they to leave, or be banished, they'd relinquish their role as storyteller. In laying themselves before a receptive host, what does the guest do but exchange the time granted to them, and convert it into a time outside temporal constraints, the temporality of reading? Because this exchange is non-equivalent—the act of reading posits not only the virtual convergence between text and reader, but also the collapse of time and duration into a "living event,"[53] a phenomenology of reading that is necessarily unlocatable—the guest thus offers not only the primal scene of narrative, but more importantly, I want to insist, a *reinterpretation* of narrative framework.

In this new conception of time and textual structure, we are met by a process that is no longer static or linear but rather undergoes rapid changes, a temporality in flux and out of joint, a temporality presupposed by the reality of our own changeable self—unknown to us even in the moment of making—who we were and might become, the ingress of possibility that insists we probe deeper. Is this not always the experience of reading and listening, in which we both attend to the other and, in the pursuit of empathy and imaginative investment, also become them? If it is true that the guest relinquishes all authority at the behest of the host, the host, too, as the recipient reader-listener, must inevitably give themselves up. The prospect of giving ourselves up and over to another depends on considering how we might also temporarily abandon a system of circulation and capital. In accepting hospitality as readers and listeners, we also accept an experience of time that desires generosity and excess, the permission to take time—and *waste time*—on behalf of one another. In our devotion to the cultivation of a pleasure outside of operational production or utility, how might hospitality propose a method for its own undoing as a conditional practice, freeing neither the host, as Jacques Derrida has argued in *Of Hospitality*,[54] nor the guest, but the home—the text itself—as a site of ownership and possession?

We know that Germany's link with hospitality stretches farther back than AD 98, when Tacitus wrote *On the Origin and Situation of the Germans* (*De Origine et situ Germanorum*). His ethnographic work on the Germanic tribes outside the Roman Empire provide us with an early indicator of the mutability of host and guest, as well as the crowdsourced nature of a hospitality that depends on continuous returns. "When he has finished entertaining him," Tacitus makes clear, "the host undertakes a fresh role: he accompanies the guest to the nearest house where further hospitality can be had."[55] Indeed, no nation, in Tacitus's estimation, is thought to be more welcoming than Germany,[56] where the refusal to receive another was thought to be a sin, the divine right of hospitality and the divine duty of the host, which can be traced to Homeric times and the twofold character of *hospitium* that encompassed both private and public spheres in ancient Greece and later, in Rome, inscribed into law that even empowered the conferral of full citizenship.

Simon's shift from hospitality to hermeneutics by locating literature as the third figure of language relies on its remaining "in a time of its own"; literature's ability to resist mutability—"[n]o interpretation *pays the text back*"[57]—constitutes its normalizing quality irreducible to specific contexts. And yet what does the text, and the guest, offer but the debt of *reflection*? Simon's contention that the guest is a rare figure in literature is informed by the reality of the guest worker's disappearance in a larger cultural consciousness. Just as the guest eludes literary representation, the Gastarbeiter has today eluded literal representation as a forgotten figure of a still-divided Berlin. Simon says that the guest always comes too late; in contradistinction, I argue that the guest, and here the guest worker, only ever anticipate, returning as both harbinger[58] and vestige, pointing toward the future of inhospitality and internal exclusion while forcing us into a reassessment of Cold War geopolitical narratives and Western European colonialism that illuminates today's flow of migration.

Lest we forget that metaphors, or their common usage, too often obscure the lived realities they qualify, that theory and practice have a tendency to surge in opposite streams, let us imagine the guest as more than a symbol, and the narrative they offer as more than the sign, or signature, of authorship. Let us consider the 108 million displaced persons in 2022—only an estimate, and a number that's risen by 59 percent in the last six years[59]—more than half of whom are children, and their stories, which are both individual and collective; let us consider how these partial and postdated reclamations speak to a larger cultural condition, while retrieving the intensely personal.[60] Autobiography, or "the writing of the self as living,"[61] as Derrida would later write, in a book published after his death, is always problematized by the dislocation and deferral of the author's own presence, which is their own absence—a spatial-temporal discrepancy that would like, nevertheless, to mirror the play of revealing and re-veiling as a mark of dis/closure. If something is made clear by the interface of inscription, it is that the self is in fact composed double *and* nothing. In this sense, the force of any autobiographical text is located in its proclivity for recounting, and thus destabilizing, its own auto-authority. Doesn't autobiography begin in the gaze or guise of the other? Isn't all autobiography composed of such ensemble performances—in which the *autós* should be read, also, as automatic: the self-reflexivity that relies on relation, where what is written in the *first* person is merely the invitation or invention of a second, third, fourth ... to follow? If the performative relationship between host and guest intervenes in the narrative frame, I'd like to think of the migratory text as the stage or surface where hospitality may unfold.

## PRODUCTIVE DEPRIVATION AS TEXTUAL EDGING

My father says he'll never go back. He says he only ever returns to Cuba in his dreams and that's enough. In the spring of 2017, we engaged in storytelling exercises.[62] Juan told me about his dreams of Cuba and I wrote them down in English. I didn't know what I'd find and what I found was that he was able to speak again about his home. About the day he left. Sometimes the reality of dreams leaks out into the reality we call our everyday life. "Dreaming has a share in history,"[63] Walter Benjamin writes. What is forgotten, I think, is that history, too, must have a share in dreams. And what I mean is that what remains to be written is not the history of the dream, as Benjamin argued, but the dream of history. That history can be re-written through dreams, coincidence, trance, and fantasy, the residue of our unconscious that alters the trajectory of our waking, conscious life. What, I often think, does the world look like when you read it in reverse?

In posing this question, I want to think about how memory might serve, not as a monument to the past, but as an instrument that informs our capacity to analyze the present. Memory, from Latin *memoria*: mindful, connected to Late Latin *martyr*: witness, related to the Greek *mermēra*: care. To be mindful is to be aware, to attend to, to devote attention and concern, to *keep* a thing or person *in mind*. But how to reaffirm the agency of memory in the face of cultural erasure without reproducing the self-silencing and trauma so common in diasporic communities? Maybe it begins by sidestepping the binary of silence and testimony. Maybe these storytelling exercises with my dad also imagined a proposal: to reimagine the historical unconscious.

Edgar Garcia, in *Skins of Columbus*, may have started from a similar premise. In his 2019 "dream ethnography," Garcia assembles diaristic accounts of his travels, shuttling from the United States to family in Guatemala, El Salvador, and Nicaragua; brief histories of CIA interventions in Central America through familial anecdotes; personal photographs and pre-Columbian illustrations culled from archival explorations; excerpts of a fictional mixed-media collaboration between Garcia and another artist about a post-cataclysmic planet Earth; rough Nahuatl translations of Ezra Pound's cantos—Modernism's ghosting of aboriginal cultures fed back to itself—and finally, slippery, verse-like annotations of his own dreams, recorded during the evenings in which he read the journal of Christopher Columbus before sleep. "Later, he transformed his dreams into a poetic record of what his memory, in its half-sleep, had forgotten it remembered," Garcia writes, embedding himself in the veil of the third person, "the gash, shock, glamour, void, punctuation, and spell of origins."[64] In a single paragraph, on the book's first page, Garcia moves from the "you" to the "our" to the "he," a movement which traces the project's shift—and its self-reflexive critique—from the interiority of the individual to the distance of an objective, historical "source." And this movement foretells another: the fact that what Garcia is reading, and what Garcia is writing, has already been translated at least twice, and each time, for vastly different ends. As Garcia himself notes: "The history of Columbus's journal is awkward."

> The extant version is a précis—evidently faithful (excluding navigational minutiae), made by de las Casas—that incorporates first-person narrative quotes from a copy of the original log. Its shaky Spanish reflects de

> las Casas' editorial commitment to originary dialectic, that is, either the Genoan's in a language foreign to him, or a semi-literate scribe's doing his best to copy. Garbled tones also complicate who comes first. Columbus writes to satisfy and elicit royal investments [...] de las Casas writes a history, and decidedly one to disentangle these dreams from the vanity of human enterprise [...].[65]

These mediations, indeed, are flattened in most accounts of the event in question. The recording of Columbus's journal is replaced by its substantiation as record (as historical), a processual detail that is seldom questioned in other texts devoted to the colonizer. In *Skins of Columbus*, however, the flattening of the past returns as a re-marking of the present; each poem in the text begins with the dual-date stamp of the moment Garcia is recording his dreams and the moment Columbus is orating his first voyage to the Americas. January 13, for instance, begins on Wednesday *and* Sunday, a self-conscious collision of *then* and *now*; in that crash what rift is produced for a narrative historical timeline so accustomed to dictating a reading of linear progression? If this diaristic (sk)etching conflates time, it also expands experience into multiple and heterogeneous temporalities; heterochrony materializes, not in the visual medium of film, but within the landscape of alphabetic text. In the book's closing section, which takes the form of contextual endnotes, Garcia links the Aboriginal concept of "Alcheringa" to the movement between emotion, gesture, dream, and historicity fundamental to a dream ethnography. In the Indigenous Australian Aranda language, "*Alcheringa*," also known as "*Alchera*," refers to the "time out of time," or, alternatively, an "everywhen"; in this moment, which is all moments, the articulation of borders between past and present, between individual and collective histories, stutters into dust, which is to say it stutters into an encounter with our own origin. What aesthetic form might render such a multi-temporal experience but the collage?—whose "underlying political theory," Garcia points out, "is that of the totalizable fragment."[66] What could it mean to reinvent a history that has misremembered, or totally forgotten you; to grant yourself permission to tell an altogether different story of nativity, one not premised on national myth?

The accidental agency arrived at via the vellum of a rough translation informs this chapter's interest in pursuing what I call the hidden legibility of the text: the charge of interference, self-abstraction, and redaction, particularly in works that redraft passages of migration or which respond to the static condition of exile. In carving a space for a productive deprivation, I contend that the space for such possibilities depends on an authorial self-effacement, the abandonment of information for the haphazard breakdown of words. To see *inside* the story, then, to see it *from the other side*, the author would have to become the specter, too, to do nothing but preside, subservient to the text and observant, watching while waiting, a nascent awareness brought about by inaction.

What is realized for the meaning of a work, and the work of meaning, when it *isn't* transmitted but perhaps deterred, perhaps disrupted, perhaps displaced?—if, perhaps, the transmission is *out of order*? And I mean this as a matter of flight *and* function, an evasion of representational logic and rank and sequence and acceptable standards. What would it mean to read—and write—for something other than for meaning?

Garcia's performative use of the archive—the language of history, the court, the law, the institutionalization of the past—can be described as an "archival autofiction,"[67] the mediation of memories, even ones not belonging to the author, that is provoked by playing the documentary authority of the archive alongside the fragile materiality of traces and objects left out of its repository. This practice of recycling, as Anna Forné has noted, privileges both fragmentation and repetition, activating the reader as an accomplice who is tasked with retrieving what has been dismantled and, moreover, I suggest, what has been reconstructed. A "spectator consciousness" thus mutates into an archivist consciousness, whereby the reader is invited to examine the divisions and connections between the material (of the past) and its manipulation (at present), subject and object. Forné asserts that such work might dismantle "the certainties of official historiography from a collective position"[68] by opening these records to the public. I argue that a migratory text like *Skins of Columbus*, which doesn't erase the original context of the material but in fact discusses its remediation in depth, goes further, and, in doing so, asks its readers whether every archive is not only found but constructed, not only factual but fictional. The moment an archive turns from a site of excavation into a site of ex(-)citation (a site of construction) is the moment that time contracts: belatedness passes into becomingness. A related question: can disturbing the origin provoke other points of departure?

I return to the mystery; the mystery of the text and the text as mystery. Recall Benjamin's call to preserve each original work's "intention": the certain pressure and deformation required as a matter of drilling, rather than excavating. To move beyond representation then is to move beyond narrative and national limitations. And to move beyond representation, it becomes necessary—as writers, as readers—to move beyond rational, objective, discursive language, toward the polyglossia of non-sense, a negation of law and logic, so suspect in a world where the law is so often used against us.

Craig Santos Perez's *from Unincorporated Territory [hacha]*, the first book in the Chamorro poet's series of re-memberings of Guam, serves not as a poetics in translation so much as a poetics of translation, and it does this through exactly these deferrals, a continuous interplay between distance and proximity. Perez's book, in a recipe comprising fragments from oral folk stories, history and medicine books, familial conversations, Chamorro dictionary entries, articles of the US constitution, and nautical charts and trade routes, presents a counter-map of language and form, one that contests and contradicts Guam's extant history of imperialization and colonization by various aggressive parties. Perez's decision to not distinguish between historical knowledge and familial understanding, legal, biblical, and literary citations, the English, Spanish, Japanese, and Chamorro, mirrors the book's interrogations of the cartographic practices that reproduce difference by visually demarcating boundaries while at the same time symbolically flattening local, non-locatable cultural traditions, that which gets passed under, below, and against the current of history, a crucial point when considering that *[hacha]*, soon after its publication in 2008, went out of print.

"The First Horse arrived," Santos Perez writes, in "*from* ta(la)ya," "mounted by damian de esplana [1673]," before shifting, two stanzas later, to a reflection of a grandfather, who "explains how to minimize your shadow/depending on the angle of the sun."[69] The historical and personal become part of the same transmission, a polyphonic relation interceded by quoted passages that have been stripped of source. Source, in Santos Perez's poetics of retrieval, has been displaced by *stream*, the productive flow of "tidelands" that captions eighteen of the collection's forty-four poems. Who or what is being heard, or overheard? And how do these interferences produce meaning through being played, as if an audio track, and picked up again, later, overlaid as if a refrain—to break up, an alteration of Latin *refringere*; more at *refract*, to subject something to alteration. Given minimal information, readers are asked to draw upon a vast network of references—historical, political, cultural, regional, familial—or to be sated with the pleasure of unknowability by reading such brief digressions as suggestive gestures, as glances meant to be carried out and on in passing—the movement of the eye as it scans the page—but not brought to fulfillment, closure.

The moment we are asked to accept an unnoticed detail is the moment we dominate it. Gaston Bachelard understood that the minimal and maximal were intricately linked; that the details of the thing could open up an entire world. That the "[m]iniature," as Bachelard has explained, "is one of the refuges of greatness."[70] What's the difference, ultimately, between a cropped image and a catalog? Detail, from Old French *détaillier*: to cut in pieces, which furnishes me with *tailor*. Every time I zoom in, I dislocate the whole. Every focus desires such fragmentation, the way a sight asks to be forgotten in the memory of its gaze. How can these poetics of the detail inform our reading of the migratory text, which builds itself on scarcity and excess, expansion and obfuscation?

*from Unincorporated Territory [hacha]*'s titular emphasis on movement, displacement, the *from* that etymologically signifies passage (to go) but also the payment, the toll of such movement—by way of Old English *faran* (the fare)—also instructs readers to return to this text as a series of excerpts: the preposition or pre-position that is used to indicate a condition of removal, abstention, exclusion, subtraction, release. "My hope," Perez writes, "is that these poems provide a strategic position for 'Guam' to emerge from imperial 'redúccion(s)' into further uprisings of meaning. Moreover, I hope 'Guam' (the word itself) becomes a strategic site for my own voice (and other voices) to resist the reductive tendencies of what Whitman called the 'deformed democracy' of America."[71] *Redúccion*, here, is a reference to the term used by the Spanish to name their efforts of subduing, converting, and gathering natives through the establishment of missions and the stationing of soldiers to protect these missions. If the poems that follow are only the beginning movements to reterritorialize the contours of a drowned language, then they necessarily have to be placed in relation to the author's own body—mobile, reflexive, repetitive—but also the body of the page, a restationing that realizes Stéphane Mallarmé's conception of another composition, parsed out a year (1897) before his death—"nothing new," the Symbolist poet was quick to make clear, "except a certain distribution of space *made within the reading*."[72] The migratory text, as an act of mobility, relies on its uncertain redistribution.

This endeavor, for Santos Perez as for others, escalates through undulation: between the compulsion to present and the desire to preserve the opacity and turbulence of history's wreckage, beginning at the verbal level, as if to say, *the words we use* to account for *do not add up*. "*from* lisiensan ga'lago," for instance, comprises a series of italicized Chamorro words etched across the page. In a boxed glossary cutting across the poem proper are the approximate English renderings:

> taiguaha: having nothing
> taiguia:
> tailagua:
> tainini: no light
> taipati: no shore
> taisongsong: no translation
> taiaan: no name
> taifino: no language[73]

I want to think about how Santos Perez's use of legends mobilizes "turning,"[74] a strategy for changing the meaning of words through creating spaces where languages and cultures are not only related to each other but entangled: nothing gets replaced, only altered via the coexistence of presences, voices, and stories. Elsewhere, Santos Perez abandons language lessons, forestalling any approximate translation until the very end of the poem. Absent a semiotics, readers are forced to encounter a word's sonic utterance, an attempt at a phatic communion with the text that has less to do with communication and more to do with the transmission of sense and experience, as in "*from* tidelands," when he writes: “night/displaces our ‘retrievable/history’—the ‘sky impaired’ by smoke—/‘skin’ ‘grain’ ‘psalms’ ‘what saved us?’—one/storm bent/[tinaitai] in the sand [...].”[75] We are required to keep reading, to turn the page, before we learn that “tinaitai” means “prayer”—and thus these poetics also and at the same time force readers to go back, to return, to reencounter what one has just read, so as to open it, in due time, for further inquiry, as one negotiates the productivity of losing one’s place. A poetics of focus and concentration, ushered in through delay. A poetics of clarity and clarification, positioned, not coincidentally, in a narrative frame in which no “I” exists—only the collective and collected—the *from* of collaboration and crowdsourced retrieval—only the anonymous “he” and “she,” only the plurality of the undetermined “they,” and, moreover, the “we” of the past, present, and future of organized unincorporation.

Guam, in this sense, as both “unincorporated” and “organized” territory of the United States, becomes the material remains of a migratory aesthetics, the excess which is also an absence, a deferral, a desire which gets repeated (each title, too, iterates throughout the book as a set of serial accountings) and whose repetitive process of non-attainability—non-arrival—displaces discursive content. The necessity to go again, to do it over, to keep doing it, is worth repeating; it is only by *repeating* absence that one can articulate presence, the way water is molded into shape by its successive contact with the earth, even as the water washes away the tracks of its own movement—not a negation but a substitution, in which an undoing occurs *without fully obscuring* its process or trajectory.

Why is the undetermined and indeterminate *we* important to such “ambivalent shapings”[76] that constitute the migratory; or rather, how does *we* work in and on the crisis of representation, the precarity linked with speaking for and speaking about? Santos Perez allows the reader to occupy a series of positions, but what effect does this plurality have for producing an ethics of copresence, an empathy that is also a form of organization, and an organization that is an activism? “We want to speak for a group. We want to show the danger of group think. We want to feel solidarity. We want to expose fracture [...],” Gayle Brandeis writes in “#WeToo,” an article whose title alone suggests the flow of crowdsourced publication across social media, the individual user displaced by the productive traffic of swarm to which one both belongs and recedes. "The first-person plural can be a way to tell the truths we hold."[77] As Brandeis suggests, the employment of the first-person plural can tell the truths we hold while also holding the telling accountable for its claim to a truth—a self-reflexive inquiry not only into narrative frame, but subjectification. The choral voice of de-individualized community might expand the possibilities of "story" and, moreover, the permission to transmit it. Such communication—which doesn't "speak" so much as assembles, overlaps, and integrates—can expand the singular or static position of storyteller. "We" doesn't just implicate the reader as witness-accomplice, it invites readers to ask fundamental questions of the text's author(s) and of the text's own armature and configuration: to work out layers of culpability, to engage in unasked questions about the power dynamics of storytelling and translation, which also includes the oppressions and privileges embedded in any act of writing, any act of speaking.

Recall our earlier attention to a reading of autobiography that begins, not in the self-knowledge of testimony and witnessing, as has been traditionally ascribed to life writing, but in the unknowability of self-experience and the fraught passages between event and its transcription, moments redolent with multiplicity and displacement. We can apply this understanding of autobiography as simultaneously capacious and effacing to our analysis of the migratory text by paying close attention to the frequency by which modes of address therein oscillate between self and other, while the borders between narrative frames—the first, second, and third-person perspectives—conflate or disintegrate. These maneuvers suggest an "I" that does not equate identity with individuality, a "we" that does not pretend an artificial commonality. Instead of following the fiction of the solitary, stable, and unified first-person singular and the universalism of the first-person plural, the migratory text strives toward a radical empathy, always unconsummated, always attainable through the *failure* of apprehension, which is to say a radical empathy attainable through intention: a practice, a direction, an exercise that demands repetition and attention and movement toward—in relation to and for—another.

Building from both Catherine Malabou and Pierre Bourdieu in her forecasting of "the futures of Auto/Biography studies" in 2017, Eva

C. Karpinski locates *plasticity* as a central component of life writing, where plasticity serves as a "practice of transformation," and "life-writing praxis" is understood as interactive and multimodal, changing "its trajectory and tak[ing] new directions while it also changes its form, allowing for new materializations of becoming."[78] To think life writing through process and affect is to consider not only how the genre is always en route to change, but, moreover, how these formal shifts—what Karpinski calls "their migrations and metamorphoses"—can change the *habitus* which defines the rules and practices of legitimacy and possibility in the arena of thinking, feeling, and imagining. If life writing has indeed stretched the terms of "life" and "writing," as Karpinski contends, then I want to think about how the migratory text, as a problematization of these terms—a *life* that is not just "a property of the subject of consciousness and perception"[79] and a *writing* that is collaborative, open-sourced, mediated in multiple—has altered the possibilities for autobiography and the larger field of life writing by turning such metaphors of "plasticity" and "migrations and metamorphoses" into material acts of passage and mobility.

## THE ARCHI-TEXTURE OF THE CITY AS A NETWORK OF TRANSLATION

Translation is a practice fraught with unequal power relations, a site where belonging and exclusion are negotiated and legitimized, and one in which existing ideologies are often reproduced. Yet, as I've shown in chapter 1, it also can serve as a mode of access and collective experience, an aesthetic and ethical strategy that can challenge hierarchical structures and create alternative versions—not just of the text but of the economy of literature and language to which it belongs. Brent Armendinger's 2019 textual assemblage, *Street Gloss*, makes this collaborative act explicit, while opening up its strictures to the archi-texture of the city. Accomplishing this requires letting go of one's authority-as-interpreter but, moreover, it demands taking in the vocabulary of the streets, which is where Armendinger relocates himself in order to comb the whereabouts of certain words, "problems" of translation that become reconfigured as possibilities. That there are gaps in transmission is *beside the point*; the point, or one of them, is that translation necessitates a poetics of contiguity, a *being around* a person or place or thing—a being around the text—which moves us closer to a heightened awareness of indeterminacy, an intimacy with the person and words with whom we gyrate, gathering tone, feel, mood—a frequency we couldn't otherwise receive, if, say, we were too close. Intimacy requires this distance, but also the missteps in the continuous play of approximate unveiling, slippages and the stripping of words, to get inside their coded information.

Paul Valéry also understood the significance of approximation for the work of translation, the coarse murmuration—imaginary and nevertheless granular—that would allow us "in some way to try walking in the tracks left by the author; and not to fashion one text upon another, but from the finished work back to the virtual moment of its formation, to the phase when the mind is in the same state as an orchestra whose instruments seem to waken, calling to each other and seeking harmony before beginning their concert."[80] Translation as textual deconstruction, as synergetic performance. Valéry's retrospective meditations on the challenges and impulses of translating Virgil's *Eclogues* insists upon a fundamental decomposition: the desire—the necessity—to relocate to the *before beginning*, a retreat from crystallization to consider a text's preparatory coordinates. We return to an original, then, to understand not the thing made but the act of *making*. To distill the moment of origin, of formation, is also to seek out, and regraft, the various and multiple conditions—both the other bodies of the orchestra and their instruments, but also the many moments of affective response between them—that would otherwise exceed the text.

As Armendinger attempts to translate the work of five contemporary Argentine writers—Alejandro Méndez, Mercedes Roffé, Fabián Casas, Néstor Perlongher, and Diana Bellessi—he confronts these gaps; for every word he doesn't know, he goes looking for the definitions in places that intuitively resonate with the poems they come from; for every word he can't translate, he forces himself to walk in parallel with the poem, the number of blocks corresponding with the word's lineation, its position on the page. If the word precedes a stanza break, he forces himself to change direction. Everything that comes after—the semiotic cruising, the interactions with strangers, the haphazard and accidental encounters, the misheard words and miscommunicated responses—all of these become collaged into a series of lyrical notations that appear in between the Spanish originals and their English renderings, as if to remind us of information theory's founding premise: there's no possibility of communication *without noise*. As if to remind us of the many mediations comprising sensory experience, so many of which are illegible, inaudible. And so this book returns language to the precarious tract of the streets and the bodies that move through them, an ethical-erotic dissemination that is as much about the meeting of strangers as it is about the estrangement of one's self. In this newfound unknowability, translator and subject cross-pollinate to produce an excerpt that resists citation. "The old man cups his ear, and when he opens his mouth, the T becomes a P," Armendinger writes, in search of Diana Bellessi's word "esteras," on the corner of Venezuela y Fortunato Devoto:

> [I]t means you have to wait. *Hay que esperar*. There is having to wait. There is no indicated pronoun, there is only the having to wait. If I were to translate his translation, if I were to take one hundred photographs, I would choose the moments where his mouth were closed, tape them together, and feed them into the projector. I wait until my errors start breathing. [...] The girl wants to provide the perfect definition. I try to reassure her. There is crawling across the mind. She says *to put a blanket down. In the soul.* She says *to take the time to reflect on something.* She says *that's what it means to me.* I don't want to use quotation marks. I want to put down the mistake, like a blanket, in the soul.[81]

Here translation becomes the actualized pre-text for action, connection, and bodily contact—without the stipulation of or desire for producing. This point is underscored by Armendinger's own prefatory acknowledgment: "I have so many 'field notes' that I ultimately had to accept that I would never be able to transcribe them all."[82] Instead of striving toward a definitive version or a static, uniform reading, *Street Gloss* performs as a mobile text that remembers itself upon every peregrination, becoming a transdiscursive, metatextual archive, a somatic map, whose coordinates are hardly localized sites but networks of phatic communion, haphazard gestures, and slips of tongue that are both erotic and error-laden: translation as lapse, and overlapping. Here it is again fruitful to recall Benjamin's theorization of the story that not only requires the ability to exchange experience but, moreover, the occasion for this story's continuous and crowdsourced reinvention. The "web in which the gift of storytelling is cradled"[83] depends on its unplanned and arbitrary translations, and even more, on transparency, the ways in which storytellers reveal the framing, including their own reception of the story they are about to tell—"unless," as Benjamin wrote, "they simply pass it off as their own experience."[84] This passing on by passing off is an appropriation that strives toward what Benjamin calls the "perfect narrative," which can only be revealed "through *the layers of a variety of retellings*."[85] Let us confront an alternative proposal, which *Drift Net* takes as axiom: narrative's achievement is not located in the meaning transmitted but in the transmission of meaning—the act of transmission in and of itself, which is inherently multiple, heterogeneous, and displacing. To show the "tracks" of narrative, as Nikolai Leskov, the subject of Benjamin's essay, achieves, is to invite a reading (and a reader) that is self-aware and self-reflexive, a reading that is curious about trace and residue and even more, how these versions of the past manufacture the present representation.

Likewise, Armendinger's insistence on capturing the spatial circumstances of each verbal rendezvous is also a maneuver to resignify urban relics, signs that have been evacuated of their historical or social value, names that have ceased, as Michel de Certeau has written, to be proper.[86] However, these remainders—as trace, as vestige—are always greater than the whole, which here becomes productively displaced by its embryonic offspring.[87]

Some poems, like Néstor Perlongher's "Vapores," generate twenty-seven intermediary interpretations before readers arrive at Armendinger's "Steam." *Street Gloss* thus serves as glossary but also should be read as gloss: an interlinear translation; and also: a transparent preparation for achieving luminosity, radiance; and finally, as glossy: the highly reflective objects—filmy and ephemeral minutiae—that adhere to surface, ricocheting from people to places as sounds, as words, as gestures, as silence, which is to say as mute possibility.

*Street Gloss* confronts the legacy of the Videla dictatorship in Argentina and *los desaparecidos* overseen by the military junta with the support of the US government and its *Guerra sucia* through enacting a poetics of mobility and an ethics of translation less concerned with fidelity than transparency; of showing translation's fallibility and the several different actors involved in its production. Gayatri Spivak reminds us that translation is the quickest way to get out of the confines of one's self.[88] Perhaps translation should also be read as a way to get out of the confines of narrative and a subject-centered ontology. The many different waypoints intervening in the space between the Spanish and the English don't just "add up" to an eventual translation, but also show the steps, detours, digressions, and mistakes—the processes of rendition, and I mean the movement of language but also the clandestine seizure and transfer of suspect bodies—that are often hidden, erased or washed clean but which here are elevated, even allotted their own space as assemblages of an original that exists to be opened up, and called into question. If this rendition is moved it moves by *feeling*, which becomes, in this text, both sense and caress. I want to linger here for a moment, on the subjective and sensual, if only to remind us of the politics of memory that were played out during the first decades following the mass abduction and disappearing of dissidents in Argentina and the end of the Videla dictatorship, in which the construction of historical truth and the public demand to remember—*Ni olvido, ni perdón*—worked hand in hand to interrupt and discredit testimonies of witness that included sensations, impressions, and reflections, all considered unreliable elements that undermined the imperatives to show and to prove.

Armendinger first migrated to Buenos Aires in 2011 to collaborate with Eloísa Cartonera—a collective of writers, designers, and activists activated in the wake of the economic crisis in 2001, and whose members make books out of cardboard bought from cartoneros, persons named after the material they collect on the street. The climate and landscape of Argentina at the turn of the new millennium was literally and literarily transformed through cardboard, which had become a kind of currency as the peso's value continued to sink. Poets reproduced their compositions using a photocopier and had them bound between hand-painted cardboard covers. As traditional publishing houses went out of business, poetry became more accessible, more sensitive to its materiality but also its environment; poets were (t)asked to imagine the poem's function and presentation within the ecology of the city, in the aftergrowth of Cold

War and dictatorship, and in the midst of renewed neoliberal precariousness. How can this redistribution of power in and as publication be read alongside Armendinger's own procedural, durational, instructional poetics, from which every translation begs further revision and self-critique? "I lean into the fact of my complicity," he writes, while on the hunt for Perlongher's "fólego" and "fuellante" on the corner of Olga Cossettini y Mariquita Thompson. "The stranger says he doesn't know exactly, but maybe it's like this, like what a plant does, his hands cupped and softly opening, unfolding. The poem keeps returning the heavy breath it gathers, thrusting, shaking off its own gesture after gesture bending down: this unextinguished blossoming."[89]

The untranslatable presents new opportunities and challenges; the persons Armendinger meet respond with synonyms, or metaphors, or illustrative anecdotes, or their own bodies, as demonstrated above; the "original" is always and endlessly deferred, to make room for copies derived from partial and piecemeal second-hand transcriptions. What makes a translation, *Street Gloss* asserts, is not what can be ferried across the borders of language—what can be shown, what can be proved—but everything that can't. Something erotic, something unseen, something covered up, something uncovered and naked, something erroneous and extrasensory—as when Armendinger describes another stranger's attempt to articulate "fracaso": "He says he can't concretize it, he cannot find a synonym, it's not poetry but ... and then his voice trails off beyond the edges of my memory,"[90] or when, in service of "reguero," on Independencia y Solis, he writes:

> It's not a word, he tells me, so I push it back against the roof of my mouth. [...] He says his name is Nicolás, and then, *do you like to read*? Maybe it all comes down to this. A name leads one question to another, or the pattern of these bricks, an imprint that is not a word. It's something on the ground but he doesn't know for sure. Maybe it is this, an unmarked path between the tongue and paper.[91]

What happens to the framework of translation—what is made possible—when the translator troubles their own role and function; when the translator accounts for the residue of the body—theirs and those around them—and insists upon these multiple and intersecting subject-positions within an environment which now becomes more than contextual data but the scene of mediation, the friction by which something new emerges? What happens to such a framework when the translator shows the limitations of the craft so as to open up the possibilities for translation? And how can *Street Gloss* be read as an organizing principle for the conditions and possibilities of other migratory texts, from the turn of the twentieth century through today, works which not only question their own single authorship but also resist the terms of translation that begin and end without correspondence and negotiation, without disclosing the recurrent and continuous modulations between persons that make all renderings, I argue, possible? I am thinking again of Bachelard, whose work on the phenomenology of poetry—a poetics of space—requires revisitation today through the lens of migration and hospitality, the ecstatic reversibility between guest and host:

> The print house awakens a *feeling for the hut* in me and through it, I re-experience the *penetrating gaze* of the *little window*. But see now what has happened! When I speak the image sincerely, I suddenly feel a need to underline. And what is *underlining* but *engraving* while we write?[92]

If to copy out is to capture the trace of an earlier work and also to transform it, then the reader's marginal notes can be understood as a literal sub-text, a peripheral palimpsest, made possible only through the unseen interactions between persons, an inscribing that flattens the time and space between them in a text, which is not timeless so much as nascent and belated, dated and also momentary. Once again, repetition becomes crucial to this communal act of reinscribing; we read so as to re-read, and with each reading, we confront the text as an experience of emerging; and what emerges, at the very least, is the joy of creation in which readers can participate. No longer can we say authors (recall Hugo Ball's encounters with Kropotkin, Bakunin, and Merezhkovsky, amid the ruins of Fort Manonvillers) ghost their readers, but readers, too, ghost the persons they are reading, which is to say the present ghosts the past by putting language itself in a state of emergence. What is an engraving, after all, but an indistinct notion or remembrance,[93] or an act of communicating through another source? And when we *scratch things out*, we produce a text through just this series of alterations, the pressure of stamping and pressing, the meeting of surface and material, a deposition produced by various recorders, I-witnesses who've abandoned their sense of self. Through errantry and errancy we get closer to, and in the process, move further from the (original) text, so as to remember it differently when we return, so as to show how translation always begs, not one, but a multitude of meanings, so many of which are involuntary, inadvertent, desultory.

One reads *Street Gloss* and more associations gush forth. No one—not anyone—can walk in another's path, especially in a different language, as Armendinger makes clear, without changing where it takes you. I read *Street Gloss* and return to Buenos Aires as I put the words in my mouth, as I try them out or taste them. Whose words? "My consciousness gets heavy," Armendinger admits, drilling inward in pursuit of "*sacude*," on the corner of Catamarca e Independencia. "[...] What if the feelings I call my own have fallen upon me, like particles of dust?"[94]

On the edge of Medrano and Rivadavia, right on the curb, I am several blocks away (in memory, which is another sort of translation, or a counter-museum: non-catalogical) as I write this. To be at two (or more) places at once, and always to be around things; to make one's self a relation, which is to say to make one's self an account; to be put in touch, to touch, to tell or be told. I can place myself there, on that corner, and now I can envision Armendinger too. It helps to have him at my fingertips; I search his name by typing out each letter; a name, we remember, leads one question to another. This is how it starts. Hold the finger here and then hover. How many times did we pass each other on our cruise around Avenida de Mayo? Between Monserrat and San Telmo, San Telmo and the Parque Lezama, where I am winding a path around jacaranda trees that reach the sky. How many times did we look at each other, and look away? When I map the distance between us, the shape becomes an *L*, except upside down and reversed, so that I forget who it is I've really switched places with, and when. Some shapes are impossible to reproduce with a keyboard; they exist, instead, to be projected across another screen. And every screen—every mask—implies a multiplication. The deferral, or dispersal, of self as guise.

I have a habit of reading books in the places in which they were composed. I read Walter Benjamin's seven-year exile in letters, I write letters back, at every point of departure. When, a year later, I return to the unreturnable (Berlin), a return that is an arrival, to a city where I've never been, I am reading his *Berlin Childhood*. Each passage is a coordinate, in which I find myself, in relation to another. Underneath de Certeau's "planned and readable city,"[95] we should remind ourselves, is the city of migration. Underneath legibility is another kind of text, but to alight upon its gradations requires contributing to a choreography that is organizational and unrehearsed. Walking, which suggests or enacts the consequences of a hyperspatial here-there location, also invites others to participate in its discontinuous drift. If it's true, as de Certeau asserts in *The Practice of Everyday Life*, that walking necessarily moves, from a solitary action to a cooperative practice, then this practice can be compared to a poetics of collaboration and anonymity, the gradual shedding of individual authorship and one-to-one translation for the rhythm of multiple bodies, heterogeneous and variable parts, enfolded and imbricated—a dance, which is itself a documentation: a way of documenting the movement of a body in time and space.

## THE BLUR OF MOVEMENT: BEYOND VISIBILITY

Beginning from the premise that *making visible* is itself a political act, and that empowering experience is contingent upon the medium of video, Mieke Bal proceeded in 2008 to think through four key concepts of migratory art: movement, time, memory, and contact.[96] In doing so, the Dutch video artist and theorist sought an aesthetics, not explicitly of migration, but of the situation brought by it. I would like to further characterize such conditions with attention to the permutations of subjectification, a doubling and a reversibility that solicits a way of looking, a way of reading steeped in virtual and physical encounters, intimacy and empathy, memory and the veil of forgetting that allows new subjectivities to take shape. By invoking forgetting, I also want us to recall the tension between fragment and detail in the itinerant personal accounting that parallels the tension between measurable time and continuous duration at work in migration. One does not cancel out the other but in fact allows new possibilities of perception and experience, of performing memory in the present (and in the presence of) forgetting; the erasure of time and life etched on, and through, the body.

In his call for re-reading Holocaust diaries and memoirs as narrative constructions grounded, not in factuality, but in the *act*uality of inscription—which includes the relationship between writer and text, the apprehending of experience—James E. Young suggests that migration and the documentary narrative are inextricably linked.[97] Because of its tendency to usurp events, narrative is not capable, Young argues, of documenting the facts so common to documentarian literature, an assertion that helps us reconceptualize our own strategies for interpretation, our own readerly translations. Without a doubt, it is not just narrative that neutralizes events by reducing and resolving them as narrative structures, by assimilating them into plot; strategies of representation must also be called into question. We are forced to consider how narrative can very often erase the underlying political rhetoric that structures migrants' lives, in the very media that is purportedly meant to serve them, as is the case with a recent Swedish instructional video[98] (commissioned by the country's national board of forensic medicine: Rättsmedicinalverket, or RMV) that promotes the practice of Sweden's voluntary medical age assessment. The examination involves biometric observations of kneecaps and molars as a "scientific"[99] way to establish asylum seekers' eligibility for basic state rights like education and healthcare. Set against the succession of scenes involving characters going about their lives without risk, as a soft-spoken voice-over discusses the benefits of ritual submission to biometrics, the video obscures the precarious realities of such persons in Sweden, including the fact that its medical age assessment is "voluntary" in name only; asylum seekers will be automatically assessed as adults if they do not agree to take the test, information that is curiously lacking in the instructions.

In contradistinction, by subverting self-representation and a predatory and exoticizing representational economy through employing multiple points of view, which shift, as we've seen, without distinction, the migratory text endeavors to dodge the appropriation of the singular I into the politicized we, whereby stereotyping, misrepresentation, and voyeurism proliferate, as well as the fraught democratic logic employed in the service of *speaking for all others*. Bal asserts that movement is always a struggle with the frame; I argue that the migratory text offers a textual encounter that changes all participants, not through Bal's techno-logic of video, which is to say the knowledge of one's role as viewer—the screen that separates subject and object—but in fact through our desire to abandon the vibrant image for the silence of the text. This movement—this mediation—engenders an intimacy, and the potential for radical empathy, that arrives when the one looking truly becomes the one looked at: the imaginative *transfer* promised—recall the classical Latin *auctor*—by the etymological tracings of the author.

Young's 1987 call for an alternative hermeneutics of literary testimony—coinciding with the emergence of refugee studies in the academy and its subsequent aim to align political policy with objective research—is likewise a call for greater sensitivity in our reading practices of such personal accountings; to trouble the privileging of documentary fact over retrospection and proximity, to enter into the immediacy of experience as it becomes restructured: marked but also shaped by imperfections, all of its discrepancies and adaptations. "[N]othing," Young writes, "can be more authentic than the ways in which the diarists' interpretations of experiences gathered the weight and force of agency *in* their lives; nothing is more authentic than the *consequences* for a life that issue from the manner in which this life may have been narrated the previous day."[100]

Actuality is always ephemeral and infinite; ephemeral because it is a becoming, a process, a modulation, a going toward, which exists or occurs *at the time*—I am writing to you, I've already begun, I have not yet ceased—infinite because in receiving this, you have *caught me in the act*. The time of our communion—"original" receiver/sender being both inextricable and interchangeable—is always hospitable because this moment can only attract, can only welcome mutually and unconditionally.

I am looking for the moment a past becomes a post. Or rather, when *past* and *post* become part of the same transmission, belonging to the same space, the same breath, a moment to read and be read in all its dimensions—awaited and remembered and hallucinated and hypostatized—this thin paper surface as Möbius strip. The migratory text evokes a nearness, a presence that does not diminish with the passage of time but intensifies because of this heterochrony: the then and there of event, the here and now of its reconstruction—the text's production of an alternative space-time in which *before*, *after*, and *now* tangle and conflate into unresolvable tension, whereby meaning is produced in the overlapping and intermingling of stories and selves. The migratory's agential potentials are indebted to the incongruencies of form, as well as its periodic and haphazard inscription: the habitual activity of keeping a journal, of accounting for one's own passage through this life, actualized through the contradictions of recording lived time. Actuality, too, is absence, the interchronic pause when nothing is actual, when nothing is actually happening, when nothing occurs, when everything occurs or is about to. Informed by the ambiguous temporalities activated by migration, I want to re-read actuality as *about to*, *aboutness*, an act that is aware of itself, that anticipates itself; an act which relies on both approximation and proximity, the close caress the hand makes on any instrument, and yet the precision of inscription, of the mark that relates—nothing, if not one's own relationship to this world.

## THE MIGRATORY TEXT IN AND AS TRANSLATION

In the 1995 edited collection *Writing Across Worlds*, editors Russell King, John Connell, and Paul White set out to investigate the ways in which creative work may inform the work of sociology, and in particular, how "'non-academic' literature, written often (but by no means exclusively) by migrants, can offer insights into the nature of the migration process and the experience of being a migrant," a narrative, they contend, that is commonly accounted for—and delimited by—social-scientific research that "fails to capture the essence of what it is like to *be* a migrant."[101] To understand international migration, which is identified as "a dominant feature of world literature from both post-industrial and developing countries," the editors contend that it is necessary to bring together "the social scientist's concerns with explanation and the student of literature's expertise in the handling of text."[102] Lest we take this disciplinary intervention as anything more than an entry point into parsing the artificial distinctions—"'non-academic' literature," "fully-fledged creative literatures," or any other[103]—brought by the academy, while continuing to place migrant literature and art more centrally in analyses of migration, we should read any attempt by white metropolitan scholars to "capture the essence of what it is like to *be* a migrant" as another conquest—an embodying and an erasure. Stories, as Edward Said has noted, "are at the heart of what explorers and novelists say about strange regions of the world; they also become the method colonized people use to assert their own identity and the existence of their own history."[104] Yet far too often, the *story* of colonization, as the first half of Said's observation suggests, replaces the people who have been colonized or otherwise marginalized, becoming a second erasure announced through a fetishized version of embodied experience that gets written down and passed on. This production turns colonial encounters into colonial histories, and the literature of a specific exile into a generic and universalizing world literature, that ever-expansive field reduced, nevertheless, to the national model; encompassing, in David Damrosch's oft-cited definition, "all literary works that circulate beyond their culture of origin, either in translation or in their original language."[105]

*Refugee Tales*, the 2016 anthology produced by UK publisher Comma Press, and in conjunction with the Gatwick Detainees Welfare Group, became so popular it produced a sequel one year later, signaling its value to world literature and an audience of consumers by publishing the "unabridged reality of refugees" while aligning itself with an ongoing political praxis that includes, as its website in 2020 described, guided walks "in solidarity [...] [to] reclaim the landscape of South East England." These "pilgrim routes," as the books' editors describe them, all include landscapes of nation-making and securitization, including 2017's passage from Runnymede to Westminster and 2018's passage from St. Albans to Westminster, the stage set for the drafting and agreement of the Magna Carta. Rather than foreground the assembling of empire made possible by such routes, as Santos Perez does, in *from Unincorporated Territory*, here they recede into the text, not to be contested, not to be interrogated, only to be accepted, or ignored, as imperial and imperializing scaffold. In drawing from the structure and, at times, the content, of *The Canterbury Tales*, *Refugee Tales* falls into the proto-nationalist project to which its source material, and Chaucer himself, in the centuries since its publication, have been linked. Each story—a selection that includes "The Migrant's Tale," "The Unaccompanied Minor's Tale," "The Detainee's Tale," along with several others—is prefaced by the authorial displacement of the displaced person, a mirroring of appropriation that resolves itself in the phrase, *as told to*. Unlike Berger and Mohr's collaboration, these life stories are not narrated in the third person but from the assumed proximity of a manufactured I that remains voyeuristic to the subject it has subsumed. The author, the scholar, the citizen, the nation, subsumes the migrant, in *Refugee Tales* as in so many clinical studies of migration. If we are attentive, we can hear Édouard Glissant's reminder that "the first thing exported by the conqueror was his language"[106] as we turn the page.[107] Only once, among the book's fourteen stories, does the writer recognize the manufacturing of this exploitative "pseudotranslation,"[108] even in the act of transposing the person into a specific representation cut and wedged into the fictive pretext and the superficial frame of narrative, the subject which becomes merely a suspect to be studied—or surveilled—by the state:

> Maybe the real story begins here
> in this office, before you press record
> and we look in the mirror of each other's eyes, we're
> first time meeting; maybe you say the word
> 'Refugee' in your head when you call me Farida,
> Refugee, what is that burn mark on your hand?
> You already have a story of the torture
>
> ("The Refugees Tale")[109]

The effect of a story or image so often depends on where one puts the frame. The location, or the unlocatability of the "I" here is cast off and further complicated by the authorial assumption of the second-person point of view, which assumes both a distance and also a newfound intimacy, a gesture which begets the arrival of realization, and the reversal of subject and object in the story's next stanza: "But these marks are from cooking breakfast for my family,/this is the first time I'm cooking in my life!"[110] At other moments, as in "The Migrant's Tale," the reality of a Syrian refugee named Aziz is conflated by the literary past, as author Dragan Todorovic merges present-day scenes of Aziz's self-disclosure inside a detention center with excerpts from Chaucer's "The Man of Law's Tale," "*as retold by the author*."[111] What is lost both in translation and in the telescoping of over six hundred years is the political and social context, a deeply complicated geography, the location of the subject and their objectification by the state, which, as we must acknowledge, controls both the movement of people and also and especially, the movement of people into texts, an alchemy that involves marking and reinscribing marginalized individuals through legislation or, as is evident here, against the various narratives fostered through a person's cultivation as world literature—"nothing," as Glissant has remarked, "but an ingenious destructuring and a hasty recomposition [...] [an] idea of the world [which] takes advantage of the imagination of the world."[112] Readers of this anthology—this series of anthologies—are thus invited to consider Glissant's own revision, that smuggled in his language, the first thing exported by the conqueror is the West's systems of thought, its systematic thought. Readers of these anthologies are tasked with negotiating the opaque layers of telling, translating, and editing: what has been cast and what has been cast out, to make room for an invented English in a performance that is not collaborative so much as it is coercive.

In other stories, such as "The Lorry Driver's Tale," it becomes clear that the goal of the project is not "to call for an immediate end to indefinite immigration detention in the UK,"[113] as co-editor David Herd points out in the book's afterword, but, on the contrary, to entertain its editors' and authors' own mystique as privileged spectators and authoritarian figures who are allowed to speak for their subjects and, more problematically, speak *as* their subjects. What is divested in such scenarios is not just one's story and voice but one's dignity, a word, not coincidentally, that became a rallying cry for self-representation among Syrian refugees in the spring of 2011.[114] A word indicated by the collective voice of the insurgent Indigenous of southeast Mexico, Subcomandante Marcos, as he ritually signed each letter, to declare the Zapatismo mission and rallying cry: "respect for ourselves, for our right to be better, our right to struggle for what we believe in, our right to live and die according to our ideals." Dignity, he writes, in a letter to Eric Jauffret dated June 20, 1995, "cannot be studied [...] dignity is the international homeland we often forget about."[115] And later, lest we forget *dignity*'s call for a self-sovereignty divested of institutions, exclusions, flow charts, utopic theorizations, and global programs for world revolution: "dignity," Marcos makes clear, "won't acknowledge passports, visas, and other absurdities."[116] The same word—*dignidad*—became the birth of a new Chicano literary movement in the early days of 2020, spawning the hashtag #DignidadLiteraria to encourage conversation and engagement in the wake of the publication of *American Dirt* by Jeanine Cummins, a novel critiqued, in large part, because of its lack of cultural literacy, including an inaccurate, voyeuristic, and sensationalized representation of border-crossers.[117] What is dignity but the conditions to be counted—as human, as worthy of subjectivity—what is dignity but the permission to take back *control* of one's self?[118] Not surprisingly, Cummins's 2020 novel, an Oprah's Book Club selection and a *New York Times Book Review* editors' choice, remains cataloged, today, as "Immigrant Fiction" and "Border Fiction."

Unlike the personal stories told by refugees that are collected by organizations such as the Amsterdam-based VluchtelingenWerk Nederland, which serves asylum applicants by publishing their accounts and turning them into official state records to aid in the processing of asylum claims, these *Refugee Stories* are addressed to readers, and thus employ narrative tropes that degrade material realities into immaterial entertainment. "And on this trip we had a journalist along, too. I'll call him Clark Kent but you know his name—-he's famous," Chris Cleave writes, writing about himself while ventriloquizing the voice of an unnamed lorry driver. "[...] And once every six months he writes about a burning social issue."[119] Clark Kent, after this auspicious introduction, becomes a central character, overtaking the titular story-subject of the lorry driver while signaling the self-referential "name value"[120] that denotes currency in the literary market. Italian multicultural and migration studies theorist Graziella Parati might call this an "act of talking back," which constitutes, in her formulation, the groundwork for resistance as well as a site of compromise, "whether it is in collaborative writing projects or in catering to the demands of the publishing industry."[121]

Yet how can we further unpack this act of *talking back* and complicate the alleged compromise through the literal interruption of voices? How can this transitory and translational intervention stage the grounds for troubling not only the traditional concept of the single author, but also the national literature for whom this single author writes? In this scenario, the intentional or unintended disturbance, the interruption, what Parati calls in her 1995 study, *Migration Italy*, the "background noise,"[122] is not only a residue of the resistance to literary-political discourse as a homogenizing project but becomes its own counter-discourse; indeed the migratory text can *only* become constructed (and thus reconstructed) through the "noise" it produces.

The problematic nature of texts such as *Refugee Tales*—its seamless translation of migrants' oral stories into written tales—presents us with a specific lens that informs a larger structural issue in the academy. Any question of refugee representation, and especially refugee self-representation, is necessarily intertwined with the question of a national literature. And yet by reappropriating their own deployment by authors, scholars, and other cultural producers, I want to insist that migrant self-representations, in redirecting the normalizing logic of "national literature," have also reevaluated nationalistic discourses of migration.

Consider the framework posited by *Princesa*, Fernanda Farias de Albuquerque's autobiographical novel published in 1994, but produced through a series of translations and collaborative renderings while its transgender author was in the Roman prison of Rebibbia, a processual drift that actualizes the agency of a personal text in transit.[123] Fernanda, a Brazilian who migrated to Italy in the nineties, tells her story in a mixture of Portuguese and Italian to another inmate, a Sardinian shepherd who transcribes the narrative in his native dialect and then passes it on to another inmate, who ultimately drafts it in an Italian that is only as homogeneous as its source code: the heterogeneous nation of Italy. Despite the fact that its author is Brazilian, and that the majority of the book's story is set in Brazil—Alagoa Grande, Campina Grande, João Pessoa, Recife, Natal, Salvador, Rio, and São Paulo—*Princesa*, which was translated (again) and published in Brazil a year later, is considered contemporary Italian literature. Yet the construction of subject-positions that are not tethered to national, ethnic, or gender identities are in fact revealed through such acts of translation, in which simplistic formulas of language and selfhood are transgressed and undone, to make room for linguistic, affective, and bodily interconnectedness. This last marker can be understood quite literally, as when Fernanda, immobilized due to the prison boundaries separating transsexuals (then referred to only as "transvestites") from political prisoners, gives her notebooks to Giovanni, the Sardinian shepherd, who transfers her testimony from one cellblock to another; this textual interaction performs as a material infiltration, whereby areas and actions deemed forbidden are pursued and accessed—a mobility made possible, not through the work of art but by the art of collaborative and remediated work, in which language no longer singularly alters the text; the text, too, effectively alters the language by introducing the texture and conditions of its own production as piecemeal and hybrid.

We might think of translation here as not serving any kind of mimetic or reproductive faculty, but in fact witness how it generates a quality or condition *within the artwork* that would otherwise not have been possible. In this sense, translation renders a migratory aesthetics. Put another way: translation makes the migratory text possible as a series of conditions, rather than the other way around. Like Lawrence Venuti's vision of translation as "a cultural means of resistance"[124] that might transform our contemporary political economy—the political institutions to which the global economy is allied—I understand that such possibilities are contingent upon the critical reflexivity of the reader-interpreter, but also upon improvisation and collaboration, and the risks that accompany each; such possible resistances are not limited to methodical corrections of a source text in translation but, as we've seen, through the celebration of error, accident, and coincidence. Here the testimonial instinct both solicited by and expected of documentarian narrative—a slippage between "authored" and "authorized" that is, as Young reminds us, so often linked with national obligation—is problematized by the imperfect reproductions characteristic of the migratory text; documentary realism is undermined by the migratory's fuzzy realism, which, in making visible the text's own mediation, also provides its readers with the opportunity to juxtapose and attend to the interpenetration between events, experience, memory, and narrative.

Thus, among the problematic aspects of *Refugee Tales* is not that its translators cover the original but that its translators cover the process of translation itself. What happened between the oral recitation and the written testimony, here collected as a series of "refugee tales"? This lack of transparency is not just a move toward the diminishment of instructive returns; the book's obscuring of the material conditions of its subject-authors has the dual function of turning the hypermediated process of sharing, telling, reception, and interpretation—those storytelling markers of dynamism and participation from which I began this chapter's analysis—into a blanket narrative divested of agency on behalf of the already marginalized storyteller.

Transgressing the distinction between writing and speech, Félix Guattari and Gilles Deleuze contend that narrative consists in communicating hearsay. The migratory texts under consideration in this study respond to this assertion, which is a challenge, and a challenge, moreover, to language: to move beyond the formula of "necessarily go[ing] from a second party to a third party, neither of whom has seen,"[125] to its opposite: making visible, and available, exactly this *going*—which is an act or instance, as well as a condition (of the ground, as for walking) and an advance (toward an objective), a drawing near or to, but also a proposition: the expectation of indefinite continuance. This tenuous movement requires that we think of translation as rendering not information, but intimacy.

Translation, as we already know, is not just a matter of words, but about the body. Walter D. Mignolo and Freya Schiwy, in their 2007 study on "Transculturation and the Colonial Difference," have shown how translation in service of conversion was used, as early as the Renaissance, to also break away from medieval conceptions of gender as necessarily ambiguous and capable of sudden change, and to establish the idea of fixed and singular bodies. This "translation machine"[126] ultimately serviced the nation-state with the binary of civilized and uncivilized, self and other. The "colonial difference" of the essay's title attests to how translation is inextricable from an ethnoracial, gendered, and epistemological foundation at the heart of the modern world-system, a foundation that "transculturation"[127]—or the multiple and nonlinear exchanges of cultural influences, ways of speaking, talking, and thinking *in between* languages—upsets and unsettles.

To witness a parallel intervention within the field of life writing, one need only return to 1992, when Caren Kaplan revisited the Eurocentric genealogy of autobiography to theorize an "out-law" genre capable of co-opting the power dynamics embedded in normative literary production, distribution, and reception. "Out-law genres [...] mix two conventionally 'unmixable' elements, autobiography criticism and autobiography as thing itself," Kaplan explains, employing the language of hybridity.[128] Through collaborative practices that emphasize an awareness of both process and of the power differences between participants, these texts—a list that includes cultural autobiographies, testimonial literature, ethnographic writing, and prison memoirs, all of which might be used to classify *Princesa*—evade the discourse of individual authorship to serve "a discourse of situation; a 'politics of location.'"[129] Kaplan links the out-law genre's deconstruction of the "individual bourgeois author" associated with autobiographical narrative with the emergence, or I would argue, the return, of a "collective consciousness that 'authorizes'"[130] the identity of the writer whose name might appear on the front cover, as well as the hybrid testimony they have reenacted.

I want to read Kaplan's "out-law genre" and its properties of autobiography (practice) and autobiographical critique (theory), alongside the migratory's embedding of its own transitional material relations (process)—key ingredients of this corpus—in order to continue pursuing the ways in which the migratory text reformulates the framework of narrative. Rather than "perform a work of domestication," such *translations in the original* call into question the adaption of cultural norms and values that can be read under the regime of assimilation. It is because the migratory text complicates the very concept of the "foreign" and "domestic"—the rubric of those translations "that work best" in Venuti's assessment[131]—through the syncretic processes of its formation and makeup that we might read this corpus of literature and media alongside contemporary projects for migrant activism, including alternative refugee integration and public housing maneuvers that critique the "target language" and nativist logic of aid and hospitality. What the migratory text provokes is indeed an altered reading pattern through a specific revisionary encounter, not, in Venuti's terms, with a foreign text, but with the text as foreign: a belonging not situated *inside* but *elsewhere*. Here, I want to insist, is where translation makes good on Venuti's thesis of redefining authorship in literature and in law while creating identities receptive to cultural difference; here—in the space without center and periphery—is the revisionary encounter, and it is indeed multiple and heterogeneous: an encounter with the dialectic of the "major" and "minor" as literary coordinates and methodologies, with the concept of original authorship and subordinate (and suppressed) translation, and with the fetishization of language tethered to nation that work in tandem to produce the "scandals" that Venuti, in his 1998 study, nevertheless endeavors to analyze.

The lesson of a migratory text like *Princesa* is not that its publication in Italian was an "invention" of the author's Brazilian Portuguese and their transcriber's Sardinian dialect that somehow cuts across cultural and lingual divisions and hierarchies but that, to tell one's story of exclusion and detainment, the processes of mediation—exposing the invention of assimilation, of fluency—would have to become a part of the story itself. Whereas Venuti's treatment of "minoritizing translation" as an ethical, political agenda—an opposition to the global hegemony of English—requires the signification of cultural and linguistic differences of the text in order to preserve, and thus restore, an otherness opposed to and juxtaposed with what has replaced it as translation, I want to assert that the relation of mediation as a kind of textual source code in works like *Princesa*, *Street Gloss*, *Skins of Columbus*, the untitled artwork of *Nest*, and *from Unincorporated Territory* does not aim to restore the identity positions disturbed by translation but in fact works to account for their extant transitioning, reflecting back to the nation its own colonial and imperializing past, alongside the labor exploitation and extraction of resources that makes empire possible. Reading such writing, Parati explains, "demands strategies, *contaminated by different disciplines*, in order to be investigated. The creation of a new language for migration is necessary for talking not only about migration, but also about its protagonists."[132]

Yet matters return, always, to flow. Even as Parati calls for a new language from which to talk about migration and migrant literature, she acknowledges its global regulation by "market strategies dictated by rich Western countries," a situation in which migrant literature becomes the literature of migration, subject to redesign while redesigning "a world map from below."[133] Whether under the pressures of the normative structures of "a destination culture"[134] or recolored as an object of study in the fieldwork of scholars, the self-representations of migrants are often at the whim of a world economy and an erudite intellectual scholarship that, as Goethe says bluntly, while coining "Weltliteratur" in 1827, allows one the opportunity of "appropriating to ourselves what is good, so far as it goes."[135]

In Pascale Casanova's *La république mondiale des lettres*, published in 1999 and translated into English by M.B. DeBevoise as *The World Republic of Letters* five years later, the success of "dominated spaces"—Latin America as Casanova's prime example—is measured by how well they can be integrated with the center.[136] While such structural dependence is seen by Casanova as the impetus for formal reinvention—what she conflates with the creation of "modernity"—writers from dominated spaces can only, within *La république mondiale des lettres*'s limited scope, produce revolution for the sake of nationalization. Modernism here does not only become a Western construction but a fundamentally colonial one. Perhaps more troubling, however, is not that, in Casanova's estimation, writers on the periphery are only capable of writing certain works for specific ends, but that writers on the periphery are only capable of *reading* their work—and all others—under the rubric of realism, a readerly interpretation that can be characterized, she clarifies, as "more historically grounded."[137] Belonging in this scenario is tethered to the nation and thus to a national literary cause; in contrast, to be a "foreigner," which Casanova links to the absence of national independence in her analysis of "The Assimilated," is to be "someone without history, without literature, without country [...] without tradition, without a culture of his [*sic*] own."[138]

What are we to think, for instance, when the publication of a book in English, by an Indian writer, is celebrated as the moment in which a continent has found its voice?[139] Which continent, I wonder, was the *New York Times* book reviewer characterizing, except the United Anglo-Americas of the World? And if it's the whole of Asia which has found its voice, why does it sound so much like imperialism and colonialism in 1981, as in years past, as in today? "It's a good time to be an Arab writer," Kevin Blankinship remarks, in a 2019 essay in *The Millions*, and to elaborate, he notes the recent "spike in supply and demand" for English translations of Arabic titles.[140] The "institutional boons to translation" are seen as "happy developments" that "bless" non-Western literatures, as if the success of a work in the world republic of letters depends upon its homogenization.

Through rooting the task of the translator in the essential echo of imitation—a transference presupposed by listening to fundamental differences—Gayatri Spivak locates the practice of translation somewhere in between "the coming into being of the subject of reparation [...] [and] the generalized commodity exchange" of the international book trade.[141] Tracing the rise of literary translation since the 1970s as "a quick way to 'know a culture',"[142] Spivak earlier showed how NGOs, replete with foreign aid and international solidarity, and specifically concerned with health, environmental, and gender issues, have paved the way for a literary-art cultural industry buoyed by capitalist globalization *and* liberal humanism. More contemporary slippages between various nongovernmental organizations and state actors function as both shield and mask in the big business of migration management and the co-production of refugees, as I've shown elsewhere, but such partnerships can be traced to the interwar period, in which government and private domains converged in the arenas of culture and art, most conspicuously in FDR's appointment of Nelson Rockefeller to head the wartime Office of the Coordinator of Inter-American Affairs in 1941, and its efforts to promote Pan-Americanism across Latin America.[143]

In negotiating the imperative of care and attentive response with the fetishization of both the migrant and their languages, the conventional translator inevitably implicates themselves as agents, either in the reproduction of existing ideologies or in their resistance. Nevertheless, the universalizing logic of the "Western way" so commonly employed in aid organizations, as I will expand upon in my final chapter, is prevalent not only in the camps sheltering migrants during their application to asylum but also commonplace within immigration inspections and asylum interviews, where translators interpret accounts and explanations of the "foreigner" through their own worldview.

If our work as researchers and instructors is constrained by our assumptions underlying this limited understanding of the individual, our efforts to relocate a Weltliteratur begin by reorienting our own individual positions within the environments in which we live and work. Perhaps we also need to rethink our role, not just as citizen-readers, but as linguistic, cultural, and social translators; in doing so, we might think to remind ourselves, as I've observed here, that translation is not merely collaborative but also interactive, an act that necessitates the third voice of the recorder-witness: At the border (a crossroads), we might sketch out a pedagogy invested in unthinking earlier modes of reading works and categories of belonging; displacing a chronological national or linguistic tradition means, also, to displace ourselves within coordinates that are invariably shifting. If world literature might be redesigned, not from an inside-outside dialectic (the center, the periphery), nor from above or below (major/minor literatures), what better rubric to begin the revision than the one offered by the transitional and relational migratory text?

Under these conditions, translation's lesson is not that it risks effacing its original author, as David Damrosch argues, after citing Goethe's supersession of his own biographer—a situation in which Goethe, in translation, becomes the author of his own death. It is not that, as Damrosch insists, "[a]ll too often [...] things slip in the process, and we can gain a work of world literature but lose the author's soul,"[144] but, on the contrary, that every translation requires both a fundamental loss *and* a revelatory convergence or consummation, opening a space in which the fundamental characters of each language resound, interfere, and gush forward: a choreography which is always virtual, always on the verge.

To think through these implications, it is necessary to move beyond Benjamin's initial task, troubling the *origin* and the *original* through recognition and repetition, a "rhythm," Walter Benjamin writes, three years after "The Task of the Translator," "[that] is apparent only to a dual insight. On the one hand it needs to be recognized as a process of restoration and reestablishment, but, on the other hand, and precisely because of this, as something imperfect and incomplete. [...] Indeed," Benjamin concludes, "this is where the task of the investigator begins."[145] It begins then, by disavowing; it begins through dis-integration, dis-assembly; it begins by offering a story, which is our own, and yet belongs to so many others, so many others. It begins with notation, and in this we are reminded, taking up or taking in Roland Barthes, that no text is original, but only "a tissue of citations,"[146] and in being a tissue, a text both absorbs and sheds—lightweight and soft, the better to be held or hauled, recast, carried.

If it is true that today "language" no longer equals "nation," and that even hegemonic languages such as English and Spanish can be appropriated to articulate positions of subaltern subjectivity, as the Zapatistas have done, then might we consider how a corpus such as the migratory text offers another opening to such a global practice, both a theory and a method, neither a "world literature," nor a rendering grounded in dichotomies or one-to-one assimilation, but a practice that advances through the ambiguity articulated by the coexistence of languages, the break or dash when two or more cultures come together. Translation can take place here, and through this alternative model, through an intervention that is political as well as ethical, translation can *take the place* of structures of power that rely on the hierarchization of languages, the modern "presupposition of the unity and uniqueness of certain languages"[147] based on their grammar and geopolitical location.

If we understand, following Eve Tuck and K. Wayne Yang, that decolonization is not an "and"—nor an end—but an "elsewhere," then this also means that decolonization is not a utopic aspiration or an abstract theorization but an ongoing practice that is and has been happening somewhere else.[148] It's this *somewhere else* I want to hold on to, or more accurately, reach for; this *something else* that the migratory text, for this book and beyond it, wants to approach, draw from but also put forth. As I seek out the somewhere in elsewhere, I can't help but be reminded of scholar and multidisciplinary artist Ashon T. Crawley's frequent call for "otherwise possibility": "a concept of internal difference, internal multiplicity [...] a movement towards, and an affirmation of, imagining other modes of social organization, other ways for us to be with each other."[149]

Otherwise, though, does not have to be relegated to the registers of a dream, but recognized, too, as its waking memory, which is to say what has already happened and what will happen again; both testimony and imminence. Otherwise—in contrast to the utopic vision of a queer futurity—isn't *not here*; otherwise *has been here*; it is only our task to remember it in the body; it is only our task to remark upon its presence in the present.[150] Otherwise, in other words, is not just sensory but subliminal, not just spatial but temporal. And a migratory text is not just a text to be read but a way of reading, which is to say, a way of listening.

Crawley's essay "Otherwise, Ferguson" was written in the aftermath of a summer that witnessed Michael Brown's murder and the paramilitary police response in Ferguson, Eric Garner's murder, and the deaths of over 2,000 Palestinian civilians during the IDF's seven-week assault of Gaza dubbed "Operation Protective Edge," a string of violence that informs today's increasingly normalized murders of unarmed Black persons by police, as well as Israel's continual attempts, intensifying in October 2023, to cleanse Palestine of its name and its people. Such uninterrupted sequences of dehumanization and dispossession of Black and brown bodies on distant shores by similar neocolonial forces underscore the "economy of occupation through policing" that allows us to glimpse the interconnections between unequitable distribution of financial, educational, health, and food resources; access to free, clean, available water; and structures of incarceration, sexism, homophobia, and racism; that all of these are grounded in the dream, the nightmare, of the white supremacist capitalist patriarchal ordering, necessary to its elaboration, elaborated by the individual who either receives or is refused its institutional rights and cultural entitlements; that all of these actors assume various roles—paramilitary police power, governance, economy, media—yet all unequally administer the disciplinary power of the state. Within this frame, which is both a border and a body, how have persons on the move—persons immobilized, persons on the margins—articulated an "otherwise possibility"; what, and who, exceeds the political ontologies of the state?

Writing of and into the limits that shape the narratives we might call "counter-histories," Saidiya Hartman, in her 2008 essay, "Venus in Two Acts," seeks an aesthetic mode adequate to render the untold and the untellable: "to tell an impossible story," Hartman proposes, "and to amplify the impossibility of its telling."[151] But how to do both? Hartman's interrogation of representation, violence, social death, and the requirements of narrative, "the stuff of subjects and plots and ends," necessarily implicates itself, and in implicating itself, asks to perform "the future of abolition [...] on the page."[152] In doing so, Hartman strives toward a hypothesis that this study insists upon: if translation, like the archive, can be repositioned, not as an elaborated institutional practice but as an improvised, open-sourced collaboration—vulnerable to unplanned contributions, unsanctioned participants—then it can appropriate the transnational institutional space, so as to transform it into a truly public commons.

"How," Hartman asks, "does one revisit the scene of subjection without replicating the grammar of violence?"[153] I want to say that the limit can also be the edge, a necessary precipice, the threshold from which *something other than the historical past* ghosts the history of our present. The archive is not, in these migratory texts, *not* "a death sentence"; on the contrary, it is because the archive functions as "an inventory of property"[154] that such texts can exploit the archive's constitutive limits, the terms of collection and catalog, a death sentence on the level of the word, which renders transparent the myriad processes by which persons have been disappeared, not once, but time and time again. In this reading, the migratory text asks us to mobilize the evidence of exploitation for the exploitation of evidence. In the archive, an impasse can become a passage, in which the limits of the archive are not confined to their materiality.

Between experience and narrative is neither an impediment, as Sarah C. Bishop argues, nor an aporia, in Hartman's view, a boundary that begins and ends in refusal, but a fault line, an articulation of the non-equivalence of all acts of translation, all acts of documentation and retrieval. The migratory text understands this fault line as its architectural framework, through which the scene of documentation converges with the scene of retrieval, through which, nevertheless, we "write our now as it is interrupted by this past."[155] In the works under investigation here, we are tasked with reading—and writing—the archive as a testament to the impossibility *and* possibility of representation.

I want to recall the potential for empathy produced by the migratory text—imaginative engagement that resists information consumption—a *feeling* that goes beyond gesture, and a sense of touch, of haptic contact, in Mieke Bal's original formulation, that is not erased by mediation, but heightened by it. Each of the migratory texts under consideration in this chapter proposes a reinterpretation of narrative framework while provoking viewers to engage in a radical empathy by moving beyond recognition and the terms of representation, beyond the desire to see and to grasp, when knowledge and information too often disconnects and discredits; when visibility reveals debasement and celebrification. Set against the techno-utopian promise of virtual reality as an empathy machine—an outlook that prevails in both empathy studies and technology news reports—the migratory text, as a media that can only operate within the terms of collaboration, and by recognizing the processes of its mediations, its channeling of a "spectator consciousness," provides a counterpoint to a technology that relies on the fabrication of unmediated experience, which is to say, a technology that relies on surpassing mediation itself, via direct transmission and the absorption or assimilation of the other.

"A lot of what we're trying to do here," Mark Zuckerberg told the *Washington Post* in 2016, reflecting on the future of social media and its convergence with virtual reality (VR) not two years removed from Facebook's purchase of Oculus Rift, "is give everyone in the world the power to share exactly what they're experiencing and thinking with anyone else."[156] The framelessness of the VR apparatus collapses the signifier into the signified, representation into referent, producing a borderless worldview, a way of seeing that is an optical illusion, in every direction from which one casts their gaze: a world of one's making. For the CEO of Facebook, even language is seen as an obstacle rather than a compass for the circuitous path in which we encounter ourselves, and, moreover, the others with whom we travel. The gap between self and other, author and reader, actor and audience, is not an impediment, but as the migratory texts discussed here make clear, a precursor.

Empathy—a *feeling into* (from the German *Einfühlung*) that demands imagination, exchange, and participation—is not just a bridge but the act of walking, a traversal that is neither singular nor straightforward but constitutive of the manifold attempts to renew such a subjectivity. The work of empathy thus requires us to shift, and to mark each veer in transit—a maneuver that, not unlike translation, is never one to one, never fully capable of total restitution or replication, never capable, in the parlance of translation, of fidelity and purity, nor liable to dissolve otherness into the subject or the subject into otherness.

It is because the guest offers us the gift of narrative that we are all implicated in the story we are told and thereby also telling. As I type these words, as I transcribe my notes from months and years past, I become acquainted with Elaine K. Chang, who recounts her mother's role as storyteller, and specifically, the Korean folktale about a disobedient blue frog, which her mother regularly recited to Elaine as a child. I alight upon Elaine K. Chang's essay, "A Not-So-New Spelling of My Name: Notes

Toward (and Against) A Politics of Equivocation," whose organizing anecdote further illuminates the productive failures of translation. Years later, it becomes apparent to Elaine that the "blue frog" central to the folktale, and, moreover, central to her own childhood fascination—her identification, as a child, coded and recoded, between two cultures, with the blue frog—is in fact just her mother's misinterpretation of the English word for "green." "[S]he had not yet mastered colors in English," Chang relates, "when she first told me the story."[157] Yet Chang's anecdote reveals how misinterpretations are never *just* incidental to the production of meaning; on the contrary, each misinterpretation has the potential to enact new meanings, latent instructions-for-use that may not be legible within the time and space of the present. "The blue frog is a (by-) product of cultural and linguistic cross-fertilization," Chang explains, before applying her familial experience in and of translation to public scholarship and the production of knowledge. "Do blue frogs have a place in academic discourse?"[158]

I wonder, as I repeat Chang's question, if we might take the story of the story of the green frog that turned blue, in translation, as the real lesson of the Korean folktale about the frog who, thinking of his mother's body, cries every time it rains. Like the ever-contradictory son, who, at her death, finally heeds his mother's instructions about her burial, and, in doing so, alters her final wish, the storyteller who passes along their story—which is never only theirs—inevitably and unconsciously alters the source through the act of reception, which is never *just* reception but *another* rendering.

A related question we might pose to ourselves, as instructors and scholars, as writers and readers, is how we might further interrogate our own relationship to the transmission and safeguarding of knowledge and language—to remember that every act of sending, every correspondence, relates nothing if not an instability intrinsic to the operation; to remind ourselves, as poststructuralism[159] has reminded me, that semiosis, too, relies not on reading, but on misreading. Elsewhere, Alan Bass writes in his own translator's introduction to Jacques Derrida's *La carte postale* (*The Post Card*): "What we call a text always implies supplementary, unpayable debts."[160] But these debts are not burdens; such absences in the text are in fact spectral presences: invitations to read between the lines and across the margins. You will recall that Derrida likes post cards because of their essential reversibility, an elasticity that is somatic but also spatial: "one does not know what is in front or what is in back," Derrida writes, in Bass's translation, "here or there, near or far, the Plato or the Socrates, recto or verso."[161] But still more significant is that these distinctions no longer matter: in that radical obscurity, passage—translation as correspondence, as mobility, as anonymous encounter, both ethical and erotic—bares itself. When we return, as we will, to the question of the migratory text's function for revitalizing discussions on world literature, national literature, and the normative role of translation as both colonizer and cultural gatekeeper, I would like to think of the story of the blue frog as a parable for paying heed to our scholarship and instruction with the cross-fertilization of languages, cultures, and histories so necessary for seeing the various shades of blue in green, green in blue.

# CHAPTER THREE: ABSTRACTION. /

## DOCUMENTING DISAPPEARANCE

### *Self-Forgery and Erasure as a Means of Mobility*

> *Against Being, which asserts itself, let us show being, which attaches itself. Let us challenge both the returns of the nationalist repressed and the sterile universal peace of the Powerful. In a world where so many communities find themselves mortally denied the right to any identity, it is paradoxical to propose the imagination of an identity-relation, an identity-rhizome. I believe however that this is indeed one of the passions of these oppressed communities, to believe in this moving beyond identity and to carry it along with their sufferings.—Édouard Glissant*[1]

How to pass when nations decide to put a tariff on entry? In 2018, Moroccans spent more than $44 million on 662,586 Schengen visa applications; $8 million collected by government officials were from applicants whose visas were denied. In the early days of 2020, the price per application raised by 25 percent,[2] a filtering technique that is rooted in a larger narrative of exclusionary measures. Shortly after May of 1991, when Spain signed the Schengen Agreement and imposed an expensive visa on citizens from the Maghreb, these people—emanating from Morocco, Mali, Mauritania, and Senegal, among other countries—became burners (*herraguas*), leaving Tangiers after taking leave of themselves, or their identities, by setting their documents ablaze.[3] Unable to pay for an application and unwilling to submit to the required biometric scan, rather than risk deportation, these individuals undergo de-subjectification in so many senses of the word, abandoning their own signification as citizens within a national polity and as migrants within a human rights regime that will attempt to sort them upon arrival by becoming anyone but who they are, or were. In doing so, they become no longer subjects or objects, no longer legible except as humans.

I want to return to Edward Said and Jean Mohr's collaborative scrapbook, *After the Last Sky*, to the importance of appropriation, resignification, collage, the sometimes intentional, sometimes involuntary blurring between memory and imagination, memories and photographs; it is not just, as Said acknowledges, that in the absence of a coherent narrative from which to tell one's story, "we borrow and patch things together," but that, indeed, "[o]ver the missing 'something' are superimposed new realities."[4] This means endless improvisation and inevitable forging, this means staged testimonies and fragmentary compositions—not the overcoming of the generic and formal limitations of narrative and documentary and fiction, but, as I've shown in chapter 2, the self-reflexive acknowledgment of such parameters—when one can no longer find a place for one's self, a sense of self, a history for one's self and one's people, it must be forged. "Constructed and deconstructed," Said says, "ephemera are what we negotiate with, since we authorize no part of the world and only influence increasingly small bits of it."[5]

How can this gesture toward the "minor literatures" that Félix Guattari and Gilles Deleuze theorized, after Kafka, allow us to locate exactly such a collective enunciation—one not housed "within the terms of its [own] institutionalization," one not "profoundly individuated,"[6] but, on the contrary, an account that is unauthorized, amateur, and self-actualizing, a media that is indeed minor and thus mobile? That autofiction was first diagnosed by the French novelist and theorist Serge Doubrovsky in 1977, a year after the US-backed military coup in Argentina and at the same moment that the guest worker as a source of migrant labor intensified, along with the growth of several aid organizations tied to managing migration,[7] is not coincidental. The specific blurring between author and protagonist, and the reclaiming of the epistemological and intertextual advantages of fiction should be seen as more than an aesthetic move by literary theorists and metropolitan authors, but as a subversive detour with specific political and social aspirations by migrants and minoritized subjects. To understand the convergence of creative expression and political maneuver at the heart of this study is to read the transformation of the camp and the reimagining of collective participation as part and parcel of the transformation of the migrant as both subject and object—laborer and commodity—to an author who might reclaim their subjectivity by repurposing their objectification.

And it begins with the question of naming, the question—who are you, where are you from, where are you going?—of names. Said explains that the sudden resurgence during the Cold War of names like Abu Ammar, Abu Jihad, Abu Firas was in fact a search for an autonomous, colonially untethered Palestinian identity; "these noms de guerre," Said writes, "symbolized the act of taking possession of ourselves in *our* way [...]. The recuperation of our past by its *partial re-creation* in the present was obviously a political act."[8] This political act relies, of course, not only on partial re-creation but on the relative anonymity and collective identity that a name like Abu Ammar (father of Ammar) suggests, referencing familial history while at the same time overcoming the specificity of and allegiance to one's own inheritance and genealogy—the transformation of the present through a fabrication of one's past. When "blocks of speech," as Jacques Rancière has written, circulate "without a legitimate father," they fail, and in failing, they generate other lines, which move by fracture, toward disincorporation. Instead of the production of a polis, however, these "blocks" have the potential to produce "*imaginary* collective bodies."[9]

I would like to pursue this political characteristic of the unreal or irreal or hypostatized real, and the agency engendered by its production of unlimited options; the ability to choose. When Glissant, with whom I begin this chapter, seeks to move beyond a universal humanist vocation, what he is also after is a certain detour from the universal's opposite: to avoid the trap of a differential identity that is both oppressed and empowered as an identity of difference. But how to reclaim or reform one's subjugation, one's marginalization, without naturalizing or centering it?

We know that Odysseus calls himself *Nobody* in order to escape from Polyphemus's cave. The Cyclops, unable to identify his own detainee, or rather, only able to identify him in such a way that negates Odysseus's identity, is rendered powerless. Nobody, in this sense, makes himself visible only by absenting himself, only by becoming imperceptible: the mobilization of self-forgery. We see a parallel maneuver at work in Amitava Kumar's *Passport Photos*, a book of mixed media published in 2000 and organized, in its author's own words, as "a forged passport,"[10] an appropriation which endeavors to "restore a certain weight of experience, a stubborn density, a *life* to what we encounter in newspaper columns as abstract, often faceless, figures without histories. And, having done that, to *then* remark on the limits of even that act."[11] We see a similar undertaking in Souvankham Thammavongsa's 2007 collection *Found*, an account which begins, or ends:

> In 1978, my parents lived in building #48. Nong Khai, Thailand, a Lao refugee camp. My father kept a scrapbook filled with doodles, addresses, postage stamps, maps, measurements. He threw it out and when he did, I took it and found this.[12]

Autofiction's common and most pronounced characteristic is "the introspective preoccupation with the self, specifically the self as a writer,"[13] yet what is demonstrated through the scrapbook aesthetic of the migratory text is in fact just the opposite: a heightened preoccupation with *abandoning* the self through a strategy of superficial visibility, an attention, not to the self but to the ways in which the self becomes mediated, dispersed, and disappeared—a critical image which both enacts and interrogates the terms of its own representation. The missing, the absent, are here retrieved as *preconditions* to the production of self and story, as when, for instance, Thammavongsa, who was born in the Nong Khai camp, shows us the scrapbook's postage stamps: "What each had/carried/here/isn't here/only/the black ink/stamped/across their face"[14]—or when, an entry earlier, she describes how the recording of such material disappearances, and the gathering of their residual violence, bear the seeds of restoration:

> When bombs
> dropped

here
we buried

the dead
then took

the metal
for stilts

to lift
our homes

above
the ground[15]

As I read these lines, I am reminded of the story of migrant laborers, who, while constructing social housing complexes in Algeria and Morocco in the 1950s, would salvage, before leaving, the materials trashed at the building site to construct their own homes, replicas of state originals produced through reappropriation and renewal.[16] I am reminded, too, of an anecdote shared with me by a fellow researcher in Korea, who passed along an anecdote told to her in turn, about a Korean immigrant factory worker in the United States who, instead of giving his supervisor, line boss, or coworkers his birth or given name, provided them with the Korean word for "boss": 사장님 (*sa-jang-nim*). He never translated it for them. Whenever they called to him, whenever he was hailed, he would hear: "hey, boss." Recall Thammavongsa's own emphasis on retrieval and reclamation: "I found this." Recall, especially, the fact of the source's attempted annihilation: "He threw it out," she writes, and here we might read the degraded original as more than just personal trash but as the reinvention of Soviet and US-orchestrated violence throughout the Laotian Civil War (1959–1975), all the persons, like Thammavongsa's mother and father, who fled overland into Thailand after the fall of Long Tieng, and who, like Thammavongsa herself, found a life.

In the 2009 adaptation of *Found*, a short film directed by Paramita Nath, Thammavongsa narrates over a montage of images; photographs of people and visual re-creations of the refugee camp where she was born and the scrapbook that she'd found there intermingle.[17] And yet, Thammavongsa insists: "there are no photographs of my mother here, just her name, her real name. Her real name looks like her: quiet and reaching for my father's." A name, in this narrative and for this text, is anything other than fixed. Indeed, even as representation speaks its true form—absence—it serves as resemblance, as mute possibility, as *more than absence*, more than quiet, extending itself outward, longing for contact, for connection. "I was never given a birth certificate when I was born," Thammavongsa announces during the film's closing minutes. "It was a refugee camp and anyone born there isn't exactly staying, so you aren't recognized as a citizen."

This chapter wants to work out the act of abstraction in service of passing, the ability to stay or move. How have migrants and other displaced and internally excluded persons used both erasure and documentation in service of mobility? Following Rancière, I understand that such aesthetic acts are capable of creating "new modes of sense perception"[18] and, in doing so, produce alternative forms of political subjectivity. This shift—from sense perception to political subjectivity—necessitates another: from the binary of viewer-spectacle to the porous and interactive frame of a subject who attends to the processes of their mediation—and exposure—to the public. In this dyad, sense perception is equally dependent on the viewer *and* the subject. Not content with locating a space of resistance within certain migrant self-representations and creative practices, I also position the extraterritorial space of the camp itself, concurrently inside and outside, as a site of question and crossroads, a self-organized refuge and a paradigm for preserving invisibility and anonymity, the endeavor of becoming imperceptible. Through comparing Eastern Bloc self-portraiture prior to the fall of the Soviet Union with contemporary glitch art, I wish to demonstrate common markers across different generational fabrics—returning to the scrapbook aesthetic to attend to aspects of transmedia, self-forgery, resignification, and, moreover, the performance of documentary and the documentation of performance.

If 1989 saw the collapse of the Berlin Wall and the diffusion of democracy across Europe, then two years later, the Strait of Gibraltar became another border, a perilous, suffocating, one-way route for people—some separated only by nine miles—who could no longer travel freely to fortress Europe. The Schengen Agreement, which proposed open borders and mutual policies in the parlance of internationalism, elides other questions of mobility: open borders for whom? The discourse of transnational fluidity forgets that what a border means, and how it operates, depends on a perspective that is also shifting, unstable, and contingent upon where one is looking; from what side of its confines one approaches or from where one withdraws. And yet it is exactly this erratic aspect—the border as various and variable—that might inform the project of its circumvention by those persons the state and its homeland infrastructure refuses, or fails, to recognize. In the face of omnipresent surveillance and compulsory enrollment, I want to insist, moreover, that an aesthetics of non-legibility introduces a different articulation of the political subject and their participation in a community of others *like and unlike one another*. What is at stake is not just the ability to pass, but the possibilities and attendant challenges of redistributing power and agency within sites of cross-cultural exchange, informing extant issues of privacy but also raising questions about public space.

In conceptualizing a mobile commons and a migrant sovereignty premised on documentation, self-forgery, countersurveillance, and anonymity, it becomes imperative to parse the distinctions between *effacement* and *erasure*. In this project, what is the final reformulation of space and self? The migrant who refuses to consent to the national discourses of migration and the international framework of refugee—the narrative tropes of the (un)deserving migrant—the migrant who refuses to participate in the construction of their own debasement or celebration, is not erasing their material experience as a person displaced, exiled, or in transit, but in fact returning it to the public as a political inquiry: a critique of the system of collection, categorization, supervision, documentation, and assimilation that colludes to keep them in place. In this context, effacement becomes a visible mark, the stroke of redaction or remediation that is also a blur, and a blur that signifies the tempo of an attempted mobility. To efface is not to erase because what is made clear by these marks is the processes by which a migrant returns themselves to autonomy; this heightened transparency, I argue, is only possible through the repetition of effacement, and the imbrication of selves and artistic forms from which to re-present the individual as unnamed collective. To respond to the either/or of repatriation and naturalization is thus to be visible as something other than migrant-refugee or national citizen-subject; to efface *one's self as such* is to enact different modes of identity, which is to say different modes of appearance and presence, and ultimately, a different representation of community.

## THE EAST AND THE WEST MEETING (AGAIN)

### Romanian Surrealism, Brazilian Concretism, and the Fractured Body (as) Politic(al)

In conversation with Sylvére Lotringer in 2005, Paul Virilio explained that "[y]ou can't understand Dada or Surrealism without World War I."[19] In this way, Virilio also can't understand abstraction, as he elaborates, without war, and in particular, without death. The disappearing face, the disfigured subject, could only be, for Virilio, an expression of the war victim, which was also a representation of the war victim. Yet what Virilio's argument, in *The Accident of Art*, ignores, is the mass displacement that occurred prior to and as a result of the First World War; the migratory drift of Central European minorities following the collapse of the Austro-Hungarian Empire that converged in actual parts—myriad denationalization, and through the adoption of multiple pseudonyms—to produce the kind of abstract art Virilio and Lotringer are here attempting to theorize.

As early as 1915, Zurich became a makeshift refuge and a seat of exile for the future Dadaists, including Tristan Tzara and Marcel Janco (Romania); Hugo Ball, Emmy Hennings, Richard Huelsenbeck, and Hans Richter (Germany); and Hans Arp (Alsace). It was not just words that were being knotted together, a particular action Tzara (real name: Samuel Rosenstock) designated as his favorite method of composition,[20] but languages—a break with the grammatical and semantic fabric that joins language with a fixed visibility, a detour guided by a word's aural resonance: the suggestions provoked by the fragile and secondhand translations that get repeated, passed on, and which gather, and drop, information in the process. This transposition of reality relied on new conditions and possibilities brought by the spectator, from which "I," as Tzara has remarked, becomes the equivalent of "not-I."[21] If it's true that abstraction emerged through a global movement, I argue that the development of an avant-garde by both Eastern European minorities and colonized subjects across the Americas and Asia cannot be understood without specific attention to a mobility predicated on exchange and imitation, which made it necessary for those without papers to also abandon their names, names which cease to be proper in a moment of cultural and ethnic disintegration, of persons dislocated and interned and on the move. To seek to elucidate the possible uses and usefulness of a diasporic avant-garde for articulating experiences of displacement and denationalization, flight, refuge, and detour is also to understand such forms of artistic production—coded as "divergent," "innovative," "experimental," or otherwise—as a response to representation (nationalist markers of identity and membership as well as pure lineage) through the recombination of language and text.

In the investigation of the liminal and imitative apperceptions that can only occur through passage, perhaps there is no greater practitioner than Tzara's fellow Romanian Ghérasim Luca (born Salman Locker), poet, theorist, visual artist, whose attention to the framing and staging of bodies, and their often indecipherable movement—the passage from the whole to its kaleidoscopic pieces, the melting of subjects in a scene where bodies, or one's own body parts, inextricably converge—brings forth a ritualistic transgression toward self-effacement. In Luca's hands, or mouth, to stutter is to wend *error*'s etymological drift: to err, to wander—toward unnatural and denaturalized subjectivities, a disability that kinks, and links, alternative representational systems with alternate modes of access, inclusion, and embodied experiences.[22]

Luca's final work, the 1991 collection *La Proie s'ombre*, translated from the French a decade later by Mary Ann Caws as *Self-Shadowing Prey*, is a text that seeks to investigate the inadvertent and involuntary permissions of our physical makeup. "Madeleine" begins with this surgical focus on the body and its dynamic arrangements—"passes her right hand/under her left elbow/hides half her face/with her left hand"—before accelerating into productive ambiguity, rendering a palindromic identity that plays on the repetition, and substitution, of the subject, an expression which ultimately converts to zero: "without hands or face/arm in arm/Madeleine hides Madeleine."[23] "The Resting Whirlwind" engages a similar sleight of hand, the alchemical outcome of which depends not on perception, but what remains unseen; what *appears* to move beyond the grasp of the spectator, a choreography organized as a series of feints:

> What passes as perfectly immobile
> pushes what seems strangely mobile
> to pretend it's fixed and unmoving
>
> So what appears to stop despite everything
> passes as flitting crazily around[24]

Despite the fact that Ghérasim Luca—the name itself, chosen from an obituary notice—was born in death, his work is a continuous exploration of how one might reinvent life, and in life, love and language together, in all of their volatile and velocitized connective tissue. Born Jewish in Romania during a time of increasing antisemitism, state repression, and eventual Soviet occupation, Luca eventually escaped to Israel en route to Paris in 1952, returning to the city he had first encountered with Surrealist countryman Victor Brauner twelve years earlier. He would remain in France, an exile, stateless, victim of the nation-state, or its transgressor, until his suicide in 1994. In opposition to fluency and clarity, Luca's poetics defamiliarizes language, destabilizing a mother tongue through exophony and continuous self-refractions: language's relation to itself, its affinity for referring to its own production, a material composition accounted for through *depriving* communication—through cutting it off while at the same time repeating it.

In this practice, we should remember that a murmuration is also a collective, a swarming that signals a cooperative movement; Luca's poetics, too, must necessarily be thought of as a politics of language, a breakdown of identity toward the prismatic and de-subjectified I or eye that constitutes an a-representational reinvention of optics and anaerobics, of seeing and moving and breathing, of breathless movement. To hear Luca read his poetry is to hear this estrangement—and strangulation—of words, the bruising play of the vowels airing out through the canal of one's throat, the architecture of the esophagus, the flexion of syllables which desire flow, to squirt onto the page or through the lips, a passage predicated on the rhythm of the heart; form reinvents itself as the stutter of content, the bating, the edging of its own completion. Language faces its own reflection, which is to say language comes *face to face* with itself, death and life commingle in the breath between lips; the tongue rolls forward, the larynx opens up, the body speaks, unless it is only listening to itself: *what we say when we say* nothing. And nothing, here, is abundance, profusion, the spit that dribbles across one's cheek when one can't seem to get it out. Stuttering makes clear the words or phrases—in, on, as in, ass, pass, passing—that already live with/in Luca's "passion."[25] To stutter is to call and to call off, to gather, to retreat and advance, to suggest all.

How do Luca's close considerations of the mechanical work of the body endeavor to dodge the stable, unified, bodily self-as-subject? As he explains in the uncategorizable *Le Vampire passif*, a lyrical, theoretical, fictitious autobiography-cum-notebook, itself a product of a falsified press (Éditions de l'Oubli, or "Forgotten Editions"), published in 1945 and translated into English decades later by Krzysztof Fijałkowski: "I refuse all forms, all categories, all acts, all plans, all laws, all your castrating scents [...]."[26] This formal assertion of redaction prefigures Édouard Glissant's right to a shared obscurity, and offers us in its refusal to be singular and unilateral, "the instinctive denial that has not yet been structured into a conscious and collective refusal,"[27] as Glissant would later write in "An Exploded Discourse." It is indeed the text's preparatory nature that provides any right to a shared obscurity with the variegated rhythm of self-creation and *métissage*, the ploy or play of diversion and deconstruction, the impure opaqueness that is, as Glissant reminds us, "opposed to any pseudo-humanist attempt to reduce us to the scale of some universal model."[28]

To the extent that self-expression can herald the moment in which we break, not only with the constraints of a single language and a common way of writing, but, moreover, with the generic catalog of identification, Luca's work reminds us that these maneuvers must be continuously repeated in order to be successful, and, furthermore, that success itself depends upon a certain regimen for failure. Indeed, the enriching contradictions made possible through phonetic chance encounters, the inversion of language, or linguistic in-versions, are not just evident in Luca's stuttering lyricism, for which the tension between forgetting and repetition is both annulled and resolved, but explicitly aspired to in *The Inventor of Love*—written in Romania during the National Legionary State regime of the 1940s—in which Luca lays out, not only an alternative poetics, but an alternative mobility. "I am forced to invent a new mode of ambulation, of breathing, of being [...]," he writes, in the 2009 translation by Julian and Laura Semilian, and this reinvention is contingent upon repetition with difference. "I salute my double, my triple. I peruse myself in the mirror [...] I am indeed indiscernible."[29] If the world is to be remade, it must happen in the absolute uncertainty of sensory perception brought by the blurring of reproduction, a slurred forgery, or not at all; it is, above all, necessary to understand that what hides is also what seeks, what carries or is carried by, what evades. "Anything," Luca insists, "can occur in this world without a past, without points of reference, without knowns."[30]

While detained indefinitely in Romania during the Second World War, "lug[ging] about a disgusting and devastated figure that the house windows reflect back to me as an insult," Luca writes of his own separation, his own scattering—and those of others—about the globe. To be separated *is* to be dispersed, and thus the worst state one can find themselves in is to find *only* themselves: to be "confined and convicted, alone [...] always alone [...]."[31] To be *by* yourself is to deny, not only the companionship of others, but the prerequisite of collaboration for authorship of one's text. By contrast, Luca's cubomania collage technique, in which an image is cut into squares that are then reassembled indefinitely, further complicates the question of origin and the single source. These cubes repeat and re-form into discontinuous grids, all of which depend on chance and association, and the multiplicity of meaning embedded in what remains outside the logic of the frame, "deliberate blockages"[32] that stage an invitation for viewers *to play*, playing off our own propensity to rationalize and hypothesize. In its lure of hypnotic disorientation, in which we are asked to become both audience and author, cubomania fosters an aesthetics of arbitrary contiguousness, liberating objects from their original contexts while relishing the beauty of a body's breakdown.

To be fractured, after all, also means to be doubled. To stammer also means to start, after stopping, after starting again; stammer from the Old Norse *stama*, from the Old English *stǫmmettan*: the source of a river or stream, or an opening or fissure in the earth; to keep a course—I mean to *flow*, an outpouring that is as choreographed as it is haphazard, as discontinuous as it is persistent, a move toward forgery and self-redaction through errantry and errancy. I stutter, not out of choice but because in stuttering, my body has decided to relinquish control. The stutter, then, is both involuntary and inevitable, becoming both a repetition and a negation, an annulment and an accretion, both approximate and proximal, by the echo of my voice's rapid succession of sonic utterance: no meaning, unless it is multiple, and here, or hear, I mean self-reproduction. The encounter between language and voice, which, as Roland Barthes explains, brings forward the former's materiality, also introduces a relation that is erotic and individual. In its depth and profusion—"am I alone in perceiving it? am I hearing voices within the voice? but isn't it," Barthes asks, "the truth of the voice to be hallucinated? isn't the entire space of the voice an infinite one?"[33]—the grain abandons the subject, and its representation, which is meaning. How does this performance of self-reflexive iteration inform postwar projects that dodge the trope of fixed subjectification, where production is tied to visibility, communication, and the disciplining of control and correction?

As freedom of speech and political opposition became stifled in Brazil with the rise of fascism amid the US-assisted dictatorships of the 1960s, the torturing and disappearing of dissidents also became commonplace, a physical silencing that rematerialized in bodily disappearances. It became necessary for internally exiled poets to seek out disappearance themselves, on their terms, a crisis of the object that spurred Brazilian Concretism into literal formation, as Noigandres poets like Haroldo de Campos turned toward the silence of the text and the secret language *within* words for the means of self-expression and representation, a negotiation born from the paradoxes of everyday life in o Estados Unidos do Brasil, in which the utopic architecture of Brasilia—including the capital city's sweeping boulevards—was co-opted by the military as a simple means of control. Likewise, de Campos's poetics are scaffolded on principles of scarcity and abundance, on proximity and redundancy, on fragment and detail, on textual coincidence and architextual meticulousness, a "cosmopoetics"[34] that, as Antonio Sergio Bessa and Odile Cisneros write in their introduction to de Campos's *Novas: Selected Writings*, reimagines the model of the poem-as-constellation, to be replaced by the text-as-nebula, a nebula that must be read in its capacious expansiveness as well as through its intentional obfuscations.

De Campos's work on display in the retrospective and collected *Novas*, translated from the Portuguese in 2007 by Bessa, begins from this disidentificatory premise, substituting discursive information for the aesthetic temperatures of the text: information about structure. Thus, the goal of Brazilian Concretism is to enmesh appearance with existing form, not for the poem to convey language but for the poem to invent language. In this way, the poem is made to deconstruct in service of the semiotic self-assertion: the poem is language becomes the poem *as* language. There is no pre-text or urtext but only the imminent—which is to say hidden, nascent, emergent—charge of the signifier mutating into its signified until the two are indistinguishable. By communicating itself, Cold War Concretism becomes self-sufficient, but also and especially, self-reproducing, abandoning and accreting meaning through its arrangement on the page, the juxtaposition of words stripped of their semantic content, a juxtaposition which relies on proximity, and a proximity which relies on approximation and difference, or the occasion for comparison, coincidence. Toward the final turn of "The Essence of Omega," the mobile "car" becomes the excrement of "caca" as well as "carcass," a bodily trajectory intimated by the "assassin" running vertically down the page, cutting the verbal constellation but also unfolding it, allowing syllables stripped of their words to fan out and fatten. Elsewhere, "speech/silver" responds to "silence/gold," becoming fractions divisible only by substituting one another's variables, culminating with the "clarity" of reversibility, the alchemical turn of "silver/silence" into golden/speech."[35]

De Campos's poetry asserts its re-semblances through an experiment of curiosity and chance: *if I put one thing next to another, I can see how they might begin to merge, converse, or oppose each other; I can see what emerges.* The space between words and between letters in a word become both bridge and gap, a silence and an invitation, the cultivation of a relationship between text and reader that is as much about entropy—breakdown—as it is about harmony. But this cultivation does not begin and end in the dyadic interaction that constitutes reading; the Noigandres poets—against the oppression of an eventual twenty-one-year-long dictatorship that would become a model for other Cold

War military coups in the name of United States democracy and Latin American securitization—were also interested in the relationships words have with themselves. In moving language away from its aesthetic political function within a culture of repressive fascism, the Concretists could now mobilize these architextual associations—the found material of the text; the language that had been used against them—for other reasons. As de Campos discusses in his 1957 essay "Concrete Poetry-Language-Communication": "Learning how to see and hear structures will thus be the key to the understanding of concrete poetry. [...] This implies, obviously, in a revision of the reader's habitual semantic reactions, which are accustomed to looking in the poem for objects other than its object, to making the artwork a pre-text for meta-artistic divagations."[36]

We can see this play of pulse and tactility at work in de Campos's work written immediately after 1964, when the first of the dictatorship's authoritarian Institutional Acts, which provided legal justification for the Brazilian military's assumption of greater power, were put in place. "Tabitexto" ("stuttertext") plays on both the orality of poetry and also how we visualize words on a page, the joyous and brilliant outburst of the eye when covering or discovering a word next to another, below or above, indicated by the almost parenthetical "yes! scintillations!" which interrupts the opening line, so as to force readers into (at least) two readings: "TO LIVE this entire world is to di" and "TO LIVE this entire world is to di/scover that the [...]."[37] The stutter here, as elsewhere, both conceals meaning and opens it up, forming a relationship through abridgment and accumulation, the divagation made once again permissible within the utopic landscape of the text. In seeking out a "total communication"[38] through Ferdinand de Saussure's anagrammatic model—the acoustic image that presents itself through phonetic mimesis, a repetition of sounds whose combination imitate certain words—Brazilian Concretism enacts a convergence between objects and their associations, or recasting this in semiotics terms, forms and meaning, enabling the emergence of Roland Barthes's *signifiance* (adopted from Julia Kristeva) and its accompanying shifts in understanding. This emergence, crucially, is contingent upon partial concealment, deprivation, and distortion, the groundswell against which dis/simulation can be measured and processed.

How to empty words of their content except by turning their structures into content, so that all other verbal proximity or all approximations born from associative gestures by the reader-writer become a part of the meaning, now multiple, now intersecting and redundant, now exploding in its receptivity, its desire to take all, and to take all in. This version of Concretism, to use the example of one of de Campos's own works—"Fome de forma"—is a hunger of form through inversion and alliteration, the "tension of word-things in space-time"[39] elucidated in his 1958 "Pilot Plan for Concrete Poetry" that must be re-read on the level of internal displacement, from which de Campos and others wrote their way out, manifesting, at all times, a form of hunger, and its many modulations:

more more
less more and less
more or less no more
nor less nor more
nor less less[40]

With a verbal pattern such as this "Hunger of Form," which develops through textual disappearances, Brazilian Concretism unsettles the logic of language so as to put the unitary subject and the law of one on trial, a performed negation that can be read through Kristeva's postulation of the signifying processes of poetic language, the process, which is a movement, that "dissolves the linguistic sign and its system [that] dissolves [...] even the earliest and most solid guarantee of the unitary subject."[41] In carving a space for mobility, Haroldo de Campos's work is also a response, at once veiled and graphic, to social censorship (the unitary subject) and the stasis of meaning (the signified). Today we can see how "the right to a shared obscurity" can be used as the creation of self-expression, and to write one's word into existence is to write one's world: an aesthetics of rupture and connection, an aesthetics of disruption and intrusion, each and all at once, but more than anything else, an aesthetics of movement, to be always on the move, toward refuge and fugitiveness. And it's important to not know where. The reader, the writer. Métissage's consequences as necessarily unforeseeable: "rambling [...] [as] an absolute challenge to narrative."[42] The itinerary as a diary of itinerant passage. If we understand a "counterpoetics" as a Caribbean discourse that is instinctive and unconscious, as Glissant has clarified,[43] it is also necessarily fragmentary and recombinant, properties that inform a broader stroke of artwork produced by persons on the move during the Cold War.

Writing of the art and life of Aubrey Williams, Kobena Mercer has described the "diasporic abstractionism" by which the Guyanese artist converged postwar European abstraction with ancestralism, contemporary science with pre-Columbian symbols and imagery: a double-facing trace structure indicated by the Amerindian word *Cenote*, "imbued with the pastness of ancient petroglyphs while at the same time radiant with future pluripotentiality," which Williams used to conclude his periodization of Caribbean art.[44] At stake in these persistent investigations into the afterlife of modernity's rupture is not just a novel art form but another representation of the postcolonial condition, in which what is unrepresentable is not the same as what is nonexistent.

I want to assert that this version of the avant-garde—double-facing; drawing from the front, approaching from behind—could *only* be produced in movement, the traversal between geographies and generational epochs, where "border-crossing" serves as more than metaphor but as methodology and autobiography. Born in British Guiana, Williams eventually moved to London to live and work, while establishing studios in Jamaica, Florida, and, after its independence, in his native Guyana. As Mercer explains, in his life and work, Williams—who led the early Caribbean Artists Movement in London—not only countered the either/or of the abstract and figurative but also confronted national and nativist leanings, resisting the romanticization and exaltation of Indigenous culture within the landscape of the West Indies, while desiring to locate his own body of "the unrecoverable" through a current of Latin American art that connected North America with South America and the Caribbean. The question of "what 'Africa' stands for," as a question of representation, a question of ecological belonging and hauntological trace, a question of rupture that is not final but formative, when "aftermath" is not finite but reoccurring, is thus negotiated by Williams—as well as by those contemporaries with whom he linked his work: Roberto Matta, from Chile; Rufino Tamayo, from Mexico; Wifredo Lam, from Cuba—through reversing the logic of Western universalism: not to make everything available (that is to say: visible, sortable, graspable, consumable) but to convert the well-rehearsed historical past into the realm of the unspeakable; to silence the dominant and dominating narrative of history, as well as modernism's reification of cultural difference through primitivism, such that affective experience serves quiet contemplation in place of visual (de)termination and binary thinking. If common conceptions of *diaspora* privilege an origin—as well as an undetermined degree of distance—then what is enacted by the migratory text is not the search for source or singularity but a commitment to waystations and shared differences. What happens when we recalibrate the terms of visibility in relation to Mercer's conception of a "diasporic abstractionism" and Williams's artistic practice of an "interstitial ambiance"? What other histories emerge? What futures?

## BECOMING ANIMAL; TRANSFORMING THE GEOGRAPHY OF THE CAMP

Before Clarice Lispector took on the task of writing *crônicas* for the largest newspaper in Brazil, at around the same time that de Campos was enacting his vision for Concretism, she wrote about her fear of circulation and availability, the notion that in using words, we also lose their inherent charge. "Writing too much and too often can contaminate the word," she insisted, echoing the thoughts of Portuguese poet Fernando Pessoa, who believed that "speaking is the easiest way of becoming unknown."[45] In delaying revelation or postponing its consummation, *productive deprivation*, as I've demonstrated throughout chapter 2, heightens one's inner connection of a subject through the fact of their obscurity, their diminished presence.

In the movement between perception and imperceptibility, it follows that, only when a person has *nothing* to conceal can they be safely concealed in the refuge of self-disclosure and undiscoverability—nothing left with which to be outed—a becoming that is equal parts simulation and dissimulation, to become, as Félix Guattari and Gilles Deleuze have written, "like everybody else [...] to no longer be anybody. To paint oneself gray on gray."[46] Movements, too—recall Luca's "Madeleine," or *what passes as perfectly immobile*—might be below or above levels of perceptions; to remain clandestine, to remain protected, to remain *here*, one must necessarily remain *on the move*, in process—*en procés*, on trial, in Julia Kristeva's words—to know one's self so as to escape oneself, the form and texture of our own image, a cultural apparition that ghosts our biometric present, wherein those whose bodies do not conform are coded as *problem*.

The struggle for survival can mean the sacrifice of one's very humanity, a negotiation between the right to live and the right to be seen; for many migrants and internally excluded persons, one forbids the other. The perils of recognition are unrelenting for the refugee whose representation so often becomes monetized and mobilized, exploited, fetishized, or otherwise distorted. In the face of this, it becomes necessary to perform the alchemical oscillation between appearance and disappearance. Such are the instructions given to the narrator of Nadine Gordimer's short story "The Ultimate Safari," written during Gordimer's encounters at a Mozambique refugee camp and first published in 1989, about a young woman displaced from her village in southeast Africa. "He said," she repeats, "we must *move like animals among the animals*, away from the roads, away from the white people's camps."[47] So says her guide, echoing Deleuze and Guattari's abstract for becoming. It is no coincidence that, to reach the refugee camp—"where there were no bandits and there was food [...] such a place; away"[48]—the migrants must first pass through a popular tourist safari, a site of labor for many men in the village, a site of leisure for many travelers, "white people [who] come to stay and *look at the animals*."[49]

It is, without question, the act of *looking* that interpellates and interns the migrant. And yet in this scenario, no act of mimicry or camouflage can actualize agency for those who have been deprived of it. In imitating an animal, the displaced persons inevitably resign themselves to no longer being viewed as what they truly are, a double bind that is as much about self-effacement as it is about dissimulation: "If they saw us," the narrator makes clear, "all they could do was pretend we were not there; they had seen only animals."[50] Ultimately, the very act that protects the unprotected person—turning one's self into an animal—is also the act that precludes them from protection within a fraught framework of human rights. Consequently, the narrator's utopic aspiration of finding refuge *somewhere away* becomes consummated, at the very end, only in the regulated, degraded, circumscribed space of the camp: a whole village encased within a tent. It's the late eighties. The Eastern Bloc is about to collapse, is collapsing. Mozambique's Marxist government (and the country's recent independence) is in the process of being overthrown with the support of South Africa and its white ruling class. The tonal shift in the story's setting, from the optimism of migration to the stark grounding of detainment, reaches a crescendo in the closing page's series of dialogue, and the grandmother's responses to the documentary film crew's insistent questions:

> And what do you hope for the future?
> Nothing. I'm here.
> [...]
> But when the war is over—you won't be allowed to stay here? Don't you want to go back home?
> [...]
> There is nothing. No home.[51]

The refugee bears a trauma that can no longer exist within the state—the polis that both necessitates and requires a future—and this is because for the stateless person, there *is* no future as it is designed and designated by governing bodies, only a past, which continuously interjects in the present; one cannot even remember what one has lost, only that one has lost it. The trauma of exile and displacement is in fact this residue, which can only operate outside of the state, which can only operate outside of the state's temporal logic that insists upon a trajectory of history that is linear and progressive, a timeline that *adds up* to (without accounting for) a future that is inevitable and foreclosed. Returning to Immanuel Kant in his attempts to seek a new form of cosmopolitanism—"a new cosmo*politics*"—Jacques Derrida believed that in order to imagine a new politics of the state, it would be necessary to imagine a new city. In developing a right of asylum absent of repatriation or naturalization, he envisions a city "equipped with new rights and greater sovereignty, open[ing] up new horizons of possibility previously undreamt of by international state law," understanding that "nowadays international law is limited by treaties between sovereign states, and that not even a 'government of the world' would be capable of sorting things out."[52] In criticizing both formal legislation of and after 1951, as well as Enlightenment thinkers of the French Revolution, Derrida identifies a considerable gap in the right to asylum and its actual implementation, forcing readers to consider what it would mean to take up meaning in a system without owning, or owing, residency to it; to consider, too, that the foreigner, as a question, puts into question the state, the sovereign code, and even language, which both creates and shapes a discourse of "sorting things out." If we consider the undocumented migrant as a persistent figure of becoming by their straddling of borders and identities, by their unwillingness to submit to fixing by the state, we must also understand the undocumented migrant as becoming what refuses to be grasped: a becoming that is itself ungraspable. Becoming animal, becoming outside or beyond the liberal and limiting framework of human rights, is not just a necessary maneuver of survival; this act should also be read as a critique of the system that can only protect those humans that fall into the specific categories of exception.

In his earlier discussion in *Of Hospitality*, Derrida acknowledged that the role of master-prisoner was just as reversible as citizen-foreigner. The host becomes the hostage, the guest becomes the host, a reversibility revealed by the word's roots from Late Latin *hospes*, from which *gospodĭ* (lord, master) and *gosti* (stranger, guest, host) both derive: power dynamics between subjects that are equally obscured and reproduced within today's human rights regime. We know that through the sacrificial rite of the Eucharist the host is one that receives but also one that is received; a victim, in its Latin (*hostia*) origins, or the sacrifice itself. A host can also be a network: the manager that administers a database or a computer that controls communications within a server. To be a host means to manage or negotiate an inevitable power dynamic. And then again—the host becomes something ingested, taken in, turned into something else: no meaning except a multitude. This transubstantiation is the answer—the flesh made word—turned into a question: the refugee as calling into question the relationship of the individual to the state.

The border, too, and the very idea of the "camp" might also be transformed, so as not to succumb to it. Here we must confront the possibility of the camp, not only as a site of authority but also a crossroads of resistance and creativity. "This is the place," anthropologist Michel Agier writes, "that each displaced person seeks to recompose, with the shelter as condition of survival. [...] [T]hey represent the principle according to which it is possible to conceive a social refoundation on the basis of mobility and chaos. If the idea of the refuge could only be separated from the camp, then refuges could be considered as towns in the making."[53] Agier's fieldnotes in 2008 on self-organized camps are especially useful in questioning the ability, and willingness, of citizen-subjects to surrender themselves to a space—social, cultural, communal—outside the constraints of the state. These spaces, as being-between-borders, might become grounds of resistance within the state and cities of true refuge—cities that act to preserve autonomy and anonymity. "The survival communities may all be different," Agier continues, "but they tend towards the formation of *communities without identity*."[54] And yet, to mobilize the local is also to respond to the totalizing project of the universal; to resist the locus of the nation-state *and* the international is to probe a form of refuge and asylum that is tethered neither to repatriation nor naturalization. If resistance takes the form of a return, such emergent encampments remember an ontology that is ante-capitalist, ante-modernist: a subject not beholden to the inclusionary disciplining (the disciplining of inclusion) of formal and formative membership.

What does it mean, in the context of alternating currents of colonialism, racism, fetishism, and dehumanization, to take on the animality that has been projected onto one? To *become the animal*, which is to say: to become lower than the citizen-subject and also higher, because by being lower than, by bending down, by walking on all fours, one becomes no longer an object but an animal like and unlike the gawking tourists, like and unlike the predatory bandits and military police, like and unlike those citizen-subjects (all spectators, all witnesses), because by becoming animal, one is no longer subject to the authority of empire, the violence and atrocity of war.

Becoming, I want to make clear, is not about arrival but rather the interstitial awareness of a not-yet that evades—exceeds—finitude: to surpass something through a lack, which isn't a lack at all but a gift (dislocation, threshold, the freedom of insecurity). In this encounter, one becomes neither subject *nor* object; similarly, this imitative act is not just performative but stridently political. In silence, the one who has been dispossessed of humanity speaks. Yet it is only by showing one's self in full view that one can remain unmarked. It is only by marking one's self with the characteristics of another that one can remain illegible. And it is only through this certain illegibility that one can reconstitute one's self as sovereign. I contend that the fugitives of Nadine Gordimer's "The Ultimate Safari," in their migration across territories both corporate and national, seek more than material refuge. Their flight is also about transcending the universal and national subjectivities that have attempted, in so many ways, to seize them.

What if the camp became a place where the present was held, so that it could be reimagined? What if the camp itself could be reimagined, not only as a site of security and incarceration, but as a zone of social intercourse and refuge, interactions that revise governing practices of identification and enrollment? Cannelle Gueguen-Teil and Irit Katz's analysis of the makeshift camps constituting the Calais Jungle demonstrates how, before its demolishment in October 2016, the Jungle's inhabitants—who described themselves as both "guides" and "citizens"—generated a certain approach to appropriating space based on belonging, hospitality, and learning, a form of unstructured and informal self-development which included the refugee-run Ecole Laïque du Chemin des Dunes in 2015.[55] I want to emphasize that these often overlooked creative practices and the possibilities they produced emerged as a specific response to the camp's restrictive policies and deplorable conditions; instead of countering their reality by opposing it, these "citizens" fostered their own mobility by reorganizing the space to which they'd been relegated, a radical revision that did not reproduce social and political norms but, in contradistinction, subverted them from the inside.

"Democracy," as Gayatri Spivak has said, "must have an abstract subject [...] a position without identity."[56] And this is because in order to fulfill the promises of equality suggested by the *dêmos*, it is equally necessary that democracy's constituents move beyond the metrics of the individual-as-subject while speaking for none other than one's self, revealing, in turn, how fraught singular and static foundations of both space and self are. I want us to observe these same relational characteristics of subject-identity formation—moments in which self, other, connection, experience, and agency constellate and refract—on the improvisational grounds of the camp.

From 2015 to 2017, a timeframe that parallels the response provoked by Calais's makeshift camps to the city's isolated formal container camp, nineteen centers situated in key locations along the Balkan Route emerged. The proliferation of these provisional camps can be linked to the reluctance—the refusal—of migrants to become formally registered and incorporated into the Serbian hospitality system, a processing which would increase the likelihood of their transfer to camps away from the borders of the countries to which they aspire to pass through. These "open camps" become, not sites of identification and collection, but, as Claudio Minca, Danica Šantić, and Dragan Umek have described: "accidentally [...] temporary destination[s]" and "unplanned waiting area[s]," in which persons are allowed to enter and leave with no fundamental restrictions. The Balkan region as a whole transforms into "a grand informal route, with endless ramifications, walls-and-holes, entry points, borders, and mobile unregistered bodies."[57] The camp's function is not incorporation; it is, on the contrary, to produce a geography of mobility.

We know that when the largest makeshift refugee camp in Europe was dismantled by Greek police, on May 24, 2016, 75 percent of the Idomeni camp's total population—an estimated 14,000 people—disappeared from all legal framework, refusing their relocation and registration at formal institutional camps elsewhere in Greece to remain nameless subjects on the move, to find or forge a mobile, spontaneous, ephemeral, and unstable landscape, taking refuge but also transforming space in previously abandoned sites. This was the case, months later, when volunteer-run Baobab Experience workers helped migrants turn an alleyway near the Tiburtina train station into an open-air community center and shelter. In the municipality of Rome, under Italian law, there is only an "asylum seeker" or a "clandestine," an illegal migrant. There are no transitory migrants. There is no in between, only either; only or. There is no language, under the law, to articulate these persons, literally unidentified until becoming known, at the same time as Baobab's emergence, as "*transitanti*": persons who manage to avoid being fingerprinted after their rescue from sea or their arrival at reception centers and who, resolutely, are passing through, seeking hospitality elsewhere, or with no intention to settle into permanent residency within the nation, a break between the false equivalence of arrival and assimilation that is consecrated in language. What we are considering here is nothing less than a form of mobility that must be invented through the body that would otherwise contain or restrict. Baobab's makeshift camp—first located in Via Cupa, and after police disbanded it and arrested the inhabitants for identification processing in September of 2016, reorganized on a small square behind Tiburtina station—remains a useful case study for theorizing the camp as a site of critique and contestation, an ephemeral and yet highly visible, accessible, public rendezvous that converges stateless and citizens, unprotected and minoritized subjects.

Rome, situated halfway between southern and northern Italy, has long been a hub for migrants moving between Africa or West Asia and Northern Europe, while at the same time serving as an enduring settlement for the Roma community dispersed throughout Western Europe. The Romani people,[58] who have never claimed the right to national sovereignty in any of the lands where they reside, and whose ideal of freedom is expressed by having no ties to a homeland, nevertheless saw the *transitanti* occupying the Tiburtina train station in 2016 as a threat to their continual existence on the fringes of Italian society. An explanation provided by one Romani woman reveals the ways in which minoritized populations subjugate one another by reproducing the segregationist tactics, exclusionary rhetoric, and contagion insecurities of the state:

> The last time they stayed here, the police cleared their camp, and we were forced to leave, too. We don't want to be kicked out again. We don't want their diseases. Their children are sick, and they are dirty. We keep it all clean here, look at the floor [...].[59]

Nevertheless, rather than remain unseen or unseeable, the persons living and creating in Baobab's open-air camp, became, along with Baobab's volunteer staff, increasingly visible, vocal, and political, organizing rallies and speeches to advocate for hospitality and state-administered housing, long absent in various cities across Italy, including Rome. The camp's eventual political action, its conversion from community center to center of critique, can be tied to a specific solidarity that I would like to linger on, a combination of care and protest, a care for life that surpasses ethnic, national, and social allegiances. This identification with the other that goes beyond any identifying markers, or identity politics, might provide a theoretical foundation and a foundational practice for just the kind of subject-less democracy Spivak described in her keynote address referenced above. It is not just that the migrant, as both storyteller and translator, is inherently a hybrid being—a being between temporal, spatial, and narratorial borders, as I've outlined throughout this study—but that the camp, too, generates the possibilities for cross-pollination and hybrid exchange, a collaboration that resists the reproduction of "any socio-spatial form," in Agier's words, "that already exists"[60] through the appropriation of space within an indefinite temporality.

The stateless person who remains uncategorizable is not just unrecognizable but illegible; assimilation into a nation-state requires both a visibility and legibility that is at odds with one's refusal to be marked, to be coded, to be categorized and counted. My fieldwork in Berlin at the largest queer refugee center in the world reminds me that closer attention to queer migration and the queer migrant is instructive for any aspiration of an alternative paradigm of appearance; of being simultaneously perceptible and imperceptible. One Schwulenberatung resident, twice deported (from different countries) and, at the time of our conversation, awaiting a temporary German work permit, describes not only their continuous shifts in name and birthplace—ethnicity, race—but also their gender, enacting a liminal mutability that has allowed them to remake the terms of identification in sites of catalog and collection. These persistent acts testify to the shifting location of an identity in motion, a fungibility and fugitivity that moves beyond the self-evident acknowledgment that we may not be the same person in different spaces. This becoming—not, as Deleuze and Guattari had theorized, an extraordinary phenomenon but, in contradistinction, an everyday occurrence—has the potential to be both infinite and unassimilable. Read in the context of migration, we can understand the processual act as constituting a refusal to be recognized and reified within the normative values of citizenship, not by resisting but by *reworking* the conditions of recognition.

Fugitivity—not to be conflated with "passing," which C. Riley Snorton has identified as a form of agency premised on the "promise of restoration" to "a natural-cum-biological mode of being"[61]—is a performance *for* freedom, capable of mapping the affective terrain for other mobilities. Such are the fugitive maneuvers for persons who have been marked for captivity and thus been made capable of changing form, from person to property, from man to woman, a condition of possibility that revises binary systems of gender and racial classification and which, as Snorton has shown in his 2017 study, *Black on Both Sides*, is inherently revisable within Blackness. I want to continue to insist that such alternative and indeterminate mobilities remain contingent upon an evasion that specifically escapes clarity. Speaking of the relations between Blackness and transness, and informed by Guattari's "transversality" as an aesthetic, ethical, and political operation that brings together disparate forces through crafting, shifting, and relating, Snorton explores how race and gender, *under* captivity, articulate "submerged forms of relationalities that *need not be visible* to have effects."[62] The potential for such an alternative politics—one that does not direct itself toward a planning for the future but a tending to each other in the present, that form of solidarity situated in a care for life—can be read alongside Karma R. Chávez's 2013 investigation into a queer migration politics, in which "queerness" is linked with "coalition": the moment in which "distinction between entities blends and blurs"—that moment that resists "permanent incorporation into one body."[63] If *passing* can indeed be read as a restoration, then we might read *fugitivity* in this context as a resistance: not only a reimagining of the normative system and logic of race and gender, but also as a reimagining of the terms of belonging and community—to flee citizenship so as to reinvent it.

Reworking the conditions of recognition—scopic, civic—requires us to continue probing the efficacy of translation, not as a form of cultural imperialism or the accumulation of literary resources through importation but, on the contrary, as a mode that exceeds the parameters of the territorial and the individual. Jean-Luc Nancy's attempts to reorient community, to reorient the social and the individual by releasing each from the "indeterminate multiplication of centripetal meanings, meanings closed in on themselves and supersaturated with significance,"[64] inform translation as an ethos and a praxis—to be together in difference as a mode of address *and* a way of thinking—in which the refusal to begin with absolute opposition (the division between self and other) and its enclosure paves the way for a thinking and a feeling that is shared, meaning that can only ever be on behalf of and in the presence of another: mutual exposure. Even more potent, however, are the moments in which "connection" falters; when connection falls short, to the extent that everything that passes between us performs as an operation of distension, a stretching out that interlaces differences even as it preserves singularities. True contact, Nancy insists, "is beyond fullness and emptiness, beyond connection and disconnection."[65]

As we have already observed throughout this study, the process of translation as a collaboration premised on co-incidence and copresence, on imbrication and interaction, a togetherness that is kin to the anonymous, moves not by continuity, but contiguity, where touch is not nearly or never penetration but simply the failure to consume fully; to be in touch with another, to touch one another, is to acknowledge this shared separation, an unknowability (or better, untranslatability) and the urge for nearness, which is intimacy. The point is not to find one's self in another through the production of love or language and literature, but to *lose one's self*. This is why the untranslatable begets translation as a point of disconnective contact: an endeavor to record the sensation of each caress, the friction of touch which can also be the failure to render, the inability to convert, to assimilate all the way. This is why translation can be its own resistance. To resist the terms of translation in its most normative framework means to reconceptualize the role and function of the translator, which necessitates, of course, reimagining the work itself. To be born in translation, as the migratory text has instructed us, is to be born illegal—illegitimate, unauthorized and unauthored, if *to author* is construed as a solitary and finite activity—where birth puts into question not the subject, but the law.

## IMPERSONATION AS A MEANS OF DESUBJECTIFICATION

The nameless narrator of Anna Seghers's autobiographical novel *Transit* wants only to remain where he is. He can only do so by displacing himself, by becoming someone else. To escape Paris, he assumes the identity of another refugee, Seidler, who is mistaken, in Marseilles, as the nom de plume of Weidel, an author who has, unbeknownst to everyone else besides the narrator, committed suicide. Death, in this scenario, presents new opportunities for reorganizing life; it is not just that the dead ghost us, the living, but as I've argued across chapter 1's evaluation of the form and function of the notebook as correspondence, that the living can also ghost the dead.

Completed in 1942, when its German-Jewish author, born Netty Reiling, had made her own escape from Paris to Marseilles en route to Mexico, aboard the same ship that included André Breton and Claude Lévi-Strauss, *Transit* informs a proximity between the interwar period and today's mass statelessness[66] while provoking us to think about impersonation as a means of desubjectification. The haphazard and bureaucratic management of movement is illuminated by the paradoxical "transit visa" of the book's title: a piece of paper that grants permission to travel through a country, *under the condition that the person plans to keep moving*. And yet any documentation that makes mobility possible also produces the power of its denial. "It has nothing to do with World Order, the old one. It is a kind of control," one aspiring visa applicant tells the narrator. "The Germans are not going to miss the chance to thoroughly control and check all people leaving Europe."[67] The man speaking, an orchestra conductor, already has a work contract in Caracas, "and because of the work contract, a visa, and because of the visa, a transit visa, but it took so long for the exit visa to be issued that the transit visa expired in the meantime, and after that the visa and after that the contract."[68]

The act of transit, today as well as in 1939, requires a complex network of prerequisites contingent upon the authority and authorization of others, the manufacturing of a certain form of power doled out as duration. The physical manipulation of time serves as a form of psychic torture. And Marseilles, indeed, is here depicted as "the last of all the waiting rooms,"[69] the last waiting room in a world that has nearly had its final appointment, and gone under. The absurdity of running in circles is not lost on any of the characters occupying this Greek-like tragedy, in which everyone is at the whim of a conditional, mercurial hospitality. "That's right," a doctor tells the narrator, amid the confusion of visa applications, between places and proper names, amid the conflation between staying and leaving, exit and arrival, "I think it's all a lot of nonsense—exchanging one burning city for another burning city, switching from one lifeboat to another in the middle of the bottomless sea."[70]

If Marseilles does in fact represent the "last home for people" without a home, "a last refuge on this continent" separated from "the first gleam of the African world on its white southern walls,"[71] Seghers's point, perhaps, is that it is Western civilization, its wholesale management of minority populations, which allows dehumanization on the global scale to flourish. Is it any wonder that the difference between sorting one's self and killing one's self is only two letters in French? *Je me tue et je me trie*. Organization, denaturalization, exportation: the production of displacement, and, moreover, the desire to manage a space without movement. "All discussion about the refugee problems revolved around this one question," Hannah Arendt remarked in 1951's *Origin of Totalitarianism*, "how can the refugee be made deportable again? The second World War and the DP camps were not necessary to show that the only practical substitute for a nonexistent homeland was an internment camp. Indeed, as early as the thirties this was the only 'country' the world had to offer the stateless."[72] Years later, the upshot of all capitalist distribution is exactly refuse and refusal: material waste and wasted humans, persons reprocessed as labor or commodity.

And yet, as Western Europe was being remade into a hell by the advancing Germans and the complicity of the French government against its own people, Marseilles could be thought of as a purgatory populated by persons who have been divested of proper names—the conductor, the doctor, the Corsican, the Legionnaire—as well as authentic selves, dissimulating in a desperate attempt to pass and so be passed on:

> She carefully typed out my answers, all the facts of my past, my goal in life. [...] All the details were in order. What did it matter that the entire thing wasn't true? All the subtleties were there, giving a clear picture of the man who was to be given permission to leave. Only the man himself wasn't there.[73]

What is a greater disguise than hiding under the false appearance of the no longer living? It is only by absenting himself that *Transit*'s narrator can present the paperwork necessary to stay, a temporary disappearance toward ultimate dispersion, evidence not only of the ability to pass, but to transfer oneself: self-transformation through imitation and a radical revision. This moment cannot be read as mere plot point but in fact as a disruption of the politics of representation, and, specifically, a visibility through invisibility, an act which is inherently aesthetic, because it is about looking, about a perceptibility and a consciousness contingent upon appearance, upon an approach that probes its own effects upon a normalizing gaze. Is it any wonder that the only moment in which the nameless narrator can recognize *himself* is when he begins to read the unfinished manuscript inside the briefcase of the man whose identity he assumes? Within this found and fictional narrative, the refugee refuses affiliations both national and filial, recognizing, instead, as he continues to read, "that *this* was my own language, my mother tongue, and it flowed into me like milk into a baby."[74]

And thus Marseilles as waiting room, as site of indefinite detention, also underscores its function as a stage for storytelling. After all, as one character tells another, during the text's own adaptation: "Marseilles is a port. Everyone has the right to tell their story. And be listened to."[75] In the 2018 film, directed by Christian Petzold, the protagonist (here named Georg) and his failure to both integrate into the local community and actualize his own self-identity is contrasted, in the end, by his ascension to the role of anonymous storyteller, who tells his story to the bartender—another person unnamed—from whose mouth we hear the story (of the story) unfold. In passing on his story, which isn't his, to a community of listeners within the diegetic space—the bartender's café, the hearth of the kitchen's pizza oven (a commonplace, if not classical site from which to kindle a chronicle)—we, too, become implicated in the events from which these intertextual stories derive, each of us a witness and an accomplice to the knitted rhythm of history, from which "destiny" is no longer or never solitary but collective. Just as Anna Seghers' novel—written in German but originally published in English—had to be born in translation, so too did Petzold's film adaptation require the repeated staging of mediation in order to tell its transgenerational story.

In an interview, Petzold described the experience of adapting the book to the screen as a procedure of memory, or forgetting. "[W]ith *Transit*

I wrote down what I could remember from the book, what was important to me, without reading Anna Seghers's work again."[76] Indeed, the film moves with the muted stillness and gauzy vision of a dream, an impression heightened by Petzold's use of long takes, his absence of establishing shots, both of which magnify Georg's drift, his wandering and idleness, the vastness, and waste, of bureaucratic paperwork, our protagonist literally retracing another's steps, or only walking in circles: a rehearsal for a transit that never comes. Years ago, Polish exile Zygmunt Bauman suggested that "the meaning of the 'underclass identity,'" speaking about the class of people—the stateless, "the non-territorials"—who are denied the right to claim an identity different from the one they have been ascribed, "is an *absence of identity*; the effacement or denial of individuality, of 'face'."[77] Such persons, Bauman wrote, are denied the right to a physical presence, "except in specially designed 'non-places'."[78] How else might we characterize the sets of *Transit*—both film and book—except as a series of "specially designed 'non-places'"—modernity's liminal zones: the space of the traveler, of haste and waiting, cafés, trains, freight cars, hotels, consulates, the waiting rooms of conditional hospitality, in which interactions are as myriad and ephemeral as identities.

It is exactly this voided sense of self—to be made illegal; the fact of one's inability to be anything (other than who they are)—that invites reader-viewers to empathize with *Transit*'s protagonist, an empathy rooted in imagination and resemblance: To be nothing is also to be *like anyone*. Georg (played by German actor Franz Rogowski), who speaks French with a German accent, is coded as an outsider from the film's opening scene. Such is the plight of the foreigner, or *l'étranger*, signaling both stranger *and* foreigner in the French that Georg has adopted or has had imposed on him, the plight of the foreigner who, as Derrida knew well, always "has to ask for hospitality in a language which by definition is not his own [...]."[79] Because he understood that hospitality is not individual so much as ancestral—given on the conditions of one's proper name, the basis of family or filial fidelity—Derrida knew that unconditional hospitality required moving beyond identification, toward the non-legible or non-linguistic, toward murmur, toward silence: the right to a consensual opacity.

When he first paces Marseilles' le Panier, Georg is shown to viewers via surveillance footage; we are reminded of his status as illegal and of the state's securitizing gaze, but also of the film's intermixing of technologies from vastly different periods. No cell phones, laptops, or even digital cameras are shown throughout *Transit*'s 102 minutes. Halfway through, Georg, a self-taught technician, repairs his young friend's transistor radio through a complicated procedure involving a spoon, a lit candle, a screwdriver, and a pair of scissors. Viewers are asked to consider the slippage on screen within our larger cultural narrative of historical silences: This world resembles our own—the world of the Second World War, or the atrocities it endured and oversaw, are still happening. In the film, twenty-first-century clothing, cars, and cops serve as props for a vaguely historical plot involving the sealing off of Paris and the city's escalating occupation by German forces. The first sounds we hear, in fact, are police sirens. Our protagonist encounters another man at a bar who mentions his danger visa: "a visa," he describes, "for people in great jeopardy. They're building camps in Aix and Cassis," he explains, as more sirens blare in the background. "The cleaning will begin." "Your papers," a French-speaking, heavily uniformed, automatic rifle-clad officer demands in the next scene, grabbing Georg from behind, between discussions of mandatory alien registrations. The "occupation" is suggested; people are shown informing on their neighbors. "They've set up camp at the Vélodrome," a friend tells Georg as he returns to the Paris apartment that he shares with another family, having narrowly escaped the police. "They're scouring the district. They call it 'Spring Cleaning.'"

Such pedestrian conversations remind viewers that we may be out of place, or out of time, but that the alternative dimension of *Transit* is, not unlike the experience of déjà vu: unrecognizable and yet entirely familiar. Was it that long ago when France was rounding up its own citizens in football stadiums? Two years after the conversion of the first of fifteen occupation camps across the Occupied Zone, the French police conducted a mass arrest of Parisian Jews in a procedure called Opération Vent Printanier (Operation Spring Breeze). After being taken to the Vélodrome d'Hiver, an indoor bicycle racing cycle track and stadium located near the Eiffel Tower, almost 14,000 persons were deported on July 16, 1942, to Auschwitz. Or less than two decades later, when several hundred Algerians were sent to detention centers throughout Paris, while others were beaten by French police on the streets of the City of Lights before being thrown to their deaths in the Seine. When Georg arrives safely in Marseilles, stowed in the shipping compartment of a freight train, it is not coincidental that he befriends another pair of illegals: a mother and son who had emigrated to France, we learn, from the Maghreb. History is revealed to be a nightmare, linearity its great catastrophe.

How to relate generational trauma, cultural amnesia, and the bigotry of both institutional classifications of migrancy and liberal humanist ideas about "refugees worthy of our protection," except through bringing viewers closer to our present moment by manufacturing distance? Whereas the novel relies on the trope of impersonation—a survival tactic premised on misidentification—the film adds the conceit of mistaking the historical past as static and immutable. The anomalous setting's "shock value" relies on the audience's ability to identify, if not the film's source material, then the genocides of the twentieth century; to connect the events leading up to and extending past the Second World War with today's conditions of drift and dispersal, the largest human displacement since the interwar era.

When Georg, traveling under the identity of the dead writer Weidel, is interviewed during his many meetings with various consuls, he is accused of writing an article for a communist newspaper. In another critical revision of the novel, Petzold updates the original scene's reference to the Spanish Civil War's Badajoz massacre to redirect our attention to the CIA-supported shooting of unionists in Almería, the Spanish district dubbed "El mar de plástico" (the sea of plastic), today responsible for Europe's largest production of fruits and vegetables, a site of transnational and temporary low-paid and dangerous labor by Moroccan migrant workers.

The "migrant crisis," so often magnified—brought closer, dramatized—and, alternately, truncated—distanced, distorted—on our touchscreens, is shown here to be the product of various and mutually constitutive processes involving national and international polities, technical system and software designers, manufacturers, distributors, retail conglomerates, local markets, and consumers. As we've already acknowledged, borders have expanded and also vanished, receding into digital infrastructures of arrest and detainment, the invisible and algorithmic violence of biometrics. Georg, too, who performs in Petzold's adaptation as both character and storyteller, frequently melts the divisions between the event of narration and the narrative event. When he arrives at a hotel in Paris at the film's opening, tasked with delivering a letter to Weidel, he sees the days-old blood of the dead writer he will soon become sprayed across the bathtub. Before he exits with Weidel's passport, his gaze catches a manuscript on the table. "Die Entronnenen" (The Escaped), announces the underlined title. Yet as the camera lingers on his fingers, as he gradually flips the pages, viewers familiar with Seghers's novel notice that "Die Entronnenen" is in fact the film's source material, *Transit*, remediated here and typeset in Seghers's native German: "Die 'Montréal' soll untergeganen sein zwischen Dakar und Martinique," reads the first line. (They're saying that the *Montréal* went down between Dakar and Martinique.) The *Montréal*, of course, is the same ship that Georg, in the film's finale, will attempt to board, before abandoning all plans for escape. He is reading his own story—a what-if future—a present found and then forged, or vice versa.

In the film's closing moments, Georg leaves the bartender the manuscript he'd retrieved back in Paris—instructions for adaptation of the story they've each entered, or produced—as Walter Benjamin once did, passing off his seminal "Theses on the Philosophy of History" to Hannah Arendt, who brought it in her baggage when she herself passed through Provence and into Portbou, months after Benjamin died. As if to punctuate the film's leitmotif of immobility, "Road to Nowhere" by Talking Heads heralds the closing credits, consummating a mostly muted movie with David Byrne's strident croon, but not before Georg looks up one last time from his seat at the bar, at someone unseen, someone unshown: us. The migrant, the displaced, the stateless, the exiled, the absolute other is the body subject to omnipresent surveillance and utter abandonment. In beginning, and ending, on the gaze, we, too, take up the experience of the film's protagonist—arrested, unsettled—we are forced, not *only* to look but to *look back*, to become aware of our own complicity, and complacency, of watching.

Anna Seghers, whose mother died in a concentration camp in Poland, was arrested by the Gestapo in 1933 for being a Communist and chose, instead, to live in exile in Paris before fleeing to Marseilles. Like her book's protagonist, Seghers was able to escape Gestapo officers, who were searching for her in Paris under her pen name. Although she was denied temporary entry into the United States in 1941 at Ellis Island, she later secured her exit visa, and finally, the transit visa her narrator never could—by using her husband's last name, Radvanzi—remaining in Mexico until returning to a fragmented Germany in 1947, ultimately choosing to defect to the German Democratic Republic (GDR), where she would remain until her death in East Berlin, six years before the Walls fell. As she writes in her later autobiographical novel *Crossing*,[80] translated from the German by Douglas Irving: "There's nothing like departure. No arrival, no reunion."[81] To privilege departure—and to resist reunion, repatriation—is to understand that dispersal allows a person to leave a part of the earth, and themselves, behind, a material loss that can only be reconstituted in fiction, or rather its transformation of the facts, a self-production meant to be transmitted:

> *Why does Triebel tell me such a thing?* I asked myself. And at the same time I thought of the answer: *because he wouldn't tell it anywhere else but here on the ship.* Then I thought again: *It's quiet all around us. Triebel needs this place. You need a place, in order to tell a person everything.*[82]

Everything told to us in *Crossing* is told to us in secondhand, sometimes even through a more distant frame—as when, for instance, Triebel relates the specific contents of another character's letters to the narrator; the "I" here becomes disintegrated and multiplied, and the narrator, if there is in fact a stable narrator, performs as audience member. The audience, in this sense, serves as more than witness or recorder, but shapes the direction of the story being told. Between the storyteller and the listener is in fact this third voice of the ship's other passengers, all those who are responsible for relating or revealing the mediations of storytelling, the rhizomatic crossing between departure and arrival. "The passengers," the narrator explains, "looked out for Triebel and me. [...] It was apparent that Triebel's talking and my listening had become an integral part of the crossing for them."[83] The *form* of itinerancy—the ship; the boat; the mobile, slippery surface—creates the *occasion* for the collaborative writing act. The migratory text here becomes both occasional and an occasion, denoted and determined by the common time stamp of a correspondence or a journal entry, by the date of one's voyage in relation to its trajectory. *Occasion* suggests the instantiation of presence (time, space) but also a need (futurity) fulfilled by its own usage as verb (to bring about, to happen); and yet, *occasion* also connotes accident and haphazard transmission, a now and then discontinuity that elides standardization and routine, the habitual and predetermined reproduction of what one already knows in advance. The *occasion* thus performs as an unstable site of unforeseen eventuality, both undetermined and inevitable as a ritual of self-inscription in departure, which is both an act of leaving and an act of turning away, the failure to follow a normative or original course. If the storyteller needs a *place* in order to tell their story, then the migratory text requires that it be marked by exactly this ambiguous, mobile, and shifting landscape.

Today the institutional camp and the city have in some respects become indistinguishable, the former melting into the latter in the form of formerly abandoned sites of transport and militarization, like Berlin's Tempelhof camp, the Nazi-built airport that became a center of containment in 2015, and which, at its peak, held nearly three thousand migrants. Six years earlier, the UNHCR estimated that about 60 percent of the world's displaced population lived in urban areas. That number has only risen today,[84] a statistic informed by the increasingly common disassembly of community centers like Rome's Baobab or Calais's Ecole Laïque du Chemin des Dunes, and the identification and deportation of its residents, an intensification of local police presence that parallels a surge in national securitization and border control, and, ultimately, the many ways in which migrants have been able to evade their own recognition as categories to be contained.

The vast majority of today's institutional refugee camps are overseen by a combination of government agencies, military personnel and police, and international humanitarian aid organizations, a complex for population management that Kelly Oliver has called "carceral humanitarianism."[85] Under this regime, there is little difference between rescue and restrain, when, once rescued, migrants are identified, sorted, surveilled, and indefinitely immobilized.[86] Against a growing anti-immigration agenda and the rise of populist right-wing governments across the West, the ability to move requires, not surrender or admission, but, on the contrary, the insistence to be someone other than what—or who—one is.

Is that not, after all, an impetus for migration? The ability to imagine something beyond one's own conditions: another life, on the other side of this one. "The image, the imagined, the imaginary," Arjun Appadurai writes, "these are all terms which direct us to something critical and new in global cultural processes: *the imagination as a social practice*."[87] As Appadurai, in 1990, distinguishes the imaginary from "mere fantasy," "simple escape," and "elite pastime," I would like to recall the form of work that the imaginary engenders as a locus connecting other agential practices, including ones that harness autobiographical subjectivity and its psychic, temporal, spatial, and material dimensions. Far from moving beyond our fantasies and elite pastimes, I see these acts of autobiographical imaginary as utilizing both, and, in doing so, to radically revise the parameters and power structures of the documentary and, more broadly, documentation.

Edward Said's "Reflections on Exile," and in particular, his contention that the experience of exile risks in some way becoming trivialized—and monetized—into a genre through the "literature of exile,"[88] are useful in questioning and critiquing the reader-viewer's role in undermining a possible politics of the refugee via our willingness to bow down to its representation. What is at stake here is more than just mapping one's territory of experience but learning to read one's history, and in learning to read one's history, resolving, as James Baldwin wrote, to step out of the book.[89] At the heart of this endeavor is the ethical question of the role of the artist and the function of artistic production in a time of war; to move beyond the binary of human commitment or creative expression, the political question of poetry and its confusion, as Mahmoud Darwish has written, with the documentarian "notion of event."[90]

Darwish's non-narrative, dialogic, interstitial, hallucinatory, and granular *Memory for Forgetfulness* is one such response to the literature of exile and the commodification and fetishization of the refugee. More specifically, *Memory for Forgetfulness*, which Darwish wrote in a three-month trance shortly after the siege of Beirut and the invasion of southern Lebanon by Israel in 1982, is a response to "that traditional poetry [which] should know to hold its humble silence in the presence of this newborn"[91]—another form of remembering, of representation. "Yes," Darwish attests, embedding his own editorial published in *Al Karmel* in the midst of 1982's cataclysm, "there is a role for literature, and severing the relationship between the text and those for whom it is transformed into power is the very alienation of letters which the prophets of the final defeat of everything are now extolling."[92] For Darwish, as for other unprotected and exiled persons, there is a discovery in defeat, the beginnings of an approach born out of divestment, dispersal, and in that hole that signals not only absence but an opening: a political subjectivity that flees the polis, a newborn poetics as a form of refuge, the fugal text as migratory. Even as the state inspires writing as a statement of record, even as the revolution insists upon a "direct, daily service to the political program," even as the counter party proposes a depoliticized "pure literature" to divorce reality from literary expression, the new poetry Darwish conjures within the contrapuntal *Memory* must evade the state and its compulsion for power, control, and stewardship; it must evade, too, the public and its craving for familiar lexicons of resistance, facialized symbols of revolution that fall prey to their own celebrification; heroic modes of the lyric and the complacency carried by an unheeding art.[93] But how to evade a surveillant state and a culture of self-surveillance, a world multiplied by and reduced to screens, and their soporific audiences, their voyeuristic producers?

In a long sequence arranged by the repetition and invocation of "Video. [...] Video. [...] Video. [...]" extending across several pages, Darwish's winding, recitative prose, translated into English by Ibrahim Muhawi over a decade after its original publication, compels readers to consider the many different ways the exile's territory of experience "has been transformed from a homeland into a slogan, not for action but for use as a tool to make statements about events and to embellish the discourse of the coup d'état industry."[94] "Is there anything more cruel than this absence," Darwish asks, "that you should not be the one to celebrate your victory or the one to lament your defeat? That you should stay offstage and not make an entrance except as a subject for others to take up and interpret."[95] In this and all scenarios, Beirut and the refugees contained within the invaded and occupied city have become merely a text co-opted by various producers. And so it is impossible to read *Memory for Forgetfulness* without thinking of the conditioning of Beirut as a stage set dually refashioned by both Arab allies and the West; it is impossible to read *Memory for Forgetfulness* and Darwish's intentional merging of the observations of the present, memories of the past, and unceasing fantasies of a future outside the frame without remembering that the audience for this re/presentation of refugee generation is not, in fact, those under siege in war-torn Beirut, but Western viewers, safe in their homes, switching from *Dallas* to the siege—the siege which is itself *a seat of distinction*, in its Old French origins—when the former cuts to commercial:

> A cinema of revolutions in speeded-up motion. Video for instant application. The new leader or new star in any field was nominated as Beirut's leader or star. [...] Therefore, the reign of stars and leaders was short here, not because the audience was easily bored—the audience in fact was not here—but because the race was run on the American pattern even if its goals were anti-American. What we had were permanent representatives of every new consciousness, every new tune, and every new trend [...] This was Beirut: the global transformer station that converted every deviation from the norm into a program of action for a public busy securing water and bread, and burying the dead.[96]

How, then, to dodge a history that is only legible the moment it is recorded or published in a newspaper at the behest of the highest bidder; how to resist the reality repackaged by the amateur North American reporter who supplies and is supplied by the suffering "not available to others"; how to disregard the collapsed "nationalist thesis" and "the residue of the majority's project"; how to dismantle the discourse of the "coup d'état industry"; how to forsake a tradition of nationalism, a docile history that you've inherited?[97] Darwish makes a movement into effacement when he reimagines himself "turn[ing] into words,"[98] a contrast from the ideological impulses and socialist realism (*Adab al-Iltizam*, or the "literature of commitment") that characterize his early work and, more specifically, his speaker's desire, in the well-known poem "A Lover from Palestine," to "Restore to me the colour of face":

> And the warmth of body
> The light of heart and eye,
> The salt of bread and rhythm,

The taste of earth ... the Motherland
[...]
Take me as a verse from my tragedy[99]

Decades after, amid ongoing Palestinian dispossession, Israeli invasion, Syrian occupation, and Lebanese civil war, Darwish understood too well the dangers of being taken as a verse from tragedy, of becoming, moreover, reduced to violence or victimhood, reduced to the either/or of "defending the lineages of this coast against the mix-up of meanings [...]." Moments later, in the amorphous diegetic space that constitutes *Memory for Forgetfulness*, Darwish speaks, without a mouth, without a voice: "I no longer have a country. I no longer have a body."[100] In that ephemeral transfiguration, there follows elemental bodily rites; within that silence, there is an explosiveness that can be more resounding than the endless "chatter" of the media and the insistent cry for drawing "this war on the walls of the city,"[101] the objectification and politicization of suffering; and within the right to experience, one might re-write theirs from their own lips, with their own voice.

*Nothing comes from nothing* but to understand that we would need to take seriously the unintended proposition of Edward Said, or to read, rather, his statement in "Reflections on Exile" at face value: "because *nothing* is secure."[102] We would need to take him at his word, whether or not he meant that security might be found in the insecurity of negation, disavowal, effacement, the incompletion of transition, of incohesive transit. And in doing so, we might also reconsider Said's "perilous territory of not-belonging" posited as the ultimate end point of every exile caught between nowhere and one's nation, Said's contention that exile is nothing if not a state of jealousy, ownership, a reinscribing of borders around one's self in the pursuit of relentless restoration, tuned to the "triumphant ideology" that inevitably follows "an exile's broken history."[103] We should hold up a broken history to see how it can be redeemed by the fact of its defects; we should see how the territory can itself become aterritorial, concurrently inside and outside; a belonging unconquered by filiation, a life that is intermittent and imminent rather than ascendant. It is in this gaze where the banished outcast and the fetishized refugee can once again become a human.

## THE DOCUMENTATION OF PERFORMANCE AND THE PERFORMANCE OF DOCUMENTATION

"Why is it," Nancy Hartsock writes, "that just at the moment when so many of us who have been silenced begin to demand the right to name ourselves, to act as subjects rather than objects of history, that just then the concept of subjecthood becomes problematic?"[104] This chapter serves as an attempt to call into question just this concept of subjecthood, to assert the concept that, on the contrary, subjecthood, particularly a construction of subjectivity tied to a "nurturing" nationalism like the one Hartsock is here theorizing, is inherently problematic, and that these "problems" may become resignified as opportunities for the subjectified persons. To elaborate this argument, I want to return to *Drift Net*'s discussion of spectator consciousness, to the performance and the perception of its staging at present; to the possibilities of a self-reflexive and critical engagement of representation; to the resignification of one's own surveillance; to the generative potential of accident and failure, all for the attainment of a presence made possible only through absence, only through appearance; ultimately, only through the act, the endeavor, of looking. As Judith Butler, in her 2004 study, *Precarious Life*, delineates such a "critical image," she adds that it must go beyond the failure to capture its referent.[105] For an image to be "successful" in this sense, it must fail to capture its referent, and *in failing to show, reveal this failing*. Failure, then, becomes both ethics and aesthetics: the negative which, taken together with its exposed representation, might illuminate the subject and also their subjectification.

Put another way: when Aimee Carrillo Rowe, on a trip to India, on a car ride back to her friend's home in a suburb of Bangalore, encounters the face of a young girl on the side of the road asking for money, she retreats. And yet, even in retreat, even in one's own rejection, even in each other's failed connection, the critical moment in which one learns of limitations, the critical moment in which one learns of possibilities, is brought forth. "She remains with me," Carrillo Rowe writes, "even as I turn."

> She teaches me about the limits of my political alliances, the limits of where we might meet as allies, the limits of the category "woman of color." She teaches me these things *through* my failure to turn to face her.

> So while I refused to meet her gaze and to engage her humanity in the moment of our encounter, she has continued to hold a powerful space in my imaginary. She is my teacher, remapping my reading of her "outrageous" actions as her expression of agency and my own circumscription within the folds of empire.[106]

In this moment, the windshield through which occurs this encounter with the face becomes, not a border, or a screen, but a window. In this moment, one's begging for money becomes one another's *asking for change*. Power relations are reversed, even briefly, because only a moment is necessary for us to share such a silence, to engage in such a self-reflexive critique, to trouble the ways in which we read others, and to think about how an aesthetics of disappearance can be the best—the only—way to map one's body as a visible text.

How might this critical image and this turn toward failure inform maneuvers by migrants to negotiate the parameters and power structures which attempt to fix them as subjects? Here we might return to Nancy Hartsock's oft-quoted inquiry, to consider the problem of subjecthood as the source of one's potential to traverse and transgress the terms of their own naming, their own compulsory identification. Such decentering "tactical subjectivities,"[107] as Chela Sandoval has called them, are problematic in the sense that they trouble the very categories of identity and the very taxonomies of knowledge that the democratic subject—and the various institutions to which we are tied—desire or in fact require in order to exist. Juana María Rodríguez, following Butler's *The Psychic Life of Power: Theories of Subjection*, reflects this critical awareness, writing that "identity politics, formed in resistance to state power, must also reflect on the implications of its own power to construct political subjects."[108]

What better way to reflect on these processes than by directing one's gaze to the cracks in the representation—to what Renaissance designers called "fractura"[109]—and to how such viewing experiences conceal, and so might reveal, these power structures, as well as the ways in which they make and unmake us. By calling attention to the documentation of performance and the performance of documentary, I wish to return to the ways in which migrants have implemented a scrapbook aesthetic in the creation of their own self-representations, a strategy that not only destabilizes the borders between autobiography and fiction but also undermines the power structures of identitarian subjectification. As I proposed at the outset of this book: an analysis of specific strategies of migrant self-representation can illuminate structural shifts in user interaction and co-production in digital culture; this might also inform the ways in which users and readers approach increasingly liminal and liquid modes of textual production. That the refugee is the vanguard of their peoples, as Hannah Arendt once wrote, is readily apparent; I understand that migrants must also be considered as vanguards of the cultural phenomena that have today become increasingly commonplace and which will, in years hence, be virtually normalized. However, contrary to Arendt's statement, which, repeated in full, reads: "Refugees driven from country to country represent the vanguard of their peoples—*if they keep their identity*,"[110] I understand that all agency, all potential for autonomy, is contingent upon the migrant effacing their identity as such: a re-writing or a *writing over* that is akin to the author who produces work by scratch: by scratching out words, or one's own image. This study's inversion of Rancière's formulation—my insistence that one need take control of their own image as an aesthetic subject, in order to construct their political subjectivity—is a call to consider the significance of mediation as an act of transmission *and* the network produced in its wake.

Migrants' specific interests in material that can be appropriated and repurposed informs the endeavor to remake the terms of representation, not only of one's life but of one's death, the virtual commemoration of which has produced public evidence and social engagement, performing simultaneously as sites of memorial *and* activism. Exploring the act of memorializing for the private and public lives of diasporic communities, Karina Horsti has asserted that digitally mediated memorials are not separate from the material world, nor do they make mourning less human or less authentic; more significant to this study is that such migrant memorialization, in blurring not just the private and public but also the local and global, planned and spontaneous, and formal and vernacular, testifies to a broader shift in how digital technologies, the reproduction and resignification of objects, and collaborative production have worked to cultivate transnational relationships and intermedial experiences.

Horsti, in 2019, demonstrates these processes by tracing a single photograph through its multiple mediations, not the least of which include her own, as she photographed the photograph—a studio portrait of a woman and her son—that had been placed inside a Sicilian family tomb after the Lampedusa disaster of 2013. In detailing the unexpected phases of this image's afterlife, Horsti also shows how refugee organizers have repurposed mass media images of death through cutting and pasting and collage, transforming news photographs into "digital memory object[s]" as an invitation to demonstrations or as a visual headline to welcome friends and family members to enter into the space of archived memorialization.[111] Here, as elsewhere, materiality and digitalization are intertwined and indistinguishable, and the hierarchies between "original" and "copy" are similarly obscured, as is the case whenever paper copies of digital photographs of "original" portraits of the deceased "return" to a physical form which they never actually had, ghosting a body—and a past—that they have ultimately altered. The very meaning of commemoration (which is always a call to the past) alters as the significance of the event becomes continuously shaped by and ultimately displaced by the process of its making: ever-present and participatory acts by survivors and family members which insist upon molding and modification.

Of course, it is not just the contours of death that are redrawn through these amateur brushstrokes but the mode of life writing; in such endeavors by migrants, the expectation to tell the truth becomes rearticulated as a permission to evacuate the distant, objective, and self-evident documentarian realism by which they've commonly been represented. Walid Raad's 2001 experimental documentary, *Hostage: The Bachar Tapes*, which combines real news images of American captives in Lebanon with those of a fictional character named Souheil Bachar—played by an actor, who claims to have shared a cell with the Americans—exploits this molding of memory, which becomes more than fiction or nonfiction but a revelation about how the two are mutually constituted. Five years later, Raad's exhibition at the Museum of Modern Art (MoMa) in New York (Walid Raad, October 12, 2015 through January 31, 2016), which included a decades-long project exploring the contemporary history of Lebanon, combined "fictional" photographs, videotapes, notebooks, and lectures related to real events with audio, film, and photographic "archival" footage. The work, collected between 1989 and 2004, was attributed to the Atlas Group, a fabricated foundation. I insert quotes around the fictional and the archival to indicate their intentional conflation and redeployment throughout the exhibition; for instance, the self-portrait snapshots of Dr. Fadl Fakhouri, an amateur Lebanese historian, are actually of Raad's father, taken from a family photo album. Regardless of each source's format, Raad processes all of his work digitally, so that all his exhibited work has already been mediated prior to exhibition. Meanwhile, information across the artist's website is frequently redacted, including the home page's succession of questionnaires, each one containing biographical data about other artists. One could write a book about Walid Raad's uses of self-forgery, dissimulation, and a scrapbook aesthetic, and how it responds to the unrepresentable events of the Lebanese Civil War and the offices of "official truth" in a splintered country which has never engaged a truth and reconciliations commission (TRC), and how, notwithstanding, Raad's production of the production of history, memory as prophecy, forgery as a form of politics also critiques the TRC logic that *truth* is supposed to reveal what can be repaired; that *reconciliation* is synonymous with justice and forgiveness; that acknowledgment necessitates accountability; that intragovernmental juridical commissions are capable of sowing social, economic, and governmental transformation. This is not that book.

Nevertheless, I want to linger on the processual elements of these compositions; to a meaning that defers to the making, and arrangement, of the text. Just as Edward Said can only recognize Mrs. Farraj, the "first beautiful woman," as he says, "I encountered in real life," once the photograph has been placed outside of its origin or original context—that of the scrapbook that comprises *After the Last Sky*—a new awareness, which is necessarily coded, comes to light during mediation and collaboration, not in the writing or the visual representation, but through its reorganization. Mrs. Farraj thus becomes connected, not only to Said, but to a whole community of persons, and indeed, "her picture," he writes, "seems like a map pulling us all together [...]. But all the connections only came to light, so to speak, some time after I had seen the photograph, after we had decided to use it, *after I had placed it in sequence.*"[112] Like James E. Young, whose 1987 essay, "Interpreting Literary Testimony: A Preface to Rereading Holocaust Diaries and Memoirs," critiques the need for unmediated facts in documentarian literature, and the simultaneous incapacity of narrative to document these facts,[113] I want to reassess the devaluation of fiction as a form to represent experiences of trauma. Fiction's perceived inadequacies are rooted in the representational logic of evidence—of what was seen, of what *has to be seen* to be believed. Yet as this chapter and this study makes clear, rather than posit fiction and testimony as oppositional and mutually exclusive, the migratory text reveals their affinities and interconnections through reorganizing each source code as unrecognizable, as unravelable.

How do you restore a history for which there is no historical record? Nearly a decade after Raad's eponymous exhibition at the MoMa, I came across his series *No, illness is neither here nor there* at the National Museum of Contemporary Art Athens, stepping out from the conference proceedings at Derrida Today in the sweltering June of 2024, at which time I was still under the foolish assumption that monographs were meant to be completed. Raad's series of fifteen color photographs of office signs that more closely resemble ornamented folding doors or strips of Scrabble tiles stacked in various orientations is accompanied by the artist statement masquerading as documentarian preface: "Between 1976 and 1978, Dr. Fakhouri was in the habit of carrying a photographic camera with him wherever he went. He exposed a frame of film every time he came across the sign for a doctor's or dentist's office. The resulting trimmed photographs were pasted in Notebook Volume 57 and organized by medical or dental discipline." And below that, in the gloss of the aforementioned "Atlas Group," to which the fabricated Dr. Fakhouri bequeathed his amateur snapshots: "In this endeavor, we produced and found several documents including notebooks, films, videotapes, photographs and other objects."[114] The mingling of "produced" and "found"—and their temporal reordering—underscores the representation of the past, like the experience of the present, as always already mediated; smuggled in the repositories of Walid Raad's archives is the assertion: to produce *is* to find, that is reclaim, the loss that would otherwise be immemorial. For the reader of the archive as for the archivist, the labyrinthine nature of parsing fictional found footage undoes any expectations of history's site-specific horizon. History, neither here nor there, is neither fulfilled nor definitive.

On The Atlas Group's digital database, viewers can watch a twenty-second Super 8 mm cut of *No, illness is neither here nor there* alongside the series' twin exhibit, aptly titled *New beginnings*, which purports to show a frame of film taken by Dr. Fakhouri "every time he thought the Lebanese wars ended." Here, family photos evaporate into household objects, religious monuments, and the talking heads of TV news. War, reconstruction, and trauma are re-presented by the amateur and imaginary archivist through a verbal-visual field that is outside—not so much beyond as underneath—the temporal currents of a linear historical narrative. How else could one intend to periodize the war that is permanent, the reconstruction that is always ongoing, the trauma that is already embedded in the bodily logic of the generations to come? Nothing is lost; everything is absent.

The scrapbook as method always disturbs the rules and structure of representation, that hierarchy which, according to Rancière, establishes "a relationship of correspondence at a distance between the sayable and the visible."[115] What is "pure" and what is "decorative," subject and object, central and peripheral, are instead continuously dislocated, replaced by the "mute surface,"[116] whose force is located not only across the depthless beauty of the page, not only within the "community without legitimacy" formed "by the random circulation of the written word,"[117] as Rancière has argued, but, moreover, upon the interface forged between various mediums when they meet, react, and invent a new way of seeing, which is to say: a new way of being seen.

The migratory text signals just this movement, necessitating a shift from discussing who makes art (producer) to whom art makes (subject): the production of self, in view of an/other, where, as we know, politics is played out, in the gathering between stage, audience, and the material body and experience of the performer. And yet, it is not just that aesthetic acts have the potential to produce novel forms of political subjectivity, as Rancière understood, but that, in order for the latter to be true, the equation needs to be reversed: political subjects *must first be recognized as aesthetic subjects*, individuals open to and capable of rendering sensory input. For persons who have too often been seen as powerless and valueless, the right to be looked at—interpreted and evaluated—through a different set of criteria is also a break from conforming to hierarchies of Western perception and, moreover, as in the realm of politics, the relationship of representation to visibility. In this sense, the disappeared anonymous will be represented *as* art and *in* art, or not at all. I want to insist that this rendering—a visibility through non-visual means—has to be *placed in sequence*, that is, reworked, before it can be reactivated as a political act. In other words, in order to be considered, the real must first be fictionalized, before becoming real (again).[118] Here this transmogrification should not only be read as an iteration toward a desired result, but in fact as a transmedial approach to reinventing mobility, a maneuver contingent upon an amorphous subject, and their persistence under the intense pressure of deformation. Forced to negotiate overexposure and omission in the public sphere, migrants have returned to the aesthetic forms that have too often represented them by producing *themselves* on their terms—a break from the oscillation between subject and object, whereby political subjectivity is enacted through the evacuation of subjectification; to reorient the terms of visibility, it becomes necessary for subject-producers to *stage the gaze* that would otherwise objectify them. Rancière reminds us that "[t]o pretend is not to put forth illusions but, to elaborate intelligible structures."[119] I wish to be reminded of the ways in which the narratives of historical time and those of personal time are inextricably wound up—not parallel streams but interpenetrating currents. Testimony and fiction, facts and stories, evidence and myth, are each proposals for considering who and what gets counted, who and what is made accountable, who and what is thus made possible.

In her 2016 analysis of the "playful aesthetics" and uses of autofiction in the literature and art of Argentina's post-dictatorship period, Jordana Blejmar argues that the collaging and modifications of documentary archives with the fictionalization of the self has produced a "*new cultural formation of memory*."[120] I want to suggest, furthermore, that the cultural memory of trauma across Latin America—our history of revolutions, annexations, incorporations—can *only* be processed through its fictionalization in various forms, an obliqueness that merges subject and object, self and other, history and myth. Blejmar says that autofiction offers what testimony, autobiography, and history-as-narrative cannot: "it allows [a generation] to imagine not only their own childhood memories but also the memories and experiences of the 'other,' of those who carried out the crimes."[121] Recall the empathic action produced by migratory art, a *feeling* that goes beyond gesture, a haptic contact that is not erased by mediation, but in fact heightened by it. Isn't all empathy an encounter with vulnerability, and specifically, with the presence of an uncertainty, an unknowability that allows the subject to shift or slip, to lose themselves, to find another? I want to insist that the montage or "cut-up" behavior of the scrapbook can be read here as an ideal form from which to represent trauma for migrants and exiles and, moreover, their children: a trauma in which there is no whole picture, only pieces—and the desire to reassemble the scraps, to participate in what one has inherited or been orphaned into in this generation.

Rebecca M. Schreiber traces the specific strategies of migrant self-representations involving documentary photography to the intensifying regimes of compulsory documentation and surveillance in the wake of 9/11 by looking at how Mexican and Central American migrants have produced, curated, exhibited, and circulated photography, film, video, and audio. By paying particular attention to the artistic and political potency of personal and family photographs collaged with other media, Schreiber, in her 2018 study, *The Undocumented Everyday*, also demonstrates how migrants have combined performance with documentary to subvert the genre, while responding to its history of racialized documentation and detection.[122] It is this translocal "counter-documentation"[123] that I would like to pursue here, while continuing to probe how new avenues for production and viewership have also reflected today's textual distribution while ultimately reshaping it.

The work of representation, particularly for marginalized and excluded persons, for those of us who simultaneously belong to multiple locations, is similarly not limited to exhibitions, screenings, or the bandwidth of a video cassette and the margins of a book or journal; no longer contingent upon media and cultural institutions and the availability of an organized and assembled audience, autobiographical activism, such as "*Si No Nos Invitan, Nos Invitamos Solos*" (footage from members of the No Papers, No Fear campaign) transfers and becomes retranslated across mobile phones and other personal devices. These reproduced texts thus become no longer duplicates but originals of varying quality and format;

the genre of "home video" is critiqued and resignified when produced by displaced persons and undocumented migrants, persons who are not recognized within the nation-state and unrecognizable within mainstream immigrant rights discourses and organizations.

Although these acts of autobiography and countersurveillance by migrants are intensely personal, they are not just about the documentation of their everyday lives but a re-storying of self that challenges citizenship by challenging the terms of representation tethered to visibility; in doing so, they not only remake the traditional scope of autobiography and documentary but also evade what Sandra Ponzanesi has called the "postcolonial cultural industry"[124] rife with exoticism, tokenism, fetishization, and, ultimately, the cultivation of cultural difference-as-commodity. I contend, moreover, that these strategies of migrant self-representation involving a scrapbook aesthetic and the intentional overlapping and intermingling of selves and stories can be traced farther back than the early twenty-first century, the Bush administration's war on terror, global neoliberalism, and digital technology. Indeed, charting the reevaluation of archive and autobiography by migrants necessitates a return to the different hemispheric valences of postwar geopolitical alliances.

Just as Cuban filmmaker Tomás Gutiérrez Alea intermixed the amateur and the official to reenact the discontinuous experience of exile in 1968's *Memorias del Subdesarrollo*, as I've analyzed elsewhere,[125] a corresponding pattern of scrapbook art production by migrants was also emerging across Warsaw Pact nations, as the expansion and integration of these socialist republics' military forces coincided with the escalation of their internal borders. What can different hemispheric and generational legacies of border control, compulsory surveillance, and forced exile tell us about the social and political agency of the migratory text, whose function as a self-reflexive and processual "critical image" prefigures today's always-already-mediated representations? Closer inspection of Eastern Bloc self-portraiture prior to the fall of the Soviet Union can yield a connection between internal migration and exile in a divided Germany and today's capture and detainment of persons endeavoring to move between the Americas, especially through the United States-Mexico borderlands, a point of inquiry that requires greater attention outside this study. At stake is a more comprehensive understanding of the multiple, intersecting, and extant repercussions of the Cold War, at the turn of the twenty-first century and beyond.

The prevalence of blurs, glitches, obfuscation, illegibility, scratching, desaturation, overexposures, and overall ambiguity in today's photography reveals a broader turn from realism to visual noise. I want to consider how such images, in becoming *representationally unreadable*, are thus able to allow their author-subjects to circulate in ways that would not have been possible otherwise. To understand the exigencies of transforming the composition of the camp it becomes crucial to read, once again, aesthetic autonomy—the reclaiming, and repurposing, of one's own image—alongside the political agency rendered through the creative act. In an era of unprecedented collection and curation, the performance of documentation—and the relation of its non-indexical assembly—provoke a framework for undermining the securitization of the individual and the fact of our compulsory incorporation into an aggregate of governable subjects. To be *on the move* here is thus to be conscious and open to the potential of mediation as more than just a movement between platforms but as a platform to foster changes within space, and our relationships therein.

Mixed-media artist Cornelia Schleime, who was not allowed to exhibit in the GDR, and was expelled in 1984, employed the equivalent of visual noise in various formats while under state surveillance and against a regime of censorship.[126] Schleime, who was born in East Berlin in 1953, also translated her earlier work—re-creating pieces, in the absence of money and traditional materials, with coffee grounds, glue, sand, shellac, and ink—after being stripped of citizenship, during which almost all her art, apart from a few drawings, was lost or destroyed. Instead of conforming to the GDR-sanctioned socialist realism, her abstract "horizontal pictures" and overpainted paper prints include cautionary, ironic, and critical messages scribbled between disintegrating and heterogeneous figures, body parts overlapped or imbricated, or partially melting into the canvas as vanishing, unidentifiable persons.

Without question, however, Schleime's greatest repurposing projects are the ones in which her found material was herself. Through the documentation of performance and, alternatively, countersurveillance tactics that perform as documentary, these self-representations problematize the conditions of mobility contingent upon parameters of identity and visibility, attesting to an altogether different "identifying mark." After 1981, when she could no longer show her paintings in public exhibitions, Schleime turned to temporary, unannounced body-painting and self-staged performances in unmarked warehouses, circumventing the censorship of government authorities while documenting the communal experience, remediating scenes in which ropes and ribbons entangle her naked body, first by photographing them with a self-timer and then by painting over the photographs: an original reproduction made more ambiguous, more public, with each mediated intervention. The series of overpaintings, *open your Mouth, close your Eyes*, completed between 1981 and 1982, obscure her already indistinct and reproduced figure with overlapping strokes while simultaneously revealing the various frames of its perception and re-presentation, exemplified and exaggerated with geometric precision as rigid blocks, windows, and film sprockets frame the central figure of the body or the face, the mediated present intervening in the murky and mercurial past of Stasi-operated surveillance and organized raids on free expression. Each "finished" piece's movement, from staging to photography to painting, calls attention to the complex representation of the material body, as well as the processual elements that *make up* one's mobility.

As surveillance of her person and censorship of her work intensified (forcing her, eventually, to operate under a pseudonym), Schleime employed strategies of subversive self-exposure, a counter-gaze that does not nullify but in fact works to transform through encountering one's own supervised suppression, by turning *toward* the surveillant eye, by soliciting its gaze. As she explains, "they robbed me of my freedom of art; that's why I have completely exposed myself. I made myself naked because they also made me naked. The GDR left nothing behind me." And so Schleime, too, leaves nothing behind, not even her own Stasi files, which she obtained following the collapse of the Soviet Bloc and the destruction of the Berlin Wall. In reoccupying her biography, she returns the invasive state records back into her life, a double movement from superficial information to interior fantasies and wishes, the consummation of Spivak's secret: what one *desires* to give up. Schleime, in this fifteen-part series, *Bis auf weitere gute Zusammenarbeit* ("I am looking forward to our continued cooperation"), completed in 1993, becomes author as well as subject; repeating the miracle of Goethe authoring his own posthumous biography, the artist here authorizes her own translation, rendering a crowdsourced and classified original and making it public. The conflation between private and public, author and subject, reflects the omnipresent gaze of official and unofficial civilian employees of the state police, tasked with monitoring their own neighbors, their own colleagues, their own family: a vast network of mistrust and deceit which could only be undone by re-presenting it, by blowing it up, by exhibiting the extent of everyday terror and control. "The work," as Schleime remarks, "could only be realized with the help of the Ministry for State Security of the GDR and its numerous helpers who painstakingly contributed to the texts. To them, I extend my thanks."

Literature written, copied, and circulated as samizdat—roughly translated as "we publish ourselves"—flourished throughout the Soviet Union following Joseph Stalin's death in 1953. "Unlike the underground of Czarist times, today's samizdat," the *New York Times* reported in June of 1970, "has no printing presses."[127] Instead, samizdat owed its existence to remediation, the dutiful duplication of typing out what's already been produced in other formats and for other audiences. Schleime, in *Bis auf weitere gute Zusammenarbeit*, extends the legacy of samizdat while subverting the practice of secrecy, provoking the gaze of the public as well as the individual reader-viewer who becomes implicated as both potential informant as well as aspiring accomplice. In these reports—each of them stamped with the disclaimer, or invitation, of iteration: KOPIE—certain words and names are redacted, while, in scrapbook fashion, personal photographs overlay and interrupt the narrative proper: the amateur gaze displacing the formal and official, the language of the unprotected uprooting the language of the state. The images, all but one in color, disrupt the monochromatic Stasi files in more ways than one; Schleime's self-conscious staging—posing on a lounge chair in a vaguely tropical setting; toasting to the viewer as she stands behind a portrait of a smiling, applauding Erich Honecker (the portrait itself remixed: the lips of the former GDR leader sewn shut with marker); standing regal, clad in a velvet dress and a makeshift crown, with a German shepherd on one side of her and a fat tiger cat on the other—enacts the ever-shifting game of identity. Schleime, stripped of freedom and mobility, appropriates the terms of her detention to inhabit several different spaces, several different roles, all of them fictional, all of them real.

Schleime's appropriation of her own (found) archive should be read as a personal response to containment and surveillance in East Germany at a historically specific moment and, moreover, as a maneuver that undermined the long-standing Eastern Bloc use of autobiography as a tool of confession, and confirmation, to the state. As early as 1920, compulsory autobiographic practice in Soviet Russia was used to advance the international communist moment; autobiography was seen as both an exercise of humiliation and a ritual of self-regulating cleansing, the permission necessary for a person's participation in public life as a member of the party.[128] And yet, Schleime is able to subvert this psychosocial ritual while using its cultural and literary markers: the common methods of self-construction, the alterations and compromising of voice—in fact, *avtobiografia* was required to be presented orally—the Soviet system's call to the party member to transform themselves, and to do so repeatedly throughout the various stages of their life. Indeed, if autobiography as a mode of textual production is nothing if not remedial, processual, and subjective, Schleime's self-conscious stylizing in *I am looking forward to our continued cooperation* must also be read as an attempt to recover autobiography as an engine of individual empowerment, and a vehicle for the microhistories stamped out by institutions and ideology.

The charge of this series, like so much found footage, is located in the discrepancy between "original" setting and "intended" audience. It is not just that the migrant proposes a reformulation of narrative frame, as I've discussed throughout chapter 2, but does so through rapidly shifting modes of address. Schleime's files, thus, are both stripped—laid bare—and clad with a meaning that has been reorganized on the basis of montage and voyeurism: the curiosity of the viewer, who fills in what's been redacted, what's been overlaid, and does so in a way that forces a proximity between the then and now of internal exile, the before and after of event, which remains in progress. If Schleime's body of work during the Cold War can be read as one of the earliest examples of migrant self-representations involving a scrapbook aesthetic and the reevaluation of autobiography and archive, Moscow-born Kon Trubkovich's short films, paintings, and drawings probe the aftereffects of Eastern Bloc containment, disinformation, and control.

Trubkovich, who moved to the United States as a child after the Chernobyl disaster, begins his multimedia work by combing through his own source footage—home videos he's filmed or found and which he pauses repeatedly, isolating each fragment before re-creating it as a grainy, distorted still: video submits to analog static in oil and graphite; each second—the artist's mother at a party on her last night in the USSR before migrating to America; the sky at various stages of day and night—produces twenty-four paintings. "I looked through hours and hours of footage," Trubkovich explains, describing his meticulous process in advance of his 2014 exhibition, *Snow*, which ran at Manhattan's Marianne Boesky Gallery from February 20 to March 22. "I was looking for something that I felt was *true*. You know? You need some element of truth to the image, because when you pause the tape, something happens. This kind of pathos enters them, a narrative that isn't perhaps there when you're watching in real time."[129]

In other words, true and authentic experience can only arrive, in Trubkovich's diasporic glitch art, through manipulation and interference; narratives are found, not between the lines but within the language of the text itself, which must be excerpted, opened up, drawn out, annotated—as when Trubkovich overlays cue marks and flecks, drawing onto the material of the film—authorial notes that distort so as to reveal. In these disruptions of vision, Trubkovich relates an indexical awareness of his own process, which is to say the mediation of memory (cultural, personal, anonymous), through which "recognition"—much like identity itself—is inevitably discomposed, displaced, and returned as suspect. Trubkovich's portraiture is rooted in this engagement, and juxtaposition, of art modes; his portraits' subjects, thus, are not only persons but also the portal of the screen, the media itself, whose malleability and fragility are here on full display. I am interested in reprocessing as a form that fashions content but also shows its material degradation; to show the stutter of a source code when it duplicates, transfers, and disperses across different media is to mark, repeatedly, one's own itinerant passage, which is to say: to re(-)mark upon, and revise, the representative territory of the collective—memory, citizenship, belonging, community—and the individual.

If all representation today comes always-already-mediated, then these migratory texts vibrate their repetition and fragmentation—indeed, the repetition of fragmentation, cuts, crops, buffering glitches—to reveal, not that the medium is the message, but that the materiality is the message: no longer a binary between semiotic meaning and aesthetic information but their gradual enfolding. As I turn toward my final chapter I am reminded, in a Facebook reminder-cum-advertisement—a digital "memory"—of the "Under One Roof" immersive installation I experienced in the Lower East Side's Tenement Museum, on this date (March 22, 2020), two years ago. Paper sons and paper daughters were persons who adopted the surnames of Chinese Americans; these paper children abandoned their flesh and blood identities and families to form another lineage, another relation, in the wake of the Chinese Exclusion Act of 1882, which prohibited all migration to the United States from China. I'm reminded, too, of the conditions necessary for their mobility, to circulate as freely as actual paper, as actual currency does. It was not merely about passing themselves on, but about leaving themselves behind, a production of truth that insists that all history is as fragile as paper, and as susceptible to fabrication. The buildings which housed state birth documents were destroyed in the 1906 San Francisco Earthquake and the ensuing fires—a catastrophe that fostered the occasion for coincidental returns. All public records were burned.

# CHAPTER FOUR: COLLABORATION. /

# REMAPPING THE STATE AND THE ACADEMY FROM WITHIN AND WITHOUT

## *The Queer Refugee Camp as a Space for Alterity and a Site of Critique*

"Not everyone deserves to see every part of you," says Yousive, a poet who two years ago fled his home in the Republic of Gambia, the smallest nation in mainland Africa, nexus of the slave trade in part because it straddles both sides of the Gambia River. The Republic of Gambia, or A Gâmbia, which was colonized by the Portuguese and then again by the British Empire, so important is the river that courses through the country's center until it melts into the Atlantic. The Gambia Colony and Protectorate, almost completely surrounded by Senegal until it was folded, in 1982, into Senegambia, a confederation of multiple ethnicities and cultures; the upshot of a centuries-long competition between the French and English in the region. Yousive asks if I'm writing this down—"you know," he points to my notebook as if it were a map, "over 70 percent of the population today live in poverty." The Gambia, where the definite article was deemed necessary, in part so that the Western world would not confuse *Gambia* with *Zambia*, a country two hours ahead and about one hundred and thirty-one hours southeast of the Gambia, if one were driving, if one were to drive for days on end. "Is the confusion," I ask, "that Zambia gained independence a year after Gambia?" Yousive shakes his head and corrects me. We are sitting across from one another outside a bakery in Walter-Benjamin-Platz, just a few blocks east of the refugee shelter where we'd been introduced hours earlier. "The confusion," he says, rubbing his right hand over his head, "is no one outside of Africa knows the Gambia exists."

And this is why Yousive, who writes in Wolof (which uses the same pronoun for both sexes) as well as Arabic and English, wants to make sure he calls himself a Gambian poet, not an African poet, not a poet who will write and be translated and circulate the world as a "foreign-born artist"—the guise of world literature, I think, but I hesitate to cut in. Behind us, children take turns darting through a water fountain. The air is cooler today, cool for August, and the breeze makes the papers shake beneath my palm. I think of the world republic of letters as it emanates from the West, the clamoring for diversity but especially, for the periphery: for the metropolis to absorb the marginalized and *make it new* (as in neotraditional; as in neo-mestizo; as in hybrid); for the market to absorb the artist's life into the work itself, while flattening the material experiences from which the artist works. "I need to remind myself," Yousive says, "and remind all the others, where I come from, where I am writing from." And I know Yousive, who has been a resident of the Schwulenberatung Berlin for the last ten months, and before that—"I was nowhere yet"—does not mean Berlin, nor Germany, nor the African continent or the hyphenated experience of Blackness outside of Africa—"I am African American," he explains, "when I came to you—over there—and visited the United States"—but the Gambia, and its history of colonizations, its history of dispersals (so important is the river that courses through the country's center until it melts into the Atlantic). The Gambia, where homosexuality carries a punishment of a lifetime in prison; where persons found living with HIV are deemed "serial offenders."

Months after we meet, outside this text (if we believe the lie of surfaces), Gambian state forces will launch a covert homosexuality crackdown. Persons including teenagers will be arrested by the National Intelligence Agency and the Presidential Guards; they will be held in unidentified locations, prevented from accessing a lawyer, threatened with rape by security personnel. Their identity cards will be confiscated;

they will be banned from traveling outside the district in which they've been detained. More names will be collected: a growing list compiled by state authorities for the purpose of future arrests. Those that are suspect will be targeted. Those that are targeted will become suspects. Those that do not confess to the charge of homosexuality will be told that they are required to submit their bodies to a device meant to test their sexual orientation. But I'm not thinking of that now, even as Yousive is, or must be, even as we speak about art and literature and which of the nearest *bäckerei* makes the best schnecken, in a country that is unfamiliar to both of us, in a city I have only known in dreams, a city whose routes I am learning by getting lost, even as I've mapped these paths from such an early age, like invisible ink; a city of borders, where I could be closer to Cuba, to Poland, not in spite of the relative distance between each but exactly because of it.

"There are so many countries in Africa," Yousive says, as I read his poetry, written in dashes of prose, following the hand-written words in English, a self-translation from the Arabic on each opposite page of his journal. "And what does it mean to be an African poet?"

At stake is the question of power, but also the potential for agency and the reclaiming of subjectivity; the question of an authentic Africa outside or in parallel with a general and generic African syncretism or a specific model of pan Africanism and its mobilization for a possible politics, as it has been enacted in years past—the federation and fragmentation of French West Africa—and as it could still be enacted in the future. At stake, too, is the reverse; the question of being an African poet begs the question of one's ability (one's challenge) to negotiate allegiances—national, ethnic, regional, religious—and systems—transnationalism, the world literary-art market—while accounting for multiple and often conflicting identity formations; to be a Gambian poet and a queer refugee in Berlin and to be Black is to recognize, as Yousive has, one's codification as always already (and at the same time) fragmented, compartmentalized, and dispersed.

◆

Today's issues of integration and hospitality are each informed by the specter of Cold War colonialism but also and especially Cold War capitalism, its manufacturing of bodies and labor. Paying heed to the ways in which today's politics of asylum and immigration reform have each been shaped means also positioning the literary and cultural representations of migrants alongside the network of publishing and academic agents that have helped certify them. Just as Fredric Jameson, writing in 1986, insisted that "the reinvention of cultural studies in the United States demands the reinvention, in a new situation, of what Goethe long ago theorized as 'world literature,'"[1] I argue that Jameson's fraught discussion of "third-world literature" should be placed beside today's resurgence of a world literature that is itself strapped to an attendant swell of migration and refugee studies within the academy. Critiques of migration scholarship and migrant-assimilation models, I repeat, inform a critical reading of world literature and universalizing trends in the publishing and translation industries.

## A DECONSTRUCTION OF LANGUAGE AND LOGIC

### Reading Critiques of Migration Studies through Gender and Sexuality

"Let's make it clear. Those who land in Lampedusa aren't 'illegals,'" Giusi Nicolini, the mayor of Lampedusa from 2012 to 2017, tells a French reporter in the 2018 HBO documentary *It Will Be Chaos*.[2] "They are refugees. We are talking about asylum seekers."

By the time the documentary airs, Nicolini, who had proposed a new European law on sanctuary and immigration rules in the wake of the 2013 migrant shipwreck near the shores of Lampedusa, will already be a former mayor, voted out by a man who will call for the whole island to strike after declaring that Lampedusa "can no longer cope" with a migrant emergency that can no longer be "managed."[3] In the film, she's still the mayor, a fierce advocate for environmental protection and migrant-integration, a recipient of a UNESCO Peace Prize.

Back on screen, Nicolini pauses as the reporter repeats her question. She shakes her head; she looks at the camera operator, who is framing her in profile. In this way, when she turns, Nicolini is looking at the viewer.

"I know what your question was," Nicolini responds, "but I have to correct you otherwise you'll report that these are 'illegals.'" Again she turns her gaze. Again she confronts us, too. "Well, if you don't get it, neither will your audience ... those who land on Lampedusa are not simply 'undocumented.' These people are refugees," she repeats. "You know," she adds, after a long exhale, "words are important."

To think through what a migrant sovereignty and a migrant commons makes possible is to also consider the array of social, cultural, and political factors that have impeded their progress. Attending to the queer migrant and the role and function of the queer refugee camp requires that educators and activists alike engage in a critical examination about the limits and inadequacies of our own language and logic, a structural reassessment of the interconnected and mutually constitutive forces that work to divest the migrant of their subjectivity in fact and in fiction. Recent work in different disciplines has contributed to a discourse that Yên Lê Espiritu has called "critical refugee studies," addressing the field's inadequacies on a broad scale—the frequent absence of theoretical reflection, for instance[4]—while also attending to the field's reliance on problematic terminology.[5] Espiritu's shift from a cultural critique to an institutional challenge, by demanding scholarly attention to unasked questions about history, identity, and power, reminds us that tracking the relationship between research centers—like Oxford's Refugee Studies Centre, which would go on to found the preeminent *Journal of Refugee Studies* in 1988—their donor collaborators, and the international bodies that govern economies of flow may yield a larger critique within our own departments and the everyday negotiation of academic independence. The coupling of scholarship and intergovernmental organizations can be traced farther back than the emergence of the United Nations High Commissioner for Refugees (UNHCR) and the coinciding founding of the Association for the Study of the World Refugee Problem in 1950 to the interwar period's International Refugee Organization, which, following the terms established by the League of Nations, did not recognize persons displaced or denationalized as refugees on account of the "purely temporary movement" facilitated by the First World War. Although it is difficult to pinpoint the very first scholarly inquiries into "possible ways out" of the "refugee problem," as a 1939 special issue of the *Annals of the American Academy of Political and Social Science* on refugees described its central aim, we can at least acknowledge the tail end of the Cold War as a turning point for the intensification of refugee studies. As Richard Black's retrospective study of the refugee in 2001 shows, the year before the fall of the Berlin Wall saw the creation of the *Journal of Refugee Studies*, the *Refugee Participation Network* (which would become *Forced Migration Review* in 1998), the *International Journal of Refugee Law*, and the *World Refugee Report*, which was established by the US Bureau for Refugee Programs, the humanitarian bureau of the US State Department.[6]

Years later, Oliver Bakewell's 2007 introduction to "researching refugees" urges us to consider how, just as the growth of the field has been tied to the growth of the United Nations and its multiple and conjoining entities (many of them assembled under the United Nations Sustainable Development Group), the scope of refugee studies has hardly strayed from the UN's own policy categories and bureaucratic labels.[7] This imitative gesture, I argue, produces a mirror effect between *policy* and *research on policy*, a theorizing that is self-contained and foreclosed. Bridget Hayden, a year earlier, suggested a similar contestation, explaining that efforts to classify migration are much more about ourselves than about the migrants we are attempting to arrest and sort.[8] As Hayden returns to the UN Protocol's definition of the refugee, she also complicates the defining aspect of *volition*, which is used to distinguish refugees from all other migrants. In this scenario, volition assumes a free will and an economic variable that is at odds with the *forced migration* of political terrain. Because so much of migration studies resolves itself through this base separation, racial and ethnic conflicts are privileged, legitimizing certain forms of migration and certain migrants while devaluing other issues, especially economic—or, lest we forget, sexual and bodily—considerations.

This aporia of logic, premised on Euro-American democratic capitalism and the individual actively produced by citizenship, has far-reaching consequences outside of the academy and the world outside of world literature. In the framework of the United Nations, economic rights are not considered human rights, and this problematic distinction reinforces the division of academic fields—refugee studies or forced migration in one corner, and migration studies in another—but also reflects the separation of responsibilities between the UNHCR and the World Bank Group, who each manage the flux of displacement and mobility in different ways.

Yet the conceptual separation of economics and politics that has prevailed in both policy and academia elides their intertwining. Starvation, too, is another form of violence. This untheorized gap implicates not only politicians, publishers, and members of the academy, but all of us, citizen-subjects who, in exclusively focusing on the absence of "freedom" for refugees worthy of our attention, also neglect the uncomfortable facts of the social and economic inequality we ourselves are implicated in and often complicit with in the "free world." It is once again the migrant who is tasked with the responsibility of teaching us, not only about their conditional humanity within our state-controlled milieu, but also and ultimately about the conditions for our own resistance of the same dehumanizing system.

As a research field, migration studies has developed rapidly in the last decade, drawing from several disciplines, including economics, sociology, anthropology, history, geography, psychology, and political science. Likewise, the characteristic lack of an intersectional analysis of migration has also been identified by those scholars not working with migrants on the ground and their specific patterns of im/mobility. In her 2015 call for reorienting the discipline through a theoretical and methodological frame that actively accounts for the structural nature of race and ethnicity within immigration, sociologist Vilna Bashi Treitler shows that sociology's prevailing model of assimilationism—even recent assimilationist theory—falls prey to an interpretation vulnerable to and complicit with a white supremacy that, I would add, undergirds immigration policies and the politics of migration.[9] In this scenario, what is at stake is not just a disciplinary field but the disciplining (and punishment) of particular people on the move.

Human displacement does not just contribute to Western economic and political practices, but also to the production of proto-nationalist narratives, through which the state controls its own role as a representative agent by controlling how its citizens are written. Control by the state begins with reworking the text of its citizens, identifying bodies and marking them, reinscribing them into an inside-outside dialectic.

Just as the naturalization process has been shown to produce a discourse of otherness at the same moment that it grants the right to belong,[10] the asylum system has been understood as a generator of new-old essentializing constructions of sexuality that function within nationalist logics. By *new-old* I mean to call attention to the antiquated aspect of "immutable" sexuality that persons must revive and, later, reaffirm, to gain asylum based on being persecuted for their sexual orientation.

The logic so often used to exclude queer persons was now, as sociologist Lionel Cantú Jr. pointed out at the turn of the millennium, being used to establish their eligibility.[11] Such are the terms of limitations and limitations of terminology for persons applying for asylum, which has been available in the United States since 1980 to those fleeing persecution on account of five criteria: race, religion, nationality, political opinion, or membership in a particular social group, a category that, beginning in 1994, included lesbians and gay men. What is missing among this roll call is the material relations of race, gender, class, sexuality, economic status, and geopolitics. What is missing is closer attention to the ways in which asylum testimony risks reinscribing the same structures of inequality from which applicants seek refuge. Into what system are migrants welcomed? What are the prescriptions of the request? The double-bind offered by asylum is to produce a testimony that will grant you legal residence while also fueling racist, homophobic, and colonialist relations that will be detrimental to your newly "protected" life. Yet it is not only life that is sanctioned by such a universalizing norm of rights but death, the metrics of identification and recognition, of *being out*, against which non-legibility—non-visibility—is equivalent to humankind's passing into disposability.

As Cantú has shown through his first-hand investigations limning the ways in which the testimonies of individual asylum applicants are elicited and embedded within larger national structures, in order to gain asylum, "Third World supplicants must paint their countries in racialist, colonialist terms, while disavowing the United States' role in contributing to the conditions that they fled. If the US government decides to 'save' the supplicant by granting asylum, this easily reaffirms the notion of the United States as a land of liberty and a bastion of progress."[12] Asylum thus can be read as an invitation: for the nation to be absolved of its past through reproducing the script of liberal progressiveness and liberating savior, a reenacting of the scene of rescue (the scene of violence) of the "developing world."

## THE SPECTER OF THE BERLIN WALL AND THE CONTEMPORARY *GASTARBEITER*

In seeking to investigate the representations of migrants across the arts and in the media, we should look not only at the source—the point of origin, the documents of passage—but also the host. Germany, which has taken in the largest number of migrants since 2014, has also far exceeded its European Union partner nations in granting asylum to persons on the move.[13] Conducting research on refugee integration throughout Europe requires us to look at the challenges of integrating East and West German citizens after the dissolution of the Berlin Wall. Thirty years after the reunification in 1990, there are people from each end of the German capital who still refuse to cross the spectral walls,[14] remnant bricks which exist today as either a mile-long street art installation or an interactive monument. This "hauntology,"[15] as Jacques Derrida understood, constitutes a politics of memory, which is a politics of inheritance. Racism, discrimination, and xenophobia, too, are subject to historical cycles that flow along migratory drifts, in Germany as elsewhere. And it isn't just the collective refusal to talk about a reunification-without-integration that haunts today's refugee culture in Berlin; deconstructing diaspora within a generational framework means looking at the border closure's immediate effect on immigration to Berlin, an influx of "guest workers" that was spurred, as so much refugee generation is today, by the need for cheap labor: young people mainly from West Asia and Southeast Europe who were recruited by the West to fill the gaps left by the sixty thousand border-crossers who could no longer reach their workplaces when the West was sealed off on August 13, 1961. Coincidentally, it was not just the West German economy that relied on cheap labor; up until the fall of the Berlin Wall, it was common practice for East German companies to staff prisoners, utilizing forced labor for the manufacturing of goods to be purchased in the West: a state economic plan that could not otherwise be fulfilled.[16]

I want to remember a coinciding system of labor exploitation enacted across the Atlantic: the United States Bracero program (1917–1921 and 1942–1964), which, during the first decade of the Cold War, annually imported an average of 333,000 persons from Mexico and Guam to fill labor shortages with low-wage and vulnerable temporary workers, many of whom were deemed "illegal" when the program ended in 1964.[17] What the Cold War inaugurated, besides a fragmentary three-world system and the attendant solidification of its borders, was the importation of deportable labor as a post-industrial norm. To trace the flow of migrant workers during the interwar period through the Cold War is to understand the production of immobility naturalized by the precarious and temporary labor contracts so common in the Gulf states today, where labor brokers (*dalal*) exploit foreign workers' lack of resources and knowledge about the nature of employment while sponsorship systems (*kafala*) bind migrants to single employers who retain workers' passports, precluding them from leaving the country and suspending their pay at will.

What are we to think of the cost of a Football World Cup celebration when that ledger includes over six thousand migrant bodies? Low-paid and unprotected workers from India, Pakistan, Nepal, Bangladesh, Sri Lanka, Kenya, and the Philippines who, over a ten-year span, had been hired to massively redevelop the city of Qatar, were stripped of their identity documents upon arrival in the Arab peninsula. Without renewed residence permits, which were simultaneously withheld, the workers were prohibited from leaving the country or changing jobs. To construct eight World Cup stadiums, a new airport, new hotels, new roads, and a new public transportation system, these men and women were paid, on average, roughly two hundred and twenty dollars a month. Six thousand and five hundred deaths is only an indication; like all figures, six thousand and five hundred is an outline, a cipher, and also: a prophecy; no statistics are available for the workers from Kenya or the Philippines.

Here we are forced to imagine, or reconsider, the definition of the "guest" in today's world as in the past: what does it mean to be a guest whose primary role is to work? What does it mean to "invite" someone to be in service of another? The *Gastarbeiter* is exactly the specter that haunts today's regime of national points-based systems[18] from which to measure internally excluded migrants, all those who risk everything to arrive into a freedom that is provisional and limited. A matrix of race, surveillance, migration, and labor extraction emerges alongside "liberty" and "liberal ways of understanding" at the end of the eighteenth century[19] that, today, is not obscured by the discourse of modern liberty so much as the transnational ideals of neoliberal governmentality and its market-driven exceptions, including Special Economic Zones (Special Administration Regions, Export Processing Zones, et cetera), where floating populations of stateless people are converted into subjects of a globalized economic system that benefits state powers and their consumer-citizenry, under the auspices of providing potential citizenship or the legitimacy of World Bank-backing.

The difference between many asylum seekers and refugees, and those who have been recruited to work beyond their borders, is often only the difference between economic and political motivations of host countries, and the power wielded by such nation-states to serve geopolitical interests and residential ones—the management of residency—at the expense of human rights. Karl Marx's oft-quoted assertion that "working men have no country. We cannot take from them what they have not got"[20] is turned on its head by today's unprotected workers, who are not liberated from nationality by any political program but might yet provide the rubric from which to consummate Marx's manifesto; the crucial distinction, however, is that the conditions for the emancipation of the proletariat pivot not on united action by "the leading civilized countries"[21] and the reconstitution of the nation, but on the desire—and possibility—of escaping it. That the guest worker and the asylum applicant are reversible is only overshadowed by the potential agency such liminality suggests for dodging not only national boundaries but the origin narratives that such boundaries enclose.

Just as postwar guest workers, after being offered long-term contracts, challenged an unprepared education system by putting down roots in West Berlin and applying for their spouses and children to join them, so, too, do their contemporaries arrive in Berlin to meet untrained aid workers. And just as in 1975, when the West Berlin Senate saw a "threat of infrastructural collapse" and imposed a settlement ban for foreign workers in the migrant-heavy districts of Kreuzberg, Wedding, and Tiergarten that lasted until 1990,[22] today we are encountering the effects of alternating radicalization and disenfranchisement in much of the world, thirty years later. The asylum applicant, the refugee, the unincorporated migrant, become both specter of the past and pressing reminder of the present.

## PUBLIC SPACE AS A SITE OF REFUGE: A SELF-REFLEXIVE FRAMEWORK

Any discussion of the challenges of refugee integration requires us to reckon, too, with the ethical question of refugee representation, not only in the media, the arts, and the academy, but also within the state and local institutions that reproduce knowledge production as a matter of policy. I want to continue to read the queer migrant and the queer refugee camp as points of relation, which elucidate the problem of representation on the individual and collective levels: in political and cultural spheres, as well as within public and institutional spaces. Marcel de Groot, who helps run Berlin's first—and the world's second[23]—LGBT+ refugee center points to this same question, and the reluctance of German citizens to think critically about their own practices and to question their own ways of thinking, a self-reflexive framework which, I assert, needs to be applied globally to understand and support migrants and asylum seekers. "The way we are living and working is the Western way and we know it—but we only know this way of life," de Groot says. "And this way of life is often unrecognizable to the people we serve, the people we shelter. And if it's not working—and it's not working—we need to find new ways of solving problems."[24]

For the Schwulenberatung Berlin, which offers housing for up to one hundred and twenty-two refugees, that has meant the genesis of a new project: the government funded Betreutes Wohnen program, which began in June of 2018, promoting domestic interaction by offering four apartments for thirty people and mandating mutual living spaces: at least two refugees reside with German citizens within each unit. Prior to its launch, no such programs in Germany existed solely for LGBT+ persons. It isn't the first time the center has had to reorient its practice; Schwulenberatung's staff, which include one hundred and twenty employees and several other volunteers, had no experience living with refugees prior to 2015, when, during the year's final quarter, nearly one hundred instances of violence against queer migrants were reported to the Lesbian and Gay Federation in Germany. Berlin, too, had no formal experience accommodating queer refugees until one month later, when Schwulenberatung transformed from the largest queer organization in the city to the largest queer refugee center in the world: a shelter with rehabilitation, therapy, housing, employment, and social services.

"Difficulties is all we have," de Groot, who has managed the center for over twenty years, tells me when I ask about the specific challenges of helping the persons who walk through the Schwulenberatung's doors. Whenever I read my notes back, I don't retrieve events so much as try to reconstruct them by adding other annotations, backdated: an attention to interval.

It is Friday, August 3, 2018. In three days, the media will report that the United States government is expected to issue a proposal that would make it harder for legal immigrants to become citizens if they have ever used a range of public welfare programs. The following week, Austrian officials will reject the asylum application of an Afghan teenager because he did not "walk, act, or dress" like a gay man, forcing him to return to Afghanistan, where homosexuality remains illegal.[25] Four weeks later, nearly eight thousand far-right German citizens in the eastern city of Chemnitz, just south of Berlin, will march to protest their nation's immigration policy, flashing Nazi salutes, and stoking hatred against foreigners that will lead to the stabbing of a migrant as he sits with his family in a café.[26] Meanwhile, in Greece's largest refugee camp, in the four months since April, there have been at least twenty-one reported cases of sexual assault; nearly half of the cases at Moria in Lesvos involved boys and girls under the age of eighteen; two incidents involved five-year-old children.[27]

De Groot tells me that the reality of chronic debilitation and the omnipresence of violence remains unchanged for LGBT+ refugees who apply for and ultimately receive asylum in Berlin. Landlords don't want to rent to them; employers don't want to hire them;[28] daily surveillance and security is required at all times at the shelter's entrance, a complicated fact obscured by the hostility and harm that pervades daily life *outside* the shelter's doors. For many of the Schwulenberatung residents, the goal, in fact, is to continue moving, this time farther north. Despite their tradition of social welfare, and the emergence of organizations like the

RFSL (Sweden) and the LGBT Asylum group (Denmark), once hospitable Scandinavian governments are increasingly becoming more right-wing, less welcoming to migrants. Within the bureaucratic and social whirlpool that migrants must wade through, the "choice" is merely to remain in spare living quarters devoid of privacy while outside, among the public, to risk enduring potential abuse, poverty, and sexual exploitation.

Today, same-sex relationships are currently criminalized in sixty-four countries, twelve of which punish offenders with death. Fourteen jurisdictions criminalize the gender identity and expression of transgender persons.[29] The arrival to Europe, "even to a cosmopolitan city like Berlin," de Groot points out, does not represent the end of violence—both physical and psychological—for so many LGBT+ refugees. But out of all the issues he cites, the one that seems most germane to the question of representation and the challenges of a mobile commons and a migrant sovereignty is the lack of an inclusive comprehension of what it means to be queer in a global context for so many of the refugees who arrive from countries such as the Gambia, Nigeria, Cameroon, Iran, and India, which only legalized homosexuality months after my visit to Schwulenberatung in August of 2018.

Writing at the dawn of the twenty-first century to think through globalization's function for reshaping the *proximate* and *intimate*, alongside the transnational subject's forms and practices of desire, Elizabeth A. Povinelli's and George Chauncey's analysis about the fissures and flows between social normativities and the discursive technologies that mediate them bears repeating: "Web sites," they write, "provide gay pornography to browsers where there are *hjira*, *travesti*, and *kathoeys* but no gay men."[30] It isn't just desire that has been reconfigured through migration and mediation, but the subjectivities that desire produces, even and especially the senses of self that evade or ignore universal categorization. Not surprisingly, during our conversation decades later, De Groot speaks about shelter residents who are thrown into a crisis of self upon being thrust into a world where to be queer does not fit their local scope of homosexuality—the tension between global discourses and institutions and local attitudes and embodiments, which rims a different or even resistant sexual subjectivity: the idea that the transcultural and diasporic subject-position refuses the opposition of "global" and "local," the assumption of any neat binary to position signifiers of similitude versus difference; yet unable to identify with other manifestations of queerness, many refugees call into question their own identity. It is this difficulty for many of the shelter's residents to understand themselves and their sexuality that parallels the world's broader understanding of migration as it is articulated in the media, across scholarship, and within literature and the visual arts; at stake in each instance is a discernment of the many divergent qualities that "make up" a migrant, provoking the call for greater intersectionality within and outside the field of migration and refugee studies.

And yet, *a general understanding of sexuality* needs also to be called into question when the conception of a generalizable queer identity is imported by the West. It is not just the limits of Western conceptions of selfhood that are reinscribed in migration discourse, but the limits of Western conceptions of queer selfhood, and moreover, the limits of the pursuit of recognition when it follows the logic of likeness, the logic of sameness—a common strategy of mainstream lesbian and gay activism at the turn of the twentieth century and beyond.[31] The "mounting insecurity about 'gay identity,'" as Scott Long, the founding director of the LGBT Rights Program for Human Rights Watch, has written, so often results in the mounting desire "to ground it in something secure," an assimilation of another's experience under "the appeal to a 'gay' universality."[32] Is not Marcel de Groot's assessment of the queer refugees he shelters susceptible, too, to the fraught Western framework of the "cosmopolitan city" of Berlin from which he offers hospitality? What, more broadly, are the limitations of any certificate of a "cultural citizenship" when the exclusionary operations of the state are nevertheless reified in its terms of resistance? I want to continue to advance the queer refugee camp as a site of productive discord, a site of crossroads, where such issues are related and returned as questions; where we can limn connections between sites of refuge and resistance and sites of control and surveillance.

To understand how authorities monitor and control the influx of migration at the border through specific and sexualized orientations,[33] we must also acknowledge the legal precedents that queer migrants are required to negotiate *as* they move. Explore, for instance, how "family" as a structural governmental formation organizes the conditions for gay asylum, while producing a racialized and gendered labor migration. Remember that since at least the 1980s—punctuated by the Family Reunification Act of 1986—the United States has been able to extend and institute "heteronormative community structures" by requiring immigrants to attach themselves to the family unit and, moreover, to the welfare provisions it allows. This conditional hospitality fosters the recruitment of low-wage workers while relocating the responsibility to provide them with economic and social resources within the state's reorganization under neoliberalism. As an entitled citizen-subject becomes increasingly securitized, low-cost immigrant laborers—akin to guest workers—are either forced into patriarchal and heterosexual mandates or forced to survive at the limits of society, as unprotected and ineligible, as undesirables whose queerness can neither enter the national record nor preserve the liberal narrative of universality that provides the nation's origin story, its foundational myth. In Chandan Reddy's assessment, the "gay Pakistani immigrant" marks the tension within this national record and the governmental practices that extend from it; as such, the figure becomes both a site of contention and a symptom of globalization and transnationalism, a critique of the national model of "family," and a reminder of the state's strategic deployment of sexuality.[34]

Calling for the increased role of sexuality in migration research in 2006,[35] Martin F. Manalansan also acknowledged the immense amount of work to be done in a field that is largely unconcerned with understanding how the framework of sexuality and gender might provide a better understanding of global flows—a void in scholarship, I want to clarify, that remains unfilled. Nevertheless, Héctor Carrillo's earlier treatment of "sexual migration" allows us to reconceptualize its trajectory, moving migration from the heteronormative processes of the family and the familiar nation and toward alternative subjectivities that inform other motivations for moving. In showing the "two-way traffic of ideas and practices related to sexuality"[36] that migrants circulate between their homelands and their host countries, Carrillo, in 2004, noted the especial transmission of agency; instead of adopting a method of assimilation, persons on the move, he argues, have provided examples of how to subvert norms while creating new spaces in which to fit, reshaping not only their lives but the lives of others in their community.

Given these considerations, de Groot's self-reflexive acknowledgment about reorienting the Western practices and logic of aid workers and shelter volunteers is perhaps undercut by a general reluctance on the organizational level to follow theory with practice. The failure of integration, I repeat, is not that migrants cannot socially and culturally translate themselves into their host communities, but that host communities are unwilling to surrender to their own act of translation—an adjustment and accommodation that is necessarily in flux, always on the move, fixing only to the demand of assiduously challenging one's self.

The call for a queer treatment of migration research is also a response to the prevailing bias of both academic and health researchers who each depend upon categories and practices that are themselves dependent upon Western conceptions of selfhood and community. Far from rooting their reasons for moving in terms of marital, reproductive, or productive (labor) roles, Manalansan asserts that non-Western sexual ideologies do not follow unilinear assimilative processes, "but rather are involved in syncretic processes that create alternative sexual politics, cultures, and identities."[37] Closer attention to sexuality returns an atypical representation of the migrant, a turn from racialized, classed, sexualized, and gendered images of migrants or universalized rationales of migration. The queer refugee camp, I argue, can be read not merely as an aterritorial space outside the state, but also as a potential site of critique, in which "the tensions, irresolutions, and contradictions" that layer the experience of membership and belonging in Espiritu's call for a critical refugee studies are both enacted and interrogated. The queer migrant provides a model for unsettling not only the network of the family but the very idea of settlement. And this mediation informs not only migrant-integration models by state actors and NGOs, but also provides a paradigm for reorienting migration scholarship and research.

Schwulenberatung's citizen-refugee living project underscores a synergistic model that has become increasingly common in recent years, with initiatives such as Startblok, which launched in Amsterdam's outskirts in the summer of 2016 when nine blocks of shipping containers were transformed into housing for 565 refugee residents, and Copenhagen's

Trampoline House: a public, educational, creative, and social space gathering asylum seekers, refugees, artists, scholars, journalists, and citizens. Morten Goll, who helped found Trampoline House in 2010 and who serves, today, as its executive director, speaks about the value of the weekly house meeting, or what he calls "our parliament," during my visit in 2019:

> It's derived from the basic democracy where we want to create equality in between all participants so that we don't have victims and experts or actors and subjects. We wanted to set up this relation where we sort of deprogram the racism we are all engulfed in. If they [migrants] come in from the camps, and they are treated and viewed as victims, it becomes unavoidable to perceive them as anything more. That is why we've said from the beginning: we aren't here to save anyone; we are here to solve problems together.[38]

Trampoline House's commitment to critiquing systemic racism and its own corridors of power flips the savior script common in the non-profit industrial complex. Instead, all discourse—scaffolded through skill-enhancing internships, counseling, and democratic practice—moves from the first rule of the house and its governing baseline: unconditional mutual respect.

To explain the transformative potential of each house meeting, Goll sketches the scene. Seven circles constellate what Goll calls an amorphous blob, and inside each circle is a smaller circle: the culture that each person carries into a shared space. "The key," Goll explains, pointing to the arrows leaking from each larger ring, "is that everybody has to sort of leave their culture a little bit in order to enter into that space in between us where we have this polymorphic weird thing: a new culture."

The new culture Goll describes requires both abandonment and surrender, the necessity to return and to return differently. Trampolines are nothing if not receptive, elastic, adaptable; the Trampoline House's parliament works as a metatextual instruction manual, a user guide that reads its own information, questions those processes, tries to alter its operations in real time, by altering its source code. If Trampoline House were a machine, we'd call this activity *feedback*, a learning algorithm. Sometimes such local transmissions are returned elsewhere in Europe.

Further south, young Dutch migrants also employ alternative strategies of identification, an effort at creating opacity through a specific refusal. Rather than pledging a sense of self to host nation or home nation, race or ethnicity, these migrant youths define themselves locally (Amsterdammer, Eindhovenner, et cetera), or through a certain music scene, or through a professional role, or through their membership in arts or sports groups. A new sense of "Dutchness" emerges through circumventing an identification with the Netherlands as nation. By evading representational aesthetics and national practices of integration, these daily counter-strategies of alternative identification demonstrate how migrants have reformulated a different territory of belonging as a method of survival and play.[39] Derrida, too, believed that sites of true refuge would need to be glocal; conditioning what he called, in one of his final works, "*the* Great Law of Hospitality—an unconditional Law, both singular and universal" would also require the refusal of identity, of identification.[40] Establishing a "world government," he insisted, in *On Cosmopolitanism and Forgiveness*, would necessitate establishing a city of the world: a civic territory that could skirt the state, union, federation, and nation, while critically reflecting upon them.

And yet, could this "city of the world" advance the rights of migrants from the inside *and* the outside? And, if so, where might we observe such a local project for *expérimentation* and reflection, for "a new order of law and a democracy to come to be put to the test?"[41] We already know that integration without modulation can only reproduce instead of respond. Through informing the public about the conditions faced by asylum seekers and refugees in Denmark, the Trampoline House also advocates for structural change on the policy level by working closely with the municipalities that are responsible for the problematic conditions of asylum seekers and refugees.

Perhaps nowhere is this emphasis on activism more evident within Trampoline House's holistic curriculum than in its attached Center for Art on Migration Politics (CAMP). CAMP, a self-governing exhibition venue founded in 2015, houses work by more established artists alongside those produced by refugees and migrants, becoming a site of inquiry and critique that explores questions of displacement, asylum, and passages.

"We try to map key factors in migration politics," CAMP's Creative Director, Frederikke Hansen, explained during *We shout and shout, but no one listens: Art from conflict zones*, a 2017 exhibition presenting installation, photography, painting, readymade, collage, and performance works that culminated with a public discussion. "And we have been talking in exhibitions with events about camps, how they function, *what they keep in, what they keep out*, what it is like to be in a camp."[42]

Hansen's choice of words forces us to think more closely about the economy of images, particularly those that circulate narratives of migration and detention. What images are received, and how they are received, inform the ways in which persons are treated in the asylum system; whether they are admitted, or whether they are ignored and obscured. It is this negotiation of the gap between perception and observation that ultimately provoked Trampoline House to expand from workshop to civic center. "From the beginning when we started out as a thinktank, we decided that we wanted to engage with asylum seekers in order to figure out what their lives were like because they were constantly being used as scapegoats by politicians," Goll says. "Everybody was talking about refugees but no one was talking to them. And actually, it was impossible to meet them, because they were stored away in camps, in remote areas that you couldn't even access." Goll's reflections echo responses by the migrants interned at such camps, including a reflection that offers an experiential comparison between the Calais Jungle and the city's container camp located meters away:

> Outside [i.e. in the Jungle] there is a certain atmosphere, people pass by and say hello, the Europeans come, pass by and say hello. But in the containers [...] the Europeans cannot come in, it's a problem [...]. I want to communicate with the Europeans, flirt, I don't know, say hello; I don't want to stay in the containers; the Europeans are very curious, they ask a lot of questions. There is more Europe in the Jungle because you have the contact with the Europeans [...] Outside you make ties with friends and Europeans, you do many things, but it's not possible in the containers.[43]

The logic of isolation precludes unforeseeable encounters, productive discord, and spontaneous interactions, so fundamental to this study as both theory and practice. The logic of isolation, as Goll affirms, also has the function of making it very easy for politicians to abuse domestic crises by misrepresenting a certain person or group of people, to whom the public has limited access. Trampoline House and CAMP's commitment to unpacking migration politics makes visible the self-representations and life experiences of refugees, asylum seekers, and other migrants, and, moreover, places their testimonies within a larger political and historical arena, in which shared space means more than just the staging ground of a gallery venue.

This performative-political endeavor is echoed by the "Welcoming Museums" project in Puglia, a community initiative aimed at promoting and training refugees in intercultural dialogue and eventually aiding them in securing positions of power and instructional roles at the Sigismondo Castromediano in Lecce and the Ribezzo in Brindisi. The year-long program involved the co-production of multimedia storytelling—including writing, art, photography, video, and audio recordings—the sharing of self-narratives, and the fostering of membership that decenters the state, culminating in the appointment of "certificates of cultural citizenship" to migrant participants on April 18, 2019. Ten years earlier, Giorgio de Finis, an art curator based in Rome, decided to provide security through art for displaced people in Italy's capital by turning an abandoned salami factory and slaughterhouse into a contemporary art museum and educational center providing language lessons, open to the public every Saturday. Until it was shut down and restored to property conglomerate Salini Impregilo in July of 2018, the Museo dell'Altro e dell'Altrove di Metropoliz (MAAM; Metropolis Museum of the Other and the Elsewhere) also housed two hundred people, including families from Peru, Morocco, Romania, and Ukraine. The court ruling did not just mean the replacement of the creative-cultural refuge with residential apartments but also the eviction of the two hundred children and adults living inside the museum.

By fostering cross-cultural exchange between migrants and their host communities through its hybrid composition of public space and communal residency, MAAM serves as another case study for creative approaches to addressing civic issues, including the lack of public housing, alongside the isolation of disenfranchised and marginalized persons. Such a revision of public space as a site of refuge implies an interruption—or more specifically, a reversal—of the violence inherent in the production of these institutions, museums, and metropolitan squares alike, like Berlin's own Alexanderplatz, which was built by enslaved laborers, including concentration camp prisoners.[44] How can we rethink the value and function of institutional venues for communal engagement and the advancement of "inclusion" and "diversity"? And how might such changes within our public institutions change the public, not as a community of *being-in-common*, but as one of mutual difference? It was the art space, after all, which became a locus of refuge in September of 2014, when the Diyarbakir Arts Center in Turkey opened its doors to the Yazidi refugees who'd escaped ISIS attacks a month earlier. In these scenarios, the museum does not serve the nation through organizing its narrative with rituals of collection and display but, on the contrary, provokes a form of non-denominational belonging.

## BETWEEN TRANSITIONAL INTEGRATION AND TRANSNATIONALISM

### The Limits of Aid, Activism, and "the Alternative"

In any discussion of the representations of humankind who are viewed as sub-human, it is important to limn the distinction between visibility (what we see) and visuality (what is shown): the *politics* of such representation, which necessarily implies a struggle over what, and who, gets to be represented.[45] Threat and victimization, each in their own way, adjust viewers' attentions toward an ethics of care or a policy of denunciation while static migrants become vehicles for discussion and study in popular culture and in academia, spoken about and spoken for but never permitted to speak for themselves, possessed as objects or objectified images and yet dispossessed of what Hannah Arendt has called "the relevance of speech,"[46] the precursor for becoming a political being; these ethics of public participation necessitate a greater understanding of our vastly different subject-positions in the world. "Being seen and being heard by others," Arendt remarked in *The Human Condition*, "derive their significance from the fact that everybody sees and hears from a different position."[47] Underscoring these different positions is a degree of ownership and possession that may no longer be geographically fixed, today when capital is global. Decades before, immigrants arriving at Ellis Island at the turn of the twentieth century had to prove that they were "clearly and beyond a doubt *entitled to land*."[48] It is no coincidence that during the interwar era, denationalization became the political precedent that allowed European nation-states to establish undesirables as *less than human*: without the right to have rights, as Arendt has said. It is no coincidence that in ancient Rome, too, it was property that constituted citizenship; in antiquity as in our current moment, one loses their location in the world and then their right to be in it.

For us to become better supporters, better learners, better instructors, better scholars, we need not necessarily gain anything, except the ability to relinquish our own roles. And in questioning our practices within and without academia, other questions must necessarily be reckoned with. How to tell without being told by others? How can exile reroute trauma and move us toward empathy? How can a "migrant consciousness" be seen as symptomatic of the estrangement of "free citizens" within post internet culture? If it is true, as I've argued elsewhere, that migrants are the hidden face of capitalism,[49] what is at stake in any circumstance involving migrant representation is the limited resources many migrants have to articulate or transmit their own experiences, whereas the desire to encounter the migrant as an interviewer, as a researcher, suggests that any attempt to accumulate knowledge on human subjects insists upon a power imbalance. The performance of asylum interviews is a negotiation between applicant and interviewer, an interpretation fraught with bias and stereotypical assumptions: the perceived presentation of sexuality, as already discussed, or the degree of danger from which people are escaping. Applicants are forced to prove their victimhood, a debased candidacy bolstered by offering documentation or offering one's self up to medical examinations, often below the standards required by international human rights law.[50] The stakes have risen so much during the application process that nations like Germany have established separate centers for investigators—"refugee detectives"—tasked with deciding who gets to leave and who gets to stay, a sorting of persons administered through techniques and procedures that demand narratives devoid of generic details, yet ones that also include a level of journalistic specificity and emotional resonance—a story fit to a predetermined form.[51] Recall the eponymous story of *Refugee Tales*, a fictionalization of the real event of asylum interviews, which are themselves rooted in the act of storytelling, not by the asylum applicant but by their reviewer: "we're/first time meeting; maybe you say the word/'Refugee' in your head when you call me Farida,/Refugee, what is that burn mark on your hand?/You already have a story of the torture [...]."[52] Without question, if deconstruction as a methodological framework offers this chapter a "lesson," it is to pursue its internal and relational possibilities while foregrounding its limitations—the extent of the Western perspective from which deconstruction privileges its approach to understanding the relationship between text and meaning.

The self-interest of writers and scholars meets a fetishization of suffering that so often turns a human into a human interest story, in journalism as in so much fieldwork. Ruben Andersson, in his 2014 study, *Illegality, Inc.*, goes as far as to assert that researchers' intense interests in suffering foreclose the field of refugee studies into a study of refugees who most fit or are willing to perform a certain sensationalized image of refugee life.[53] Asylum seekers, like those housed in the Schwulenberatung, must demonstrate their fear of persecution; in claiming injustice and insecurity, they are placed in a position of defense and testimony, whereby they must provide supporting evidence. In this presentation of self, what is on display is less a human being than the migrant requiring human security, the signifier of "refugee" connoting absence and lack that has been continuously produced—and refashioned—to fit various geopolitical narratives; recall, for example, that the refugee as a cultural figure shifted from a humanitarian victim and political byproduct of state failure in the wake of the Cold War to a person alienated and uprooted from a fixed home. Today, repatriation has replaced resettlement as the popular storyline, in coordination with particular organizational and political interests. Georgia Cole's 2018 assertion, that "[f]or each desired durable solution, interested parties can [...] create an 'ideal' refugee to validate its application,"[54] should be read in connection to the system of scholarship, literature, mass media, and policy that has continued to conflate key differences between migrants while proliferating new connotations associated with the refugee label. Cole, who locates the desire to categorize as a founding principle within the field of Refugee and Forced Migration Studies—remember that the *Journal of Refugee Studies* launched, in 1988, as a forum "to explore the rich research agenda established by the label 'refugee'"[55]—also argues that the field still lacks a clear theoretical framework from which to engage in critical observations around naming as such.

Just as the scopes of forced migration studies and refugee studies were framed, especially at their outsets, by UN policy, media representations of refugees and other displaced persons have been shown to derive from the descriptions offered by police and politicians. Closer attention to these power dynamics reveals the intertwining of institutional forces at work to reproduce not only knowledge, but the policies and rhetoric of border control. Such practices of symbolic bordering operate in tandem with the policies of border control implemented by national and supranational governments.

At stake in this system of refugee generation is not only the degradation of life, but the degradation of death. Between 2014 and 2018, nearly 18,000 people drowned trying to cross the Mediterranean.[56] From a legal point of view, nobody is a refugee at sea, in the sense that in order to claim asylum one must land on land to be recognized as a human being and not as an anonymous victim. If, as Moira Inghilleri asserts, "[it] is only when bodies are washed up on a beach, lost at sea, or when remains are discovered in the desert that we are reminded of the relationship between migration and the topographical spaces that are integral to the journey,"[57] then what is obscured in our limited collective imagination is not just the body of the migrant but the fact of their movements. Mobility itself is called into question once we no longer recognize its processes in everyday life.

In contrast to static and passive images of the refugee, Khatharya Um, in her 2015 study of Cambodian diaspora, *From the Land of Shadows*, called for a greater awareness of the state, conditions, and consciousness of *being* a refugee.[58] I want to read "refugitude" as intervening in both the continual circulation of refugee likenesses and the prevailing refugee scholarship devoid of comprehensive analysis of the elastic and interminable experience of migration. Through an attention to microhistories of survivors comprising over 250 first-hand accounts, Um's retrieval of a history untold—a history, in some senses, untellable—is rooted in these same questions of identity, belonging, and the possibilities of intergenerational connection through collective memorial. Narratability—the ability to tell, to be told—as we have already seen, can be meaningfully rendered in the act of reciprocal narration. "Put simply," Adriana Cavarero writes, "I tell you my story in order to make you tell it to me."[59] The alchemy of consensual exchange is thus this: that a life is not merely recounted but made real. Politics and narration conjoin in the creation of this relational space. We also know that texts, like photographs, construct subjects through particular points of view. Yet to narrate one's self as a person is to legitimate for one's self a representation that is outside the gaze of the other, where the other is the standard gaze (the standards of the gaze) one has been simultaneously produced by and subjected to.

Cavarero, in *Relating Narratives: Storytelling and Selfhood*, reminds us of the crucial difference between writing the story for another and writing the story in their place, while accounting for the polyvalent effects of the text within this alternating "economy of desire."[60] Yet contrary to her analysis, *Drift Net* understands as imperative that identification with another and identification of the other (as irremediably unlike any other) *are not necessarily antagonist but coordinate*. It is precisely during that moment of exposure—when someone tells their story in order to be heard, which is to say in order *to hear it repeated*—that absence (the first condition of all representation) is returned as intimacy, and intimacy encounters an empathy that requires absolute contact, absolute abandonment. The intersection between autobiography and biography desires an "I" but an I, nevertheless, that is multiple, susceptible, obscured, transparent; an I who relates the experience of dispersal as flux and disintegration, movement that includes, *before all*, the activity of one's story (skin, sensation) *taking place*.

In the endeavor to assimilate foreigners into host communities, are government and volunteer aid workers reproducing the fiction of reunification, while forgetting the possibilities and productive discomposure offered by the ones they wish to welcome? Today, in place of assimilation and integration as means to an end, transnational norms and increasing circular migrations have provoked new models of internationalism, a "cosmopolitanism from below"[61] that informs and potentially formulates new identities, while ushering in, as this study has shown, a reformulation of the narrative frame.

I began this chapter's analysis with Fredric Jameson's call for a theory of third-world literature founded on the national model; in recognizing today's mobilization of "world literature" (capitalized, hyphenated, or otherwise) in response to transnational economic realities, we should acknowledge the many ways in which this reanimation of Goethe's phrase is itself inescapably attached to the nation and to the state's nationalizing agenda. How does world literature as an interpretive paradigm reproduce exclusionary and normative practices *on the ground*? In exploring this question, my hope is that we might begin to envision the migratory text as an alternative to the fetishization of exile and displacement as a subject, and the global circulation of national literatures in translation as a method.

## A QUESTION OF POWER: REDESIGNING WORLD LITERATURE THROUGH DECENTERING THE NATION AND THE TRANSNATIONAL

When Djelal Kadir, in his 2004 essay "To World, To Globalize," traces world literature further than Goethe's "coining a phrase" in 1827 and toward the territorial displacement and concomitant national revisioning of Herodotus in the fifth century BC, he also forces us to think about the parallels between the fragmentation of Goethe's Europe and the surging imperialism and nationalism that was produced in its wake. These conditions serve as a stage set for the dawn of *Weltliteratur* that resembles our own social and political climate today, too often obscured, nevertheless, within the halls of academia, a site of objectivity and neutrality that parallels the imperial hegemony underneath the universalizing of the world. "Our engagement," in Kadir's words, "in notional or narrative acts of worlding,"[62] become the byproducts of our limited imaginations.

Rather than differential identities—elements too often thought to be fixed, such as nationality, race, and gender—might we reformulate our examinations vis-à-vis *differential subjectivities*? Joaquín Barriendos Rodríguez, in his 2011 investigation of the transcultural shifts in the international art system, calls for closer attention between subjectivities that coexist and make sense because of and despite "their relation of proximity to a specific cultural context or their synchronicity with a given moment-space."[63] By linking transcultural art practices to a cartographic system of representation and, moreover, to colonial and postcolonial technologies for the management of mobility politics, Barriendos Rodríguez also shows how the marginal and the migratory become alternately fetishized and depoliticized as they become absorbed into the market, a pattern that has only intensified during the last two and a half centuries:

> At every turn, we see biennials, fairs, round-tables, and exhibitions materializing. Each and every one of them is explicitly international and asserts a "harmonious" coexistence between artists from the Maghreb, sub-Saharan Africa, south and central Asia, South and Central America, the Mexican-American border, eastern Europe, and (apparently) elsewhere with artists from North America and central Europe. In a very short space of time, the mainstream has given up its limited territory and gone in search of the periphery. As in the old days of colonial expansionism, alterity, the exotic, the diverse, or, in one word, the Other, have aroused the interest of museums, galleries, macro-exhibitions, and commercial contemporary art fairs. [...] In the blink of an eye, the scenification of the multicultural has turned into the raw material of every international exhibition.[64]

Perhaps nowhere is the "raw material" of the Other more emphatically fleshed out as a form of cultural currency and redistributed at auction than in *The Man Who Sold His Skin*, a 2020 film from Tunisian writer-director Kaouther Ben Hania about a man who escapes imprisonment in Syria in 2011 and becomes a refugee once he crosses over, inside the seat of a car, into Lebanon.[65] A year passes in Lebanon, where Sam Ali watches the war on TV, while working at a factory farm and sneaking into gallery openings at night to forage for supper at the tables lined with decorative hors d'oeuvres. But after repeated visits, he's marked as a Syrian refugee, asked for his name—which he declines to give—and slips into the gallery behind a couple who has just checked in. He isn't denied admission because he's a Syrian refugee; it's the reason he's allowed to pass, and as he wanders around the exhibition space holding a flute of gratis champagne, Sam is invited, by the artist's assistant, to try the caviar and, when he declines, offered a package of the buffet's leftovers, which he rejects with slightly harsher language—"Don't take it badly, okay. Fuck you"—a foreshadowing of the film's remaining eighty minutes, or its narrative's parables concerning the discrepancies between pity and dignity. Sam's outburst at the viewing turns him further into a spectacle, and the spectacle into a commodity; it is because he is "an angry young man" that Sam attracts the gaze of Jeffrey Godefroi (a caricature of Belgian artist Wim Delvoye), "the most expensive living artist" and a renowned provocateur, he who, a news report explains, "turns *worthless objects* into works that cost millions and millions of dollars.[66]

Afterward, over a drink, the artist continues to draw from stereotype, asking Sam if he'd like a flying carpet, to travel as freely as anyone else who is born, as Sam points out, "on the right side of the world." When Jeffrey refers to himself as Mephistopheles, Sam asks if what he wants in exchange is his soul. "I want your back," Jeffrey says, and he purchases it, but not before he tattoos the entire length of Sam's dorsum with an image of the Schengen Visa, which is later scanned, for insurance purposes. Unable to apply for legal transit to Europe, Sam obtains the elusive Schengen by merging his body with the visa's signifier and thus becomes a breathing artwork, convertible and portable, contractually obligated to be present—that is, to appear—at every viewing, for every institution, private or public, who has acquired him for collection.

The inscribed back of the refugee serves as promotional lure for national galleries and private collectors; when Sam first witnesses the enormous fanfare surrounding his back—lines for admission snaking around the corner, more crowds exiting a tour bus—his face is framed by the oval openings of a stone colonnade, as if, even before he is to be put on display, he is already and inherently contained within a limited grid of representation. After a series of viewings at the Musées Royaux des Beaux-Arts de Belgique in Brussels, Sam encounters the chair of the Organization for the Defense of Syrian Refugees (a fictional organization), who is worried about Sam's exploitation by wealthy Westerners. "I'm sleeping in a five-star hotel," he responds, from the doorway to his hotel suite, a mound of caviar, which he won't eat, plated behind him. "I don't feel exploited." "They tattooed your back and put you in a museum," the chair insists, incredulous. "Is it a circus or a zoo?"

Meanwhile, communication with his old world—the other side of the world—occurs exclusively in grainy, lagging Skype video. The persons across the screen—family members, like his beloved mama—are remembered through the violence that pervades their daily present, as when Sam discovers, as the camera unintentionally swerves during a buffering call, that his mother has lost both her legs in an explosion. As I've analyzed elsewhere, the "refugee" can only be seen in the West as a body that is fragmented; it is, moreover, only when such persons become decimated and defective that Western viewers can begin the task of reassembling them as a branding exercise of charity and compassion.[67] Abounaddara, the anonymous video art collective formed in the wake of the Syrian civil uprising in the same year (2011) that opens *The Man Who Sold His Skin*'s diegetic space, says that pity is Syria's first enemy.[68] Abounaddara, in their production of short films that bear witness to everyday stories about ordinary people—neither martyrs, nor heroes—which contradict the tropes of violence and victimhood that pervade their cultural representation, assert their right not for dignity, but for *a dignified image*. The specificity of "image" is critical: image as semblance, imitation, duplicate, copy, model, example, manifestation, personification, appearance, shape, and symbol—but also, in the classical Latin imāgō: as a death mask. Again, I ask: what is dignity but the conditions to be counted—as human, as worthy of subjectivity? Again, I ask: what is dignity but the permission to take back control of one's self?

By his Rolodex of acquirers, Sam is referred to, in the same breath, as an "it" and "a masterpiece." Asked why he could not resist Sam as his latest purchase on loan, a collector explains, with equal horror and glee: "this work of art bears the signature of the devil." The repetition of violence and the violence of repetition is seen here as the banality of evil. Every morning, Sam strides through the museum's halls garbed in a blue silk robe, advancing toward his assigned gallery space to assume his customary position—head bent low, the emblazoned back to the viewer-audience—under strobe-lit ribbons of metallic light. On one occasion, however, as Sam stops his habitual procession to look at the art on the walls to which he will once again, in due time, join, he is struck with a cascade of tactile memories—fingers interlocked, anonymous limbs clasping—meditations triggered by proximity. Diaphanous embraces of Sam's fragmentary past in Syria continue to perforate the present in symphonic montage, each time the camera zooms in on the painting, which is to say, each time Sam looks closer, as if to remind the viewer of art's potential for immediation—the immediacy of affect and its necessary excess—even as Sam himself is a living object-witness of its system's necrophiliac underpinning.

Is it any wonder that in order to hatch his elaborate escape plan, Sam must first return himself to the stereotype of "angry young man"—and eventually, suspected terrorist, to become, once again, the victim of racist prejudice and easy conclusions—when he feigns a bomb threat during an auction in which his back garners a five million euro bid (by an unnamed businessman played by Delvoye himself) and, later, when he ultimately falsifies his own death via ersatz ISIS execution video? "I had to die," he tells Jeffrey, a year afterward, over a phone call's voice-over. "So that I can finally live." Sam lives, even as his lab-grown skin—his back's biometric scan—begins to circulate among the public, now even more valuable, encased in a gilded frame, because of the presumed death of its subject. "Of course, it's a nice story to tell. For posterity," Jeffrey tells Sam, during the same phone call, as a slow-pan of the flesh-toned Schengen Visa objet d'art is positioned against a pristine white wall. "How we beat the system, Sam." So signals the film's jubilant finale—and yet, is it not the same system which, nevertheless, dictates the rules of the game, since even the endeavor to hoodwink collectors with a forgery of Sam's back requires that all of the players consent to the unequal value of a life, the exorbitant value of the dead?

Thus, among *The Man Who Sold His Skin*'s unintended appraisals is not that for those who are "persona non grata" in Western culture, it is necessary to turn one's self into a commodity, to perform the alterity that is asked, that is expected of you, and that, in becoming aestheticized and exchanged as merchandise, one might return themselves, according to the standards of Western time, to the appearance of humanity; but that it is the art system, and its entanglement with transnational and humanitarian capitalism, the strategic twinning of marketing and militarization, who profit from each death or disappearance. In the parable of a human turned into an artwork, a carcass turned into a canvas, what is more tragic than the realization of one's own submission to a fate worse than death: infinite life as a legacy of being seen as less than human? "Are we going to sit like this all day?" Sam asked Jeffrey, during the introductory photoshoot that would eventually herald his introduction to the artworld at large. *Well, from now on, it will be forever.*

In the past I've called these curatorial tactics *the fetishization of hybridity as aesthetic asset of internationalization for the cultural market at large*.[69] Years earlier, Kwame Anthony Appiah, writing during the expansion of refugee studies in the early 1990s, described *syncretism*, and understood the clamoring for diversity, the genre of the *neotraditional*, and the intensification of aesthetic individualism as a consequence of the international exchange of commodities. In this scenario, the market, desiring such distinctions, absorbs the artist's life into the work itself; modes of identity become "modes of identifying objects."[70] While "neotraditional art" may get produced in Africa, or elsewhere in the Global South, Appiah clarifies that it is art that is produced for the West. In the same fashion, the first generation of "modern African novels," epitomized by Chinua Achebe's *Things Fall Apart* (1958) and Camara Laye's earlier *L'Enfant noir* (1953), championed by Western publishers, can be read as a legitimation of the nationalist project that thus rationalizes Western legitimation. Appiah's critique of both the *neo*, which begs attention to elements that are recognizably postcolonial, and the *traditional*, which implies actual or imagined precolonial techniques, informs later critiques of the postcolonialism produced in academia, "emanating from the West," as Ania Loomba has more recently argued, "and of questionable relevance" to the actual persons living in the Global South, their own lives and struggles.[71] Recall this chapter's earlier assessment: scholarly efforts to classify migration are much more about the individual actively produced by democratic capitalism than about the migrants these individuals are attempting to research and qualify. These power dynamics require further investigation of the interconnected and mutually constitutive relationship between the literary-art market, the academy, and public policy, and their various absorption or apprehension of the migratory.

World literature, taking its cue from the international contemporary art system, reorders the literary market according to the logic of globalization, circumscribing the world into manageable global boundedness while retaining the preeminent model of the nation from which to reflect upon or reify.[72] The movement of the world novel, too, as scholars such as Michael Denning have shown, coincided with the exportation of the national literatures of colonized countries throughout the twentieth century. "Like world music, the world novel," Denning writes in his 2003 study of global cultures that emerged as three worlds gave way to one, "is a category to be distrusted."[73] Accounting for this distrust means attending to how the world novel has been used as a marketing device that flattens and frames regional and linguistic distinctions "into a single world beat,"[74] a phenomena that Marx also predicted in his *Communist Manifesto*, the simultaneous rise of a world literature and the creation of a world after its own image.[75] Marx's observations anticipated the ways in which the world novel was eventually employed by Marxist-Leninist socialist states as the "literature of the world revolution," particularly in the decades spanning the Russian Revolution and China's War of Liberation, a thirty-year period in which world literature became not merely reflective of a larger worldview but also reduced into a self-conscious literary movement.

In other interpretations, world literature, or what the editors of *n+1*, writing in 2013, called "Global Literature," is not only produced for the so-called global West Village, but also assembled in tandem with universities, honoring the universal neutrality of the former and the liberal humanism of the latter.[76] In *n+1*'s analysis, this has served, since at least the late 1970s, a dual function: the importing of migrant writers—described revealingly as "guest workers" whose employment depended "on a permanently foreign identity"—and the reduction of third-world and migratory trauma to keynote addresses, "transform[ing] exile into professional expertise and literary theme." Clothed in its universal garb, and intent on retelling its history of trauma, today's world literature, in spite of its alleged contemporaneousness, displaces the present, degrading its own political agency—the "literature of the world revolution"—for a post-factum narrative that a liberal readership can agree with.

Perhaps it is no coincidence that even contemporary critiques of world literature risk reproducing its exclusionary measures, as well as the rationalization of the nationalist project and Western domination that world literature escorts on the level of language and expression.[77] Pascale Casanova, in her 1999 treatise, *La république mondiale des lettres*, makes this fetishization of language explicit by exposing literary value's attachment to certain languages, positing translation and criticism as "weapons in the struggle by and for literary capital" while locating specific cities of literary wealth, "centers of credit" that provide universal capital yet remain inextricably linked with their national languages, the material conditions of literature down to their very makeup.[78] However, in Casanova's analysis, writers are given only two choices: "either to affirm their difference and so condemn themselves to [...] writing in 'small' literary languages that are hardly, or not at all, recognized in the international literary world; or to betray their heritage and, denying their difference, assimilate the values of one of the great literary centers."[79]

By limiting the strategies to assimilation and differentiation, "the obligatory itinerary"[80] of every underprivileged writer, Casanova prescribes the normative features of the metropolitan center on work that has been marginalized by it, reducing the foundation of all literary struggle to the "claim to national identity"[81] while conflating politicization with nationalization, which she identifies as "one of the constitutive features of small literatures."[82] As Casanova follows Fredric Jameson in arguing that writers within literary-deprived spaces are "condemned [...] to develop a national and popular theme [...] engaged in elaborating a national literature,"[83] she forgets her earlier supposition: persons on the periphery might *change* the structure of the world of letters, not by defense or critique, but through reinvention. It is not just that the migratory text offers a site of compromise, as I've examined in chapter 2, but furthermore, that the migratory text makes viable, as a framework, a participation in host communities or dominant literatures through processes that are explicitly syncretic, the creation of alternative cultures and identities that resist traditional either/or models, neither betraying heritage nor denying difference: not merely the "act of talking back" in Graziella Parati's estimation, but the art of changing the conversation.

How do the limits of polities reinscribe themselves upon the terms by which literatures are written, read, and circulated? Of course, it is not just world literature but internationalism—as a program, as a discourse—that is contingent upon the nation-state; political organizations such as the United Nations reproduce the forms of nationalism that are also the conditions for their invitation to the global party. And yet the imperializing logic obscured by such internationalism is not limited to intergovernmental organizations. Aamir Mufti's 2016 critical literary historiography, *Forget English! Orientalism and World Literatures*, sheds light on the global power relations that world literature has enacted, a structuring "nation-thinking" that has simultaneously been obscured from the very world that world literature ostensibly represents. In this literary and political articulation of power, 1989 again becomes a focal point, in this chapter and for this study, precisely because of the illusion of comity engendered by the collapse of the three-world system, what Mufti calls "the triumphalist 'We are the world' tone,"[84] and the subsequent revival, I want to make clear, of world literature as an academic discourse, a publishing practice, and a readerly habit.

We can see this performance of self-staging at work not only in the promise of a newly reunified Germany, but in the organization and expansion of global neoliberalism that soon followed. Linking the assimilation of peripheral languages and cultures into the metropolitan model with the production—and reproduction—of world literature allows us to critically engage the terms of assimilation and integration required of many migrants and asylum applicants, in Berlin and elsewhere, an analysis that attends to the connection between the world literary system, national homogenization and hegemony, and the celebration of an advancing cosmopolitanism. The difference between "world" and "national" literature, Mufti clarifies, is only the order in which they "'force [their] way abroad.'"[85] In this restrictive and mutually reinforcing relationship, space cannot enter the world without first becoming a nation. Likewise, world literature can only recognize the national literatures it translates and transmits. All else disappears.

Instead of elaborating the national tradition in a larger context, we might start by reenvisioning our study on a non-national model; looking beyond the nation means also looking closely at the texts that complicate generic and linguistic borders through their migratory form and the terms of their inscription, of which the works examined in *Drift Net* are but a beginning list. And what happens, what is happening, when we shift the coordinates from which the locus of enunciation—the locus of knowledge production—occurs? That it is neither impossible nor new to produce culture outside capital is worth repeating. Aimé Césaire speaks of the moment when he realized the precolonial cultures of Africa and Asia were not just ante-capitalist but also anti-capitalist:

> They were communal societies, never societies of the many for the few. [...] They were democratic societies, always. They were cooperative societies, fraternal societies. I make a systematic defense of the societies destroyed by imperialism. They were the fact, they did not pretend to be the idea [...] [t]hey kept hope intact.[86]

Césaire's comments are informed by what was happening at the moment in which he was writing, the onset of Cold War colonial decampment, as the question of what alternative forms of government to colonial rule could be imagined was being posed—and enacted—throughout French West Africa. Chief among these political actors was, not coincidentally, Césaire's longtime friend and Négritude collaborator, poet and former prisoner of war in Germany Léopold Sédar Senghor, who understood that to address the conquest, exploitation, disparity, and subjection of empire, it was necessary to transform it into a pluralistic community, a community guided by integration and an integration that could hold, together, both equality and difference. What was the meaning of "real independence"? What lessons could be learned—can be learned—from our colonial past, from present-day colonization? Using Algeria's Civil War of independence as one of many possible case studies, Frederick Cooper, in his 2014 revisitation of postwar Africa, reminds us that "a total reversal of a colonial past can provide a rationale, if not a reason, for new forms of state oppression and violence."[87] This is why the political imagination is so often impoverished by nationalism, racial and ethnic apartheid, and state autocracy; this is when the catastrophe of the past catches up with the catastrophe of the future.

Yet the structure of empire could become, Senghor and others insisted, the groundwork for another polity, not the congruence of nation and state but their dissolution into a nonhierarchical federation. The choice, then, for the organizer of angular resistance—signaling a shift, importantly, from *anti-* to *de*colonial maneuver—moves beyond the conflation of independence as nationalism; it is to imagine alternatives to formal membership, to link one's independence with others, to respond to territorial politics and the independent nation-state by reassembling the governing code as self-reflexive and open-sourced. And yet the lesson, or one of them, of this same period of Cold War colonial decampment that anticipated the construction of the Berlin Wall, is that the dangers of a narrow nationalism are omnipresent, and even the most revolutionary political leaders, Senghor among them, are susceptible to its trappings: power, possession, nativity, the artificial sense of unity whereby a singular people should correspond to a single government. As Cooper details in *Africa in the World*, the dream of a multi-national state composed of multiple nationalities—a union of peoples—so palpable in the 1950s, disintegrated, only a decade later, into the serial reality of sovereign, territorial nations.

Again, we are tasked with asking ourselves to reconsider the route out of empire; to consider the routes out of empire as manifold and necessarily intersecting. What would world literature look like if we began, not in Goethe's moment of national insecurity and surging ethnonationalism, but at the juncture of national renunciation, the emergence of a collective predicated on humankind's idiosyncrasies and shared differences, on a power that is consensual, on a personality that is "ordinary," on a love that insists upon "two people mutually feeding each other?"[88] Such is the oft-repeated invocation of internationalism and mutual respect in Bessie Head's semi-autobiographical account of unprotected life in Botswana, *A Question of Power*, first published in 1973. The story's leitmotif of breakdown, of collapse—Elizabeth carries the trauma of her past amid the Cold War's ongoing South African Border War, alongside her precarious present in Motabeng—reminds us of Morten Goll's pilot plan for a "trampoline house": that the groundwork for a new culture requires risk, exposure, deconstruction. In the divisive society of Bessie's—and her protagonist's—past, in Apartheid Africa, where the mulatto is born illegal, unrecognizable to the society, whose laws nevertheless forbid the union between Black and white persons, how does one relate to one's self except through attending to the self's proneness toward disintegration?

To expose the inherent limitations of her society—and the attendant complications on the psyche of its people—Head write's Elizabeth's reality as a series of discontinuous dreams and hallucinations; if sanctuary is to be found it is by accepting that the "facts" must be intermingled with fantasy in order to be untangled, and rewoven; or, rather, that fiction's lesson—imagination as a form of responsibility—might be harnessed on the grounds of everyday life; such is the case for Elizabeth and her son, who find refuge after leaving South Africa, living and working on an experimental farm. Individual transformation cannot and will not be sustainable, *A Question of Power*'s nonlinear narrative suggests, unless it coincides with a collective shift. If we are to transform community, the potential for change and growth requires an allegiance to motion, to flight, to anonymity. Yet among all the novel's moments, one proves particularly useful for conceptualizing this remapping of world literature. In the scene, Elizabeth's young son discusses school lessons with another member of the village; his conversation moves from the gift of a paper airplane to the reality of modern jets, a special type, the boy informs his guest, that "go faster than any other aeroplane"; and yet, the certainty of acceleration is only matched by the negotiation of fear that necessitates any true shift toward a new world:

> 'I'm afraid about what happen when my jet comes to the edge of the earth [...] I will fall right off. [...] Do you think it's better then that I fly it about in the middle? [...] The goats keep on going to the edge and falling off. My mother says once they fall off they just keep falling and falling because there is no bottom. I can never go far away from home in case I fall off too.'[89]

It is not just that the protagonist's child is learning about modernity's technological encroachments of nature, but that he has not yet learned to move past a provincial nativity, the self-security of *a place of one's own*. Much later, when Elizabeth tells an American volunteer that "'Africa isn't rising. It's up already. It depends on where one places the stress. I place it on the soul [...] it's a power that belongs to all of mankind and in which all mankind can share,'"[90] readers are also prompted to relocate the logic of power and the locus of belonging, as well as our own positions within this cartography. The airplane, the jet, the sky birds, the butterflies—everything natural and artificial, mythical and machinic—each of these become emblem and evidence of this liberation, an intimation of the visible "new dawn and a new world."[91] Bessie Head, like her mixed-race refugee protagonist, straddled the edge without ever following the itinerary and trajectory of Casanova's world literary logic, neither assimilating nor manufacturing difference, electing in her lifetime to remain stateless in Botswana, living and writing in the country where she would ultimately become known as its national writer, despite not ever becoming its citizen.

## LEARNING FROM THE MYTH OF REUNIFICATION: LIMITS AS EDGES

Founded in Kreuzberg in 2004, the Kreuzberger Initiative gegen Antisemitismus (KIGA) develops new approaches for combating anti-semitism. It is not, team member Helen Müller stresses, a program that aims at fostering integration, if only because integration, as Müller points out, is a concept often used in German discourse to package nationalist desires. KIGA's slogan, "Politische Bildung für die Migrationsgesellschaft" (Civic Education for the Migrant Society), underscores the ways in which society is shaped and enriched by migrancy. "We understand it in a way that migration is natural," explains Müller, "and the main question now as in the past is how living together in a diverse society can work. Our approach is not to talk about integration but about living together in a diverse society."[92] Müller, in our discussions in 2019, echoed my conversations with Marcel de Groot a year earlier, as when she described the main obstacle of an inclusive society as a lack of knowledge and understanding of different outlooks when it comes to geopolitical conflicts or the ways we talk about and identify history. What seems evident is the necessity of cultivating both tolerance and ambiguity: to accept that different perspectives can coexist beside one another, and that tension can be productive, discomfort a salve. To recognize this celebration of difference as society's true strength: to remake a culture of consensus as a culture of hospitality.

Édouard Glissant, in his *Traité du tout-monde* (*Treatise on the Whole-World*), published in 1997 and translated into English by Celia Britton in 2020, parses the complexities of expression and acculturation by distinguishing between *langue* (the means of expression) and *langage* (the mode or manner of expression), manner of expression), capable of producing self-subversion through linguistic diversion. In Glissant's analysis, "language can no longer be monolingual,"[93] which implies, too, that all language depends on its echoes but also its traces—the way its speakers re-qualify the self through inflection and iteration, thereby appropriating, when possible, what has been imposed on them, by expressing their own voice within its sonic and semantic scale. "If the French language had been offered to me or imposed on me (they tried, it's true) as the sole experience of its only traditional space," Glissant insists, "I would not have been able to use it."[94] What seems necessary, for the survival of the speaker, the survival of the language, is neither assimilation nor standardization, but a creolization that resists both fusion and essence, and revels in the unpredictability of exchange; what seems necessary for activating the hallowed growth—and hidden revelation—of language is for its intermediaries to consult the unity of difference, where each component must be recognized, "even," as Glissant points out, "while it is already changing."[95] These are the stakes—hospitality, integration, asylum, civic activism—of any discussion about the role and function of language and translation in the migratory text.

KIGA's ongoing "Discover Diversity—between the Present and the Past" workshops, which train young refugees to become peer-to-peer instructors in various secondary schools in Berlin and Brandenburg, encourage engagement and critical self-reflection under a similar rubric. The project, when it began in January of 2016, was a response to common self-silencing and a move toward accountability on the institutional and individual levels. After a one-year phase of interviewing local teachers on their perceived needs and challenges in civic education with young refugees, "Discover Diversity" turned toward applying this knowledge in the development of workshops for schools while conceptualizing and conducting its "train-the-trainer" program. "Our goal is participation not only on a 'listening to' level," Müller says, "but on a level that gives participants agency and influence in decision-making processes." Significantly, Müller, who has worked with KIGA as a civic educator since 2017, also speaks about the awareness of an extant power asymmetry within the project, a critical self-reflection that has animated the gradual reversal of project roles with each iteration of the initiative, wherein participants have been successively granted more control and authority while KIGA's team members have become learners—learning, too, to step back and give room to each participant, to their ideas and perspectives. In challenging dominant narratives together and developing new approaches, KIGA has enacted a cooperative, collaborative, and community-driven approach that provides a different model, conceptual and operational, for migration representation, a way of working in tandem that, as Müller acknowledges, allowed the fruition of several things that would not have been possible in more hierarchical power structures:

> First, all our participants stayed with us during the whole one-year training program. By listening to their needs and giving them room to really challenge our (team's) perspectives, all decided they wanted to stay. This requires a lot of ambiguity tolerance on both sides; the project team need to accept that narratives they grew up with are fundamentally challenged, and so do the participants that have not been socialized in Germany. Our working model allows us to discover how people who have not been raised in Germany perceive discourses on history and politics; we discover gaps, dominant and marginalized perspectives, and we discuss how to close these gaps or how to talk about things without reproducing marginalization or stereotypes.

In 2019, KIGA's plan for the next three years included the introduction of additional school workshops, the advancement of the train-the-trainer program, and, ultimately, the development of learning material that further includes marginalized transnational perspectives of refugees and other migrants. In its reorientation of civic education in German society and Berlin in particular, we might read the organization as providing a framework, not for escaping the past and the specter of the guest worker, but, on the contrary, for learning from the myth of reunification, and rigorously questioning our current worldviews and logic, the customs of assimilation and ownership and conditional hospitality; our own failure, perhaps, to follow theory with practice, within and outside the academy.

And yet these aspirations, to build a more democratic union within Germany and to educate migrants in such civic practices, raise a further question about what "democracy" means in the context of contemporary pandemic and in light of the security procedures of democratic nations; across Germany and elsewhere in Europe and Asia, as borders closed, indispensable migrant workers became disposable, marked as "illegal" in the nation or state of their employment as well as in their own home, which became for many, at the stroke of midnight, unreturnable.

"The difficulty for democratic politics," Étienne Balibar reminds us, "is to avoid becoming enclosed in representations that have historically been associated with emancipatory projects and struggles for citizenship and have now become obstacles to their revival, to their permanent reinvention. Every identification is subject to the double constraint of the structures of the capitalist world economy and of ideology (feelings of belonging to cultural and political units)."[96] Balibar's scrutiny bears fruit, although we can also look to the past for further evidence of the circular problem of political resistance, the fallacy of democracy's reinvention under the constraints of democratic capitalism: Marx's investigation into the contradictory relationships between the outer form of a struggle and its social content, charted in *The Eighteenth Brumaire of Louis Bonaparte* in 1852.[97] Marx, imitating Engels, with whom he was in constant correspondence, writes that every revolution is fixed, in the sense that each attempt at a new historical consciousness proceeds from an extant model, the gift of the past which is its catastrophe. No new revolutions, only new stage sets.

This study can't ignore Marx's suggestion, which he raised early yet never returned to: that history, like language, can only be translated through assimilation, a mother tongue that would yet need to be forgotten. In our endeavors to revivify our organizational and instructional practices from the ground up, we are tasked with moving beyond institutional phraseology, the imposition of emancipatory projects, the common language and idiom of the transnational political or institutional space, the evacuation of referent into semantic superabundance and empty signifier. We are tasked, ultimately, not to render another's perspective and experience through the customs and culture we've inherited, but, on the contrary, to employ translation to change the language we consider to be our own.

Might an education of "practicing democracy" be only the initial learning outcome on a syllabus that aims to question the terms (and limits) of democratic participation?—political rights, which do not equate with social and economic rights, and a state membership, which does not, in fact, provide equal protection by the state based on gender, sexuality, ethnicity, race, and a host of other conditions. If community "finds its truth in limit situations,"[98] as Balibar has advised, has the COVID-19 virus enacted a new (counter?) logistics to supply chain management and neoliberal governance, or merely deepened its chain of command, and thus the problem of the (always) unequal citizen? Ranabir Samaddar, the Director of the Mahanirban Calcutta Research Group, states the case for an alternative foundation of power—a power emanating from the periphery, the dispossessed—in the context of contemporary pandemic:

> Without beating the bush then, we confront the question: how will the entire society be cared for? This of course calls for a new kind of public power, a new republican authority built on the sans culottes of the society—slum dwellers, neighborhood committees, local clubs and associations, associations of health care workers, workers in waste processing and reprocessing—sections in greatest danger, who will be also engaged in defending the vulnerable.[99]

The camp and the city are today indistinguishable, the former melting into the latter, and vice versa; the urban camp is not just a feature of today's cities—Paris, Berlin, Belgrade, Budapest, Athens, Rome ... — but is, in many cases, initiated and managed by these cities. We know that 60 percent of all refugees and 80 percent of all internally displaced persons live, today, in urban areas rather than organized camps.[100] The growth of cities, and of migrant populations within them, will inevitably provoke the breakdown of categories and classifications, of persons and of spaces. Perhaps this is what Balibar had in mind when he proposed, in 2004, that urban border areas weren't "marginal to the constitution of a public sphere but rather [...] at the center,"[101] to the extent that such concentrated zones are also zones of concentration, capable of assembling conflict as change.

Imagining the city as an environment—an occasion—for mobility has never been more pertinent, now when the occupation of urban space as a tactical strategy—see the examples of Rabaa al-Adawiya Square in 2013, Tahrir Square in 2011, Mustapha Mahmoud Square in 2005—has been used to actualize an alternative political future, now when pandemic and shelter-at-home restrictions have altered and interrogated the psychic geography of a public commons. As Adam Ramadan and Elisa Pascucci emphasize: "The protest camp is a project not for its own sake, but a tactic to bring about change in the national and international—as in the case of refugees protesting against the UNHCR—political order itself."[102] Such collective liberation is fostered through an allegiance that goes beyond ethnic, racial, national, and social parameters: a care for life cultivated and reinforced by "the experience of attending to each other's needs in a shared space."[103] Within that break, which is also a meeting, there is something that cannot be assimilated. In producing necessary contradictions, necessary adjustments, this excess, which is a remainder, breaks the illusion of integration.

Here it seems important to revisit an earlier point, to my assessment that employing world literature as an interpretive paradigm risks reproducing exclusionary and normative practices on the ground, in order to flesh out a proposal which began this book, if not also its research: the migratory text, through its formal qualities and collaborative makeup, provokes a conceptual strategy for reconfiguring such models built on assimilation. Indeed, the queer refugee center—and similar local migrant coalitions produced by community organizations, arts centers, and shelters—concretizes the migratory text *as a public project*. How might this social-cultural intervention, as the seeds of an alternative political ecology, contribute to the discourse of decoloniality, from which a growing body of scholarship on migration has drawn?

Between Eve Tuck and K. Wayne Yang's oft-cited affirmation that "decolonization is not a metaphor" in 2012 and Tapji Garba and Sara-Maria Sorentino's critical revision of Tuck and Yang's project eight years later is the suggestion that we might learn to read the native cosmographies emanating from Indigenous studies alongside the political-ontological interventions of Black studies.[104] The 2020 critical commentary "Slavery Is a Metaphor," in which Garba and Sorentino resuscitate the metaphor of settler colonialism to redress the structural logic of the so-called settler-native-slave triad and restore the project of recovery to those who have been enslaved—to restore, moreover, identity and political decipherability to the slave as a non-economic subject—pivots on four major points: "slavery is only ever available as semantic displacement [...] [s]lavery-as-metaphor is the being-of-slavery"; "[t]he political-symbolic structures of slavery are essential to the production of space and its meanings"; "the metaphoricity of slavery [...] provides the generative conditions for the geographies of conquest;" and "*the excision of metaphor from settler colonialism is necessarily the excision of slavery*."[105] In amending the Anglo-centrism of Tuck and Yang's analysis—the compass of Canada and the United States from which Tuck and Yang formulate the relationship between Blackness and Indigeneity—Garba and Sorentino challenge not only the structural history of our "current colonial era," but the very metaphysics that structure our characterization of reality. The move from language to geography and geography to metaphysics is neither incidental nor without precedent, informing the "pluriverse" articulated by Walter Mignolo in 1995 and attributed to the Zapatistas' own decolonial "vision of a world in which many worlds would coexist."[106] I am attracted to the pluriverse for many of the same reasons I am attracted to the interventions provoked by the migratory text: the break from the temporal-spatial ontology of the nation it realizes; the institutional reassessment it proposes for scholars and instructors.

But to understand a pluriverse is to understand its opposite: how the hermeneutics and epistemology of Western metaphysics, which prevents diversity by closing off ways of thinking and doing that are outside its own concept of universality, have long worked in tandem with the rhetorical narrative of modernity, as well as the borders between disciplines, whose territories are necessarily maintained, fought for, driven by a concept of ownership, of producing ownership as "knowledge" and knowledge as "ownership": the rationalization of the divine and divine rationalization, in Aristotle's original conception.[107]

We can trace our contemporary understanding of a pluriverse to the Cold War conceptualization of Négritude, imagined at the moment that colonialism was abolished and at the same time expanded—as former colonies were rebranded as departments and the colonial state proliferated, operating politically, economically, and culturally to establish Western domination: the past and present conforming to the generic model of the West, a spatial-temporal calibration within which we continue to revolve. Aimé Césaire may be frequently cited as the cofounder of Négritude but, as he readily acknowledges, the movement's resistance to the politics of assimilation was, by necessity, a collective project, one that is indebted, even, to the metropolitan culture from which Césaire (and so many newly "liberated" Black subjects, during the period of colonial dismantling in the Antilles and elsewhere) experienced shame and alienation. Before Négritude, there was "pre-Négritude": an enthusiastic interest in African art among white male European painters. Negroes, Césaire insisted, had to be made fashionable in France by Picasso, Vlaminck, Braque ... before the collective Black consciousness could come into focus.

Before articulation is exportation. Before redefinition is fetishization. One would have to go further, then. Not to decolonize society, but to decolonize our inner life. And this, too, was Césaire's project. In re-writing Marx in 1950, Césaire tried to re-write the cartography of liberal humanism, to make good on what the French—the West—had failed to do: "a humanism made to the measure of the world,"[108] and to do so through "plung[ing] into the depths." As he explained in an interview with René Depestre, conducted seventeen years after *Discourse of Colonialism*'s publication, "I felt that beneath the social being would be found a profound being, over whom all sorts of ancestral layers and alluviums had been deposited."[109]

Césaire's call for the discovery of the human being beneath the totalizing force of history and the abstract universalism of the humanities recalls another: Glissant's conjecture that the "confrontation of landscapes confirms that of cultures, sensibilities: not as the exaltation of an Unknown, but as that manner at last of being rid of one's skin to know one's projection in another light, the shadow of what one will be."[110] *Soleil de la conscience: Poétique I*, written in 1955, five years after Césaire's *Discourse of Colonialism*, and translated into English by Nathanaël in 2020, is a remarkable documentation of itineracy, a critique and a celebration of displacement that Chela Sandoval would refer to as "oppositional consciousness," nearly four decades later. The notebook-cum-essay's prescience should be lingered upon; several years before his theorizations of *métissage* and counterpoetics and the poetics of relation, Glissant was able to articulate a collective communion built on desubjectification, and a desubjectification that remained intensely personal: the retracing of his voyage from Martinique to Paris, where he would begin his studies at the Sorbonne, in 1946.

Recall Césaire's need to reclaim Black cultural and aesthetic values through a concrete coming-to-consciousness that does not sidestep but in fact replays the scene of colonizing trauma and shame. Recall Spivak's secret that wants to be revealed, in every act of relation, every act of reading. Recall Glissant's own embrace of opacity, as a measure to clarify, as a means to oppose "any pseudo-humanist attempt" to be reduced "to the scale of some universal model."[111] At the heart of Glissant's first and formidable rite of passage is this desire for a self-recovery that has everything to do with an-other, everything to do with becoming reconstituted through the fundamental gaps in transmission, the essential slips of tongues. "What does language matter then," Glissant asks:

> I mean if it was taught to you or whether you knew it firstly? [...] *The city is all the more secret that you offer yourself to its secret; the Measure will be the same for all; yet whoever seeks unity first crystallizes it in his own language.* And this language disproportions a new language, awkward certainly, that wants to bite. Then it slows, fulfills itself and circulates, on the black roads, at the bedside of the other moons.[112]

What is this but a proposal for knowledge, and the knowledge, not just of a potential future but what has already come to pass? And when Glissant writes "the bedside of the other moons," we are instructed, too, to think about how the retracing of his own displacement via notations that merge prose poetry and the elaboration of theory *without a prescriptive pedagogy*—notes toward a collective participation that is not, he is quick to point out, national[113]—also directs our gaze to other forms of sovereignty, other cosmologies not beholden to Western capitalism and its temporal dicta.

When I read these notes, I think of Marcel de Groot, and the Schwulenberatung Berlin, which he has managed since Germany's reunification, and I think about de Groot's acknowledgment of the prevailing logic and operational method of the "Western way" that remains unrecognizable to shelter residents and asylum applicants. National, sexual, racial, and ethnic identity—the basis of the Western, modern individual—as a categorical construction for an alternative politics will always be limited, and these limitations are inscribed in the narrative of the colonial world from which these markers come. An alternate version of this sentence, which I restrain myself from discarding: *Can we articulate any form of radical or antisystemic resistance while reverting to the terms and position of a fundamental colonial construction?*

Systemic change necessitates first moving beyond one's subject-position and singular experience. To imagine an antisystemic politics and poetics beyond the identitarian model is to imagine a global, migratory culture that is not clothed in Western universalism and disguised as cosmopolitanism; it is to consider how, when we talk of empire and the experiences of minoritized, racialized, and colonized persons, we are also talking about the experience of migration, the breaks both presupposed and instigated by movement, the epistemological impasses posed by persons on the move. For those among us who say and even believe that we are committed to these interventions, it is not a question of *escaping identity* but putting it to work; to continue to insist upon identity formations that resist the trappings of capitalism, that resist the trap of commodification, of turning ourselves into commodities. Isn't it true that political, social, and cultural coalition requires, at the same time, that we can mobilize collectively without denying our individual material realities? To coexist, then, in mutual difference and to celebrate that shared difference even as we critique and disarm the governing powers of differentiation, omission, and ostracism.

We know, following Gaston Bachelard, that only images can set verbs in motion again;[114] such is the necessity, echoed by Saidiya Hartman, to provoke abolition by first performing it on the page.[115] The struggle, as Balibar, too, has clarified, hinges on the agency borne through creative expression, the possibility of inventing "a new image of the relation between membership in historical communities (*ethnos*) and the continued creation of citizenship (*dēmos*) through collective action [...]."[116] It is this vision of a "citizenship without community"—a rethinking of the fetishization of "being-in-common" that redresses the incommensurability between *ethnos* and *dēmos*, the mythos of a shared lineage and the prefab construction of shared civic rights—that must be imagined, articulated, and otherwise performed through the radical acts of collaborative translation elicited by the migratory text. Perhaps, therefore, it has become necessary to move beyond a "citizenship without community," and toward a citizenship without citizens, or rather, a democracy without *demos*: a transformation of the relationships between state, law, and citizenship that calls into question each of these institutions, while enacting a resistance of relation: the attainment of equal rights, enjoyed by all, within a locality.

I want to recall my earlier proposition, that the limit can also be the edge, a necessary precipice, the threshold from which *something other than the historical past* ghosts the history of our present. This study, and, in particular, the moments when I was tasked to pursue its theoretical implications on the ground, in my encounters with the queer refugee, and in the issues gleaned from discussions at migrant community centers and shelters, has reminded me that systemic change requires true coalition, but it also means addressing the ways in which these movements, consciously or otherwise—whether they are situated in immigrants' rights, women's rights, workers' rights, LGBT+ rights, or any other—advance racist, ableist, heteronormative, cisgender, and nationalist frameworks in the name of equality. I want to remember, to retrieve, a common Zapatista saying: "*luchar por un mundo donde otros mundos sean posibles*." Fight for a world where *other worlds are possible.* Decoloniality, in this analysis, wants to delink from all state forms of governance, from the formation of the modern subject, from the institutional and educational paradigms that would want to "divert its pluriverse back into a universe, its heterogeneity back into a totality."[117] Queer, too, is not a metaphor but a subjectivity and a praxis. Just as conceptions of sexuality and gender have been produced through empire and employed by the nation state to enact material rubrics of eligibility and legibility, so can their deconstruction provide not just a blueprint for transforming desires—for desiring differently—but the conditions in which to transform the excess of queer desire into acts of creation, to assemble different infrastructures of social and political governance.

Through this organized and unrehearsed practice, might we see glimmers of the "diverse horizon" imagined by Mignolo in the makeshift spaces for community, conviviality, and necessary conflict that I witnessed at the Schwulenberatung Berlin, at the Sigismondo Castromediano and the Ribezzo museums, at the Trampoline House and the Center for Art on Migration Politics, at the Kreuzberg Initiative against Antisemitism; and in each of these initiative's own critical self-reflections, which signal the work yet to come? Can the queer refugee camp—as embodiment of the migratory—be read, correspondingly, as a site of critique and a space of resistance, not in its opposition to state structures, but through the ways it enacts a different temporality, a different rubric for participation on the intimate, everyday, cross-cultural, and local levels, outside the state?

And if we take up these questions, might we consider this book as only a starting point for further inquiry: to apply its theoretical analysis while calling attention to the limits of the fieldwork from which I've tested its operational potential? Despite the fact that three-quarters of the world's refugee population lives in North Africa, South Asia, and West Asia,[118] the vast majority of scholarship on the mediated experiences of migrants focuses on those in Western and Northern Europe. If we, as scholars and instructors of media, migration, and literature, hope to advance a critical refugee studies discourse, it will also be necessary to take the migratory text at its polyphonic word and decentralize Europe in the field of refugee studies and forced migration. In this pursuit, we need not abandon our language so much as address its limitations and potential for adaptation. Recall the example of the Zapatistas, whose two-way translations from Spanish and Western thought to Tojolabal conveyed Amerindian and subaltern cosmologies in the present; recall the intersubjectivity glimpsed through any act of translanguaging, the attempts to reconcile the particular and the universal through insisting upon the paradigm of transformation through interpenetration; that languages may be incompatible and incommensurable and that, moreover, it is the fact of their fundamental incongruence that orients each to every other—toward interaction, modification, exchange, continual becoming, the drift of mediation.

Where do these encounters lead us and what, mindful of the aporias inherent in engaging Indigenous thought through European tongues, are their limits? When we reorient our own notional and narrative acts of "worlding"—both a violation and a nativity—might we recover other migratory routes, other persons that are not legible to a UNHCR framework, acts of passage that do not serve and which are not guided by Western political policy or discourses of migration? This, too, was my project. Or will be.

# CODA. / "THE HOLE FROM WHICH STORIES GROW"

How to generate agency and resistance within the same system that denies us space and rejects our forms of life?

Rather than posit another label—to be recirculated on the carousel of identity positions from which capitalism derives its power as purveyor (to consume and be consumed)—my hope is that the migratory text as both a canon and a rubric fosters, on the contrary, a relation of process and the processes of relation in which to share approaches for self-reflexive critiques of the roles we inhabit and the institutions from which we yet articulate our positions of resistance, where theory is not an end but the beginning of tools and practices that might help us develop our strategies.

This study has taken as paramount that the migratory text is more than a corpus of literature or a literary theory—as if literature and language were ever confined to the pages they appear before—but a methodology that bears fruit for social and political coalition, a way of reading—reception, recognition—that might aid in the construction of other forms of intersubjective relations or alternative formulations of subjectivity. To read these texts in this way is thus to draw out and draw upon migration; not to elide cultural, regional, lingual, or historical specificity but, on the contrary, to provoke links between markers that might otherwise remain distant and distinct. In the same way that the subject of migration is never just persons on the move but the economic, environmental, political, social, and embodied conditions from which they move and through which each person continues to navigate. This is why mobility is not only a movement but a reimagining of space. Likewise, our treatment of the migratory text allows us to observe these literary-artistic developments alongside contemporary social and political interventions by migrant coalitions. The twinning of migratory and media cultures to read alternative integration and asylum maneuvers is not coincidental. As this study reminds us, the strategies of new media users to compose content and identity are neither new nor digitally native; the situational discourses inscribed through critical-creative autobiographical criticism—a celebrated hybrid poetics, or liminal poetics, or border poetics—is neither an academic phenomenon nor one that should be attributed to the "powerful white male scholars" that have adopted it in their keynotes; and the migrant who offers the primal scene of narrative also proposes a reinterpretation of narrative framework, in which what is returned is the reversibility of original and translation, source and trace. Perhaps then it is not, in Richard Rodriguez's oft-cited assessment, that "the illegal immigrant [...] is the most modern among us,"[1] but that what is overlaid on modernity's tendency to reconstitute the old is the story of migration, which calls the law into question. How did I get here?

> *Walter Benjamin walks the last few craggy passes of a makeshift trail in the Pyrenees and sets foot on Spanish soil. He's breathing heavy; one hand on his walking stick, the other holding his briefcase. A "leather briefcase like those used by businessmen," according to official court documents. He already sees the small custom house to which he'd been directed upon arrival* [...] *takes a look at the Franco-Spanish frontier and sighs, wipes his eyeglasses, directs his own worn eyes toward the bombed-out buildings and scattered rubble: another casualty of fascism, the Spanish Civil War. A deluge of refugees fled toward France. Then refugees in France fled toward Spain.* [...] *Picture it. Picture it again. Better. Picture yourself there.*[2]

And when, above, I write *you*, I am including myself. I had to picture myself there, on the trail of another's exile, in order to imagine my parents' own trails, points of exile, yes, but also sites of confluence that *Drift*

*Net* takes as central in its attempts to untangle or entangle the East and West before and long after the Cold War. And after I'd pictured myself there—an invitation from Wayne Koestenbaum, in a class I'd just entered as a first-year PhD student—I had to turn imagination into material experience; to move in parallel with Benjamin's haphazard coordinates, and then to detour: Puglia, Rome, Berlin, Copenhagen ... to draft a study of media whose scrapbook fabric nurtures elements of autobiography (practice), criticism (theory), and notebook (process), and which renders a mode, not merely a theme, of migration.

But my interest in the questions of affect, semiotics, and translation (to name only a few) that pulsate beneath *Drift Net*'s literary analysis is something with which I'd arrived, if I arrived in the corridors of academia with anything except curiosity and the impostor syndrome that follows anyone who is privileged enough to be the first in their family to do anything, to be anywhere. Several years ago, when I'd just completed my undergraduate studies, traversing that same alternating current of curiosity and shame, I worked as an editor and reporter at the *San Francisco Chronicle* and *Star-Ledger*, helping to put out three editions a night in a print newspaper industry that didn't yet know it was about to die, or become reborn, remediated across our screens, which were nevertheless still nascent. In the mornings, I'd found work by acting in daytime television soap operas—first, *All My Children*, and later, *One Life to Live*—and modeling for companies like Calvin Klein, Levi's, and Saks Fifth Avenue. I did not know it, or at least I didn't yet have the words for it, but I was beginning my investigation of a representational economy rooted in visibility that coheres an environment like the newsroom with the runway and the studio.

If there is a story behind the story of *Drift Net* it is the hole from which stories grow, the hole that begs, if not excavation, then in Benjamin's words, persistent drilling. The displacement I felt growing up as a first-generation US American citizen became also the displacement I experienced as both viewer and subject, writer and text in a culture industry that urged me to attend to the negotiation between commodification and production, and the territorialization and tokenization brought by both. At the heart of this study are these same issues of narrative frame, audience, and address, as well as the reclamation of agency and authorship over one's own representation, a constellation that serves *Drift Net*'s itinerary, and a schedule of movements that remains nothing if not preparatory, as we see from the study's last (but not final) lines: a call to be en route.

So often wanting to disclaim ownership if not also authority, I understand that this *Drift Net*, too, moves in ways I couldn't possibly envision or administer. Like many of us, I knew, or thought I knew, what it was I wanted to pay attention to, where I wanted to go, even if or perhaps because I didn't know how to get there. And when I got there—and there, and there ... guided by the ideas and exchanges of my mentors, those departed and ever-present—the suppositions I had taken as theory were unfurled on the ground, questioned, and reevaluated. Although my interactions with asylum applicants and migrant coalition organizers throughout Europe comprise my final chapter's analysis, the lessons—of a migrant sovereignty not tethered to Western rubrics—inform each preceding chapter, prompting us to question whether refugee co-authorship in the academy—integration into a structure of unequal access and representation—risks reifying the power structures regularly obscured by operations at the border, while devaluing the material experiences of persons on the move, as well as their potential for political subjectivity not beholden to institutional membership. The university, too, is a border, and the operations of translation and interpretation (interpellation, surveillance) do not end after we cross a seemingly fixed point.

Thus, I feel ill-equipped to provide a response to the common question of *what I might have done differently if I knew what I know now*—the knowing as being a part of this nearly decade-long study, but also the not-knowing—the processes of alighting upon consciousness (the swerves and repetitions) as a form of knowledge production I have hoped to retain. The tempo of this work, after all, remains collaboration, polyphony, archive, and abstraction, and it is with these formal characteristics that I began to hone my reading of literature and art but also organization and activism; it is the only way I can think to conclude this study of the migratory text—in defense of incompletion, but also invitation: to accommodate a similar rhythm as you read, too.

# *Notes*

## INTRODUCTION. /

1 See: Chris Campanioni, "In Parallel with My Actual Diary: On Re-Writing an Exile," *Life Writing* 18, no. 1 (2021): 95–111, https://doi.org/10.1080/14484528.2020.1766752. Anthologized in *Essays in Life Writing*, ed. Kylie Cardell (New York and London: Routledge, 2022).

2 Richard Black, "Fifty Years of Refugee Studies: From Theory to Policy," *International Migration Review* 35, no. 1 (Spring 2001): 57–78.

3 See: Georgia Cole, "Beyond Labelling: Rethinking the Role and Value of the Refugee 'Label' through Semiotics," *Journal of Refugee Studies* 31, no. 1 (2018): 1–21, https://doi.org/10.1093/jrs/fex021

4 See: Dick Higgins, "Intermedia," *Something Else Newsletter* 1, no. 1 (1966): 1–4, web. Retrieved from https://www.primaryinformation.org/oldsite/SEP/Something-Else-Press_Newsletter_V1N1.pdf

See also: the retrospective Dick Higgins and Hannah Higgins, "Intermedia," *Leonardo* 34, no. 1 (2001): 49–54.

5 Alessandra Di Maio, *Wor(l)ds in Progress: A Study of Contemporary Migrant Writers* (Rome: Mimesis International, 2014), 13.

6 See: Henry Jenkins, *Convergence Culture: Where Old and New Media Collide* (New York: New York University Press, 2006), and earlier: Jenkins, "Convergence? I Diverge," *MIT Technology Review*, June 1, 2001, web. Retrieved from https://www.technologyreview.com/2001/06/01/235791/convergence-i-diverge/

7 Mieke Bal, "Documenting What? Auto-Theory and Migratory Aesthetics," in *A Companion to Contemporary Documentary Film*, eds. Alexandra Juhasz, and Alisa Lebow (Hoboken, NJ: Wiley-Blackwell, 2015), 124–144.

8 Bal, "Documenting What? Auto-Theory and Migratory Aesthetics," 132.

9 Sandra Ponzanesi, *The Postcolonial Cultural Industry: Icons, Markets, Mythologies* (New York: Palgrave Macmillan, 2014).

10 Sarah C. Bishop, *Undocumented Storytellers: Narrating the Immigrant Rights Movement* (Oxford: Oxford University Press, 2019), 152.

11 Graziella Parati, *Migration Italy: The Art of Talking Back in a Destination Culture* (Toronto: University of Toronto Press, 1995), 31.

12 Eva C. Karpinski, "Migrations and Metamorphoses," *a/b: Auto/Biography Studies* 32, no. 2 (2017): 173, https://doi.org/10.1080/08989575.2017.1287898

13 See: Rebecca M. Schreiber, *The Undocumented Everyday: Migrant Lives and the Politics of Visibility* (Minneapolis, MN: University of Minnesota Press, 2018).

14 See: French novelist and theorist Serge Doubrovsky, who coined the term in reference to his own novel in 1977, a year after the US-backed military coup in Argentina and at the same moment that the guest worker as a source of migrant labor intensified, along with the growth of several aid organizations tied to managing migration.

15 For the earliest book-length examination of the user-led collaborative processes characterized by open participation, communal evaluation, common property, unfinished artefacts, and indefinite development, see: Axel Bruns, *Blogs, Wikipedia, Second Life, and Beyond: From Production to Produsage* (New York: Peter Lang, 2008).

16 Hannah Arendt, "We Refugees," in *Altogether Elsewhere: Writers on Exile*, ed. Marc Robinson (London: Faber and Faber, 1994), 119.

17 See: Martin F. Manalansan, "Queer Intersections: Sexuality and Gender in Migration Studies," *The International Migration Review* 40, no. 1 (2006): 224–249, https://doi.org/10.1111/j.1747-7379.2006.00009.x

18 Dana Diminescu, "The Connected Migrant: An Epistemological Manifesto," *Social Science Information* 47, no. 4 (2008): 565–579, https://doi.org/10.1177/0539018408096447

19 See: Oliver Bakewell, "Researching Refugees: Lessons from the Past, Current Challenges and Future Directions," *Refugee Survey Quarterly* 26, no. 3 (2007): 6–14, https://doi.org/10.1093/rsq/hdi0239; and Dawn Chatty and Philip Marfleet, "Conceptual Problems in Forced Migration," *Refugee Survey Quarterly* 32, no. 2 (2013): 1–13, https://doi.org/10.1093/rsq/hdt008

20 See: Raka Shome, "When Postcolonial Studies Interrupts Media Studies," *Communication Culture & Critique* 12 (2019): 305–322, https://doi.org/10.1093/ccc/tcz020

21 In another nod to the iterative past, the words that begin this study recall the introduction of my endeavor to re-write Walter Benjamin's exile. If my correspondence to Benjamin as a whole is lost here, it is only so that its material traces can disperse, in fragments, in each chapter to follow.

22 Kale Bantigue Fajardo, *Filipino Crosscurrents: Oceanographies of Seafaring, Masculinities, and Globalization* (Minneapolis, MN: University of Minnesota Press, 2011), 23.

23 Russell King, John Connell, and Paul White, eds., *Writing Across Worlds: Literature and Migration* (London and New York: Routledge, 1995), ix–x, emphasis in the original.

24 King, Connell, and White, *Writing Across Worlds*, x.

25 David Damrosch, *What Is World Literature?* (Princeton, NJ: Princeton University Press, 2003), 4.

26 Lawrence Venuti, *Translation Changes Everything: Theory and Practice* (New York: Routledge, 2013), 193.

27 Venuti, "Translation and the Pedagogy of Literature," *College English* 58.3 (March 1996): 334.

28 See: Caren Kaplan, "Resisting Autobiography: Out-Law Genres and Transnational Feminist Subjects," in *De/Colonizing the Subject*, eds. Sidonie Smith and Julia Watson (Minneapolis, MN: University of Minnesota Press, 1992), 115–138.

29 See: Liisa H. Malkki, "Speechless Emissaries: Refugees, Humanitarianism, and Dehistoricization," *Cultural Anthropology* 11, no. 3 (1996): 377–404.

30 Jacques Rancière, *The Politics of Aesthetics*, trans. Gabriel Rockhill (London: Continuum, 2004), 9.

31 Karma R. Chávez, *Queer Migration Politics* (Urbana, IL: University of Illinois Press, 2013), 8.

32 See: C. Riley Snorton, *Black on Both Sides: A Racial History of Trans Identity* (Minneapolis, MN: University of Minnesota Press, 2017).

33 Brian Massumi, Jacob Ferrington, Alina Hechler, and Jannell Parsons, "Affect and Immediation: An Interview with Brian Massumi," *disClosure: A Journal of Social Theory* 28 (2019): 115, https://doi.org/10.13023/disclosure.28.09

34 Massumi, Ferrington, Hechler, and Parsons, "Affect and Immediation," 116.

35 Erin Manning, "Toward a Politics of Immediation," *Frontiers in Sociology* 3 (2019): 1, https://doi.org/10.3389/fsoc.2018.00042

36 See: Percy Shelley, *A Defence of Poetry*, in *Shelley's Poetry and Prose*, eds. Donald H. Reiman and Neil Fraistat (New York and London, W.W. Norton, 2002), 535, quoted in Timothy Morton, "Ecology without the Present," *Oxford Literary Review* 34, no. 2 (2012): 235.

37 For a comprehensive overview on the entanglements of war and trade and how the "logistics revolution" of the Cold War continues to transform capitalist production, especially in relation to the securitization of spatial mobility and the restructuring and regulation of vulnerable labor since September 11, 2001, see: Deborah Cowen, *The Deadly Life of Logistics: Mapping Violence in Global Trade* (Minneapolis, MN: University of Minnesota Press, 2014). More recently, Karin Krifors' analysis of the economies of high-tech services and forestry/agriculture in Sweden demonstrates how calculations of labor costs are central to the commercialization of migration across diverse markets, making visible how people's labor and movements are fundamental to their design. See: Krifors, "Logistics of Migration Labour: Rethinking how Workers 'Fit' Transnational Economies," *Journal of Ethnic and Migration Studies* 47, no. 1 (2021): 148–165, https://doi.org/10.1080/1369183X.2020.1754179

38 See: Chris Campanioni, *the Internet is for real* (Winston-Salem, NC: C&R Press, 2019).

39 Hans Park, "The Power of Cities," *UNHCR*, November 25, 2016, web. Retrieved from https://www.unhcr.org/innovation/the-power-of-cities/

## CHAPTER ONE: ARCHIVE. /

1 Dubravka Ugrešić, *The Museum of Unconditional Surrender*, trans. Celia Hawkesworth (New York: New Directions, 1999), 26–27.

2 Ugrešić, *The Museum of Unconditional Surrender*, 214.

3 Fredric Jameson, *The Political Unconscious: Narrative as Socially Symbolic Act* (New York: Routledge, 1981).

4 As Neil Gershenfeld, director of MIT's Center for Bits and Atoms, first described it during a March 10, 2010 talk at the Museum of Science called "How To Make Almost Anything."

5 Mieke Bal, "Double Movement," in *2move: Video, Art, Migration*, eds. Mieke Bal and Miguel Á. Hernández-Navarro (Murcia: Cendeac, 2008), 13–82.

6 The best media, in the rubric of the industry, are the ones that don't appear to mediate at all, erasing the traces of their own mediation, along with the possibility of collaboration through glitch and its generative failures, as I've written elsewhere. See: Chris Campanioni, "How Bizarre: The Glitch of the

Nineties as a Fantasy of New Authorship," *M/C: Media & Culture* 21, no. 5 (December 2018), https://doi.org/10.5204/mcj.1463

7 See: Susan Sontag, *As Consciousness Is Harnessed to Flesh: Journals & Notebooks 1964–1980*, ed. David Rieff (New York: Picador, 2012).

8 Nancy K. Miller, *Getting Personal: Feminist Occasions and Other Autobiographical Acts* (New York: Routledge, 1991), 3–7.

9 For more on the complexities of migrant im/perceptibility, see: Saskia Witteborn, "Becoming (Im)Perceptible: Forced Migrants and Virtual Practice," *Journal of Refugee Studies* 28, no. 3 (2015): 354, https://doi.org/10.1093/jrs/feu036

10 For an elaboration of "networked affect," see: Susanna Paasonen, "Networked affect," in *Posthuman Glossary*, eds. Rosi Braidotti and Maria Hlavajova (London: Bloomsbury Academic, 2018), 283–285.

11 Jodi Dean, "Affective Networks," *Media Tropes* 2, no. 2 (2010): 37.

12 Dean, "Affective Networks," 21.

13 In his 2017 study of the Ibdaa refugee camp in the West Bank, Sanjay Asthana noted the emergence of a similar form of participation and identity formation through young people's social media practices, including the self-archival of blogging; such everyday motions allow refugees to transgress boundaries both social and physical while pushing beyond the reductive humanitarian representation of victimization and suffering. See: Sanjay Asthana, "Youth, Self, Other: A Study of Ibdaa's Digital Media Practices in the West Bank, Palestine," *International Journal of Cultural Studies* 20, no. 1 (2017): 100–117, https://doi.org/10.1177/1367877915600546

14 Elizabeth A. Povinelli and George Chauncey, "Thinking Sexuality Transnationally: An Introduction," *GLQ* 5, no. 4 (1999): 440.

15 For an early, pre-digital definition of "copresence," see Erving Goffman, *Behavior in Public Places* (New York: The Free Press, 1963). Goffman noted the particular psychological impacts of being together in a virtual environment, wherein individuals become "accessible, available, and subject to one another."

16 Ugrešić, *The Museum of Unconditional Surrender*, 28, emphasis mine.

17 Sarah Manguso, *Ongoingness: The End of a Diary* (London: Picador, 2019), 16.

18 Ugrešić, *The Museum of Unconditional Surrender*, 28.

19 Eve Sedgwick, *Touching Feeling: Affect, Pedagogy, Performativity* (Durham, NC: Duke University Press, 2003), 146.

20 José Esteban Muñoz, *Cruising Utopia: The Then and There of Queer Futurity* (New York: New York University Press, 2009), 162.

21 Miriyam Aouragh, "Everyday Resistance on the Internet: The Palestinian Context," *Journal of Arab and Muslim Media Research* 1, no. 2 (2008): 110, https://doi.org/10.1386/jammr.1.2.109_1

22 See: Rebecca M. Schreiber's *The Undocumented Everyday: Migrant Lives and the Politics of Visibility* (Minneapolis: University of Minnesota Press, 2018) and Rozalinda Borcilă's "The Political Aesthetics of Immigrant Protest," in *Immigrant Protest: Politics, Aesthetics, and Everyday Dissent*, eds. Katarzyna Marciniak and Imogen Tyler (Albany, NY: State University of New York Press, 2015), 45–62.

23 For an in-depth analysis of these specific tactics, see: Campanioni, "The Glitch of Biometrics and the Error as Evasion: The Subversive Potential of Self-Effacement," *Diacritics* 48, no. 4 (2021): 28–51, https://doi.org/10.1353/dia.2020.0028

24 See: Dana Diminescu, "The Connected Migrant: An Epistemological Manifesto," *Social Science Information* 47, no. 4 (2008): 565–579, https://doi.org/10.1177/0539018408096447

25 See: Sandro Mezzadra and Brett Neilson, *Border as Method: Or, the Multiplication of Labor* (Durham, NC: Duke University Press, 2013), Lilie Chouliaraki and Myria Georgiou, "The Digital Border: Mobility Beyond Territorial and Symbolic Divides," *European Journal of Communication* 34, no. 6 (2019): 598, https://doi.org/10.1177/0267323119886147, and Étienne Balibar, *Politics and the Other Scene*, trans. Christine Jones, James Swenson, and Chris Turner (New York: Verso, 2002), among others.

26 As I write this, I'm reminded of Franz Kafka's own notes, from which we glean: "From outside one will always triumphantly impress theories upon the world and then fall straight into the ditch one has dug, but only from inside will one keep oneself and the world quiet and true." See: Franz Kafka, *The Blue Octavo Notebook*, trans. Ernst Kaiser and Eithne Wilkins, ed. Max Brod (Cambridge, MA: Exact Change, 1991), 16.

27 Theodor W. Adorno, *Aesthetic Theory*, trans. Robert Hullot-Kentor (New York and London: Continuum, 2002), 243.

28 Patricia Bizzell, "The Intellectual Work of 'Mixed' Forms of Academic Discourses," in *ALT DIS: Alternative Discourses and the Academy*, eds. Christopher Schroeder, Helen Fox, and Patricia Bizzell (Portsmouth, NH: Heinemann, 2002), 5.

29 Muñoz, *Disidentifications: Queers of Color and the Performance of Politics* (Minneapolis, MN: University of Minnesota Press, 1999), 11.

30 See: Campanioni, *A and B and Also Nothing* (Atlanta, GA: Unbound Edition, 2023).

31 Examples abound: Elizabeth Ellen (*PERSON/A*), Megan Boyle (*LIVEBLOG*), Darcie Wilder (*literally show me a healthy person*), David Shapiro (*Supremacist*), Ben Lerner (*10:14*), Rachel Cusk (*Outline*), as well as Rob Doyle, Scott McClanahan, and Sam Pink, all of whom are cited as contributors to the database aesthetic of public self-construction that characterizes the broader trend of "New Autofiction" in Joseph Worthen, "Autofiction and Selfie Aesthetics," *Post45*, December 16, 2021, web. Retrieved from https://post45.org/2021/12/autofiction-and-selfie-aesthetics/

32 Walter Benjamin, "Diary from August 7, 1931, to the Day of My Death," trans. Rodney Livingstone, in *Walter Benjamin: Selected Writings (Volume 2, Part 2, 1931–1934)*, eds. Michael W. Jennings, Marcus Bullock, Howard Eiland, and Gary Smith (Cambridge, MA: Harvard University Press, 1999), 504.

33 Benjamin, "Diary from August 7, 1931, to the Day of My Death," 505.

34 Also known as "about to die" images. See: Barbie Zelizer, *About to Die: How News Images Move the Public* (Oxford: Oxford University Press, 2010).

35 *Abounaddara: The Right to the Image*, which ran at The Vera List Center for Art and Politics from October 22 through November 11, 2015, was organized by theme, each of the three weeks focusing on a specific strategy implemented by Abounaddara in the production of their emergency cinema. "LOOK AT OUR FACES: PORTRAITS OF A BECOMING REVOLUTION" was the centerpiece of the show's second week.

36 Abounaddara, "Dignity Has Never Been Photographed," *documenta 14*, March 24, 2017, web. Retrieved from https://documenta14.de/en/notes-and-works/15348/dignity-has-never-been-photographed

37 Benjamin, "Notes from Svendborg, Summer 1934," trans. Rodney Livingstone, in *Walter Benjamin: Selected Writings (Volume 2, Part 2, 1931–1934)*, 783.

38 Benjamin, "Surrealism: The Last Snapshot of the European Intelligentsia," trans. Edmund Jephcott, in *Walter Benjamin: Selected Writings (Volume 2, Part 1, 1927–1930)*, eds. Michael W. Jennings, Howard Eiland, and Gary Smith (Cambridge, MA: Harvard University Press, 1999), 217–218.

39 Antoinette Burton, "'An Assemblage/Before Me': Autobiography as Archive," *Journal of Women's History* 25, no. 2 (2013): 188, https://doi.org/10.1353/jowh.2013.0022

40 My use of the term is a marked departure from Marisa Olson's founding remarks in 2006, where "postinternet" is used to characterize a growing canon of art under the influence of the internet—work that describes and critiques nascent conditions of production and distribution; Guthrie Lonergan's "internet-aware art," which decenters the technology through critical distance; and Gene McHugh's vision of postinternet as a phenomenon

of banality. Elsewhere, I've described *post* internet practices as emphasizing textual presentation while calling attention to a presence that is simultaneous and heterospatial—the work's ability, and its invitation, to be in several places at once. This version of post internet signals, not detachment, but activity and interaction and collaboration: an awareness and celebration of ensemble. For a contrasting and comprehensive survey, see: Marisa Olson, "Postinternet: Art After the Internet," *Foam* 29 (2011): 59–63.

41 Kwame Anthony Appiah, "Is the Post- in Postmodernism the Post- in Postcolonial?" *Critical Inquiry* 17, no. 2 (Winter 1991): 336–357.

42 Ania Loomba, *Colonialism/Postcolonialism* (New York: Routledge, 2005), 2.

43 Loomba, *Colonialism/Postcolonialism*, 20–22.

44 See: Loomba's discussion of Martin Bernal's 1987 book, *Black Athena: The Afroasiatic Roots of Classical Civilization* (New Brunswick, NJ: Rutgers University Press), in Loomba, *Colonialism/Postcolonialism*, 59.

45 Francis Ponge, *Nioque of the Early-Spring*, trans. Jonathan Larson (Brooklyn, NY: The Song Cave, 2018), 23.

46 Ponge, *Nioque of the Early-Spring*, 24.

47 Ponge, *Nioque of the Early-Spring*, 24, emphasis mine.

48 Ponge, *Nioque of the Early-Spring*, 31.

49 Ponge, *Nioque of the Early-Spring*, 29.

50 Ponge, *Nioque of the Early-Spring*, 15.

51 Ponge, *Nioque of the Early-Spring*, 45–46.

52 Ponge, *Nioque of the Early-Spring*, 52–53.

53 Marcel Duchamp, *The Writings of Marcel Duchamp*, trans. Elmer Peterson, eds. Michel Sanouillet and Elmer Peterson (Cambridge, MA: Da Capo Press, 1973), 167.

54 Ponge, *Nioque of the Early-Spring*, 55.

55 Franz Kafka, *The Diaries of Franz Kafka*, trans. Joseph Kresh, ed. Max Brod (New York: Schocken Books, 1948), 191.

56 Pascale Casanova, *The World Republic of Letters*, trans. M.B. DeBevoise (Cambridge, MA: Harvard University Press, 2004), 207.

57 Casanova, *The World Republic of Letters*, 11.

58 Kafka, *The Blue Octavo Notebooks*, trans. Ernst Kaiser and Eithne Wilkins, ed. Max Brod (Cambridge, MA: Exact Change, 1991), 9.

59 Kafka, *The Blue Octavo Notebooks*, 69–70.

60 Miguel Á. Hernández-Navarro, "Out of Synch: Visualizing Migratory Times through Video Art," in *Art and Visibility in Migratory Culture*, eds. Mieke Bal and Miguel Á. Hernández-Navarro (Leiden: Brill, 2011), 191.

61 Burton, "'An Assemblage/Before Me'," 187, https://doi.org/10.1353/jowh.2013.0022

62 Wolfgang Iser, "The Reading Process: A Phenomenological Approach," *New Literary History* 3, no. 2 (1972): 285, https://doi.org/10.2307/468316

63 Matt DelConte, "A Further Study of Present Tense Narration: The Absentee Narratee and Four-Wall Present Tense in Coetzee's *Waiting for the Barbarians* and *Disgrace*," *Journal of Narrative Theory* 37, no. 3 (2007): 434.

64 Jill Bennett, "Migratory Aesthetics: Art and Politics beyond Identity," in *Art and Visibility in Migratory Culture*, 112 and 117, emphasis mine.

65 For an expansive analysis of transmedia mobilization, see: Sasha Costanza-Chock, *Out of the Shadows, Into the Streets!: Transmedia Organizing and the Immigrant Rights Movement* (Cambridge, MA: MIT Press, 2014).

66 See: "Palestinian Discusses Humanitarian Needs in Gaza," *ABC News*, October 13, 2023, web. Retrieved from https://abcnews.go.com/International/video/palestinian-discusses-humanitarian-gaza-103967824

67 Fady Joudah, "A Palestinian Meditation in a Time of Annihilation," *Literary Hub*, November 1, 2023, web. Retrieved from https://lithub.com/a-palestinian-meditation-in-a-time-of-annihilation/

68 Khatharya Um, "Exiled Memory: History, Identity, and Remembering in Southeast Asia and Southeast Asian Diaspora," *Positions* 20, no. 3 (Summer 2012): 834, emphasis mine, https://doi.org/10.1215/10679847-1593564

69 Um, "Exiled Memory," 847.

70 Jacques Derrida, *Limited Inc.*, trans. Samuel Weber (Evanston, IL: Northwestern University Press, 1988), 20.

71 Derrida, "No (Point of) Madness—Maintaining Architecture," trans. Kate Linker, in *Psyche: Inventions of the Other, Volume II*, eds. Peggy Kamuf and Elizabeth Rottenberg (Redwood City, CA: Stanford University Press, 2008), 88.

72 Paul Cilliers, *Complexity and Postmodernism: Understanding Complex Systems* (London and New York: Routledge, 1998), 42.

73 Timothy Morton, "Ecology without the Present," *Oxford Literary Review* 34, no. 2 (2012): 234.

74 Campanioni, "The Glitch of Biometrics," 41–43.

75 Anthony Cody, *The Rendering* (Oakland, CA: Omnidawn, 2023), 12.

76 Cody, *The Rendering*, 27.

77 Deferred Action for Childhood Arrivals (DACA) is a US immigration policy that protects migrants who came to the United States when they were children from deportation. United States Citizenship and Immigration Services

(USCIS) began accepting applications for the program on August 15, 2012, two months after President Barack Obama announced the policy.

78 Mary Ann Caws, *The Eye in the Text* (Princeton, NJ: Princeton University Press, 1981), 11.

79 Cody, *The Rendering*, 51.

80 Benjamin, "The Storyteller," trans. Harry Zohn, in *Illuminations*, ed. Hannah Arendt (New York: Schocken Books, 1969), 107.

81 Benjamin, "The Storyteller," 87.

82 Édouard Glissant, Manthia Diawara, and Christopher Winks, "One World in Relation: Édouard Glissant in Conversation with Manthia Diawara," *Nka: Journal of Contemporary African Art* 28 (2011): 7.

83 Ponge, *Soap*, trans. Lane Dunlop (Redwood City, CA: Stanford University Press, 1998), 7.

84 Ponge, *Soap*, 7.

85 Ponge, *Soap*, 97.

86 Ponge, *Soap*, 46.

87 Yury Tynyanov, "The Literary Fact," trans. Ann Shukman, in *Modern Genre Theory*, ed. David Duff (New York: Routledge, 2014), 39.

88 Ponge, *Soap*, 87.

89 Ponge, *Soap*, 93.

90 Boris Pasternak, Marina Tsvetayeva, and Maria Rilke Rainer, *Letters: Summer 1926*, trans. Margaret Wettlin, Walter Arndt, Jamey Gambrell (New York: New York Review of Books, 2001), 111–112.

91 Marcos, *Professionals of Hope: The Selected Writings of Subcomandante Marcos* (Brooklyn, NY: The Song Cave, 2017), 33, emphasis mine.

92 Marcos, *Professionals of Hope*, 45.

93 Marcos, *Professionals of Hope*, 46.

94 For a more elaborate discussion of "generative fictions," see: Campanioni, "Made in My Image: Co-Produced Fantasy and the Politics of Play," in *Transmedia Selves: Identity and Persona Creation in the Age of Mobile and Multiplatform Media*, eds. James Dalby and Matthew Freeman (New York: Routledge, 2023), 112–129, https://doi.org/10.4324/9781003134015

95 Hannah Arendt, "Introduction," in *Illuminations: Essays and Reflections*, ed. Hannah Arendt (New York: Schocken Books, 1969), 8.

96 Benjamin, *The Correspondence of Walter Benjamin, 1910–1940*, trans. Manfred R. Jacobson and Evelyn M. Jacobson, eds. Gershom Scholem and Theodor W. Adorno (Chicago, IL: University of Chicago Press, 2012), 256.

97 Benjamin, *The Arcades Project*, trans. Howard Eiland and Kevin McLaughlin (Cambridge, MA: Harvard University Press, 1999), 458.

98 Pasternak, Tsvetayeva, and Rilke, *Letters*, 88.

99 Benjamin, "Curriculum Vitae (III)," trans. Rodney Livingstone, in *Walter Benjamin: Selected Writings (Volume 2, Part 1, 1927–1930)*, 77–78.

100 Benjamin, *The Correspondence of Walter Benjamin*, 359.

101 Benjamin, "Notes from Svendborg, Summer 1934," 786.

102 Benjamin, "Notes from Svendborg, Summer 1934," 786.

103 Benjamin, "Notes from Svendborg, Summer 1934," 786.

104 John Berger, *Ways of Seeing* (London: Penguin, 1972), 21.

105 Benjamin, "The Author as Producer," trans. Edmund Jephcott, in *Walter Benjamin: Selected Writings (Volume 2, Part 2, 1931–1934)*, 777.

106 Roland Barthes, *The Rustle of Language*, trans. Richard Howard (Berkeley, CA: University of California Press, 1986), 147.

107 See: Umberto Eco, *The Open Work*, trans. Anna Cancogni (Cambridge, MA: Harvard University Press, 1989), 246.

108 See: Henry Jenkins, "Transmedia Storytelling 101," *Pop Junctions: Reflections on Entertainment, Pop Culture, Activism, Media Literacy, Fandom, and More*, March 21, 2007, web. Retrieved from http://henryjenkins.org/blog/2007/03/transmedia_storytelling_101.html

"Transmedia storytelling" can be traced to Jenkins, "Convergence? I Diverge," *MIT Technology Review*, June 1, 2001, web. Retrieved from https://www.technologyreview.com/2001/06/01/235791/convergence-i-diverge/

109 See also: Tunisian French cultural theorist Pierre A. Lévy, who theorized collective intelligence in 1994 as a form of "universally distributed intelligence, constantly enhanced, coordinated in real time," with the publication of *L'intelligence collective: Pour une anthropologie du cyberspace*, translated into English three years later in Lévy, *Collective Intelligence: Mankind's Emerging World in Cyberspace*, trans. Robert Bononno (New York: Plenum Trade, 1997).

110 For a broader analysis of digital modernism, see: Jessica Pressman, "The Strategy of Digital Modernism," in *World Literature in Theory*, ed. David Damrosch (West Sussex: John Wiley & Sons, 2004), 493–510.

111 Arendt, "Introduction," 48.

112 Rolf Tiedemann, "Dialectics at a Standstill: Approaches to the *Passagen-Werk*," trans. Gary Smith and André Lefevere, in *The Arcades Project*, 931.

113 Benjamin, *One-Way Street*, trans. Edmund Jephcott, ed. Michael W. Jennings (Cambridge, MA: Harvard University Press, 2016), 21.

114 Fredric Jameson, *The Modernist Papers* (London: Verso, 2007), 5.

115 Benjamin, "Unpacking My Library," trans. Harry Zohn, in *Walter Benjamin: Selected Writings (Volume 2, Part 2, 1931–1934)*, 492.

116 Tynyanov, "The Literary Fact," 42.

117 Tynyanov, 30.
118 Tynyanov, 34.
119 Tynyanov, 34.
120 Tynyanov, 41.
121 Arnaldo Calveyra, *Letters So That Happiness*, trans. Elizabeth Zuba (Brooklyn, NY: Ugly Duckling Presse, 2018), 37.
122 Sontag, *As Consciousness Is Harnessed to Flesh*, 511.
123 Calveyra, *Letters So That Happiness*, 21.
124 Calveyra, 47.
125 Elizabeth Zuba, "Translator Note," in *Letters So That Happiness*, 56.
126 Benjamin, "German Letters," trans. Rodney Livingstone, in *Walter Benjamin: Selected Writings (Volume 2, Part 2, 1931–1934)*, 466.
127 Benjamin, "On the Trail of Old Letters," trans. Rodney Livingstone, in *Walter Benjamin: Selected Writings (Volume 2, Part 2, 1931–1934)*, 556.
128 Félix Guattari, *Chaosophy: Texts and Interviews 1972–1977*, ed. Sylvére Lotringer (Los Angeles, CA: Semiotext(e), 2009), 71.
129 See: Viktor Shklovsky's *Third Factory*, an assortment of anecdotes, not all of them about the author. "I have no desire to be witty," Shklovsky writes on the first page of his autobiographical novel. "I have no desire to construct a plot. I am going to write about things and thoughts. To compile quotations." Shklovsky, *Third Factory*, trans. Richard Sheldon (Chicago, IL: Dalkey Archive Press, 2002), 3.
130 Ponge, *Soap*, 96.
131 Shklovsky, *Third Factory*, 52.
132 Benjamin, *One-Way Street*, 43.
133 See: Axel Bruns, "Towards Produsage: Futures for User-Led Content Production," in *Cultural Attitudes towards Technology and Communication 2006: Proceedings of the Fifth International Conference*, eds. Fay Sudweeks, Herbert Hrachovec, and Charles Ess (Murdoch: School of Information Technology, 2006), 275–284; and Bruns, *Blogs, Wikipedia, Second Life, and Beyond: From Production to Produsage* (New York: Peter Lang, 2008).
134 Édouard Glissant, *Poetics of Relation*, trans. Betsy Wing (Ann Arbor, MI: University of Michigan Press, 1997), 25.
135 Michel Foucault, "What Is an Author?," trans. Josué V. Harari, in *Aesthetics, Method, and Epistemology*, ed. James D. Faubion (New York: The New Press, 1998), 222, emphasis mine.
136 Benjamin, "The Task of the Translator," trans. Harry Zohn, in *Illuminations*, ed. Hannah Arendt (New York: Schocken Books, 1968), 263.
137 Foucault, "What Is an Author?" 217.

138 Foucault, 206, emphasis mine.

139 Boris Pasternak, *Safe Conduct*, trans. Babette Deutsch (New York: New Directions, 2009), 26–27.

140 Hugo Ball, *Flight out of Time: A Dada Diary*, trans. Ann Raimes (Berkeley, CA: University of California Press, 1996), 10.

141 Friedrich Schlegel, *Friedrich Schlegel's* Lucinde *and the Fragments*, trans. Peter Firchow (Minneapolis, MN: University of Minnesota Press, 1971), 196.

142 Susan Buck-Morss, "Hegel and Haiti," *Critical Inquiry* 26, no. 4 (Summer 2000): 852.

143 Buck-Morss, "Hegel and Haiti," 822.

144 Buck-Morss, "Hegel and Haiti," 865.

145 Aijaz Ahmad, *In Theory* (London: Verso, 1992), 122.

146 Edward Said, "Permission to Narrate," *London Review of Books* 6, no. 3, February 16, 1984, web. Retrieved from https://www.lrb.co.uk/the-paper/v06/n03/edward-said/permission-to-narrate

147 Available on YouTube. See: Archivos Politicos, "Ni muerto ni vivo ... está desaparecido," YouTube, April 1, 2015, web. Retrieved from https://youtu.be/ASMPYgoYueU

148 The "New Syrian National Archive" is neither backed by any state organization nor is it housed in any museum. It's found, instead, on social media, where a trove of self-shot videos, low-grade screen grabs, and other documents of various genres comprise a torrent of archived media revealing the atrocities wrought by the Assad regime. See: Ali Shamseddine and John Rich, "An Introduction to the New Syrian National Archive," *e-flux journal* 60 (December 2014), web. Retrieved from https://www.e-flux.com/journal/60/61055/an-introduction-to-the-new-syrian-national-archive/

149 *82 Names*, dir. Maziar Bahari (2018; Washington, DC: United States Holocaust Memorial Museum), film. Retrieved from https://www.ushmm.org/ar/82-names

## CHAPTER TWO: POLYPHONY. /

1 Edward Said and Jean Mohr, *After the Last Sky: Palestinian Lives* (New York: Columbia University Press, 1999), 38.

2 Sarah C. Bishop, *Undocumented Storytellers: Narrating the Immigrant Rights Movement* (Oxford: Oxford University Press, 2019), 30, emphasis mine.

3 Bishop, *Undocumented Storytellers*, 40.

4 Walter Benjamin, "The Storyteller," trans. Harry Zohn, in *Illuminations*, ed. Hannah Arendt (New York: Schocken Books, 1969), 86, emphasis mine.

5 Benjamin, "The Storyteller," 91.

6 See, for example, Fabian Hutmacher's recent examination, which looks at the historical social-cultural biases that have foregrounded the domination of the visual in Western culture, and its reproduction through scholarship, in Hutmacher, "Why Is There So Much More Research on Vision Than on Any Other Sensory Modality?" *Frontiers in Psychology* 10 (2019): 1–12, https://doi.org/10.3389/fpsyg.2019.02246

7 If seeing does indeed equate to knowing, let alone believing, then we must radically reconsider what a refugee "looks like," not the least of which includes what a gay refugee looks like, as the fraught processes of asylum interviews have revealed; we must question our own assumptions and connotations, and the worldviews they derive from.

8 Liisa H. Malkki, "Speechless Emissaries: Refugees, Humanitarianism, and Dehistoricization," *Cultural Anthropology* 11, no. 3 (1996): 382.

9 "Eyewitness Rwanda," *Life*, September 1994, 74.

10 Said and Mohr, *After the Last Sky*, 3–4.

11 See: Chris Campanioni, "Fixing Being with Likeness: Facial Recognition as the Site for Global Per-Formance," *Im@go: A Journal of the Social Imaginary* 12 (2018): 102–123, https://doi.org/10.7413/22818138129

12 See: research demonstrating the link between multiculturalism and autobiography, and nationality and autobiography, in Gabriele Rosenthal, "National Identity or Multicultural Autobiography? Theoretical Concepts of Biographical Constitution Grounded in Case Reconstructions," in *The Narrative Study of Lives: Volume 5*, eds. Amia Lieblich and Ruthellen Josselson (Thousand Oaks, CA: Sage Publications, 1997), 21–39; Benaouda Lebdai's examination of autobiography and postcolonial personal expression in Lebdai, *Autobiography as a Writing Strategy in Postcolonial Literature* (Cambridge: Cambridge Scholars Publishing, 2015); the pedagogical implications of autobiography for students in a multicultural education setting in Heewon Chang, "Cultural Autobiography: A Tool to Multicultural Discovery of Self," *Electronic Magazine of Multicultural Education* 1, no. 2 (Spring 1999): 1–5; Jenny Zhang's contention that writers of color are assumed by white readers to write only "an unimaginative extension of [their] already-limited self" in Zhang, "They Pretend To Be Us While Pretending We Don't Exist," *BuzzFeed*, September 11, 2015, web. Retrieved from https://www.buzzfeed.com/jennybagel/they-pretend-to-be-us-while-pretending-we-dont-exist; and Fredric Jameson's characterization of "third-world texts" as "*the story of the private individual destiny*" inextricably tied to a national allegory in Jameson, "Third-World Literature in the

Era of Multinational Capitalism," *Social Text* 15 (Autumn, 1986): 65–88. The constellation of an erstwhile "third-world literature," autobiography, and nationalization (or "multiculturalism" by another name) can be understood, in this study, as an extant complication for today's analyses of world literature and migrant-produced media.

13 Trinh T. Minha-ha, *Elsewhere, Within Here: Immigration, Refugeeism and the Boundary Event* (New York and London: Routledge, 2011), 28.

14 *Every Day, Every Day*, dir. Reem Karssli (2013; Romania: Passport Productions), film.

15 See: Long Bui, "The Refugee Repertoire: Performing and Staging the Postmemories of Violence," *MELUS: Multi-Ethnic Literature of the U.S.* 41, no. 3 (2016): 112–132, https://doi.org/10.1093/melus/mlw034

16 Trinh T. Minha-ha, *Elsewhere, Within Here*, 99.

17 See: Mohamadou Kane, *Birago Diop: L'Homme et l'oeuvre* (Paris: Présence africaine, 1971), 37, quoted in Minh-ha, 99.

18 Said and Mohr, *After the Last Sky*, 6.

19 Said and Mohr, 26.

20 See: Campanioni, *north by north/west* (Morgantown, WV: West Virginia University Press, 2025).

21 Said and Mohr, *After the Last Sky*, 108.

22 Undocumented narrators, as Bishop relates, discover or uncover parts of their identities they had previously been unaware of or worked to hide by countering, recording, or reclaiming a narrative and ultimately, their selfhood, mobilizing their digital identities for real-world social and political agency. See: Bishop, *Undocumented Storytellers*,117.

23 See: Campanioni, "How Bizarre: The Glitch of the Nineties as a Fantasy of New Authorship," *M/C: Media & Culture* 21, no. 5 (December 2018), https://doi.org/10.5204/mcj.1463

24 Warwick Research Collective, *Combined and Uneven Development: Towards a New Theory of World-Literature* (Liverpool: Liverpool University Press, 2015), 16.

25 *Bunker Berlin #4*, Boros Foundation, Berlin, May 1, 2022 through March 31, 2026. Accessed August 14, 2022.

26 Anna Gritz, "Klára Hosnedlová in conversation with Anna Gritz," *Cura* 36 (2021), web. Retrieved from https://curamagazine.com/digital/klara-hosnedlova/

27 See the unpublished interview with Jacqueline Lichtenstein and Gerard Wajcman conducted by Francois Rouan in May of 1997, quoted in Paul Virilio, *Art and Fear*, trans. Julie Rose (London and New York: Continuum, 2006), 15.

28 Michael Fried, "Art and Objecthood," in *Art and Objecthood: Essays and Reviews* (Chicago, IL: University of Chicago Press, 1998).

29 Barbara Freedman, *Staging the Gaze: Postmodernism, Psychoanalysis, and Shakespearean Comedy* (Ithaca, NY: Cornell University Press, 1991), 1.

30 Freedman, *Staging the Gaze*, 9.

31 J.L. Austin, "Performative Utterances," in *Philosophical Papers* (Oxford: Oxford University Press, 1979), 237–238.

32 See: Gayatri Spivak, "Can the Subaltern Speak?" in *Marxism and Interpretations of Culture*, eds. Cary Nelson and Lawrence Grossberg (Urbana, IL: University of Illinois Press, 1988), 271–313.

33 Linda Alcoff, "The Problem of Speaking for Others," *Cultural Critique* 20 (Winter 1991–1992): 23, https://doi.org/10.2307/1354221

34 Freedman, *Staging the Gaze*, 6, emphasis mine.

35 Nancy K. Miller, "But enough about me, what do you think of my memoir?," *The Yale Journal of Criticism* 13, no. 2 (Fall 2000): 422, https://doi.org/10.1353/yale.2000.0023

36 Miller, "But enough about me," 424.

37 Said and Mohr, *After the Last Sky*, 20.

38 Said and Mohr, 1.

39 Said and Mohr, 146.

40 Said and Mohr, 147.

41 Said and Mohr, 6.

42 Said and Mohr, 12–14.

43 Said and Mohr, 167.

44 See: Judith Butler, *Precarious Life: The Powers of Mourning and Violence* (New York: Verso, 2004).

45 Said and Mohr, *After the Last Sky*, 128.

46 John Berger and Jean Mohr, *A Seventh Man* (London: Verso, 2010), 225, emphasis mine.

47 Berger and Mohr, *A Seventh Man*, 225.

48 Berger and Mohr, 9.

49 Robert E. Welsh, "David W. Griffith Speaks," *New York Dramatic Mirror*, January 14, 1914, 49.

50 Berger and Mohr, *A Seventh Man*, 233.

51 Ralf Simon, "The Temporality of Hospitality," trans. Andrew Shields, in *Critical Time in Modern German Literature and Culture*, ed. Dirk Göttsche (New York: Peter Lang, 2016), 165.

52 See: Jurij M. Lotman, *The Structure of the Artistic Text*, trans. Ronald Vroon (Ann Arbor, MI: University of Michigan Press, 1977).

53 See: Wolfgang Iser, "The Reading Process: A Phenomenological Approach," *New Literary History* 3, no. 2 (1972): 296, https://doi.org/10.2307/468316

54 See: Jacques Derrida and Anne Dufourmantelle, *Of Hospitality*, trans. Rachel Bowlby (Redwood City, CA: Stanford University Press, 2000).

55 Tacitus, *On the Origin and Situation of the Germans*, trans. Thomas Gordon. The Project Gutenberg, web. Retrieved from https://www.gutenberg.org/files/2995/2995-h/2995-h.htm

56 Ironically, this same text was employed during the rise of National Socialism during the interwar period to help bolster Nazi political and racial agendas and as evidence of Germany's link to a pure, Indigenous people with nearly no history of migration.

57 Simon, "The Temporality of Hospitality," 176.

58 By paying close attention to the ancient civilizations of Egypt, Iran, and Greece, Germany was not only able to accrue literary capital but also dispossess these nations of the possibility of future internal translations, having in the meantime claimed first rights and a monopoly on Classical study. Germany's literary exploitation of West Asia would be mirrored a century later, in the literal exploitation of the Gastarbeiter—the persons farmed in for labor from these same countries.

59 UNHCR, "Global Trends: Forced Displacement in 2022," *UNHCR*, June 2023: 1–48, web. Retrieved from https://www.unhcr.org/global-trends-report-2022. In 2016, when I began this project, the number of displaced persons was estimated at 68.5 million. See: UNHCR, "Global Trends: Forced Displacement in 2017," *UNHCR*, June 19, 2018: 1–75, web. Retrieved from https://www.unhcr.org/5b27be547

60 See, for instance, migrant-led international forums like the Refugee Radio Network and Migrant Voice, or the Salzburg Global Seminar (SGS). Since 2013, the SGS, with locations in Salzburg, Berlin, and Chiang Rai, has provided a multimedia forum for such stories, which take the form of video testimonials, written essays, and oral recitations in public sessions. See also: Jose Antonio Vargas's "Define American." Vargas's website, defineamerican.com, serves as a crowdsourced digital archive, in which individuals upload their personal stories in conversation with one another, revealing fundamental differences as well as intersections between migrants' experiences and experiences of migration.

61 Derrida, *The Animal That Therefore I Am*, trans. David Wills (New York: Fordham University Press, 2008), 45.

62 See: "Letters from Santiago: Re-membering the Displaced Body Through Dreams," *La Revista Científica de Información y Comunicación* 15 (2018): 59–87;

and in Spanish, "Cartas de Santiago: Rememorando el cuerpo desplazado a través de los sueños," in the same volume: 89–118.

63 Benjamin, "Dream Kitsch," trans. Howard Eiland, in *The Work of Art in the Age of Its Technological Reproducibility, and Other Writings on Media*, eds. Michael W. Jennings, Brigid Doherty, and Thomas Y. Levin (Cambridge, MA: Harvard University Press, 2008), 236.

64 Edgar Garcia, *Skins of Columbus: A Dream Ethnography* (New York: Fence Books, 2019), 1.

65 Garcia, *Skins of Columbus*, 11–12.

66 Garcia, iii.

67 See: Anna Forné, "Archival Autofiction in Post-Dictatorship Argentina," *Life Writing* (2019): 1–12, https://doi.org/10.1080/14484528.2019.1642174

68 Forné," Archival Autofiction," 10.

69 Craig Santos Perez, *from Unincorporated Territory [hacha]* (Oakland, CA: Omnidawn, 2017), 36–37.

70 Gaston Bachelard, *The Poetics of Space*, trans. Maria Jolas (Boston, MA: Beacon Press, 1994), 155.

71 Santos Perez, *[hacha]*, 11.

72 Stéphane Mallarmé, "Preface to 'Dice Thrown Never Will Annual Chance'," trans. Mary Ann Caws, in *Selected Poetry and Prose*, ed. Mary Ann Caws (New York: New Directions, 1982), 105, emphasis mine.

73 Santos Perez, *[hacha]*, 35.

74 Manoela dos Anjos Alfonso Rodrigues encounters "turning" after she alights upon a traffic sign that had become resignified by a passerby. "Diversion Ends" became "La Diversión Ha Empezado!!!" (The Fun Has Begun) after an accent mark was placed on the "o" and "Ends" was crossed out and written over. See: "Translanguaging and Autobiogeography as Decolonial Strategies for Writing Life Narratives within Displacement," *a/b: Auto/Biography Studies* 33, no. 3 (2018): 621–642, https://doi.org/10.1080/08989575.2018.1503437

75 Santos Perez, *[hacha]*, 51.

76 I am thinking, too, of the "ambivalent shaping" parsed by Paul de Man in his deconstructive reading of Percy Shelley's "The Triumph of Life," in which de Man links veiling and unveiling to limn *forgetting* as an erotic experience. See: Paul de Man, "Shelley Disfigured," in *The Rhetoric of Romanticism* (New York: Columbia University Press, 1984), 107.

77 Gayle Brandeis, "#WeToo: Women Writing the First Person Plural," *Gay Magazine*, January 22, 2020, web. Retrieved from https://gay.medium.com/wetoo-b2b01fa2ae79

78 Eva C. Karpinski, "Migrations and Metamorphoses," *a/b: Auto/Biography Studies* 32, no. 2 (2017): 172, https://doi.org/10.1080/08989575.2017.1287898
79 Karpinski, "Migrations and Metamorphoses," 173.
80 Paul Valéry, *The Art of Poetry*, trans. Denise Folliot (Princeton, NJ: Princeton University Press, 1985), 304–305.
81 Brent Armendinger, *Street Gloss* (Brooklyn, NY: The Operating System, 2019), 96.
82 Armendinger, *Street Gloss*, 11.
83 Benjamin, "The Storyteller," 91.
84 Benjamin, "The Storyteller," 92.
85 Benjamin, "The Storyteller," 93, emphasis mine.
86 Michel de Certeau, *The Practice of Everyday Life,* trans. Steven Rendall (Berkeley, CA: University of California Press, 1984), 105.
87 See my introduction for a more elaborate parsing of the "remainder," and my divergence from Lawrence Venuti's conception of the term for the study and teaching of translation.
88 Spivak, "The Politics of Translation," in *Outside in the Teaching Machine* (New York: Routledge, 1993), 179.
89 Armendinger, *Street Gloss*, 85.
90 Armendinger, 38.
91 Armendinger, 36.
92 Bachelard, *The Poetics of Space*, 50.
93 As I write this, I am picturing the white headscarves imprinted on the coral tiles, curving a circle around Plaza de Mayo, and all the mothers who walked here, who are still walking, to honor their disappeared children.
94 Armendinger, *Street Gloss*, 19.
95 De Certeau, *The Practice of Everyday Life*, 93.
96 Mieke Bal, "Double movement," in *2move: video, art, migration*, eds. Mieke Bal and Miguel Á. Hernández-Navarro (Murcia: Cendeac, 2008), 13–82.
97 James E. Young, "Interpreting Literary Testimony: A Preface to Rereading Holocaust Diaries and Memoirs," *New Literary History* 18, no. 2 (1987): 403–423.
98 Rättsmedicinalverket, "Medicinsk åldersbedömning (SVENSKA)," YouTube, May 16, 2017, web. Retrieved from https://youtu.be/Mnv9tNWbo1k
99 In reality, no validation study for the procedure was ever conducted despite the nearly 10,000 children who were tested in Sweden in 2017 alone; examination of the third molar and the distal femoral epiphysis to determine age relies on an assumption, not science. See: Petter Mostag and Fredrik Tamsen, "Error Rates for Unvalidated Medical Age Assessment Procedures,"

*International Journal of Legal Medicine* 133 (2019), 613–623, https://doi.org/10.1007/s00414-018-1916-3. More recently, Christian Rossipal, by recovering the screenplay of the informational video, shows how the RMV rephrased language to avoid any claims about exact age-determination. See: Rossipal, "The Public Procurement of a Biometric Love Story," *Orphan Film Symposium*, May 26, 2020, web. Retrieved from https://wp.nyu.edu/orphanfilm/2020/05/26/the-public-procurement-of-a-biometric-love-story/

100 Young, "Interpreting Literary Testimony," 420.

101 Russell King, John Connell, and Paul White, eds., *Writing Across Worlds: Literature and Migration* (London and New York: Routledge, 1995), ix–x, emphasis in the original.

102 King, Connell, and White, *Writing Across Worlds*, x.

103 See the editors' model for an "evolutionary series of forms of migrant literature" laid out in the book's preface.

104 Edward Said, *Culture and Imperialism* (London: Vintage, 1994), xiii.

105 David Damrosch, *What Is World Literature?* (Princeton, NJ: Princeton University Press, 2003), 4.

106 Édouard Glissant, *Poetics of Relation*, trans. Betsy Wing (Ann Arbor, MI: University of Michigan, 1997), 19.

107 Goethe himself was adamant in his assessment that the "strength of a language is [its power] not to repel what is foreign, but to devour it." See: Fritz Strich, *Goethe und die Weltliteratur* (Bern: Franke Verlag, 1946), 57, quoted in Casanova, *World Republic of Letters*, trans. M.B. DeBevoise (Cambridge, MA: Harvard University Press, 2004), 236.

108 For an earlier instance of the term, see Anton Popovič's 1975 study, *Teória umeleckého prekladu* (Theory of artistic translation). Popovič defined a pseudotranslation as an "original work" published by its author "as a fictitious translation" with the explicit aim "to win a wide public, thus making use of the reader's expectation." See: Popovič, *Dictionary for the Analysis of Literary Translation* (Edmonton: University of Alberta, 1976), 20.

109 Patience Agbabi, "The Refugee's Tale," in *Refugee Tales*, eds. David Herd and Anna Pincus (Manchester: Comma Press, 2016), 12.

110 Agbabi, "The Refugee's Tale," 12.

111 Dragan Todorovic, "The Migrant's Tale," in *Refugee Tales*, 12, emphasis mine.

112 Édouard Glissant, *Treatise on the Whole-World*, trans. Celia Britton (Liverpool: Liverpool University Press, 2020), 74.

113 David Herd, "Afterword," in *Refugee Tales*, 133.

114 For more on Abounaddara, an anonymous group of Syrian artists whose documentary films respond to the challenge of reclaiming self-representation

and dignity through their refusal to participate in the economy of images, see Campanioni, "The Right to a Dignified Image: The Fashioning and Effacement of the Refugee within the Celebrity System," *JCMS: Journal of Cinema and Media Studies* 61, no. 1 (Fall 2021): 27–50, https://doi.org/10.1353/cj.2021.0080

115 Marcos, *Professionals of Hope: The Selected Writings of Subcomandante Marcos* (Brooklyn, NY: The Song Cave, 2017), 51.

116 Marcos, *Professionals of Hope*, 82.

117 Also: as a crass attempt to cash in on the border's humanitarian crisis, a point that was already evident, for instance, at the book's launch party, when publisher Flatiron Books embellished tables with floral centerpieces resembling high walls, or tombstones, wrapped with barbed wire.

118 Dignity's relevance for an arts-focused coalition warrants more space than this chapter—and this book—permits. Since 2009, the Zapatista communities have gathered with international artists, activists, journalists, and organizations for the annual *Global Festival of Dignified Rage*.

119 Chris Cleave, "The Lorry Driver's Tale," in *Refugee Tales*, 27.

120 It is no surprise, in due fashion, that the producers of *Refugee Tales* have recently taken to mobilizing celebrities who narrate these stories on the Refugee Tales website as part of the series' promotional campaign. "Ordinary" readers, too, can book their passage on the annual Refugee Tales Walk through payment to the University of Kent, a transaction that clarifies the interconnected relationship between the media and the academy, and their coordinated efforts to undermine the self-representation of refugees.

121 Graziella Parati, *Migration Italy: The Art of Talking Back in a Destination Culture* (Toronto: University of Toronto Press, 1995), 31.

122 Parati, *Migration Italy*, 31.

123 Fernanda Farias de Albuquerque and Maurizio Jannelli, *Princesa* (Rome: Sensibili alle foglie, 1994).

124 Lawrence Venuti, *Translation Changes Everything: Theory and Practice* (New York: Routledge, 2013), 141.

125 Gilles Deleuze and Félix Guattari, *A Thousand Plateaus: Capitalism and Schizophrenia*, trans. Brian Massumi (Minneapolis, MN: University of Minnesota Press, 1987), 77.

126 Walter D. Mignolo and Freya Schiwy, "Transculturation and the Colonial Difference: Double Translation," *IC Revista Científica de Información y Comunicación* 4 (2007): 9.

127 *Transculturación* was first coined by Cuban anthropologist Fernando Ortiz, intended to address the inadequacies of acculturation: the one-way processes

of assimilation experienced by migrant populations within host communities. See: Fernando Ortiz, *Contrapunteo Cubano del Tabaco y el Azúcar* (Havana: Montero, 1940).

128 Caren Kaplan, "Resisting Autobiography: Out-Law Genres and Transnational Feminist Subjects," in *De/Colonizing the Subject*, eds. Sidonie Smith and Julia Watson (Minneapolis, MN: University of Minnesota Press, 1992), 119.

129 Kaplan, "Resisting Autobiography," 119.

130 Kaplan, 121.

131 See: Venuti, *The Scandals of Translation: Towards an Ethics of Difference* (London and New York: Routledge, 1998), 4–13.

132 Parati, *Migration Italy*, 53, emphasis mine.

133 Parati, *Migration Italy*, 194–195.

134 Parati, *Migration Italy*, 53.

135 Johann Wolfgang Goethe, *Conversations with Eckermann 1823–1832*, trans. John Oxenford (London: Everyman, 1930), 19.

136 Pascale Casanova, *The World Republic of Letters*, trans. M.B. DeBevoise (Cambridge, MA: Harvard University Press, 2004), 184.

137 Casanova, *The World Republic of Letters*, 250.

138 Casanova, 211.

139 Clark Blaise, "A Novel of India's Coming of Age," *New York Times*, April 19, 1981, web. Retrieved from https://archive.nytimes.com/www.nytimes.com/books/98/12/06/specials/rushdie-children.html

140 Kevin Blankinship, "Lost in Translation: Classical Arabic Literature," *The Millions*, November 26, 2019, web. Retrieved from https://themillions.com/2019/11/lost-in-translation-classical-arabic-literature.html

141 Spivak, "Translation as Culture," in *An Aesthetic Education in the Era of Globalization* (Cambridge, MA: Harvard University Press, 2012), 247.

142 Spivak, "Translating into English," in *Nation, Language, and the Ethics of Translation*, eds. Sandra Bermann and Michael Wood (Princeton, NJ: Princeton University Press, 2005), 94.

143 Campanioni, "The Right to a Dignified Image," 44.

144 Damrosch, *What Is World Literature?*, 35.

145 Benjamin, *The Origin of German Tragic Drama*, trans. John Osborne (London: Verso, 1998), 45–46.

146 Roland Barthes, "The Death of the Author," trans. Richard Howard, in *Image-Music-Text*, ed. Stephen Heath (Waukegan, IL: Fontana Press, 1977), 146.

147 Mignolo and Schiwy, "Transculturation and the Colonial Difference," 20.

148 Eve Tuck and K. Wayne Yang, "Decolonization Is Not a Metaphor," *Decolonization: Indigeneity, Education & Society* 1, no. 1 (2012): 36.

149 Ashon T. Crawley, "Otherwise, Ferguson," *Interfictions: A Journal of Interstitial Arts* 7 (October 2016), web. Retrieved from http://interfictions.com/otherwise-fergusonashon-crawley/

150 See José Esteban Muñoz's prefatory assessment of "queerness" as "ideality": "Queerness is not yet here." In José Esteban Muñoz, *Cruising Utopia: The Then and There of Queer Futurity* (New York City: New York University Press, 2009), 1.

151 Saidiya Hartman, "Venus in Two Acts," *Small Axe* 26 (June 2008): 11, https://doi.org/10.1215/-12-2-1

152 Hartman, "Venus in Two Acts," 10.

153 Hartman, 4.

154 Hartman, 2.

155 Hartman, 2.

156 Caitlin Dewey, "Here are Mark Zuckerberg's full remarks about how much he'd like to (literally!) read your thoughts," *Washington Post Blogs*, June 14, 2016, web. Retrieved from https://www.washingtonpost.com/news/the-intersect/wp/2016/06/14/here-are-mark-zuckerbergs-full-remarks-about-how-much-hed-like-to-literally-read-your-thoughts/

157 Elaine K. Chang, "A Not-So-New Spelling of My Name: Notes Toward (and Against) A Politics of Equivocation," in *Displacement: Cultural Identities in Question*, ed. Angelika Bammer (Bloomington, IN: Indiana University Press, 1994), 22.

158 Chang, "A Not-So-New Spelling of My Name," 22.

159 See: Jonathan Culler, *On Deconstruction: Theory and Criticism after Structuralism* (Ithaca, NY: Cornell University Press, 1983), following Umberto Eco, *A Theory of Semiotics* (Bloomington, IN: Indiana University Press, 1976).

160 Alan Bass, "Translator's Introduction: L Before K," in Derrida, *The Post Card*, trans. Alan Bass (Chicago, IL: University of Chicago Press: 1987), x.

161 Derrida, *The Post Card*, 13.

## CHAPTER THREE: ABSTRACTION. /

1 Édouard Glissant, *Treatise on the Whole-World*, trans. Celia Britton (Liverpool: Liverpool University Press, 2020), 12.

2 Morgan Hekking, "Moroccans Spend More than $44 Million on Schengen Visa Applications," *Morocco World News*, December 18, 2019, web. Retrieved from https://www.moroccoworldnews.com/2019/12/289246/moroccans-spend-44-million-schegen-visa-applications/

3 See: Adel Abdel Ghafar, *The European Union and North Africa: Prospects and Challenges* (Washington, DC: Brookings, 2019).

4 Edward Said and Jean Mohr, *After the Last Sky: Palestinian Lives* (New York: Columbia University Press, 1999), 23.

5 Said and Mohr, *After the Last Sky*, 37.

6 Gilles Deleuze and Félix Guattari, *Toward a Minor Literature*, trans. Dana Polan (Minneapolis, MN: University of Minnesota Press, 1986), 41.

7 As the categories of migrants expanded, the United Nations High Commission for Refugees (UNHCR) also grew exponentially, moving from an office of 33 workers and a budget of $300,000 in 1951 to a staff of over 1,700 and annual expenditures of more than $500 million by 1980. See: Gil Loescher, *Beyond Charity: International Cooperation and the Global Refugee Crisis* (Oxford: Oxford University Press, 1993).

8 Said and Mohr, *After the Last Sky*, 91, emphasis mine.

9 Jacques Rancière, *The Politics of Aesthetics*, trans. Gabriel Rockhill (London: Continuum, 2004), 39, emphasis mine.

10 Amitava Kumar, *Passport Photos* (Berkeley, CA: University of California Press, 2000), ix.

11 Kumar, *Passport Photos*, xi.

12 These are the book's first words, as well as the words etched across the book's back cover. See: Souvankham Thammavongsa, *Found* (Toronto: Pedlar Press, 2007), 11.

13 Tanjil Rashid, "*On Earth We're Briefly Gorgeous* by Ocean Vuong," *The Brooklyn Rail*, June 2019, web. Retrieved from https://brooklynrail.org/2019/06/books/-Ocean-Vuong

14 Thammavongsa, *Found*, 35.

15 Thammavongsa, 33.

16 See Kobena Mercer's conversation with artist Kader Attia in Kobena Mercer, "Conceptualising Modernist Architecture in Transcultural Spaces: An Interview with Kader Attia," *Atlantica: Journal of Art and Thought* 50 (2011): 44–61, web. Retrieved from https://www.revistaatlantica.com/wp-content/uploads/ATL50.pdf

17 *Found*, dir. Paramita Nath (2009; Canada), film.

18 Rancière, *The Politics of Aesthetics*, trans. Gabriel Rockhill (London: Continuum, 2004), 9.

19 Sylvére Lotringer and Paul Virilio, *The Accident of Art*, trans. Michael Taormina (Los Angeles, CA: Semiotext(e), 2005), 14.

20 Tristan Tzara, *Approximate Man & Other Writings*, trans. Mary Ann Caws (Boston, MA: Black Widow Press, 2005), 14.

21 Tzara, *Approximate Man*, 128.

22 See also: the rejection of disability as an impairment or fixed mark conceptualized by Rosemarie Garland-Thompson as "disability gain," and disability's interventions of modern political, social, and cultural identity formations, beginning with Garland-Thomson, *Extraordinary Bodies: Figuring Physical Disability in American Culture and Literature* (New York: Columbia University Press, 1996).
23 Ghérasim Luca, *Self-Shadowing Prey*, trans. Mary Ann Caws (New York: Contra Mundum Press, 2012), 33–34.
24 Luca, *Self-Shadowing Prey*, 11.
25 See: Luca's poem "Passionnément," in *Rhuthmos*, April 5, 2011, web. Retrieved from http://rhuthmos.eu/spip.php?article332
26 Luca, *The Passive Vampire*, trans. Krzysztof Fijałkowski (Prague: Twisted Spoon Press, 2008), 89.
27 Édouard Glissant, "An Exploded Discourse," in *Caribbean Discourse*, trans. J. Michael Dash (Charlottesville, VA: Caraf Books, 1989), 163.
28 Glissant, "An Exploded Discourse," 162.
29 Luca, *Inventor of Love & Other Writings*, trans. Julian and Laura Semilian (Boston, MA: Black Widow Press, 2009), 17–18.
30 Luca, *Inventor of Love*, 20.
31 Luca, *Inventor of Love*, 132–133.
32 Krzysztof Fijałkowski, "Cubomania: Ghérasim Luca and Non-Oedipal Collage," *Dada/Surrealism* 20 (2015): 7, https://doi.org/10.17077/0084-9537.1301
33 Roland Barthes, "The Grain of the Voice," in *Image Music Text*, trans. Stephen Heath (London: Fontana Press, 1977), 184.
34 Haroldo de Campos, *Novas: Selected Writings*, eds. Antonio Sergio Bessa and Odile Cisneros (Evanston, IL: Northwestern University Press, 2007), xiv.
35 De Campos, *Novas*, 28.
36 De Campos, 243.
37 De Campos, 63.
38 De Campos, 244.
39 De Campos, 218.
40 De Campos, 30.
41 Julia Kristeva, "The Subject in Process," *The Tel Quel Reader*, eds. Roland-François Lack and Patrick Ffrench (New York: Routledge, 1998), 134.
42 Glissant, *Poetics of Relation*, trans. Betsy Wing (Ann Arbor, MI: University of Michigan Press, 1997), 25.
43 Glissant, "An Exploded Discourse," 163.

44 Kobena Mercer, "Aubrey Williams: Abstraction in Diaspora," *British Art Studies* 8 (2008), web. Retrieved from https://www.britishartstudies.ac.uk/issues/issue-index/issue-8/aubrey-williams

45 Clarice Lispector, *Selected Crônicas*, trans. Giovanni Pontiero (New York: New Directions, 1996), vii.

46 Deleuze and Guattari, *A Thousand Plateaus, Capitalism and Schizophrenia*, trans. Brian Massumi (Minneapolis, MN: University of Minnesota Press, 1987), 197.

47 Nadine Gordimer, "The Ultimate Safari," in *Ten Years of the Caine Prize for African Writing*, ed. Chris Bazier (Oxford: New Internationalist Publications, 2009), 14, emphasis mine.

48 Gordimer, "The Ultimate Safari," 12–13.

49 Gordimer, 13, emphasis mine.

50 Gordimer, 15.

51 Gordimer, 20.

52 Jacques Derrida, *On Cosmopolitanism and Forgiveness*, trans. Mark Dooley and Michael Hughes (London: Routledge, 2001), 7–8.

53 Michel Agier, *Managing the Undesirables: Refugee Camps and Humanitarian Government*, trans. David Fernbach (Cambridge: Polity, 2011), 58–59.

54 Agier, *Managing the Undesirables*, 46.

55 Cannelle Gueguen-Teil and Irit Katz, "On the Meaning of Shelter: Living in Calais's Camps de la Lande," in *Camps Revisited: Multifaceted Spatialities of a Modern Political Technology*, eds. Irit Katz, Diana Martin, and Claudio Minca (London: Rowman & Littlefield International, 2018), 91.

56 Gayatri Spivak, "Keynote Speech at CSD Department of International Relations," November 7, 2015, YouTube, January 29, 2016, web. Retrieved from https://youtu.be/-Hr_wsM5mDM

57 Claudio Minca, Danica Šantić, and Dragan Umek, "Walking the Balkan Route: The Archipelago of Refugee Camps in Serbia," in *Camps Revisited*, 56.

58 Although the Romani living in the European Union (a number currently estimated between ten and twelve million persons) are recognized as EU citizens, they do not enjoy the same rights as all other citizens, and they live, in Rome and elsewhere, in the margins of society, often in segregated settlements, under poor social and economic conditions and with the constant threat of discrimination and violence.

59 Jan-Jonathan Bock, "Grassroots Solidarity and Political Protest in Rome's Migrant Camps," in *Camps Revisited*, 167.

60 Agier, *Managing the Undesirables*, 53.

61 C. Riley Snorton, *Black on Both Sides: A Racial History of Trans Identity* (Minneapolis, MN: University of Minnesota Press, 2017), 58.

62 Snorton, *Black on Both Sides*, 10, emphasis mine. See also: Guattari, "Transdisciplinarity Must Become Transversality," trans. Andrew Goffey, *Theory, Culture & Society* 32, nos. 5–6 (2015): 131–137, https://doi.org/10.1177/0263276415597045

63 Karma R. Chávez, *Queer Migration Politics* (Urbana, IL: University of Illinois Press, 2013), 8.

64 Jean-Luc Nancy, *Being Singular Plural*, trans. Robert D. Richardson and Anne E. O'Byrne (Redwood City, CA: Stanford University Press, 2000), xiii.

65 Nancy, *Being Singular Plural*, 5.

66 A convergence intensified by the text's recent translation from German into English by Margot Bettauer Dembo in 2013.

67 Anna Seghers, *Transit*, trans. Margot Bettauer Dembo (New York: New York Review of Books, 2013), 39.

68 Seghers, *Transit*, 38–39.

69 Seghers, 235–236.

70 Seghers, 112.

71 Seghers, 219.

72 Hannah Arendt, *The Origins of Totalitarianism* (New York: Harcourt Brace & Company, 1973), 284.

73 Seghers, *Transit*, 181–182.

74 Seghers, 21.

75 *Transit*, dir. Christian Petzold (2018; Germany: Schramm Film), film.

76 Hillary Weston, "Missed Connections: A Conversation with Christian Petzold," *The Current (Criterion Collection)*, December 7, 2018, web. Retrieved from https://www.criterion.com/current/posts/6088-missed-connections-a-conversation-with-christian-petzold

77 Zygmunt Bauman, *Identity: Conversations with Benedetto Vecchi* (Cambridge: Polity, 2004), 39.

78 Bauman, *Identity*, 40.

79 Jacques Derrida and Anne Dufourmantelle, *Of Hospitality*, trans. Rachel Bowlby (Redwood City, CA: Stanford University Press, 2000), 15.

80 Seghers's shift in ideas about ethical storytelling in a time of war, from *Transit* (1942) to *Crossing* (1971), is important. The two texts serve as bookends of her own migration and exile: one the experience of waiting, the other the experience of passing.

81 Seghers, *Crossing*, trans. Douglas Irving (New Orleans, LA: Diálogos, 2016), 21.

82 Seghers, *Crossing*, 44.

83 Seghers, 93.

84 "More refugees and IDPs are moving into urban areas to avoid camp settings that may lack opportunities, such as employment and access to services." See: Hans Park, "The Power of Cities," *UNHCR*, November 25, 2016, web. Retrieved from https://www.unhcr.org/innovation/the-power-of-cities/

85 See: Kelly Oliver, *Carceral Humanitarianism: Logics of Refugee Detention* (Minneapolis: University of Minnesota Press, 2017).

86 For a more expansive exploration of the state processes and systems of capital that generate refugees—linking labor, resource extraction, militarization, humanitarian aid, and the continuous formation of celebrity—see: Chris Campanioni, "The Right to a Dignified Image: The Fashioning and Effacement of the Refugee within the Celebrity System," *JCMS: Journal of Cinema and Media Studies* 61, no. 1 (2021): 27–50, https://doi.org/10.1353/cj.2021.0080

87 Arjun Appadurai, "Disjuncture and Difference in the Global Cultural Economy," *Public Culture* 2, no. 2 (Spring 1990): 5, https://doi.org/10.1177/026327690007002017

88 Said, "Reflections on Exile," in *Reflections on Exile and Other Essays* (Cambridge, MA: Harvard University Press, 2000), 137–149.

89 James Baldwin, *Tell Me How Long the Train's Been Gone* (New York: Vintage Books, 1968), 189.

90 Mahmoud Darwish, *Memory for Forgetfulness: August, Beirut, 1982*, trans. Ibrahim Muhawi (Berkeley, CA: University of California Press, 2013), 63.

91 Darwish, *Memory for Forgetfulness*, 65.

92 Darwish, 139.

93 Darwish, 137.

94 Darwish, 49.

95 Darwish, 110.

96 Darwish, 53–54.

97 Darwish, 148, 47, 49.

98 Darwish, 51.

99 Mahmoud Darwish, "A Lover from Palestine," in *Splinters of Bone*, trans. B.M. Bennani (New York: The Greenfield Review Press, 1974). Quoted in Said, "Reflections on Exile," 142.

100 Darwish, *Memory for Forgetfulness*, 51.

101 Darwish, 65.

102 Said, "Reflections on Exile," 141.

103 Said, 140–141.

104 Nancy Hartsock, "Foucault on Power: A Theory for Women?" in *Feminism/Postmodernism*, ed. Linda J. Nicholson (London: Routledge, 1990), 163.

105 Judith Butler, *Precarious Life: The Powers of Mourning and Violence* (New York: Verso, 2004), 146.

106 Aimee Carrillo Rowe, "Moving Relations: On the Limits of Belonging," *Liminalities: A Journal of Performance Studies* 5, no. 5 (November 2009): 8.

107 See: Chela Sandoval, "Feminist Forms of Agency and Oppositional Consciousness: U.S. Third World Feminist Criticism," in *Provoking Agents: Gender and Agency in Theory and Practice*, ed. Judith Kegan Gardiner (Urbana, IL: University of Illinois Press, 1995): 208–226.

108 Juana María Rodríguez, *Queer Latinidad* (New York: New York University Press, 2003), 82.

109 See: Leon Battista Alberti, *On Painting,* trans. John R. Spencer (London: Routledge, 1956), quoted in Carolyn L. Kane, *High-Tech Trash: Glitch, Noise, and Aesthetic Failure* (Berkeley, CA: University of California Press, 2019), 9.

110 Arendt, "We Refugees," in *Altogether Elsewhere: Writers on Exile*, ed. Marc Robinson (Boston, MA: Faber and Faber, 1994), 119, emphasis mine.

111 Karina Horsti, "Digital Materialities in the Diasporic Mourning of Migrant Death," *European Journal of Communication* 34, no. 6 (2019): 676, https://doi.org/10.1177/0267323119886169

112 Said and Mohr, *After the Last Sky*, 84, emphasis mine.

113 James E. Young, "Interpreting Literary Testimony: A Preface to Rereading Holocaust Diaries and Memoirs," *New Literary History*, 18, no. 2 (1987): 403–423.

114 Walid Raad, *No, illness is neither here nor there* (1976–1990), National Museum of Contemporary Art Athens, on permanent view. Accessed June 9, 2024.

115 Rancière, *The Politics of Aesthetics*, 15.

116 Rancière, 15.

117 Rancière, 14.

118 Not unlike the lesson taught to us by the Skin Horse: "Real isn't how you are made. [...] It's a thing that happens to you." See: Margery Williams, *The Velveteen Rabbit* (New York: Doubleday & Company, 1922), web. Retrieved from https://digital.library.upenn.edu/women/williams/rabbit/rabbit.html

119 Rancière, *The Politics of Aesthetics*, 34.

120 Jordana Blejmar, *Playful Memories: The Autofictional Turn in Post-Dictatorship Argentina* (London: Palgrave Macmillan, 2016), 4.

121 Blejmar, *Playful Memories*, 9.

122 Rebecca M. Schreiber, *The Undocumented Everyday: Migrant Lives and the Politics of Visibility* (Minneapolis, MN: University of Minnesota Press, 2018), 4.

123 Schreiber, *The Undocumented Everyday*, 18.

124 Sandra Ponzanesi, *The Postcolonial Cultural Industry: Icons, Markets, Mythologies* (New York: Palgrave Macmillan, 2014).

125 See: Campanioni, "Houses in Motion: The Reimagining of Time and Space as Anomalous in Representations of Mobility," in *Migration, Dislocation and Movement on Screen*, ed. Ruxandra Trandafoiu (New York: Berghahn Books, 2024), 17–37, https://doi.org/10.3167/9781805395942

126 See: Cornelia Schleime's work on view as part of *Utopie und Untergang. Kunst in der DDR*, Museum Kunstpalast, Dusseldorf, May 9, 2019 through January 5, 2020. Accessed November 15, 2019.

127 Albert Parry, "Samizdat Is Russia's Underground Press," *New York Times*, March 15, 1970, 249.

128 See: Vera Sheridan, "Disclosing the Self: 1956 Hungarian Student Refugees Creating Autobiographies for University Scholarships in the USA," *Life Writing* (2019): 4, https://doi.org/10.1080/14484528.2019.1644210

129 Kurt McVey, "Kon Trubkovich's Transmissions," *Interview*, February 12, 2014.

## CHAPTER FOUR: COLLABORATION. /

1 Fredric Jameson, "Third-World Literature in the Era of Multinational Capitalism," *Social Text* 15 (Autumn 1986): 68.

2 *It Will Be Chaos*, dirs. Lorena Luciano and Filippo Piscopo (2018; Italy: HBO), film.

3 See: "Italian Mayor Urges 'Strike' over Migrant Arrivals," *Deutsche Welle*, August 30, 2020, web. Retrieved from https://www.dw.com/en/lampedusa-mayor-calls-for-strike-over-migrant-arrivals/a-54763386

4 See: Oliver Bakewell, "Researching Refugees: Lessons from *Welle* the Past, Current Challenges and Future Directions," *Refugee Survey Quarterly* 26, no. 3 (2007): 6–14, https://doi.org/10.1093/rsq/hdi0239; and Dawn Chatty and Philip Marfleet, "Conceptual Problems in Forced Migration," *Refugee Survey Quarterly* 32, no. 2 (2013): 1–13, https://doi.org/10.1093/rsq/hdt008

5 See: Yên Lê Espiritu, "Towards a Critical Refugee Study: The Vietnamese Refugee Subject in U.S. Scholarship," *Journal of Vietnamese Studies* 1, nos. 1–2 (2006): 410–433.

6 Richard Black, "Fifty Years of Refugee Studies: From Theory to Policy," *International Migration Review* 35, no. 1 (Spring 2001): 58–60.

7 Bakewell, "Researching Refugees," 6.

8 See: Bridget Hayden, "What's in a Name? The Nature of the Individual in Refugee Studies," *Journal of Refugee Studies* 19, no. 4 (2006): 471–487, https://doi.org/10.1093/refuge/fel021

9 See: Vilna Bashi Treitler, "Social Agency and White Supremacy in Immigration Studies," *Sociology of Race and Ethnicity* 1, no. 1 (2015): 153–165, https://doi.org/10.1177/2332649214560796

10 For more on the "double-speak" of naturalization as the enforcement of difference through the performance of equality, see: Didier Fassin and Sarah Mazouz, "What Is It to Become French? Naturalization as a Republican Rite of Institution," *Revue française de sociologie* 50 (2009): 37–64.

11 Lionel Cantú Jr., Eithne Luibhéid, and Alexandra Minna Stern, "Well-Founded Fear: Sexual Identity in the U.S.-Mexico Borderlands," in *Queer Migrations: Sexuality, U.S. Citizenship, and Border Crossings*, eds. Eithne Luibhéid and Lionel Cantú Jr. (Minneapolis, MN: University of Minnesota Press, 2005), 61.

12 Cantú, Luibhéid, and Stern, "Well-Founded Fear," 65.

13 UNHCR, "Asylum-Seekers," *UNHCR*, June 2018, web. Retrieved from http://popstats.unhcr.org/en/asylum_seekers

14 A national study conducted in 2015 concluded that half of all Germans believe there are more differences than commonalities between Easterners and Westerners. Today there are significantly less migrants in East Germany; an aversion to migrants in the east is considered by many local analysts to be a result of its citizens' lack of experience living with foreigners. See: Kate Connolly, "German Reunification 25 Years On: How Different Are East and West Really," *The Guardian*, October 2, 2015, web. Retrieved from https://www.theguardian.com/world/2015/oct/02/german-reunification-25-years-on-how-different-are-east-and-west-really

15 Jacques Derrida, *Specters of Marx,* trans. Peggy Kamuf (New York: Routledge Classics, 1993), 10.

16 Günther Birkenstock, "East Germany Relied on Forced Labor," *Deutsche Welle*, May 6, 2012, web. Retrieved from https://www.dw.com/en/east-germany-relied-on-forced-labor/a-15932840

17 See: Philip Martin, "Mexican Braceros and US Farm Workers," *Wilson Center*, July 10, 2020, web. Retrieved from https://www.wilsoncenter.org/article/mexican-braceros-and-us-farm-workers

18 See: The UK's points-based system consisting of a five-tier visa system, premised on Australia's existing model, and the recently introduced RAISE Act (February 13, 2017) in the United States of America, all of which categorize migrants based on their "value," "talent," and "skill" for work.

19 For more on the coeval global processes of settler colonialism, slavery, and imported colonial labor, see Lisa Lowe's *The Intimacies of Four Continents* (Durham, NC: Duke University Press, 2015).

20 Karl Marx and Frederick Engels, *The Communist Manifesto*, trans. Frederick Engels (London: Verso, 1998), 58.

21 Marx and Engels, *The Communist Manifesto*, 58.

22 See a visual re-creation of this in *Demolition and Protest at Kottbusser Tor*, on permanent view, Friedrichshain-Kreuzberg Museum, Berlin. Accessed August 6, 2018.

23 A much smaller LGBT+ refugee center with space for eight persons opened four weeks earlier, on February 1, 2016, in Nuremberg.

24 Marcel De Groot, personal interview, August 3, 2018.

25 Agence France-Presse, "Austria Rejects Afghan's Asylum Bid Because He 'Did Not Act or Dress Gay,'" *The Guardian*, August 15, 2018, web. Retrieved from https://www.theguardian.com/world/2018/aug/15/austria-accuses-afghan-asylum-seeker-of-pretending-to-be-gay

26 Katrin Bennhold, "Chemnitz Protests Show New Strength of Germany's Far Right," *New York Times*, August 30, 2018, web. Retrieved from https://www.nytimes.com/2018/08/30/world/europe/germany-neo-nazi-protests-chemnitz.html

27 Chantal Da Silva, "Families Live in Fear as Children Suffer Sexual Abuse at Greece's Biggest Refugee Camp," *Newsweek*, October 18, 2018, web. Retrieved from https://www.newsweek.com/families-greek-refugee-camps-live-fear-children-will-suffer-sexual-abuse-1168146?amp=1

28 A common custom in Germany as elsewhere: under the Preferential Employment Provision, a refugee or asylum applicant can be considered for a job only in cases where no German citizen or citizen of any other European country wants it. Nationals from countries who do not belong to the European Union or the European Economic Area require a residence title—a visa, residence permit, EU Blue Card, settlement permit, or a permanent EU residence permit—in order to enter the German labor market.

29 As of August 4, 2024. See: "Map of Jurisdictions that Criminalise LGBT People," *Human Dignity Trust*, web. Retrieved from https://www.humandignitytrust.org/lgbt-the-law/map-of-criminalisation/

30 Elizabeth A. Povinelli and George Chauncey, "Thinking Sexuality Transnationally: An Introduction," *GLQ* 5, no. 4 (1999): 442.

31 See: Scott Long, "Unbearable Witness: How Western Activists (Mis)Recognize Sexuality in Iran," *Contemporary Politics* 15, no. 1 (March 2009): 119–136, https://doi.org/10.1080/13569770802698054; and Nancy Fraser, *Justice*

*Interruptus: Critical Reflections on the 'Postsocialist' Origins of Sexual Orientation* (New York: Routledge, 1997).

32 Long, "Unbearable Witness," 129–131.

33 See, for example, Eithne Luibhéid's investigation of how the state regulates migratory flows through legal, political, cultural, and economic means in order to reproduce regulatory sexual identities and practices in Eithne Luibhéid, *Entry Denied: Controlling Sexuality at the Border* (Minneapolis, MN: University of Minnesota Press, 2002).

34 See: Chandan Reddy, "Asian Diasporas, Neoliberalism, and Family: Reviewing the Case for Homosexual Asylum in the Context of Family Rights," *Social Text* 23 (2005): 101–119, https://doi.org/10.1215/01642472-23-3-4_84-85-101

35 See: Martin F. Manalansan, "Queer Intersections: Sexuality and Gender in Migration Studies," *The International Migration Review* 40, no. 1 (2006): 224–249, https://doi.org/10.1111/j.1747-7379.2006.00009.x

36 Héctor Carrillo, "Sexual Migration, Cross-Cultural Sexual Encounters, and Sexual Health," *Sexuality Research and Social Policy* 1, no. 3 (2004): 61, https://doi.org/10.1525/srsp.2004.1.3.58

37 Manalansan, "Queer Intersections," 229–230.

38 Morten Goll, personal interview, August 22, 2019.

39 For more on the problematization of "tolerance" in the Netherlands, and Isabel Hoving's critique of the Dutch paradigm of reducing power differences to cultural differences, and regulating such cultural differences through unspoken segregated structures or outspoken multiculturalization, see: Isabel Hoving, "Opacity and Openness: Creating New Senses of Dutchness," in *Art and Visibility in Migratory Culture*, eds. Mieke Bal and Miguel Á. Hernández-Navarro (Leiden: Brill, 2011), 297–312.

40 Derrida, *On Cosmopolitanism and Forgiveness*, trans. Mark Dooley and Michael Hughes (London: Routledge, 2001), 18.

41 Derrida, *On Cosmopolitanism and Forgiveness*, 23.

42 Jeppe Wedel-Brandt, "Interview with CAMP," *Public Square* 25 (November 2017), web, emphasis mine. Retrieved from https://publicsquare.dk/artikel/interview-with-camp-center-for-art-and-migration-politics

43 Cannelle Gueguen-Teil and Irit Katz, "On the Meaning of Shelter: Living in Calais's Camps de la Lande," in *Camps Revisited: Multifaceted Spatialities of a Modern Political Technology*, eds. Irit Katz, Diana Martin, and Claudio Minca (London: Rowman & Littlefield International, 2018), 87.

44 For a more recent example, see Abu Dhabi's ongoing $27 billion Saadiyat Island project, featuring a new branch of the Louvre as well as, once completed, the largest of the Guggenheim museums.

45 Nicholas Mirzoeff, "On Visuality," *Journal of Visual Culture* 5, no. 1 (2006): 76, https://doi.org/10.1177/1470412906062285

46 Hannah Arendt, *The Human Condition* (Chicago, IL: University of Chicago Press, 1958), 3.

47 Arendt, *The Human Condition*, 57.

48 Moira Inghilleri, *Translation and Migration* (New York: Routledge, 2017), 49; emphasis mine.

49 Chris Campanioni, "The Glitch of Biometrics and the Error as Evasion: The Subversive Potential of Self-Effacement," *Diacritics* 48, no. 4 (2021): 43, https://doi.org/10.1353/dia.2020.0028

50 See: Claudia Torrisi, "The Double Stigma of LGBTI Asylum Seekers," *Open Migration*, March 31, 2017, web. Retrieved from https://openmigration.org/en/analyses/the-double-stigma-of-lgbti-refugees/

51 See: Graeme Wood, "The Refugee Detectives," *The Atlantic*, April 2018, web. Retrieved from https://www.theatlantic.com/magazine/archive/2018/04/the-refugee-detectives/554090/

52 Patience Agbabi, "The Refugee's Tale," in *Refugee Tales*, eds. David Herd and Anna Pincus (Manchester: Comma Press, 2016), 12.

53 Ruben Andersson, *Illegality, Inc.* (Berkeley, CA: University of California Press, 2014), 53–55.

54 Georgia Cole, "Beyond Labelling: Rethinking the Role and Value of the Refugee 'Label' through Semiotics," *Journal of Refugee Studies* 31, no. 1 (2018): 12.

55 Roger Zetter, "Refugees and Refugee Studies: A Label and an Agenda," *Journal of Refugee Studies* 1, no. 1 (1988): 2, https://doi.org/10.1093/jrs/1.1.1

56 International Organization for Migration, "Missing Migrants Project," 2019, web. Retrieved from https://missingmigrants.iom.int/region/mediterranean

57 Inghilleri, *Translation and Migration*, 4.

58 See: Khatharya Um, *From the Land of Shadows: War, Revolution, and the Making of the Cambodian Diaspora* (New York: NYU Press, 2015).

59 Adriana Cavarero, *Relating Narratives: Storytelling and Selfhood*, trans. Paul A. Kottman (London: Routledge, 2000), 62.

60 Cavarero, *Relating Narratives*, 75.

61 Inghilleri, *Translation and Migration*, 180.

62 Djelal Kadir, "To World, To Globalize—Comparative Literature's Crossroads," *Comparative Literature Studies* 41, no. 1 (2004): 7.

63 Joaquín Barriendos Rodríguez, "(Trans)Cultural Shifts in the International Contemporary Art-System," trans. Anke van Wijck, in *Art and Visibility in Migratory Culture*, 317.

64 Barriendos Rodríguez, "(Trans)Cultural Shifts in the International Contemporary Art-System," 322.

65 *The Man Who Sold His Skin*, dir. Kaouther Ben Hania (2020; Tunisia: Cinétéléfilms), film.

66 Emphasis mine.

67 See: Campanioni, "The Right to a Dignified Image: The Fashioning and Effacement of the Refugee within the Celebrity System," *JCMS: Journal of Cinema and Media Studies* 61, no. 1 (2021): 27–50, https://doi.org/10.1353/cj.2021.0080

68 Melena Ryzik, "Syrian Film Collective Offers View of Life Behind a Conflict," *New York Times*, October 18, 2015, web. Retrieved from https://www.nytimes.com/2015/10/19/movies/syrian-film-collective-offers-view-of-life-behind-a-conflict.html

69 See: Campanioni, *A and B and Also Nothing* (Atlanta, GA: Unbound Edition, 2023).

70 Kwame Anthony Appiah, "Is the Post- in Postmodernism the Post- in Postcolonial?" *Critical Inquiry* 17, no. 2 (Winter 1991): 342.

71 Ania Loomba, "Postcolonialism—or Postcolonial Studies," *Interventions: International Journal of Postcolonial Studies* 1, no. 1 (1998): 39–42, https://doi.org/10.1080/13698019800510121. For an elaborate discussion into the limitations and complications of the "postcolonial," see also: Loomba, *Colonialism/Postcolonialism* (New York: Routledge, 2005).

72 As economist Magnus Resch has shown, there are only ten institutions—all in the United States, all but one in New York City—which, together with their tastemakers, decide the market value of every working artist in the world. See: Resch, *How to Become a Successful Artist* (New York: Phaidon Press, 2021).

73 Michael Denning, *Culture in the Age of Three Worlds* (London: Verso, 2004), 51.

74 Denning, *Culture in the Age of Three Worlds*, 51–52.

75 Marx and Engels, *The Communist Manifesto*, 39–40.

76 *n+1*, "World Lite," *n+1* 17 (Fall 2013), web. Retrieved from https://nplusonemag.com/issue-17/the-intellectual-situation/world-lite/

77 In addition to Pascale Casanova's fraught analysis in *The World Republic of Letters*, see: *n+1*'s proposal for an "international literature" that doesn't cater to the tastes of a "middlebrow audience" but instead "creates the taste by which it is to be enjoyed" in the aforementioned essay "World Lite," as well as Alexander Beecroft's conceptual "ecology" of world literature grounded in processes of statecraft whose six "biomes" reduce, ultimately, to the same economic and political determinants he claims to want to abandon, in Alexander Beecroft, *An Ecology of World Literature: From Antiquity to the*

*Present Day* (London: Verso, 2015). In paving "another path" for today's world literature, *n+1*'s editors, as well as countless scholars, forget that these designs proceed from a fixed map, one that doesn't account for the works and writers who cannot be placed, or have no wish to be.

78 Pascale Casanova, *The World Republic of Letters*, trans. M.B. DeBevoise (Cambridge, MA: Harvard University Press, 2004), 23–24.

79 Casanova, *The World Republic of Letters*, 180.

80 Casanova, 207.

81 Casanova, 179.

82 Casanova, 189.

83 Jameson, "Third-World Literature in the Era of Multinational Capitalism," 191.

84 Aamir R. Mufti, *Forget English! Orientalisms and World Literatures* (Cambridge, MA: Harvard University Press, 2016), 60.

85 Mufti, *Forget English!*, 77.

86 Aimé Césaire, *Discourse on Colonialism*, trans. Joan Pinkham (New York: NYU Press, 2000), 44.

87 Frederick Cooper, *Africa in the World* (Cambridge, MA: Harvard University Press, 2014), 68.

88 Bessie Head, *A Question of Power* (Long Grove, IL: Waveland Press, 2017), 5.

89 Head, *A Question of Power*, 97.

90 Head, 143.

91 Head, 222.

92 Helen Müller, personal interview, May 23, 2019.

93 Édouard Glissant, *Treatise on the Whole-World*, trans. Celia Britton (Liverpool: Liverpool University Press, 2020), 52.

94 Glissant, *Treatise on the Whole-World*, 52.

95 Glissant, 130.

96 Étienne Balibar, *We, the People of Europe?: Reflections on Transnational Citizenship* (Princeton, NJ: Princeton University Press, 2004), 10.

97 See: Marx, *The Eighteenth Brumaire of Louis Bonaparte*, trans. Saul K. Padover (Moscow: Progress Publishers, 1937). Marx/Engels Internet Archive, web. Retrieved from https://www.marxists.org/archive/marx/works/1852/18th-brumaire/index.htm

98 Balibar, *We, the People of Europe?*, 71.

99 Monobina Gupta, "At the Stroke of Midnight, Migrant Workers Became Aliens in a Double Sense: Interview with Ranabir Samaddar," *Wire*, April 23, 2020, web. Retrieved from https://thewire.in/rights/interview-ranabir-samaddar-migrant-workers-invisible

100 Hans Park, "The Power of Cities," *UNHCR*, November 25, 2016, web. Retrieved from https://www.unhcr.org/innovation/the-power-of-cities/

101 Balibar, *We, the People of Europe?*, 2.

102 Adam Ramadan and Elisa Pascucci, "Urban Protest Camps in Egypt: The Occupation, (Re)Creation, and Destruction of Alternative Political Worlds," in *Camps Revisited: Multifaceted Spatialities of a Modern Political Technology*, 211.

103 Ramadan and Pascucci, "Urban Protest Camps in Egypt," 212.

104 See: Eve Tuck and K. Wayne Yang, "Decolonization Is Not a Metaphor," *Decolonization: Indigeneity, Education & Society* 1, no. 1 (2012): 1–40; and Tapji Garba and Sara-Maria Sorentino, "Slavery Is a Metaphor: A Critical Commentary on Eve Tuck and K. Wayne Yang's 'Decolonization Is Not a Metaphor,'" *Antipode* 52, no. 3 (2020): 764–782, https://doi.org/10.1111/anti.12615

105 Garba and Sorentino, "Slavery Is a Metaphor," 774–776, emphasis in the original.

106 Walter D. Mignolo, "On Pluriversality and Multipolarity," in *Constructing the Pluriverse*, ed. Bernd Reiter (Durham, NC: Duke University Press, 2018): ix.

107 See: Aristotle, *De Interpretatione* (*On Interpretation*), 350 BCE; and, especially, the chapter "On the Prehistory of Hermeneutics," in Jean Grondin, *Introduction to Philosophical Hermeneutics*, trans. Joel Weinsheimer (New Haven, CT: Yale University Press, 1994).

108 Césaire, *Discourse on Colonialism*, 73.

109 Césaire, "An Interview with Aimé Césaire (conducted by René Depestre)," trans. Maro Riofrancos, in *Discourse on Colonialism*, 84.

110 Glissant, *Sun of Consciousness*, trans. Nathanaël (New York: Nightboat Books, 2020), 79.

111 Glissant, "An Exploded Discourse," trans. J. Michael Dash, in *Caribbean Discourse* (Charlottesville, VA: Caraf Books, 1989), 162.

112 Glissant, *Sun of Consciousness*, 31.

113 "In any case, regarding this capacity for consciousness, for collective participation (I do not say national), the weight of history is such [...]." See: Glissant, *Sun of Consciousness*, 72.

114 Gaston Bachelard, *The Poetics of Space*, trans. Maria Jolas (Boston, MA: Beacon Press, 1994), 110.

115 Saidiya Hartman, "Venus in Two Acts," *Small Axe* 26 (June 2008): 10, https://doi.org/10.1215/-12-2-1

116 Balibar, *We, the People of Europe?*, 7.

117 Mignolo, "On Pluriversality and Multipolarity," xiv.

118 See: UNHCR, "Connecting Refugees: How Internet and Mobile Connectivity Can Improve Refugee Well-Being and Transform Humanitarian Action," *UNHCR*, September 14, 2016, web. Retrieved from https://reliefweb.int/report/world/connecting-refugees-how-internet-and-mobile-connectivity-can-improve-refugee-well-being

## CODA. /

1 Richard Rodriguez, "Illegal Immigrants: Prophets of a Borderless World," *New Perspectives Quarterly* 12 (1995), 61.

2 Chris Campanioni, "In Parallel with My Actual Diary: On Re-Writing an Exile," *Life Writing* 18, no. 1 (2021): 95–111, https://doi.org/10.1080/14484528.2020.1766752. Anthologized in *Essays in Life Writing*, ed. Kylie Cardell (New York and London: Routledge, 2022).

# *Acknowledgments*

Earlier versions of *Drift Net*'s analyses, sometimes in alternate arrangements, have appeared elsewhere.

A section of chapter 1, "Tracing Imperfections for an Amateur Aesthetic: A Genealogy," was originally published in *American Poetry Review* 53, no. 3 (May/June 2024): 33–35.

A section of chapter 2, "Migration as the Primal Scene of Narrative and a Model for its Reconfiguration," was originally published in *American Poetry Review* 49, no. 6 (November/December 2020): 41–42.

A section of chapter 3, "Documenting Disappearance: Self-Forgery and Erasure as a Means of Mobility," was originally published in *Social Identities* 28, no. 5 (2022): 658–675; and *Vestiges* 6 (2022): 140–151.

A section of chapter 4, "Remapping the State and the Academy from Within and Without: The Queer Refugee Camp as a Space for Alterity and a Site of Critique," was originally published in the *Los Angeles Review of Books*, December 31, 2021.

Thank you to my many mentors, especially Wayne Koestenbaum, Meena Alexander, Mary Ann Caws, Giancarlo Lombardi, Steven Kruger, Sonali Perera, Siraj Ahmed, Robert Reid-Pharr, and Herman Bennett, all of whom have enriched my thinking and learning in unquantifiable ways. Thanks, too, to Sean Guynes, for your editorial acumen and sage guidance, and for believing in this project. I also want to acknowledge the invaluable feedback from *Drift Net*'s anonymous reviewers, whose care and sensitivity helped me learn more about this book and, ultimately, how to hone its analyses while retaining the tumbles of consciousness that seeded them. This project would not have been possible without the support of the CHCI Global Humanities Institute, the A.W. Mellon Foundation, the Institute for Research on the African Diaspora in the Americas and the Caribbean, and the staff and students in the English and Comparative Literature programs at The Graduate Center of the City University of New York. Thank you, finally and forever, to Sophie and John Campanioni, and to Lilly, for always being my first reader.

# *Bibliography*


Abounaddara, "Dignity Has Never Been Photographed." *documenta 14*, March 24, 2017. https://documenta14.de/en/notes-and-works/15348/dignity-has-never-been-photographed

Abounaddara, *Abounaddara: The Right to the Image*, The Vera List Center for Art and Politics, New York City, October 22 through November 11, 2015. Accessed November 1, 2015.

Adorno, Theodor W. *Aesthetic Theory*. Translated by Robert Hullot-Kentor. New York and London: Continuum, 2002.

Agbabi, Patience. "The Refugee's Tale." In *Refugee Tales*, edited by David Herd and Anna Pincus, 125–132. Manchester: Comma Press, 2016.

Agence France-Presse. "Austria Rejects Afghan's Asylum Bid Because He 'Did Not Act or Dress Gay.'" *The Guardian*, August 15, 2018. https://www.theguardian.com/world/2018/aug/15/austria-accuses-afghan-asylum-seeker-of-pretending-to-be-gay

Agier, Michel. *Managing the Undesirables: Refugee Camps and Humanitarian Government*. Translated by David Fernbach. Cambridge: Polity, 2011.

Ahmad, Aijaz. *In Theory*. London: Verso, 1992.

Akella, Shastri. "Migratory Art: The Aesthetics of Contact." *World Literature Today*, September 17, 2017. https://www.worldliteraturetoday.org/2017/september/migratory-art-aesthetics-contact-shastri-akella

Alberti, Leon Battista. *On Painting*. Translated by John R. Spencer. London: Routledge, 1956.

Albuquerque, Fernanda Farias de and Maurizio Jannelli. *Princesa*. Rome: Sensibili alle foglie, 1994.

Alcoff, Linda. "The Problem of Speaking for Others." *Cultural Critique* 20 (Winter 1991–1992): 5–32. https://doi.org/10.2307/1354221

Andersson, Ruben. *Illegality, Inc.* Berkeley, CA: University of California Press, 2014.

Aouragh, Miriyam. "Everyday Resistance on the Internet: The Palestinian Context." *Journal of Arab and Muslim Media Research* 1, no. 2 (2008): 109–130. https://doi.org/10.1386/jammr.1.2.109_1

Appadurai, Arjun. "Disjuncture and Difference in the Global Cultural Economy." *Public Culture* 2, no. 2 (Spring 1990): 295–310. https://doi.org/10.1177/026327690007002017

Appiah, Kwame Anthony. "Is the Post- in Postmodernism the Post- in Postcolonial?" *Critical Inquiry* 17, no. 2 (Winter 1991): 336–357.

Archivos Politicos. "Ni muerto ni vivo ... esta desaparecido." YouTube, April 1, 2015. https://youtu.be/ASMPYgoYueU

Arendt, Hannah. "Introduction." In *Illuminations: Essays and Reflections*, edited by Hannah Arendt, 1–55. New York: Schocken Books, 1969.

Arendt, Hannah. *The Human Condition*. Chicago, IL: University of Chicago Press, 1958.

Arendt, Hannah. *The Origins of Totalitarianism*. San Diego, CA: Harcourt Brace & Company, 1973.

Arendt, Hannah. "We Refugees." In *Altogether Elsewhere: Writers on Exile*, edited by Marc Robinson, 110–119. London: Faber and Faber, 1994.

Armendinger, Brent. *Street Gloss*. Brooklyn, NY: The Operating System, 2019.

Asthana, Sanjay. "Youth, Self, Other: A Study of Ibdaa's Digital Media Practices in the West Bank, Palestine." *International Journal of Cultural Studies* 20, no. 1 (2017): 100–117. https://doi.org/10.1177/1367877915600546

Austin, J.L. *Philosophical Papers*. Oxford: Oxford University Press, 1979.

Bachelard, Gaston. *The Poetics of Space*. Translated by Maria Jolas. Boston, MA: Beacon Press, 1994.

Bahari, Maziar, dir. *82 Names*. March 1, 2018; Washington, DC: United States Holocaust Memorial Museum. https://www.ushmm.org/ar/82-names

Bakewell, Oliver. "Researching Refugees: Lessons From the Past, Current Challenges and Future Directions." *Refugee Survey Quarterly* 26, no. 3 (2007): 6–14. https://doi.org/10.1093/rsq/hdi0239

Bal, Mieke. "Documenting What? Auto-Theory and Migratory Aesthetics." In *A Companion to Contemporary Documentary Film*, edited by Alexandra Juhasz, and Alisa Lebow, 124–144. Hoboken, NJ: Wiley-Blackwell, 2015.

Bal, Mieke. "Double Movement." In *2move: video, art, migration*, edited by Mieke Bal and Miguel Á Hernández-Navarro, 13–82. Murcia: Cendeac, 2008.

Bal, Mieke and Miguel Á. Hernández-Navarro. "Introduction." In *Art and Visibility in Migratory Culture*, edited by Mieke Bal and Miguel Á. Hernández-Navarro, 9–20. Leiden: Brill, 2011.

Baldwin, James. *Tell Me How Long the Train's Been Gone*. New York: Vintage Books, 1968.

Balibar, Étienne. *Politics and the Other Scene*. Translated by Christine Jones, James Swenson, and Chris Turner. New York: Verso, 2002.

Balibar, Étienne. *We, the People of Europe?: Reflections on Transnational Citizenship*. Princeton, NJ: Princeton University Press, 2004.

Ball, Hugo. *Flight out of Time: A Dada Diary*. Translated by Ann Raimes. Berkeley, CA: University of California Press, 1996.

Barriendos Rodríguez, Joaquín. "Global Art and the Politics of Mobility: (Trans) Cultural Shifts in the International Contemporary Art-System." In *Art and Visibility in Migratory Culture*, translated by Anke van Wijck, edited by Mieke Bal and Miguel Á. Hernández-Navarro, 313–334. Leiden: Brill, 2011.

Barthes, Roland. *Image-Music-Text*. Translated by Richard Howard, edited by Stephen Heath. Waukegan, IL: Fontana Press, 1977.

Barthes, Roland. *The Rustle of Language*. Translated by Richard Howard. Berkeley, CA: University of California Press, 1986.

Bass, Alan. "Translator's Introduction: L Before K." In Jacques Derrida, *The Post Card*, translated by Alan Bass, ix–xxx. Chicago, IL: University of Chicago Press: 1987.

Bauman, Zygmunt. *Identity: Conversations with Benedetto Vecchi*. Cambridge: Polity, 2004.

Beecroft, Alexander. *An Ecology of World Literature: From Antiquity to the Present Day*. London: Verso, 2015.

Ben Hania, Kaouther, dir. *The Man Who Sold His Skin*. 2020; Tunisia: Cinétéléfilms.

Benjamin, Walter. *Illuminations*. Translated by Harry Zohn, edited by Hannah Arendt. New York: Schocken Books, 1968.

Benjamin, Walter. *One-Way Street*. Translated by Edmund Jephcott, edited by Michael W. Jennings. Cambridge, MA: Harvard University Press 2016.

Benjamin, Walter. *The Arcades Project*. Translated by Howard Eiland and Kevin McLaughlin. Cambridge, MA: Harvard University Press, 1999.

Benjamin, Walter. *The Correspondence of Walter Benjamin, 1910–1940*. Translated by Manfred R. Jacobson and Evelyn M. Jacobson, edited by Gershom Scholem and Theodor W. Adorno. Chicago, IL: University of Chicago Press, 2012.

Benjamin, Walter. *The Origin of German Tragic Drama*. Translated by John Osborne. London: Verso, 1998.

Benjamin, Walter. *The Work of Art in the Age of Its Technological Reproducibility, and Other Writings on Media*. Translated by Howard Eiland, edited by Michael W. Jennings, Brigid Doherty, and Thomas Y. Levin. Cambridge, MA: Harvard University Press, 2008.

Benjamin, Walter. "Time: On Werner Hegemann's *Das steinerne Berlin*." In *Metropolis Berlin: 1880–1940*, translated by Iain Boyd Whyte, edited by Iain Boyd Whyte and David Frisby, 358–362. Berkeley, CA: University of California Press, 2012.

Benjamin, Walter. *Walter Benjamin: Selected Writings (Volume 2, Part 1, 1927–1930)*, edited by Michael W. Jennings, Howard Eiland, and Gary Smith. Cambridge, MA: Harvard University Press, 1999.

Benjamin, Walter. *Walter Benjamin: Selected Writings (Volume 2, Part 2, 1931–1934)*, edited by Michael W. Jennings, Marcus Bullock, Howard Eiland, and Gary Smith. Cambridge, MA: Harvard University Press, 1999.

Bennett, Jill. "Migratory Aesthetics: Art and Politics beyond Identity." In *Art and Visibility in Migratory Culture*, edited by Mieke Bal and Miguel Á. Hernández-Navarro, 9–20. Leiden: Brill, 2011.

Bennhold, Katrin. "Chemnitz Protests Show New Strength of Germany's Far Right." *New York Times*, August 30, 2018. https://www.nytimes.com/2018/08/30/world/europe/germany-neo-nazi-protests-chemnitz.html

Berger, John. *Ways of Seeing*. London: Penguin, 1972.

Berger, John and Jean Mohr. *A Seventh Man*. London: Verso, 2010.

Birkenstock, Günther. "East Germany Relied on Forced Labor." *Deutsche Welle*, May 6, 2012. https://www.dw.com/en/east-germany-relied-on-forced-labor/a-15932840

Bishop, Sarah C. *Undocumented Storytellers: Narrating the Immigrant Rights Movement*. Oxford: Oxford University Press, 2019.

Bizzell, Patricia. "The Intellectual Work of 'Mixed' Forms of Academic Discourses." In *ALT DIS: Alternative Discourses and the Academy*, edited by Christopher Schroeder, Helen Fox, and Patricia Bizzell, 1–11. Portsmouth, NH: Heinemann, 2002.

Black, Richard. "Fifty Years of Refugee Studies: From Theory to Policy." *International Migration Review* 35, no. 1 (Spring 2001): 57–78.

Blaise, Clark. "A Novel of India's Coming of Age." *New York Times*, April 19, 1981. https://archive.nytimes.com/www.nytimes.com/books/98/12/06/specials/rushdie-children.html

Blankinship, Kevin. "Lost in Translation: Classical Arabic Literature." *The Millions*, November 26, 2019. https://themillions.com/2019/11/lost-in-translation-classical-arabic-literature.html

Blejmar, Jordana. *Playful Memories: The Autofictional Turn in Post-Dictatorship Argentina.* London: Palgrave Macmillan, 2016.

Bock, Jan-Jonathan. "Grassroots Solidarity and Political Protest in Rome's Migrant Camps." In *Camps Revisited: Multifaceted Spatialities of a Modern Political Technology*, edited by Irit Katz, Diana Martin, and Claudio Minca, 159–175. London: Rowman & Littlefield International, 2018.

Borcilâ, Rozalinda. "The Political Aesthetics of Immigrant Protest." In *Immigrant Protest: Politics, Aesthetics, and Everyday Dissent*, edited by Katarzyna Marciniak and Imogen Tyler, 45–62. Albany, NY: State University of New York Press, 2015.

Boros Foundation. *Bunker Berlin #4*, Boros Foundation, Berlin, May 1, 2022 through March 31, 2026. Accessed August 14, 2022.

Brandeis, Gayle. "#WeToo: Women Writing the First Person Plural." *Gay Magazine*, January 22, 2020. https://gay.medium.com/wetoo-b2b01fa2ae79

Bruns, Axel. *Blogs, Wikipedia, Second Life, and Beyond: From Production to Produsage*. New York: Peter Lang, 2008.

Bruns, Axel. "Towards Produsage: Futures for User-Led Content Production." In *Cultural Attitudes towards Technology and Communication 2006: Proceedings of the Fifth International Conference*, edited by Fay Sudweeks, Herbert Hrachovec, and Charles Ess, 275–284. Murdoch: School of Information Technology, 2006.

Buck-Morss, Susan. "Hegel and Haiti." *Critical Inquiry* 26, no. 4 (Summer 2000), 821–865.

Bui, Long. "The Refugee Repertoire: Performing and Staging the Postmemories of Violence." *MELUS: Multi-Ethnic Literature of the U.S.* 41, no. 3 (2016): 112–132. https://doi.org/10.1093/melus/mlw034

Burton, Antoinette. "'An Assemblage/Before Me': Autobiography as Archive." *Journal of Women's History* 25, no. 2 (2013): 185–188. https://doi.org/10.1353/jowh.2013.0022

Butler, Judith. *Precarious Life: The Powers of Mourning and Violence*. New York: Verso, 2004.

Calveyra, Arnaldo. *Letters So That Happiness*. Translated by Elizabeth Zuba. Brooklyn, NY: Ugly Duckling Presse, 2018.

Campanioni, Chris. *A and B and Also Nothing*. Atlanta, GA: Unbound Edition, 2023.

Campanioni, Chris. "Fixing Being with Likeness: Facial Recognition as the Site for Global Per-Formance." *Im@go: A Journal of the Social Imaginary* 12 (2018): 102–123. https://doi.org/10.7413/22818138129

Campanioni, Chris. "Houses in Motion: The Reimagining of Time and Space as Anomalous in Representations of Mobility." In *Migration, Dislocation and Movement on Screen*, edited by Ruxandra Trandafoiu, 17–37. New York: Berghahn Books, 2024. https://doi.org/10.3167/9781805395942

Campanioni, Chris. "How Bizarre: The Glitch of the Nineties as a Fantasy of New Authorship." *M/C: Media & Culture* 21, no. 5 (December 2018). https://doi.org/10.5204/mcj.1463

Campanioni, Chris. "In Parallel with My Actual Diary: On Re-Writing an Exile." *Life Writing* 18, no. 1 (2021): 95–111. https://doi.org/10.1080/14484528.2020.1766752

Campanioni, Chris. "Made in My Image: Co-Produced Fantasy and the Politics of Play." In *Transmedia Selves: Identity and Persona Creation in the Age of Mobile and Multiplatform Media*, edited by James Dalby and Matthew Freeman, 112–129. New York: Routledge, 2023. https://doi.org/10.4324/9781003134015

Campanioni, Chris. *north by north/west*. Morgantown, WV: West Virginia University Press, 2025.

Campanioni, Chris. "The Glitch of Biometrics and the Error as Evasion: The Subversive Potential of Self-Effacement." *Diacritics* 48, no. 4 (2021): 28–51. https://doi.org/10.1353/dia.2020.0028

Campanioni, Chris. *the Internet is for real*. Winston-Salem, NC: C&R Press, 2019.

Campanioni, Chris. "The Right to a Dignified Image: The Fashioning and Effacement of the Refugee within the Celebrity System." *JCMS: Journal of Cinema and Media Studies* 61, no. 1 (Fall 2021): 27–50. https://doi.org/10.1353/cj.2021.0080

Cantú, Lionel Jr., Eithne Luibhéid, and Alexandra Minna Stern. "Well-Founded Fear: Sexual Identity in the U.S.-Mexico Borderlands." In *Queer Migrations: Sexuality, U.S. Citizenship, and Border Crossings*, edited by Eithne Luibhéid and Lionel Cantú Jr., 61–74. Minneapolis, MN: University of Minnesota Press, 2005.

Carrillo, Héctor. "Sexual Migration, Cross-Cultural Sexual Encounters, and Sexual Health." *Sexuality Research and Social Policy* 1, no. 3 (2004): 58–70. https://doi.org/10.1525/srsp.2004.1.3.58

Casanova, Pascale. *The World Republic of Letters*. Translated by M.B. DeBevoise. Cambridge, MA: Harvard University Press, 2004.

Cavarero, Adriana. *Relating Narratives: Storytelling and Selfhood*. Translated by Paul A. Kottman. London: Routledge, 2000.

Caws, Mary Ann. *The Eye in the Text*. Princeton, NJ: Princeton University Press, 1981.

Césaire, Aimé. *Discourse on Colonialism*. Translated by Joan Pinkham. New York: NYU Press, 2000.

Chang, Elaine K. "A Not-So-New Spelling of My Name: Notes Toward (and Against) A Politics of Equivocation." In *Displacement: Cultural Identities in*

*Question*, edited by Angelika Bammer, 251–266. Bloomington, IN: Indiana University Press, 1994.

Chang, Heewon. "Cultural Autobiography: A Tool to Multicultural Discovery of Self." *Electronic Magazine of Multicultural Education* 1, no. 2 (Spring 1999): 1–5.

Chatty, Dawn and Philip Marfleet. "Conceptual Problems in Forced Migration." *Refugee Survey Quarterly* 32, no. 2 (2013): 1–13. https://doi.org/10.1093/rsq/hdt008

Chávez, Karma R. *Queer Migration Politics*. Urbana, IL: University of Illinois Press, 2013.

Chouliaraki, Lilie and Myria Georgiou. "The Digital Border: Mobility Beyond Territorial and Symbolic Divides." *European Journal of Communication* 34, no. 6 (2019): 594–605. https://doi.org/10.1177/0267323119886147

Cilliers, Paul. *Complexity and Postmodernism: Understanding Complex Systems*. London and New York: Routledge, 1998.

Cleave, Chris. "The Lorry Driver's Tale." In *Refugee Tales*, edited by David Herd and Anna Pincus, 25–34. Manchester: Comma Press, 2016.

Cody, Anthony. *The Rendering*. Oakland, CA: Omnidawn, 2023.

Cole, Georgia. "Beyond Labelling: Rethinking the Role and Value of the Refugee 'Label' through Semiotics." *Journal of Refugee Studies* 31, no. 1 (2018): 1–21. https://doi.org/10.1093/jrs/fex021

Connolly, Kate. "German Reunification 25 Years On: How Different are East and West Really." *The Guardian*, October 2, 2015. https://www.theguardian.com/world/2015/oct/02/german-reunification-25-years-on-how-different-are-east-and-west-really

Cooper, Frederick. *Africa in the World*. Cambridge, MA: Harvard University Press, 2014.

Cooppan, Vilashini. "World Literature and Global Theory: Comparative Literature for the New Millennium." *Symploké* 9, nos. 1 & 2 (2001): 7–19.

Costanza-Chock, Sasha. *Out of the Shadows, Into the Streets!: Transmedia Organizing and the Immigrant Rights Movement*. Cambridge, MA: MIT Press, 2014.

Cowen, Deborah. *The Deadly Life of Logistics: Mapping Violence in Global Trade*. Minneapolis, MN: University of Minnesota Press, 2014.

Crawley, Ashon T. "Otherwise, Ferguson." *Interfictions: A Journal of Interstitial Arts* 7 (October 2016). http://interfictions.com/otherwise-fergusonashon-crawley/

Culler, Jonathan. *On Deconstruction: Theory and Criticism after Structuralism*. Ithaca, NY: Cornell University Press, 1983.

Da Silva, Chantal. "Families Live in Fear as Children Suffer Sexual Abuse at Greece's Biggest Refugee Camp." *Newsweek*, October 18, 2018.

https://www.newsweek.com/families-greek-refugee-camps-live-fear-children-will-suffer-sexual-abuse-1168146?amp=1

Damrosch, David. *What Is World Literature?* Princeton, NJ: Princeton University Press, 2003.

Darwish, Mahmoud. *Memory for Forgetfulness: August, Beirut, 1982*. Translated by Ibrahim Muhawi. Berkeley, CA: University of California Press, 2013.

Darwish, Mahmoud. *Splinters of Bone*. Translated by B.M. Bennani. New York: The Greenfield Review Press, 1974.

De Campos, Haroldo. *Novas: Selected Writings*, edited by Antonio Sergio Bessa and Odile Cisneros. Evanston, IL: Northwestern University Press, 2007.

De Certeau, Michel. *The Practice of Everyday Life.* Translated by Steven Rendall. Berkeley, CA: University of California Press, 1984.

De Man, Paul. *The Rhetoric of Romanticism*. New York: Columbia University Press, 1984.

Dean, Jodi. "Affective Networks." *Media Tropes* 2, no. 2 (2010): 19–44.

DelConte, Matt. "A Further Study of Present Tense Narration: The Absentee Narratee and Four-Wall Present Tense in Coetzee's *Waiting for the Barbarians* and *Disgrace*." *Journal of Narrative Theory* 37, no. 3 (2007): 427–446.

Deleuze, Gilles and Félix Guattari. *A Thousand Plateaus: Capitalism and Schizophrenia*. Translated by Brian Masumi. Minneapolis, MN: University of Minnesota Press, 1987.

Deleuze, Gilles and Félix Guattari. *Toward a Minor Literature*. Translated by Dana Polan. Minneapolis, MN: University of Minnesota Press, 1986.

*Demolition and Protest at Kottbusser Tor*, on permanent view, Friedrichshain-Kreuzberg Museum, Berlin. Accessed August 6, 2018.

Denning, Michael. *Culture in the Age of Three Worlds.* London: Verso, 2004.

Derrida, Jacques. *Limited Inc.* Translated by Samuel Weber. Evanston, IL: Northwestern University Press, 1988.

Derrida, Jacques. "No (Point of) Madness—Maintaining Architecture." In *Psyche: Inventions of the Other, Volume II*, translated by Kate Linker, edited by Peggy Kamuf and Elizabeth Rottenberg, 87–103. Redwood City, CA: Stanford University Press, 2008.

Derrida, Jacques. *On Cosmopolitanism and Forgiveness*. Translated by Mark Dooley and Michael Hughes. London: Routledge, 2001.

Derrida, Jacques. *Specters of Marx*. Translated by Peggy Kamuf. London: Routledge Classics, 1993.

Derrida, Jacques. *The Animal That Therefore I Am*. Translated by David Wills. New York: Fordham University Press, 2008.

Derrida, Jacques. *The Post Card*. Translated by Alan Bass. Chicago, IL: The University of Chicago Press: 1987.

Derrida, Jacques and Anne Dufourmantelle. *Of Hospitality*. Translated by Rachel Bowlby. Redwood City, CA: Stanford University Press, 2000.

Deutsche Welle. "Italian Mayor Urges 'Strike' over Migrant Arrivals." August 30, 2020. https://www.dw.com/en/lampedusa-mayor-calls-for-strike-over-migrant-arrivals/a-54763386

Dewey, Caitlin. "Here Are Mark Zuckerberg's Full Remarks About How Much He'd Like to (Literally!) Read Your Thoughts." *Washington Post Blogs*, June 14, 2016. https://www.washingtonpost.com/news/the-intersect/wp/2016/06/14/here-are-mark-zuckerbergs-full-remarks-about-how-much-hed-like-to-literally-read-your-thoughts/

Di Maio, Alessandra. *Wor(l)ds in Progress: A Study of Contemporary Migrant Writers*. Rome: Mimesis International, 2014.

Diminescu, Dana. "The Connected Migrant: An Epistemological Manifesto." *Social Science Information* 47, no. 4 (2008): 565–579. https://doi.org/10.1177/0539018408096447

Dos Anjos Alfonso Rodrigues, Manoela. "Translanguaging and Autobiogeography as Decolonial Strategies for Writing Life Narratives within Displacement." *a/b: Auto/Biography Studies* 33, no. 3 (2018): 621–642. https://doi.org/10.1080/08989575.2018.1503437

Duchamp, Marcel. *The Writings of Marcel Duchamp*. Translated by Elmer Peterson, edited by Michel Sanouillet and Elmer Peterson. Cambridge, MA: Da Capo Press, 1973.

Eco, Umberto. *A Theory of Semiotics*. Bloomington, IL: Indiana University Press, 1976.

Eco, Umberto. *The Open Work*. Translated by Anna Cancogni. Cambridge, MA: Harvard University Press, 1989.

Espiritu, Yên Lê. "Towards a Critical Refugee Study: The Vietnamese Refugee Subject in U.S. Scholarship." *Journal of Vietnamese Studies* 1, nos. 1–2 (2006): 410–433.

Fajardo, Kale Bantigue. *Filipino Crosscurrents: Oceanographies of Seafaring, Masculinities, and Globalization*. Minneapolis, MN: University of Minnesota Press, 2011.

Fassin, Didier and Sarah Mazouz. "What Is It to Become French? Naturalization as a Republican Rite of Institution." *Revue française de sociologie* 50 (2009): 37–64.

Fijałkowski, Krzysztof. "Cubomania: Ghérasim Luca and Non-Oedipal Collage." *Dada/Surrealism* 20 (2015): 1–31. https://doi.org/10.17077/0084-9537.1301

Forné, Anna. "Archival Autofiction in Post-Dictatorship Argentina." *Life Writing* (2019): 1–12. https://doi.org/10.1080/14484528.2019.1642174

Foucault, Michel. "What Is an Author?" In *Aesthetics, Method, and Epistemology*, translated by Josué V. Harari, edited by James D. Faubion, 205–222. New York: The New Press, 1998.

Fraser, Nancy. *Justice Interruptus: Critical Reflections on the 'Postsocialist Origins of Sexual Orientation.* New York: Routledge, 1997.

Freedman, Barbara. *Staging the Gaze: Postmodernism, Psychoanalysis, and Shakespearean Comedy*. Ithaca, NY: Cornell University Press, 1991.

Fried, Michael. *Art and Objecthood: Essays and Reviews*. Chicago, IL: University of Chicago Press, 1998.

Garba, Tapji and Sara-Maria Sorentino. "Slavery Is a Metaphor: A Critical Commentary on Eve Tuck and K. Wayne Yang's 'Decolonization Is Not a Metaphor." *Antipode* 52, no. 3 (2020): 764–782. https://doi.org/10.1111/anti.12615

Garcia, Edgar. *Skins of Columbus: A Dream Ethnography*. New York: Fence Books, 2019.

Garland-Thompson, Rosemarie. *Extraordinary Bodies: Figuring Physical Disability in American Culture and Literature*. New York: Columbia University Press, 1996.

Ghafar, Adel Abdel. *The European Union and North Africa: Prospects and Challenges*. Washington, DC: Brookings, 2019.

Glissant, Édouard. *Caribbean Discourse*. Translated by J. Michael Dash. Charlottesville, VA: Caraf Books, 1989.

Glissant, Édouard. *Poetics of Relation*. Translated by Betsy Wing. Ann Arbor, MI: University of Michigan Press 1997.

Glissant, Édouard. *Sun of Consciousness*. Translated by Nathanaël. New York: Nightboat Books, 2020.

Glissant, Édouard. *Treatise on the Whole-World*. Translated by Celia Britton. Liverpool: Liverpool University Press, 2020.

Glissant, Édouard, Manthia Diawara, and Christopher Winks. "One World in Relation: Édouard Glissant in Conversation with Manthia Diawara." *Nka: Journal of Contemporary African Art* 28 (2011): 4–19.

Goethe, Johann Wolfgang. *Conversations with Eckermann 1823–1832*. Translated by John Oxenford. London: Everyman, 1930.

Goffman, Erving. *Behavior in Public Places*. New York: The Free Press, 1963.

Gordimer, Nadine. "The Ultimate Safari." In *Ten Years of the Caine Prize for African Writing*, edited by Chris Bazier, 11–20. Oxford: New Internationalist Publications, 2009.

Gritz, Anna. "Klára Hosnedlová in Conversation with Anna Gritz." *Cura* 36, 2021. https://curamagazine.com/digital/klara-hosnedlova/

Grondin, Jean. *Introduction to Philosophical Hermeneutics*. Translated by Joel Weinsheimer. New Haven, CT: Yale University Press, 1994.

Guattari, Félix. *Chaosophy: Texts and Interviews 1972–1977*, edited by Sylvére Lotringer. Los Angeles, CA: Semiotext(e), 2009.

Guattari, Félix. "Transdisciplinarity Must Become Transversality." Translated by Andrew Goffey. *Theory, Culture & Society* 32, nos. 5–6 (2015): 131–137. https://doi.org/10.1177/0263276415597045

Gueguen-Teil, Cannelle and Irit Katz. "On the Meaning of Shelter: Living in Calais's Camps de la Lande." In *Camps Revisited: Multifaceted Spatialities of a Modern Political Technology*, edited by Irit Katz, Diana Martin, and Claudio Minca, 83–98. London: Rowman & Littlefield International, 2018.

Gupta, Monobina. "At the Stroke of Midnight, Migrant Workers Became Aliens in a Double Sense: Interview with Ranabir Samaddar." *Wire*, April 23, 2020. https://thewire.in/rights/interview-ranabir-samaddar-migrant-workers-invisible

Hartman, Saidiya. "Venus in Two Acts." *Small Axe* 26 (June 2008): 1–14. https://doi.org/10.1215/-12-2-1

Hartsock, Nancy. "Foucault on Power: A Theory for Women?" In *Feminism/Postmodernism*, edited by Linda J. Nicholson, 15–33. London: Routledge, 1990.

Hayden, Bridget. "What's in a Name? The Nature of the Individual in Refugee Studies." *Journal of Refugee Studies* 19, no. 4 (2006): 471–487. https://doi.org/10.1093/refuge/fel021

Head, Bessie. *A Question of Power*. Long Grove, IL: Waveland Press, 2017.

Hekking, Morgan. "Moroccans Spend More than $44 Million on Schengen Visa Applications." *Morocco World News*, December 18, 2019. https://www.moroccoworldnews.com/2019/12/289246/moroccans-spend-44-million-schegen-visa-applications/

Herd, David. "Afterword." In *Refugee Tales*, edited by David Herd and Anna Pincus, 133–143. Manchester: Comma Press, 2016.

Herd David and Anna Pincus, eds. *Refugee Tales*. Manchester: Comma Press, 2016.

Hernández-Navarro, Miguel Á. "Out of Synch: Visualizing Migratory Times through Video Art." In *Art and Visibility in Migratory Culture*, edited by Mieke Bal and Miguel Á. Hernández-Navarro, 191–208. Leiden: Brill, 2011.

Higgins, Dick. "Intermedia." *Something Else Newsletter* 1, no. 1 (1966): 1–4. https://www.primaryinformation.org/oldsite/SEP/Something-Else-Press_Newsletter_V1N1.pdf

Higgins, Dick and Hannah Higgins. "Intermedia." *Leonardo* 34, no. 1 (2001): 49–54.

Horsti, Karina. "Digital Materialities in the Diasporic Mourning of Migrant Death." *European Journal of Communication* 34, no. 6 (2019): 671–681. https://doi.org/10.1177/0267323119886169

Hoving, Isabel. "Opacity and Openness: Creating New Senses of Dutchness." In *Art and Visibility in Migratory Culture*, edited by Mieke Bal and Miguel Á. Hernández-Navarro, 297–312. Leiden: Brill, 2011.

Human Dignity Trust. "Map of Jurisdictions that Criminalise LGBT People," accessed November 11, 2024, https://www.humandignitytrust.org/lgbt-the-law/map-of-criminalisation/

Hutmacher, Fabian. "Why Is There So Much More Research on Vision Than on Any Other Sensory Modality?" *Frontiers in Psychology* 10 (2019): 1–12. https://doi.org/10.3389/fpsyg.2019.02246

Inghilleri, Moira. *Translation and Migration*. New York: Routledge, 2017.

International Organization for Migration. "Missing Migrants Project," 2019. https://missingmigrants.iom.int/region/mediterranean

Iser, Wolfgang. "The Reading Process: A Phenomenological Approach." *New Literary History* 3, no. 2 (1972): 279–299. https://doi.org/10.2307/468316

Jameson, Fredric. *The Modernist Papers*. London: Verso, 2007.

Jameson, Fredric. *The Political Unconscious: Narrative as Socially Symbolic Act.* New York: Routledge, 1981.

Jameson, Fredric. "Third-World Literature in the Era of Multinational Capitalism." *Social Text* 15 (Autumn, 1986): 65–88.

Jenkins, Henry. *Convergence Culture: Where Old and New Media Collide*. New York: New York University Press, 2006.

Jenkins, Henry. "Convergence? I Diverge." *MIT Technology Review*, June 1, 2001. https://www.technologyreview.com/2001/06/01/235791/convergence-i-diverge/

Jenkins, Henry. "Transmedia Storytelling 101." *Pop Junctions: Reflections on Entertainment, Pop Culture, Activism, Media Literacy, Fandom, and More*, March 21, 2007. http://henryjenkins.org/blog/2007/03/transmedia_story telling_101.html

Joudah, Fady. "A Palestinian Meditation in a Time of Annihilation." *Literary Hub*, November 1, 2023. https://lithub.com/a-palestinian-meditation-in-a-time-of-annihilation/

Joudah, Fady. "Palestinian Discusses Humanitarian Needs in Gaza." *ABC News*, October 13, 2023. https://abcnews.go.com/International/video/palestinian-discusses-humanitarian-gaza-103967824

Kadir, Djelal. "To World, To Globalize—Comparative Literature's Crossroads." *Comparative Literature Studies* 41, no. 1 (2004): 1–9.

Kafka, Franz. *The Blue Octavo Notebook*. Translated by Ernst Kaiser and Eithne Wilkins, edited by Max Brod. Cambridge, MA: Exact Change, 1991.

Kafka, Franz. *The Diaries of Franz Kafka*. Translated by Joseph Kresh, edited by Max Brod. New York: Schocken Books, 1948.

Kane, Carolyn L. *High-Tech Trash: Glitch, Noise, and Aesthetic Failure*. Berkeley, CA: University of California Press, 2019.

Kane, Mohamadou. *Birago Diop: L'Homme et l'oeuvre*. Paris: Présence africaine, 1971.

Kaplan, Caren. "Resisting Autobiography: Out-Law Genres and Transnational Feminist Subjects." In *De/Colonizing the Subject*, edited by Sidonie Smith and Julia Watson, 115–138. Minneapolis, MN: University of Minnesota Press, 1992.

Karpinski, Eva C. "Migrations and Metamorphoses." *a/b: Auto/Biography Studies* 32, no. 2 (2017): 171–173. https://doi.org/10.1080/08989575.2017.1287898

Karssli, Reem, dir. *Every Day, Every Day*. 2013; Romania: Passport Productions.

Karssli, Reem, and Caroline Williams, dirs. *Now Is the Time To Say Nothing*. 2015; London: Young Vic's Taking Part.

King, Russell, John Connell, and Paul White, eds. *Writing Across Worlds: Literature and Migration*. London and New York: Routledge, 1995.

Krifors, Karin. "Logistics of Migration Labour: Rethinking How Workers 'Fit' Transnational Economies." *Journal of Ethnic and Migration Studies* 47, no. 1 (2021): 148–165. https://doi.org/10.1080/1369183X.2020.1754179

Kristeva, Julia. "The Subject in Process." In *The Tel Quel Reader*, edited by Roland-François Lack and Patrick Ffrench, 133–178. New York: Routledge, 1998.

Kumar, Amitava. *Passport Photos*. Berkeley, CA: University of California Press, 2000.

Lebdai, Benaouda. *Autobiography as a Writing Strategy in Postcolonial Literature*. Cambridge: Cambridge Scholars Publishing, 2015.

Lévy, Pierre A. *Collective Intelligence: Mankind's Emerging World in Cyberspace*. Translated by Robert Bononno. New York: Plenum Trade, 1997.

Life. "Eyewitness Rwanda." *Life*, September 1994.

Lispector, Clarice. *Selected Crônicas*. Translated by Giovanni Pontiero. New York: New Directions, 1996.

Loescher, Gil. *Beyond Charity: International Cooperation and the Global Refugee Crisis*. Oxford: Oxford University Press, 1993.

Long, Scott. "Unbearable Witness: How Western Activists (Mis)Recognize Sexuality in Iran." *Contemporary Politics* 15, no. 1 (March 2009): 119–136. https://doi.org/10.1080/13569770802698054

Loomba, Ania. "Postcolonialism—or Postcolonial Studies." *Interventions: International Journal of Postcolonial Studies* 1, no. 1 (1998): 39–42. https://doi.org/10.1080/13698019800510121

Loomba, Ania. *Colonialism/Postcolonialism*. New York: Routledge, 2005.

Lotman, Jurij M. *The Structure of the Artistic Text*. Translated by Ronald Vroon. Ann Arbor, MI: University of Michigan Press, 1977.

Lotringer, Sylvére and Paul Virilio. *The Accident of Art*. Translated by Michael Taormina. Los Angeles, CA: Semiotext(e), 2005.

Lowe, Lisa. *The Intimacies of Four Continents*. Durham, NC: Duke University Press, 2015.

Luca, Ghérasim. *Inventor of Love & Other Writings*. Translated by Julian and Laura Semilian. Boston, MA: Black Widow Press, 2009.

Luca, Ghérasim. "Passionnément." *Rhuthmos*, April 5, 2011. http://rhuthmos.eu/spip.php?article332

Luca, Ghérasim. *Self-Shadowing Prey*. Translated by Mary Ann Caws. New York: Contra Mundum Press, 2012.

Luca, Ghérasim. *The Passive Vampire*. Translated by Krzysztof Fijałkowski. Prague, Czech Republic: Twisted Spoon Press, 2008.

Luciano, Lorena and Filippo Piscopo, dirs. *It Will Be Chaos*. 2018; Italy: HBO.

Luibhéid, Eithne. *Entry Denied: Controlling Sexuality at the Border*. Minneapolis, MN: University of Minnesota Press, 2002.

Malkki, Liisa H. "Speechless Emissaries: Refugees, Humanitarianism, and Dehistoricization." *Cultural Anthropology* 11, no. 3 (1996): 377–404.

Mallarmé, Stéphane. "Preface to 'Dice Thrown Never Will Annual Chance'." In *Selected Poetry and Prose*, translated and edited by Mary Ann Caws, 105–106. New York: New Directions, 1982.

Manalansan, Martin F. "Queer Intersections: Sexuality and Gender in Migration Studies." *The International Migration Review* 40, no. 1 (2006): 224–249. https://doi.org/10.1111/j.1747-7379.2006.00009.x

Manguso, Sarah. *Ongoingness: The End of a Diary*. London: Picador, 2019.

Manning, Erin. "Toward a Politics of Immediation." *Frontiers in Sociology* 3 (2019): 1–11. https://doi.org/10.3389/fsoc.2018.00042

Marcos. *Professionals of Hope: The Selected Writings of Subcomandante Marcos*. Brooklyn, NY: The Song Cave, 2017.

Martin, Philip. "Mexican Braceros and US Farm Workers." *Wilson Center*, July 10, 2020. https://www.wilsoncenter.org/article/mexican-braceros-and-us-farm-workers

Marx, Karl. *The Eighteenth Brumaire of Louis Bonaparte*. Translated by Saul K. Padover. Moscow: Progress Publishers, 1937. Marx/Engels Internet Archive.

https://www.marxists.org/archive/marx/works/1852/18th-brumaire/index.htm
Marx, Karl and Frederick Engels. *The Communist Manifesto*. Translated by Frederick Engels. London: Verso, 1998.
Massumi, Brian, Jacob Ferrington, Alina Hechler, and Jannell Parsons. "Affect and Immediation: An Interview with Brian Massumi." *disClosure: A Journal of Social Theory* 28 (2019): 110–121. https://doi.org/10.13023/disclosure.28.09
McVey, Kurt. "Kon Trubkovich's Transmissions." *Interview*, February 12, 2014.
Mercer, Kobena. "Aubrey Williams: Abstraction in Diaspora." *British Art Studies* 8 (2008). https://www.britishartstudies.ac.uk/issues/issue-index/issue-8/aubrey-williams
Mercer, Kobena. "Conceptualising Modernist Architecture in Transcultural Spaces: An Interview with Kader Attia." *Atlantica: Journal of Art and Thought* 50 (2011): 44–61. http://www.revistaatlantica.com/wp-content/uploads/2016/02/ATL50.pdf
Mezzadra, Sandro and Brett Neilson. *Border as Method: Or, the Multiplication of Labor*. Durham, NC: Duke University Press, 2013.
Mignolo, Walter. "On Pluriversality and Multipolarity." In *Constructing the Pluriverse*, edited by Bernd Reiter, ix–xv. Durham, NC: Duke University Press, 2018.
Mignolo, Walter D., and Freya Schiwy, "Transculturation and the Colonial Difference: Double Translation." *IC Revista Científica de Información y Comunicación* 4 (2007): 6–28.
Miller, Nancy K. "But Enough About Me, What Do You Think of My Memoir?" *The Yale Journal of Criticism* 13, no. 2 (Fall 2000): 421–436. https://doi.org/10.1353/yale.2000.0023
Miller, Nancy K. *Getting Personal: Feminist Occasions and Other Autobiographical Acts*. New York: Routledge, 1991.
Minca, Claudio, Danica Šantić, and Dragan Umek. "Walking the Balkan Route: The Archipelago of Refugee Camps in Serbia." In *Camps Revisited: Multifaceted Spatialities of a Modern Political Technology*, edited by Irit Katz, Diana Martin, and Claudio Minca, 35–59. London: Rowman & Littlefield International, 2018.
Minha-ha, Trinh T. *Elsewhere, Within Here: Immigration, Refugeeism and the Boundary Event*. New York and London, Routledge: 2011.
Mirzoeff, Nicholas. "On Visuality." *Journal of Visual Culture* 5, no. 1 (2006): 53–79. https://doi.org/10.1177/1470412906062285
Morton, Timothy. "Ecology without the Present." *Oxford Literary Review* 34, no. 2 (2012): 229–238.

Mostag, Petter and Fredrik Tamsen. "Error Rates for Unvalidated Medical Age Assessment Procedures." *International Journal of Legal Medicine* 133 (2019), 613–623. https://doi.org/10.1007/s00414-018-1916-3

Mufti, Aamir R. *Forget English! Orientalisms and World Literatures.* Cambridge, MA: Harvard University Press, 2016.

Muñoz, José Esteban. *Cruising Utopia: The Then and There of Queer Futurity.* New York: New York University Press, 2009.

Muñoz, José Esteban. *Disidentifications: Queers of Color and the Performance of Politics.* Minneapolis, MN: University of Minnesota Press, 1999.

*n+1*. "World Lite." *n+1* 17 (Fall 2013). https://nplusonemag.com/issue-17/the-intellectual-situation/world-lite/

Nancy, Jean-Luc. *Being Singular Plural.* Translated by Robert D. Richardson and Anne E. O'Byrne. Redwood City, CA: Stanford University Press, 2000.

Nath, Paramita, dir. *Found.* 2009; Canada.

Oliver, Kelly. *Carceral Humanitarianism: Logics of Refugee Detention.* Minneapolis, MN: University of Minnesota Press, 2017.

Olson, Marisa. "Postinternet: Art After the Internet." *Foam* 29 (2011): 59–63.

Ortiz, Fernando. *Contrapunteo Cubano del Tabaco y el Azúcar*. Havana, Cuba: Montero, 1940.

Paasonen, Susanna. "Networked Affect." In *Posthuman Glossary*, edited by Rosi Braidotti and Maria Hlavajova, 283–285. London: Bloomsbury Academic, 2018.

Parati, Graziella. *Migration Italy: The Art of Talking Back in a Destination Culture.* Toronto: University of Toronto Press, 1995.

Park, Hans. "The Power of Cities." *UNHCR*, November 25, 2016. https://www.unhcr.org/innovation/the-power-of-cities/

Parry, Albert. "Samizdat Is Russia's Underground Press." *New York Times*, March 15, 1970, 249.

Pasternak, Boris. *Safe Conduct*. Translated by Babette Deutsch. New York: New Directions, 2009.

Pasternak, Boris, Marina Tsvetayeva, and Maria Rilke Rainer. *Letters: Summer 1926*. Translated by Margaret Wettlin, Walter Arndt, and Jamey Gambrell. New York: New York Review of Books, 2001.

Petzold, Christian, dir. *Transit*. 2018; Germany: Schramm Film.

Ponge, Francis. *Nioque of the Early-Spring*. Translated by Jonathan Larson. Brooklyn, NY: The Song Cave, 2018.

Ponge, Francis. *Soap*. Translated by Lane Dunlop. Redwood City, CA: Stanford University Press, 1998.

Ponzanesi, Sandra. *The Postcolonial Cultural Industry: Icons, Markets, Mythologies*. New York: Palgrave Macmillan, 2014.

Popovič, Anton. *Dictionary for the Analysis of Literary Translation*. Edmonton: University of Alberta, 1976.

Povinelli, Elizabeth A., and George Chauncey. "Thinking Sexuality Transnationally: An Introduction." *GLQ* 5, no. 4 (1999): 439–450.

Pressman, Jessica. "The Strategy of Digital Modernism." In *World Literature in Theory*, edited by David Damrosch, 493–510. West Sussex: John Wiley & Sons, 2004.

Raad, Walid. *No, Illness Is Neither Here Nor There* (1976–1990), National Museum of Contemporary Art Athens, on permanent view. Accessed June 9, 2024.

Raad, Walid. *Walid Raad*, The Museum of Modern Art, New York City, October 12, 2015 through January 31, 2016. Accessed January 10, 2016.

Ramadan, Adam and Elisa Pascucci. "Urban Protest Camps in Egypt: The Occupation, (Re)Creation, and Destruction of Alternative Political Worlds." In *Camps Revisited: Multifaceted Spatialities of a Modern Political Technology*, edited by Irit Katz, Diana Martin, and Claudio Minca, 199–214. London: Rowman & Littlefield International, 2018.

Rancière, Jacques. *The Politics of Aesthetics*. Translated by Gabriel Rockhill. London: Continuum, 2004.

Rashid, Tanjil. "*On Earth We're Briefly Gorgeous* by Ocean Vuong." *The Brooklyn Rail*, June 2019. https://brooklynrail.org/2019/06/books/-Ocean-Vuong

Rättsmedicinalverket. "Medicinsk åldersbedömning (SVENSKA)." YouTube, May 16, 2017. https://youtu.be/Mnv9tNWb01k

Reddy, Chandan. "Asian Diasporas, Neoliberalism, and Family: Reviewing the Case for Homosexual Asylum in the Context of Family Rights." *Social Text* 23 (2005): 101–119. https://doi.org/10.1215/01642472-23-3-4_84-85-101

Resch, Magnus. *How to Become a Successful Artist*. New York: Phaidon Press, 2021.

Rodríguez, Juana María. *Queer Latinidad*. New York: New York University Press, 2003.

Rodriguez, Richard. "Illegal Immigrants: Prophets of a Borderless World." *New Perspectives Quarterly* 12 (1995): 61–62.

Rosenthal, Gabriele. "National Identity or Multicultural Autobiography? Theoretical Concepts of Biographical Constitution Grounded in Case Reconstructions." In *The Narrative Study of Lives: Volume 5*, edited by Amia Lieblich and Ruthellen Josselson, 21–39. Thousand Oaks, CA: Sage Publications, 1997.

Rossipal, Christian. "The Public Procurement of a Biometric Love Story." *Orphan Film Symposium*, May 26, 2020. https://wp.nyu.edu/orphanfilm/2020/05/26/the-public-procurement-of-a-biometric-love-story/

Rowe, Aimee Carrillo. "Moving Relations: On the Limits of Belonging." *Liminalities: A Journal of Performance Studies* 5, no. 5 (November 2009): 1–10.

Ryzik, Melena. "Syrian Film Collective Offers View of Life Behind a Conflict." *New York Times*, October 18, 2015. https://www.nytimes.com/2015/10/19/movies/syrian-film-collective-offers-view-of-life-behind-a-conflict.html

Said, Edward. *Culture and Imperialism*. London: Vintage, 1994.

Said, Edward. "Permission to Narrate." *London Review of Books* 6, no. 3, February 16, 1984. https://www.lrb.co.uk/the-paper/v06/n03/edward-said/permission-to-narrate

Said, Edward. *Reflections on Exile and Other Essays*. Cambridge, MA: Harvard University Press, 2000.

Said, Edward and Jean Mohr. *After the Last Sky: Palestinian Lives*. New York: Columbia University Press, 1999.

Sandoval, Chela. "Feminist Forms of Agency and Oppositional Consciousness: U.S. Third World Feminist Criticism." In *Provoking Agents: Gender and Agency in Theory and Practice*, edited by Judith Kegan Gardiner, 208–226. Urbana, IL: University of Illinois Press, 1995.

Santos Perez, Craig. *from Unincorporated Territory [hacha]*. Oakland, CA: Omnidawn, 2017.

Schlegel, Friedrich. *Friedrich Schlegel's* Lucinde *and the Fragments*. Translated by Peter Firchow. Minneapolis, MN: University of Minnesota Press, 1971.

Schreiber, Rebecca M. *The Undocumented Everyday: Migrant Lives and the Politics of Visibility*. Minneapolis, MN: University of Minnesota Press, 2018.

Sedgwick, Eve. *Touching Feeling: Affect, Pedagogy, Performativity*. Durham, NC: Duke University Press, 2003.

Seghers, Anna. *Crossing*. Translated by Douglas Irving. New Orleans, LA: Diálogos, 2016.

Seghers, Anna. *Transit*. Translated by Margot Bettauer Dembo. New York: New York Review of Books, 2013.

Shamseddine, Ali and John Rich. "An Introduction to the New Syrian National Archive." *e-flux journal* 60 (December 2014). https://www.e-flux.com/journal/60/61055/an-introduction-to-the-new-syrian-national-archive/

Shelley, Percy. *A Defence of Poetry*. In *Shelley's Poetry and Prose*, edited by Donald H. Reiman and Neil Fraistat, 509–535. New York and London: W.W. Norton, 2002.

Sheridan, Vera. "Disclosing the Self: 1956 Hungarian Student Refugees Creating Autobiographies for University Scholarships in the USA," *Life Writing* (2019): 1–16. https://doi.org/10.1080/14484528.2019.1644210

Shklovsky, Viktor. *Third Factory*. Translated by Richard Sheldon. Chicago, IL: Dalkey Archive Press, 2002.

Shome, Raka. "When Postcolonial Studies Interrupts Media Studies." *Communication Culture & Critique* 12 (2019): 305–322, https://doi.org/10.1093/ccc/tcz020

Simon, Ralf. "The Temporality of Hospitality." In *Critical Time in Modern German Literature and Culture*, translated by Andrew Shields, edited by Dirk Göttsche, 165–182. New York: Peter Lang, 2016.

Snorton, C. Riley. *Black on Both Sides: A Racial History of Trans Identity*. Minneapolis, MN: University of Minnesota Press, 2017.

Sontag, Susan. *As Consciousness Is Harnessed to Flesh: Journals & Notebooks 1964–1980*, edited by David Rieff. New York: Picador, 2012.

Spivak, Gayatri. *An Aesthetic Education in the Era of Globalization*. Cambridge, MA: Harvard University Press, 2012.

Spivak, Gayatri. "Can the Subaltern Speak?" In *Marxism and Interpretations of Culture*, edited by Cary Nelson and Lawrence Grossberg, 271–313. Urbana, IL: University of Illinois Press, 1988.

Spivak, Gayatri. "Keynote Speech at CSD Department of International Relations." November 7, 2015. YouTube, January 29, 2016. https://youtu.be/-Hr_wsM5mDM

Spivak, Gayatri. *Outside in the Teaching Machine*. New York: Routledge, 1993.

Spivak, Gayatri. "Translating into English." In *Nation, Language, and the Ethics of Translation*, edited by Sandra Bermann and Michael Wood, 93–110. Princeton, NJ: Princeton University Press, 2005.

Strich, Fritz. *Goethe und die Weltliteratur*. Bern: Franke Verlag, 1946.

Tacitus. *On the Origin and Situation of the Germans*. Translated by Thomas Gordon. The Project Gutenberg. https://www.gutenberg.org/files/2995/2995-h/2995-h.htm

Thammavongsa, Souvankham. *Found*. Toronto: Pedlar Press, 2007.

Tiedemann, Rolf. "Dialectics at a Standstill: Approaches to the *Passagen-Werk*." Translated by Gary Smith and André Lefevere. In *The Arcades Project*. Cambridge, MA: Harvard University Press, 1999.

Todorovic, Dragan. "The Migrant's Tale." In *Refugee Tales*, edited by David Herd and Anna Pincus, 1–12. Manchester: Comma Press, 2016.

Torrisi, Claudia. "The Double Stigma of LGBTI Asylum Seekers." *Open Migration*, March 31, 2017. https://openmigration.org/en/analyses/the-double-stigma-of-lgbti-refugees/

Treitler, Vilna Bashi. "Social Agency and White Supremacy in Immigration Studies," *Sociology of Race and Ethnicity* 1, no. 1 (2015): 153–165. https://doi.org/10.1177/2332649214560796

Trubkovich, Kon. *Snow*, Marianne Boesky Gallery, New York City, February 20 to March 22, 2014. Accessed March 5, 2014.

Tuck, Eve and K. Wayne Yang. "Decolonization Is Not a Metaphor." *Decolonization: Indigeneity, Education & Society* 1, no. 1 (2012): 1–40.

Tynyanov, Yury. "The Literary Fact." In *Modern Genre Theory*, translated by Ann Shukman, edited by David Duff, 29–49. New York: Routledge, 2014.

Tzara, Tristan. *Approximate Man & Other Writings*. Translated by Mary Ann Caws. Boston, MA: Black Widow Press, 2005.

Ugrešić, Dubravka. *The Museum of Unconditional Surrender*. Translated by Celia Hawkesworth. New York: New Directions, 1999.

Um, Khatharya. "Exiled Memory: History, Identity, and Remembering in Southeast Asia and Southeast Asian Diaspora." *Positions* 20, no. 3 (Summer 2012): 831–850.

Um, Khatharya. *From the Land of Shadows: War, Revolution, and the Making of the Cambodian Diaspora*. New York: NYU Press, 2015.

UNHCR. "Asylum-Seekers." *UNHCR*, June 2018. http://popstats.unhcr.org/en/asylum_seekers

UNHCR. "Connecting Refugees: How Internet and Mobile Connectivity Can Improve Refugee Well-Being and Transform Humanitarian Action." *UNHCR*, September 14, 2016. https://reliefweb.int/report/world/connecting-refugees-how-internet-and-mobile-connectivity-can-improve-refugee-well-being

UNHCR. "Global Trends: Forced Displacement in 2022," *UNHCR*, June 2023: 1–48. https://www.unhcr.org/global-trends-report-2022

UNHCR. "Global Trends: Forced Displacement in 2017." *UNHCR*, June 19, 2018: 1–75. https://www.unhcr.org/5b27be547

*Utopie und Untergang. Kunst in der DDR*, Museum Kunstpalast, Dusseldorf, May 9, 2019 through January 5, 2020. Accessed November 15, 2019.

Venuti, Lawrence. *The Scandals of Translation: Towards an Ethics of Difference*. London and New York: Routledge, 1998.

Venuti, Lawrence. "Translation and the Pedagogy of Literature." *College English* 58.3 (March 1996): 327–344.

Venuti, Lawrence. *Translation Changes Everything: Theory and Practice*. New York: Routledge, 2013.

Virilio, Paul. *Art and Fear*. Translated by Julie Rose. London and New York: Continuum, 2006.

Warwick Research Collective. *Combined and Uneven Development: Towards a New Theory of World-Literature*. Liverpool: Liverpool University Press, 2015.

Wedel-Brandt, Jeppe. "Interview with CAMP." *Public Square* 25, November 2017. https://publicsquare.dk/artikel/interview-with-camp-center-for-art-and-migration-politics

Welsh, Robert E. "David W. Griffith Speaks." *New York Dramatic Mirror*, January 14, 1914.

Weston, Hillary. "Missed Connections: A Conversation with Christian Petzold." *The Current (Criterion Collection)*, December 7, 2018. https://www.criterion.com/current/posts/6088-missed-connections-a-conversation-with-christian-petzold

Williams, Margery. *The Velveteen Rabbit*. New York: Doubleday & Company, 1922. https://digital.library.upenn.edu/women/williams/rabbit/rabbit.html

Witteborn, Saskia. "Becoming (Im)Perceptible: Forced Migrants and Virtual Practice." *Journal of Refugee Studies* 28, no. 3 (2015): 350–367. https://doi.org/10.1093/jrs/feu036

Wood, Graeme. "The Refugee Detectives." *The Atlantic*, April 2018. https://www.theatlantic.com/magazine/archive/2018/04/the-refugee-detectives/554090/

Worthen, Joseph. "Autofiction and Selfie Aesthetics." *Post45*, December 16, 2021. https://post45.org/2021/12/autofiction-and-selfie-aesthetics/

Young, James E. "Interpreting Literary Testimony: A Preface to Rereading Holocaust Diaries and Memoirs." *New Literary History* 18, no. 2 (1987): 403–423.

Zelizer, Barbie. *About to Die: How News Images Move the Public*. Oxford: Oxford University Press, 2010.

Zetter, Roger. "Refugees and Refugee Studies: A Label and an Agenda." *Journal of Refugee Studies* 1, no. 1 (1988): 1–6. https://doi.org/10.1093/jrs/1.1.1

Zhang, Jenny. "They Pretend To Be Us While Pretending We Don't Exist." *BuzzFeed*, September 11, 2015. https://www.buzzfeed.com/jennybagel/they-pretend-to-be-us-while-pretending-we-dont-exist

Zuba, Elizabeth. "Translator Note." In Arnaldo Calveyra, *Letters So That Happiness*. Translated by Elizabeth Zuba, 51–59. Brooklyn, NY: Ugly Duckling Presse, 2018.